NATIONAL GEOGRAPHIC

Concise
Atlas of the World

THIRD
EDITION

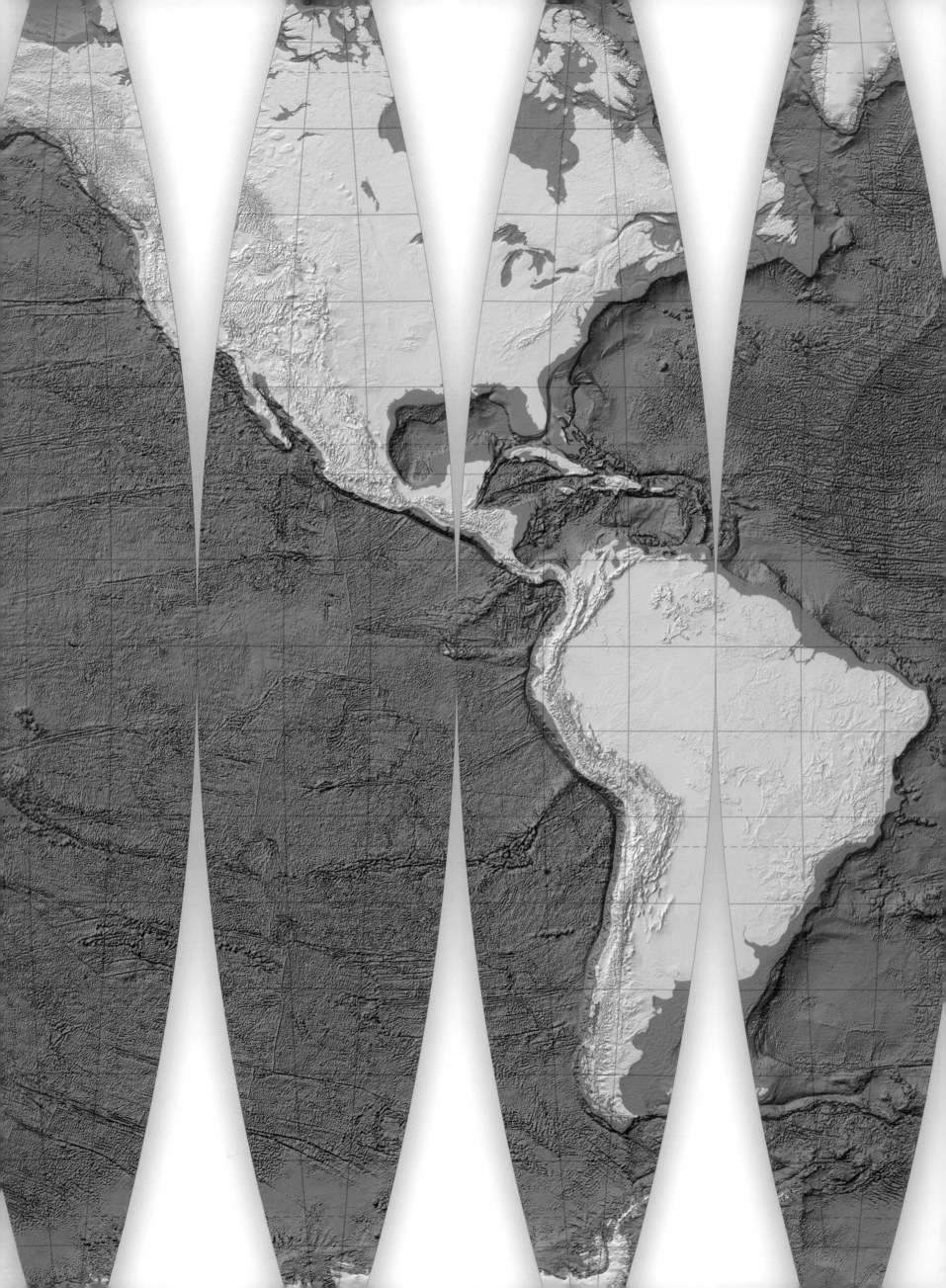

NATIONAL GEOGRAPHIC

Concise
Atlas of the World

THIRD
EDITION

National Geographic
Washington, D.C.

The National Geographic Society is one of the world's largest non-profit scientific and educational organizations. Founded in 1888 to "increase and diffuse geographic knowledge," the Society works to inspire people to care about the planet. National Geographic reflects the world through its magazines, television programs, films, music and radio, books, DVDs, maps, exhibitions, live events, school publishing programs, interactive media and merchandise. *National Geographic* magazine, the Society's official journal, published in English and 33 local-language editions, is read by more than 60 million people each month. The National Geographic Channel reaches 435 million households in 37 languages in 173 countries. National Geographic Digital Media receives more than 19 million visitors a month. National Geographic has funded more than 10,000 scientific research, conservation and exploration projects and supports an education program promoting geography literacy. For more information, visit www.nationalgeographic.com.

For more information, please call
1-800-NGS LINE (647-5463)
or write to the following address:

National Geographic Society
1145 17th Street N.W.
Washington, D.C. 20036-4688 U.S.A.

For information about special discounts
for bulk purchases, please contact
National Geographic Books Special Sales:
ngspecsales@ngs.org

For rights or permissions inquiries, please
contact National Geographic Books
Subsidiary Rights: ngbookrights@ngs.org

First Edition, 2003
Second Edition, 2008
Third Edition, 2012

This 2013 edition printed for Barnes & Noble, Inc.
by the National Geographic Society.

ISBN: 978-1-4351-4912-0 (B&N ed.)
ISBN: 978-1-4262-0951-2

Library of Congress
The Library of Congress has cataloged the second
edition as follows:

National Geographic
concise atlas of the world -- 2nd ed.
    p. cm.
    ISBN 978-1-4262-0196-7 (alk. paper)
    1. Atlases.

G1021.C76.N43 2007
912--dc22

                              2007630027

Printed in Italy
13/EV/1

This atlas was made possible by the contributions
of numerous experts and organizations around the
world, including the following:

Boston University Department of Geography and
Environment Global Land Cover Project

Center for International Earth Science Information
Network (CIESIN), Columbia University

Center for Systemic Peace and Center for Global Policy,
George Mason University

Central Intelligence Agency (CIA)

National Aeronautics and Space Administration (NASA)
    NASA Ames Research Center,
    NASA Goddard Space Flight Center,
    NASA Jet Propulsion Laboratory (JPL),
    NASA Marshall Space Flight Center

National Geospatial-Intelligence Agency (NGA)

National Oceanic and Atmospheric Administration (NOAA)
(see listing under U.S. Department of Commerce, below)

National Science Foundation

Population Reference Bureau

Scripps Institution of Oceanography

Smithsonian Institution

United Nations (UN)
    UN Conference on Trade and Development,
    UN Development Programme,
    UN Educational, Scientific, and Cultural Organization
    (UNESCO),
    UN Environment Programme (UNEP),
    UN Population Division,
    Food and Agriculture Organization (FAO),
    International Telecommunication Union (ITU),
    World Conservation Monitoring Centre (WCMC)

U.S. Board on Geographic Names

U.S. Department of Agriculture

U.S. Department of Commerce: Bureau of the Census,
National Oceanic and Atmospheric Administration (NOAA)
    National Climatic Data Center,
    National Environmental Satellite, Data, and
    Information Service,
    National Geophysical Data Center,
    National Ocean Service

U.S. Department of Energy and Oak Ridge National
Laboratory

U.S. Department of the Interior: Bureau of Indian Affairs,
Bureau of Land Management, Fish and Wildlife Service,
National Park Service, U.S. Geological Survey

U.S. Department of State: Office of the Geographer

World Bank

World Health Organization/Pan American
Health Organization (WHO/PAHO)

World Resources Institute (WRI)

World Trade Organization (WTO)

For a complete listing of contributors, see pages 158 – 159.

Introduction

THE GOAL OF REFLECTING OUR WORLD'S SHAPE AND GEOGRAPHICAL STATE in as unfiltered a manner as possible has transformed into the pages that follow. These graphical depictions of Earth in lines, colors, points, numbers, and letters, paint a vivid, present-day review of our planet and its trends. This compelling story of geographic evolution and the processes that ebb, flow, and remain in constant flux is illustrated by a comparison of the natural, physical world before human footprints to the current world political map; today's map, densely dotted and plotted with thousands of towns and city spots and illuminated by colorful country boundary tints surrounding conquered lands where humankind has planted flags.

This concise compendium of world and continental maps covering every pixel of Earth from the North Pole to its antipode—the South Pole—seeks to bring about a meaningful visual portrayal and explanation of the physical, political, and thematic landscapes of our world today. Man and nature are inextricably intertwined in a complex, dynamic web of cause and effect that makes ever-greater demands on finite resources and a growing population. As planetary stewards, we must manage and plan our environmental and humanitarian policies responsibly. With empirical, unbiased data, and the guidance of internationally respected experts and consultants, we endeavor to bring you a clear and accurate picture of the facts and stats. The third edition of this award-winning collection of maps has been completely updated using the most reliable data available from the most recognized and authoritative scientific organizations—institutions of dedicated individuals who continually strive to collect, distill, and share with the world their findings from focused areas of expertise, observation, and study. This approach, which includes the practice of gathering geographic information with technologically advanced processing and graphic projection tools, assists us in our aspirations to acquire, record, and report to you a myriad of topics concerning aspects of our intricate, intriguing, spinning world.

It was more than a half century ago that John Glenn, flying a *Mercury* capsule, *Friendship 7*, became the first American to orbit Earth three times during a five-hour mission. Yuri Gagarin aboard *Vostok I* had surpassed this feat nearly a year earlier in the Cold War's space race. Regardless of nationality, both explorers in their extraterrestrial solitude aboard their spacecrafts, likely pondered the future of their world and the fragile balance between nature and humanity in the constant struggle for conflict resolution, equitable coexistence, and preservation and management of Earth's natural resources and riches. At the time of his historic 1962 flight, Glenn looked down from his spaceship's tiny portal at a planet then inhabited by 3.1 billion people. Today, the world's population exceeds 7 billion. Who, aside from demographers, would have thought the human population of billions would more than double in number? With such incredible population growth, issues of poverty, health, availability of food and fresh water, pollution, deforestation and desertification—to name a few—become exacerbated. This dynamic and complex world calls for a better understanding, appreciation, and conservation of our finite lands and interconnected ocean, as well as our precious, limited resources—natural and human. In this edition we devote detailed coverage to world population—including growth, density, distribution, fertility, urbanization, life expectancy, and migration.

With topics ranging from plate tectonics to water availability, world economies to earthquakes, volcanic activity to tsunamis, energy consumption, and geographic superlatives, this assemblage of earthly marvels depicts a gripping story of the pulse of a resilient yet very delicate planet.

When our last edition of this work was produced in 2008, there were fewer countries in the world. With Kosovo and South Sudan's independence there are now 195 independent nations—more than triple the number since the end of World War II. What was Africa's largest nation in area—Sudan—is now divided after years of civil conflict and a 2011 referendum for independence. Today, that continent's largest country is Algeria. The world's political landscape is never static—as revealed in the *Conflicts* world thematic spread, which has been completely updated for this edition.

We hope that these pages will inspire, engage, and enrich your understanding of the world today and enhance the prospect for a more sustainable and verdant planet and peaceful existence for its inhabitants—human, plant, and animal, great and small.

At stake is the destiny of a balanced, responsibly managed world for the present and future generations. Shared efforts and technologies bring tremendous possibilities and opportunities to seek greater resource management, conservation, and international peace and stability—and thus to have an impact on solving economic, social, and humanitarian issues.

As astronaut John Glenn wisely stated, "We have an infinite amount to learn both from nature and from each other." With this in mind, we aim in this atlas to disseminate—through meaningful, realistic representations—the natural wonders and treasures with which we are gifted and endlessly in awe.

CARL MEHLER
PROJECT EDITOR AND DIRECTOR OF MAPS
CONCISE ATLAS OF THE WORLD, FIRST, SECOND, AND THIRD EDITIONS

Table of Contents

LOCATED IN THE INNER SOLAR SYSTEM, Earth is the third planet from the sun—after Mercury and Venus. Earth's oceans and continents join to form nearly 197 million square miles of surface area. Seventy-one percent of its surface is water. Although different terms are used to describe ocean depths (bathymetry) and the lay of the land (topography), Earth's surface is a continuum. Similar features, such as mountains, ridges, volcanoes, plateaus, valleys, and canyons, give texture to the lands both above and below sea level. See pages 16–17 to view the entire surface of the Earth.

Using This Atlas

Maps are a rich, useful, and—to the extent humanly possible—accurate means of depicting the world. Yet maps inevitably make the world seem a little simpler than it really is. A neatly drawn boundary may in reality be a hotly contested war zone. The government-sanctioned, "official" name of a provincial city in an ethnically diverse region may bear little resemblance to the name its citizens routinely use. These cartographic issues often seem obscure and academic. But maps arouse passions. Despite our carefully reasoned map policies, users of National Geographic maps write us strongly worded letters when our maps are at odds with their worldviews.

How do National Geographic cartographers deal with these realities? With constant scrutiny, considerable discussion, and help from many outside experts.

EXAMPLES

Nations: Issues of national sovereignty and contested borders often boil down to "de facto versus de jure" discussions. Governments and international agencies frequently make official rulings about contested regions. These de jure decisions, no matter how legitimate, are often at odds with the wishes of individuals and groups, and they often stand in stark contrast to real-world situations. The inevitable conclusion: It is simplest and best to show the world as it is—de facto—rather than as we or others wish it to be.

Africa's Western Sahara, for example, was divided by Morocco and Mauritania after the Spanish government withdrew in 1976. Although Morocco now controls the entire territory, the United Nations does not recognize Morocco's sovereignty over this still disputed area. This atlas shows the de facto Moroccan rule but includes an explanatory note.

Place-names: Ride a barge down the Danube, and you'll hear the river called Donau, Duna, Dunaj, Dunarea, Dunav, Dunay. These are local names. This atlas uses the conventional name, "Danube," on physical maps. On political maps, local names are used, with the conventional name in parentheses where space permits. Usage conventions for both foreign and domestic place-names are established by the U.S. Board on Geographic Names, a group with representatives from several federal agencies.

Political Maps

Political maps portray features such as international boundaries, the locations of cities, road networks, and other important elements of the world's human geography. Most index entries are keyed to the political maps, listing the page numbers and then the specific locations on the pages. (See page 138 for details on how to use the index.)

Asia Political, pp. 90–91

Physical features: Gray relief shading depicts surface features such as mountains, hills, and valleys.

Water features are shown in blue. Solid lines and filled-in areas indicate perennial water features; dashed lines and patterns indicate intermittent features.

Boundaries and political divisions are defined with both lines and colored bands; they vary according to whether a boundary is internal or international (for details, see map symbols key at right).

Cities: The regional political maps that form the bulk of this atlas depict four categories of cities or towns. The largest cities are shown in all capital letters (e.g., LONDON).

Physical Maps

Physical maps of the world, the continents, and the ocean floor reveal landforms and vegetation in stunning detail. Painted by relief artists John Bonner and Tibor Tóth, the maps have been edited for accuracy. Although painted maps are human interpretations, these depictions can emphasize subtle features that are sometimes invisible in satellite imagery.

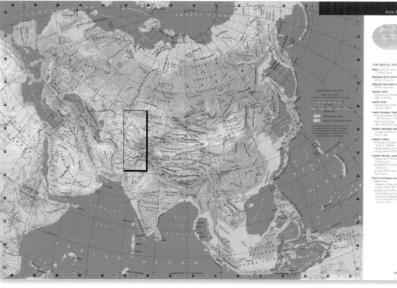

Asia Physical, pp. 92–93

Physical features: Colors and shading illustrate variations in elevation, landforms, and vegetation. Patterns indicate specific landscape features, such as sand, glaciers, and swamps.

Water features: Blue lines indicate rivers; other water bodies are shown as areas of blue. Lighter shading reflects a depth of 200 meters or less.

Boundaries and political divisions are shown in red. Dotted lines indicate disputed or uncertain boundaries.

World Thematic Maps

Thematic maps reveal the rich patchwork and infinite interrelationships of our changing planet. The thematic section at the beginning of the atlas charts human patterns, with information on population, religions, and the world economy. In this section, maps are coupled with charts, diagrams, photographs, and tabular information, which together create a very useful framework for studying geographic patterns.

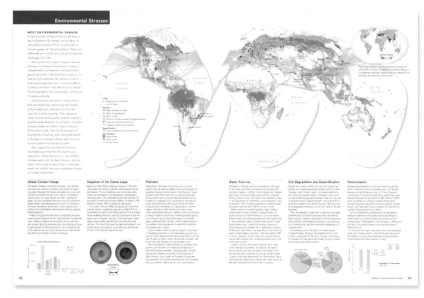

World Environmental Stresses, pp. 42–43

Flags and Facts

This atlas recognizes 193 independent nations. All of these countries, along with dependencies and U.S. states, are profiled in the continental sections of the atlas. Accompanying each entry are highlights of geographic, demographic, and economic data. These details provide a brief over-view of each country, state, or territory; they are not intended to be comprehen-sive. A detailed description of the sources and policies used in compiling the list-ings is included in the Key to Flags and Facts on page 159.

Palau
REPUBLIC OF PALAU

AREA	459 sq km (177 sq mi)
POPULATION	21,000
CAPITAL	Melekeok 1,000
RELIGION	Roman Catholic, Protestant, none
LANGUAGE	Palauan, Filipino, English
LITERACY	92%
LIFE EXPECTANCY	72 years
GDP PER CAPITA	$8,100
ECONOMY	**IND:** tourism, craft items (from shell, wood, pearls), construction, garment making **AGR:** coconuts, copra, cassava (tapioca), sweet potatoes, fish **EXP:** shellfish, tuna, copra, garments

Index and Grid

Beginning on page 138 is a full index of place-names found in this atlas. The edge of each map is marked with letters (in rows) and numbers (in columns), to which the index entries are referenced. As an example, "Cartagena, Col. 68 A2" (see inset below) refers to the grid section on page 68 where row A and column 2 meet. More examples and additional details about the index are included on page 138.

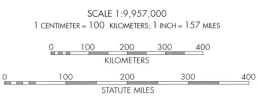

Map Symbols

BOUNDARIES

	Defined
	Undefined or disputed
	Offshore line of separation
	International boundary (Physical Plates)
	Disputed or undefined boundary (Physical Plates)

CITIES

✪ ★ ◉	Capitals
● ● ● ●	Towns

WATER FEATURES

	Drainage
	Intermittent drainage
	Intermittent lake
	Dry salt lake
	Swamp
200	Depth curves in meters
51	Water surface elevation in meters
	Falls or rapids

PHYSICAL FEATURES

	Relief
	Lava and volcanic debris
+8850 (29035 ft)	Elevation in meters (feet in United States)
.-86	Elevation in meters below sea level
✕	Pass
	Sand
	Salt desert
	Below sea level
	Ice shelf
	Glacier

CULTURAL FEATURES

	Canal
	Dam
▫	Site

MAP SCALE (Sample)

SCALE 1:9,957,000
1 CENTIMETER = 100 KILOMETERS; 1 INCH = 157 MILES

0   100   200   300   400
KILOMETERS

0   100   200   300   400
STATUTE MILES

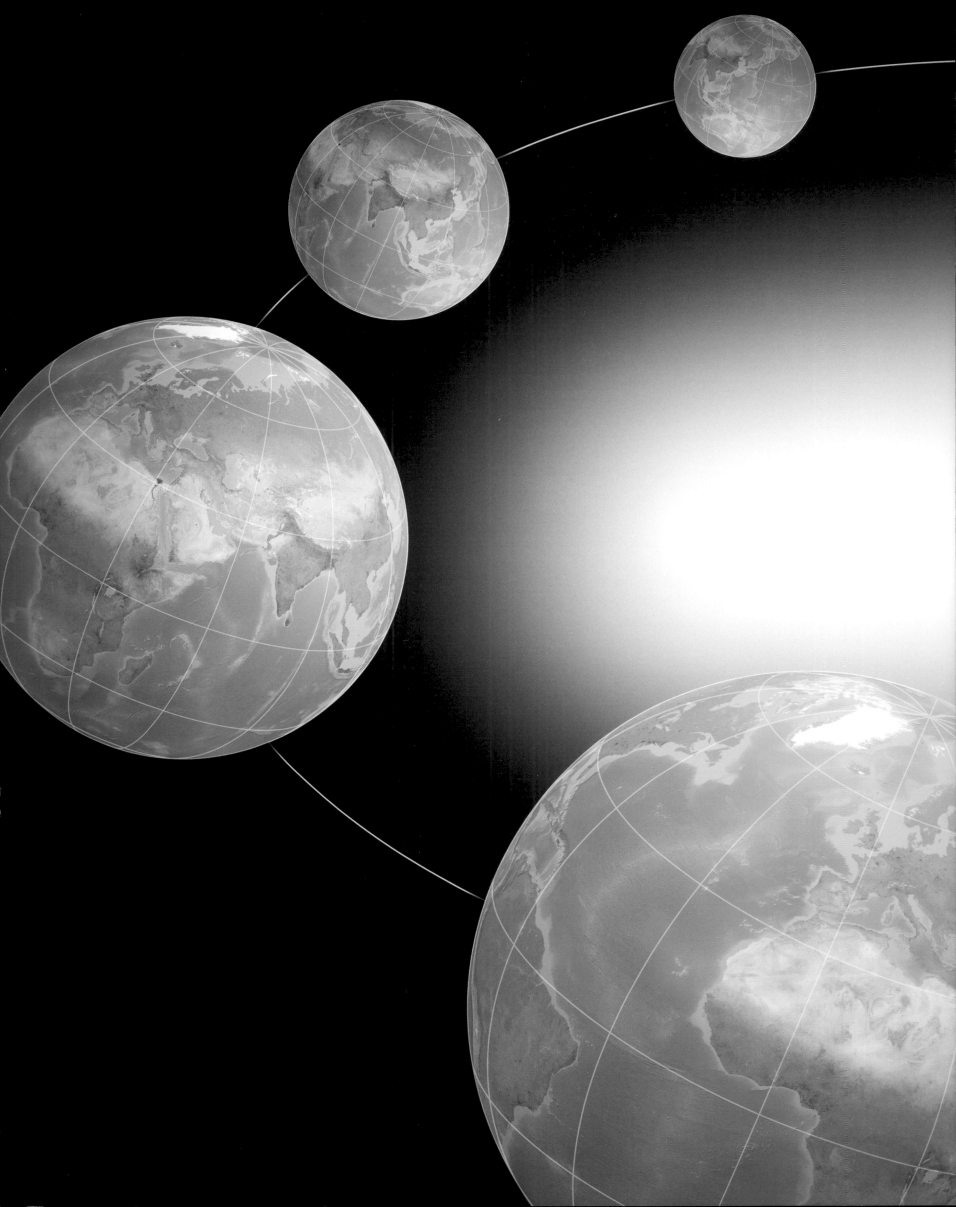

World

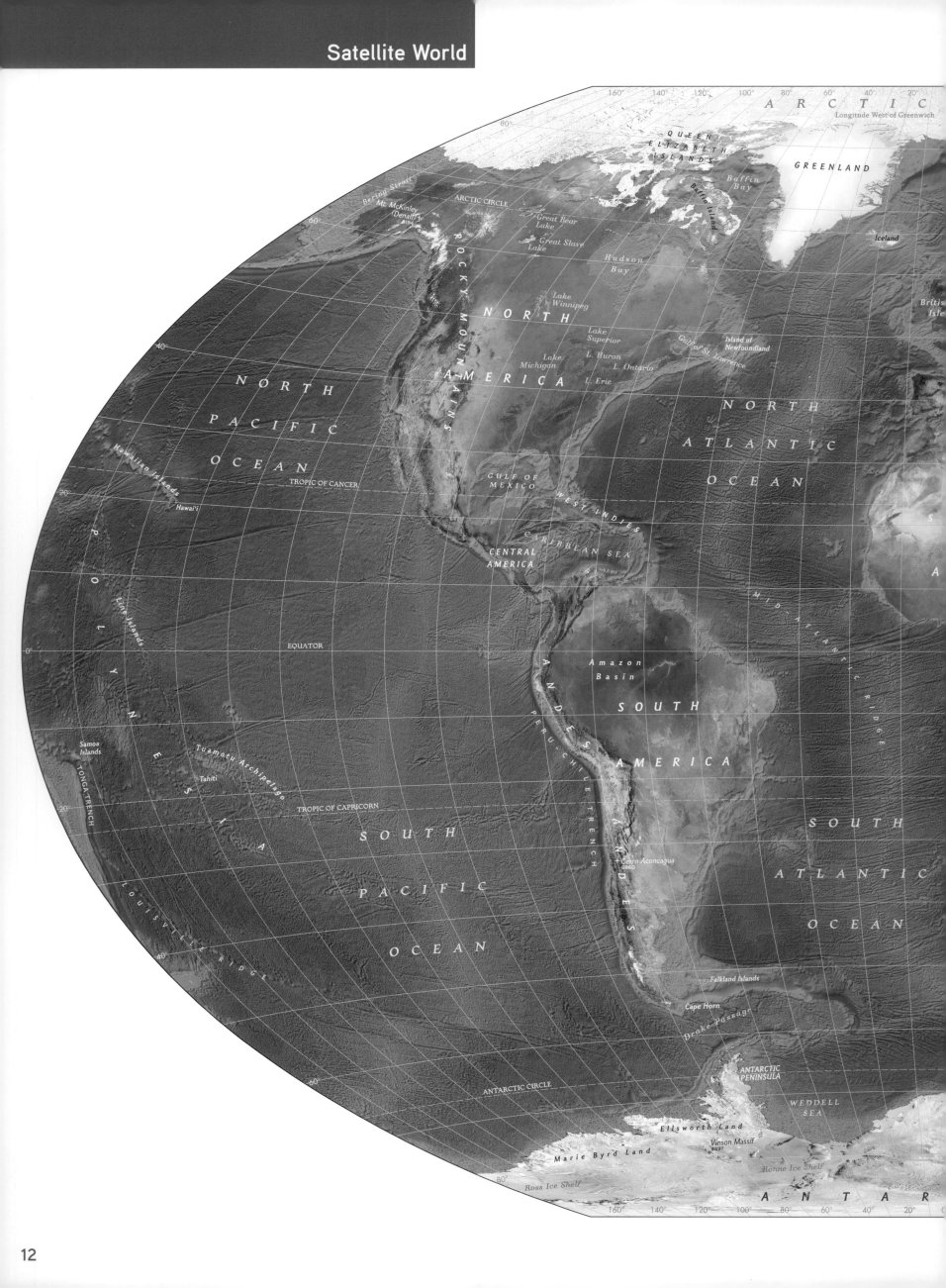

ARCTIC

QUEEN
ELIZABETH
ISLANDS

GREENLAND

Longitude West of Greenwich

Baffin
Bay

Baffin Island

Bering Strait

Mt. McKinley
(Denali)
6194

ARCTIC CIRCLE

Great Bear
Lake

Great Slave
Lake

Iceland

R O C K Y   M O U N T A I N S

Hudson
Bay

Lake
Winnipeg

British
Isles

N O R T H

Lake
Superior

Gulf of St. Lawrence

Island of
Newfoundland

N O R T H

Lake
Michigan

L. Huron

L. Ontario

N O R T H

Lake
Michigan

L. Erie

A T L A N T I C

P A C I F I C

A M E R I C A

O C E A N

O C E A N

Hawaiian Islands

TROPIC OF CANCER

GULF OF
MEXICO

WEST INDIES

Hawai'i

CARIBBEAN SEA

CENTRAL
AMERICA

P

M I D - A T L A N T I C   R I D G E

O

EQUATOR

Amazon
Basin

L

Y

SOUTH

N

Samoa
Islands

Tuamotu Archipelago

A N D E S

AMERICA

E

S

Tahiti

TROPIC OF CAPRICORN

I

SOUTH

TONGA TRENCH

A

P E R U - C H I L E   T R E N C H

SOUTH

PACIFIC

Cerro Aconcagua
6960

A T L A N T I C

LOUISVILLE RIDGE

OCEAN

OCEAN

Falkland Islands

Cape Horn

A N D E S

Drake Passage

ANTARCTIC
PENINSULA

ANTARCTIC CIRCLE

WEDDELL
SEA

Ellsworth Land

Vinson Massif
4897

Marie Byrd Land

Ronne Ice Shelf

Ross Ice Shelf

A N T A R

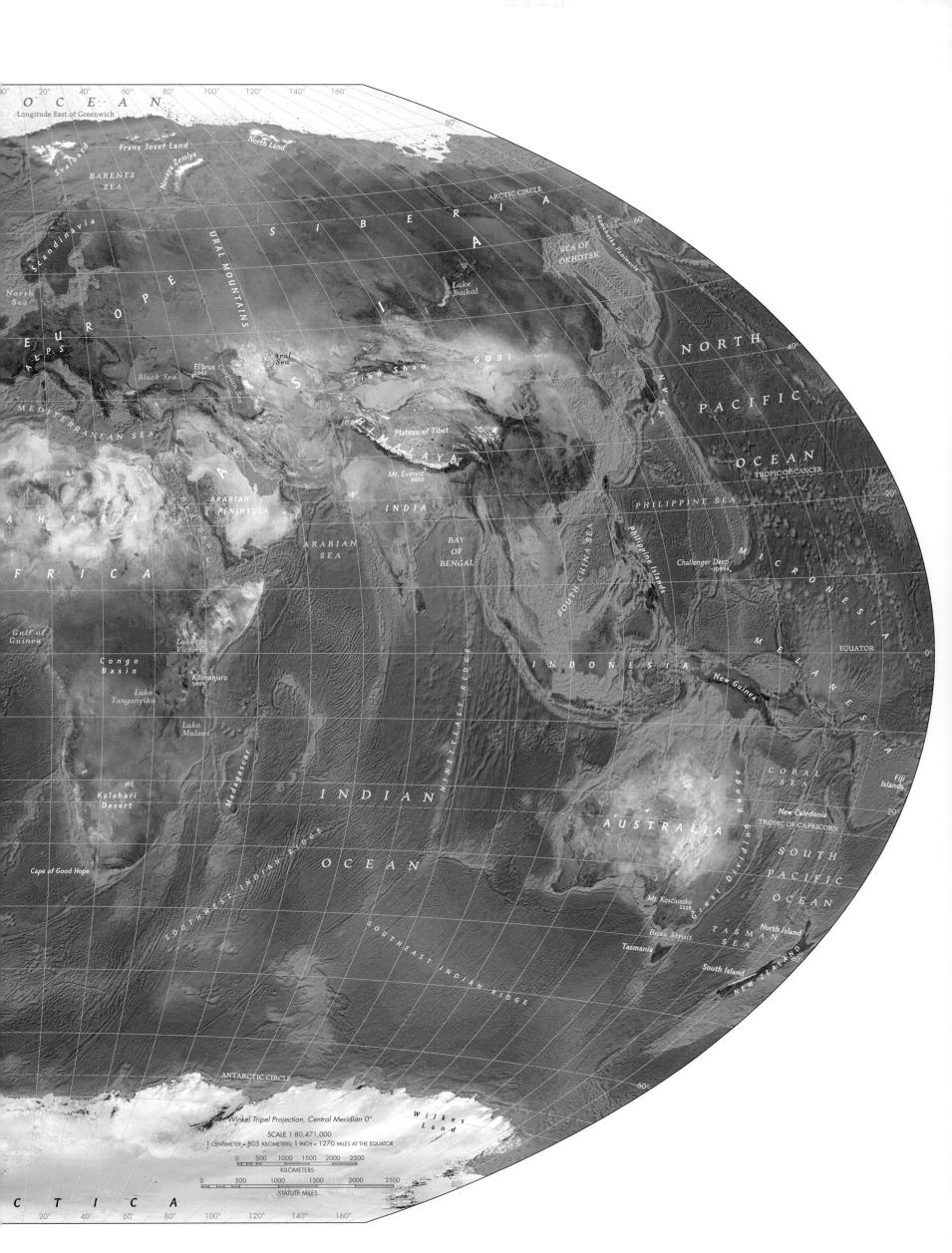

20°   40°   60°   80°   100°   120°   140°   160°

80°

Svalbard
Franz Josef Land
North Land

BARENTS
SEA
Novaya Zemlya

ARCTIC CIRCLE   60°

Kamchatka Peninsula

SEA OF
OKHOTSK

S I B E R I A

Scandinavia

URAL MOUNTAINS

North
Sea

E U R O P E

Lake
Baikal

NORTH

S
I
B
E
R
I
A

40°

ALPS

El'brus
5642   Caspian Sea

Aral
Sea

Tian Shan

GOBI

PACIFIC

Black Sea

A
S
I
A

Plateau of Tibet

JAPAN

OCEAN

MEDITERRANEAN SEA

H I M A L A Y A

Mt. Everest
8850

TROPIC OF CANCER

20°

PHILIPPINE SEA

S
A
H
A
R
A

ARABIAN
PENINSULA

INDIA

Red Sea

Philippine Islands

MICRONESIA

Gulf of
Guinea

A F R I C A

ARABIAN
SEA

BAY
OF
BENGAL

SOUTH CHINA SEA

Challenger Deep
-10994

Lake
Victoria

Congo
Basin

Kilimanjaro
5895

I N D O N E S I A

M E L A N E S I A

EQUATOR

New Guinea

Lake
Tanganyika

Lake
Malawi

Madagascar

CORAL
SEA

Fiji
Islands

Kalahari
Desert

I N D I A N

NINETY EAST RIDGE

AUSTRALIA

New Caledonia
TROPIC OF CAPRICORN   20°

Cape of Good Hope

O C E A N

Great Dividing Range

SOUTH
PACIFIC

SOUTHWEST INDIAN RIDGE

Mt. Kosciuszko
2228

OCEAN

SOUTHEAST INDIAN RIDGE

Bass Strait

TASMAN
SEA

North Island

Tasmania

NEW ZEALAND

South Island

ANTARCTIC CIRCLE   60°

Wilkes
Land

Winkel Tripel Projection, Central Meridian 0°

SCALE 1:80,471,000
1 CENTIMETER = 805 KILOMETERS; 1 INCH = 1270 MILES AT THE EQUATOR

0   500   1000   1500   2000   2500
KILOMETERS

0   500   1000   1500   2000   2500
STATUTE MILES

80°

C T I C A

20°   40°   60°   80°   100°   120°   140°   160°

North Pole

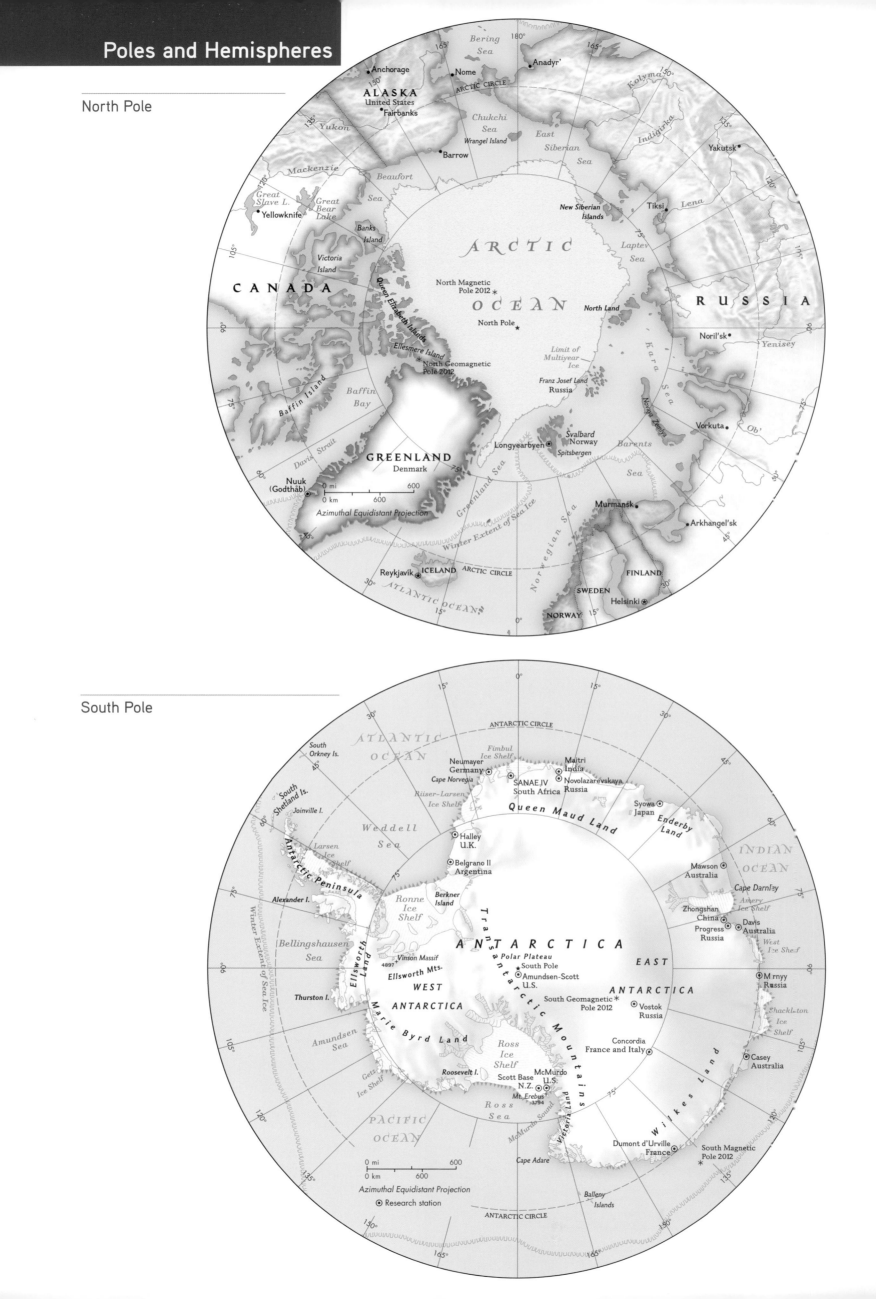

Anchorage
Nome
Anadyr'
Bering Sea
Kolyma
165°
180°
150°
ALASKA
United States
Fairbanks
ARCTIC CIRCLE
Chukchi Sea
East Siberian Sea
Indigirka
135°
Yukon
Wrangel Island
Barrow
Yakutsk
Mackenzie
Beaufort Sea
Laptev Sea
Lena
120°
Great Slave L.
Great Bear Lake
Yellowknife
ARCTIC
New Siberian Islands
Tiksi
105°
Banks Island
OCEAN
North Land
CANADA
Victoria Island
North Magnetic Pole 2012
RUSSIA
90°
Queen Elizabeth Islands
North Pole
Limit of Multiyear Ice
Noril'sk
Yenisey
Ellesmere Island
North Geomagnetic Pole 2012
Franz Josef Land Russia
Kara Sea
75°
Baffin Island
Baffin Bay
Novaya Zemlya
Ob'
Vorkuta
Davis Strait
Svalbard Norway Spitsbergen
Barents Sea
30°
GREENLAND
Denmark
Longyearbyen
60°
Nuuk (Godthåb)
0 mi   600
0 km   600
Azimuthal Equidistant Projection
Murmansk
Arkhangel'sk
45°
Greenland Sea
Winter Extent of Sea Ice
Reykjavík ICELAND ARCTIC CIRCLE
Norwegian Sea
FINLAND
30°
ATLANTIC OCEAN
SWEDEN
Helsinki
15°
NORWAY
15°

South Pole

ANTARCTIC CIRCLE
0°
15°
30°
South Orkney Is.
ATLANTIC OCEAN
Fimbul Ice Shelf
Neumayer Germany
Cape Norvegia
Maitri India
Novolazarevskaya Russia
45°
South Shetland Is.
SANAE IV South Africa
Joinville I.
Riiser-Larsen Ice Shelf
Queen Maud Land
Syowa Japan
Enderby Land
INDIAN OCEAN
Weddell Sea
Halley U.K.
Mawson Australia
Antarctic Peninsula
Larsen Ice Shelf
Belgrano II Argentina
Cape Darnley
75°
Alexander I.
Ronne Ice Shelf
Berkner Island
Zhongshan China
Amery Ice Shelf
Bellingshausen Sea
Ellsworth Land
ANTARCTICA
Progress Russia
Davis Australia
West Ice Shelf
Thurston I.
Vinson Massif 4897
Ellsworth Mts.
Polar Plateau
South Pole
Amundsen-Scott U.S.
EAST
ANTARCTICA
90°
Mirnyy Russia
WEST
South Geomagnetic Pole 2012
Vostok Russia
Winter Extent of Sea Ice
Marie Byrd Land
ANTARCTICA
Shackleton Ice Shelf
Amundsen Sea
Ross Ice Shelf
Transantarctic Mountains
Concordia France and Italy
Wilkes Land
Casey Australia
Roosevelt I.
Getz Ice Shelf
Scott Base N.Z.
McMurdo U.S.
Mt. Erebus 3794
McMurdo Sound
Victoria Land
75°
PACIFIC OCEAN
Ross Sea
Dumont d'Urville France
South Magnetic Pole 2012
0 mi   600
0 km   600
Azimuthal Equidistant Projection
⊙ Research station
Cape Adare
Balleny Islands
ANTARCTIC CIRCLE
165°
150°
135°
120°
105°

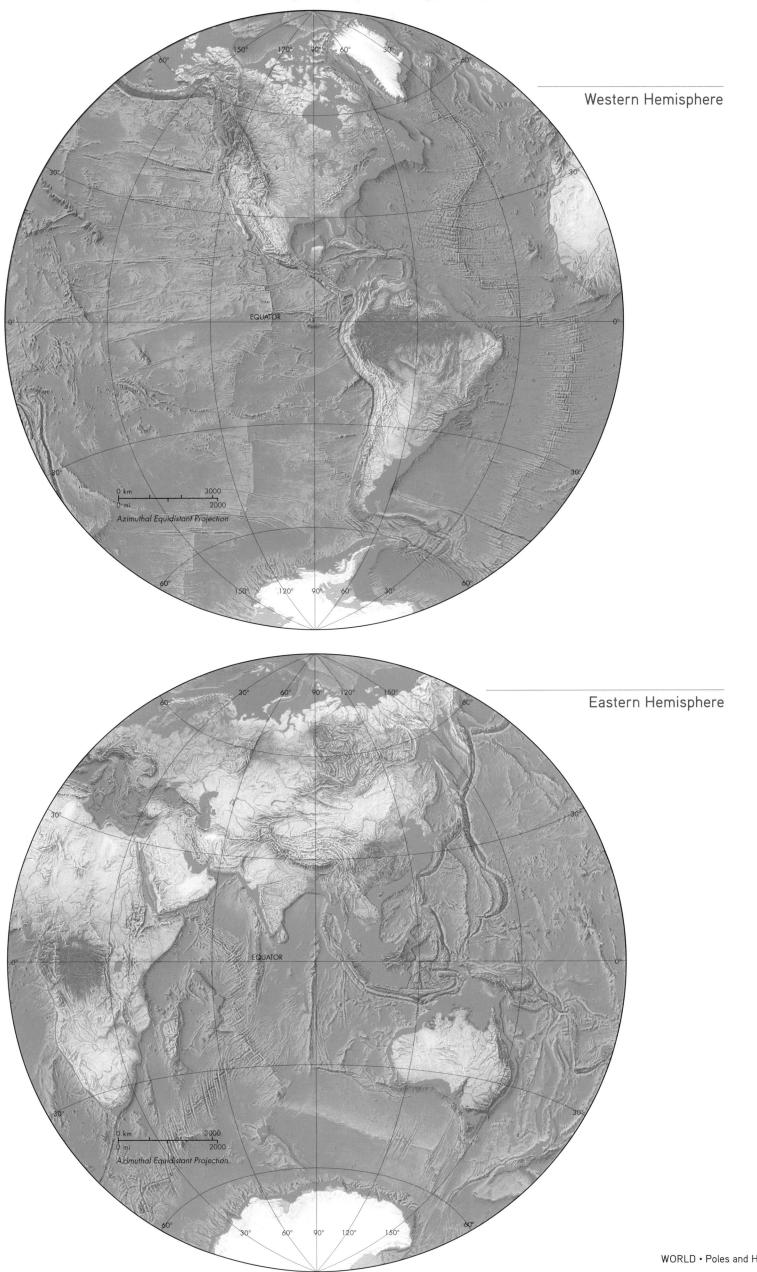

150° 120° 90° 60° 30°
60°
60°
30°
30°
0°
0°
EQUATOR
30°
30°
0 km 3000
0 mi 2000
Azimuthal Equidistant Projection
60°
60°
150° 120° 90° 60° 30°

30° 60° 90° 120° 150°
60°
60°
30°
30°
0°
0°
EQUATOR
30°
30°
0 km 3000
0 mi 2000
Azimuthal Equidistant Projection
60°
30° 60° 90° 120° 150°

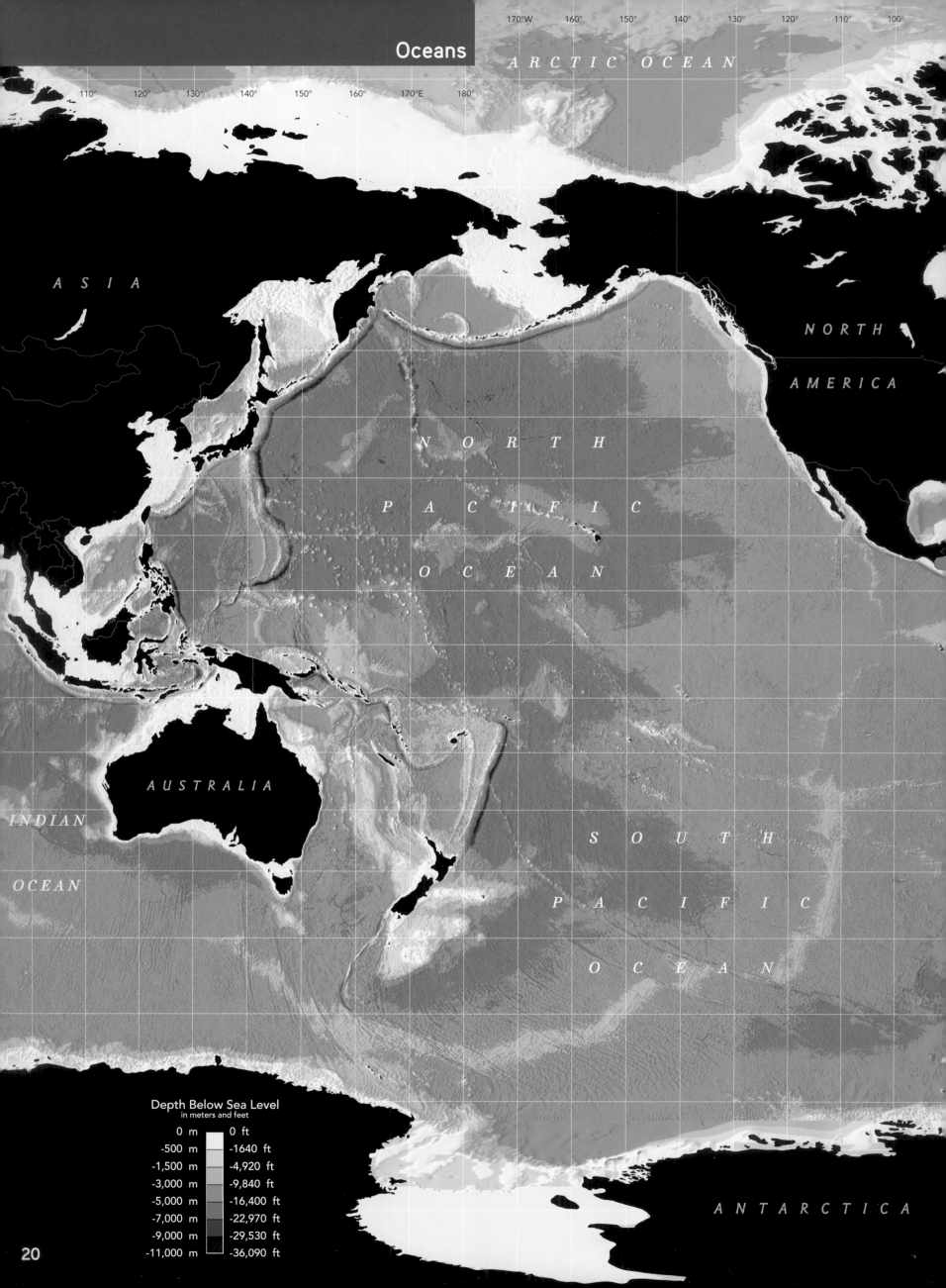

ARCTIC OCEAN

170°W 160° 150° 140° 130° 120° 110° 100°

110° 120° 130° 140° 150° 160° 170°E 180°

ASIA

NORTH

AMERICA

NORTH

PACIFIC

OCEAN

AUSTRALIA

INDIAN

OCEAN

SOUTH

PACIFIC

OCEAN

ANTARCTICA

Depth Below Sea Level
in meters and feet

0 m	0 ft
-500 m	-1640 ft
-1,500 m	-4,920 ft
-3,000 m	-9,840 ft
-5,000 m	-16,400 ft
-7,000 m	-22,970 ft
-9,000 m	-29,530 ft
-11,000 m	-36,090 ft

ARCTIC OCEAN

Greenland

EUROPE

ASIA

NORTH

ATLANTIC

OCEAN

AFRICA

SOUTH
AMERICA

SOUTH

ATLANTIC

OCEAN

INDIAN

OCEAN

ARCTIC OCEAN

World Bathymetry

Kilometers
0   1,000   2,000   3,000

Statute Miles
0   1,000   2,000   3,000

Nautical Miles
0   1,000   2,000   3,000

Scale at the Equator
Miller Cylindrical Projection

Structure of the Earth

LIKE ICE ON A GREAT LAKE, the Earth's crust, or the lithosphere, floats over the planet's molten innards, is cracked in many places, and is in slow but constant movement. Earth's surface is broken into 16 enormous slabs of rock, called plates, averaging thousands of miles wide and having a thickness of several miles. As they move and grind against each other, they push up mountains, spawn volcanoes, and generate earthquakes.

Although these often cataclysmic events capture our attention, the movements that cause them are imperceptible, a slow waltz of rafted rock that continues over eons. How slow? The Mid-Atlantic Ridge (see "spreading" diagram, opposite) is being built by magma oozing between two plates, separating North America and Africa at the speed of a growing human fingernail.

The dividing lines between plates often mark areas of high volcanic and earthquake activity as plates strain against each other or one dives beneath another. In the Ring of Fire around the Pacific Basin, disastrous earthquakes have occurred in Kōbe and Fukushima, Japan, and in Los Angeles and San Francisco, California. Volcanic eruptions have taken place at Pinatubo in the Philippines and Mount St. Helens in Washington State.

CRUST
2 to 45 miles thick

LITHOSPHERE
1 to 120 miles thick

ASTHENOSPHERE
60 to 400 miles thick

UPPER MANTLE
400 miles thick

LOWER MANTLE
1,400 miles thick

OUTER CORE
1,400 miles thick

INNER CORE
1,500 miles in diameter

Continents Adrift in Time

With unceasing movement of Earth's tectonic plates, continents "drift" over geologic time—breaking apart, reassembling, and again fragmenting to repeat the process. Three times during the past billion years, Earth's drifting landmasses have merged to form so-called supercontinents. Rodinia, a supercontinent in the late Precambrian, began breaking apart about 750 million years ago. In time, its pieces reassembled to form another supercontinent, which in turn later split into smaller landmasses during the Paleozoic. The largest of these were called Euramerica (ancestral Europe and North America) and Gondwana (ancestral Africa, Antarctica, Arabia, India, and Australia). More than 250 million years ago, these two landmasses recombined, forming Pangaea. In the Mesozoic era, Pangaea split and the Atlantic and Indian Oceans began forming. Though the Atlantic is still widening today, scientists predict it will close as the seafloor recycles back into Earth's mantle. A new supercontinent, Pangaea Ultima, will eventually form.

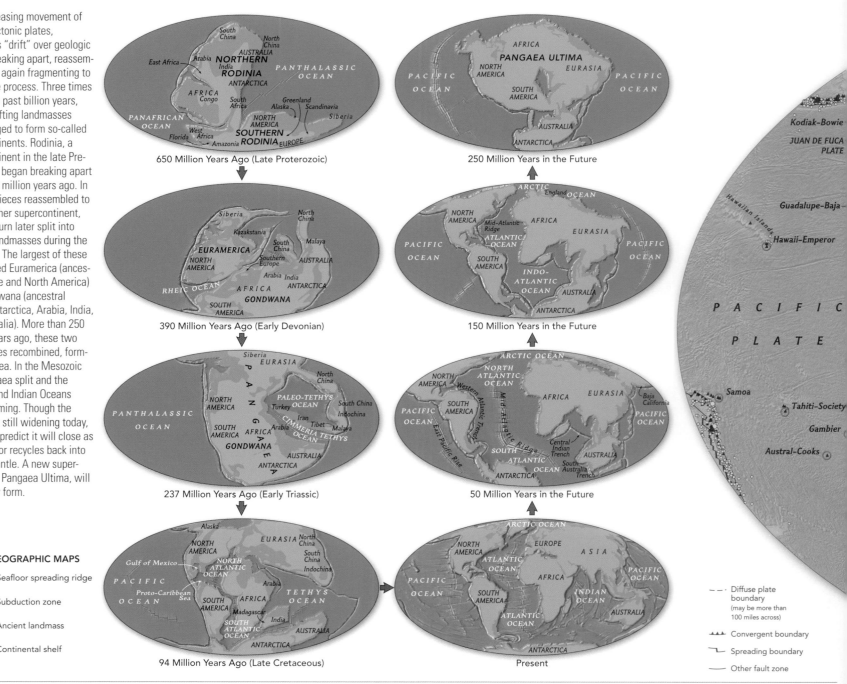

650 Million Years Ago (Late Proterozoic)

390 Million Years Ago (Early Devonian)

237 Million Years Ago (Early Triassic)

94 Million Years Ago (Late Cretaceous)

250 Million Years in the Future

150 Million Years in the Future

50 Million Years in the Future

Present

KEY TO PALEO-GEOGRAPHIC MAPS

- Seafloor spreading ridge
- Subduction zone
- Ancient landmass
- Continental shelf

– – · Diffuse plate boundary (may be more than 100 miles across)

▲▲▲ Convergent boundary

⌐⌐ Spreading boundary

— Other fault zone

Geologic Time

	4,500 MILLIONS OF YEARS AGO	3,500	3,000	2,500	2,000	1,500	1,000	
EON	PRISCOAN	ARCHAEAN			PROTEROZOIC			
ERA	EOARCHAEAN	PALEOARCHAEAN	MESOARCHAEAN	NEOARCHAEAN	PALEOPROTEROZOIC	MESOPROTEROZOIC		
PERIOD	No subdivision into periods				SIDERIAN RHYACIAN OROSIRIAN STATHERIAN	CALYMMIAN ECTASIAN STENIAN	TONIAN	

Kodiak-Bowie

JUAN DE FUCA PLATE

Guadalupe-Baja

Hawaii-Emperor

PACIFIC PLATE

Samoa

Tahiti-Society

Gambier

Austral-Cooks

Geologic Forces Change the Face of the Planet

ACCRETION

As ocean plates move toward the edges of continents or island arcs and slide under them, seamounts are skimmed off and piled up in submarine trenches. The resulting buildup can cause continents to grow.

FAULTING

Enormous crustal plates do not slide smoothly. Strain built up along their edges may release in a series of small jumps, felt as minor tremors on land. Extended buildup can cause a sudden jump, producing an earthquake.

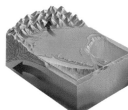

COLLISION

When two continental plates converge, the result can be the most dramatic mountain-building process on Earth. The Himalaya mountain range rose when the Indian subcontinent collided with Eurasia, driving the land upward.

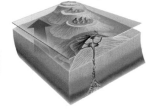

HOT SPOTS

In the cauldron of inner Earth, some areas burn hotter than others and periodically blast through their crustal covering as volcanoes. Such a "hot spot" built the Hawaiian Islands, leaving a string of oceanic protuberances.

SPREADING

At the divergent boundary known as the Mid-Atlantic Ridge, oozing magma forces two plates apart by as much as eight inches a year. If that rate had been constant, the ocean could have reached its current width in 30 million years.

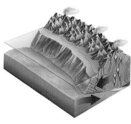

SUBDUCTION

When an oceanic plate and a continental plate converge, the older and heavier sea plate takes a dive. Plunging back into the interior of the Earth, it is transformed into molten material, only to rise again as magma.

Plate Tectonics

Tectonic boundaries mark areas of geologic change in ocean floors, on the margins of continents, and even within continents, as seen in the Great Rift Valley of East Africa. Clusters of volcanoes and frequent earthquakes indicate unstable areas.

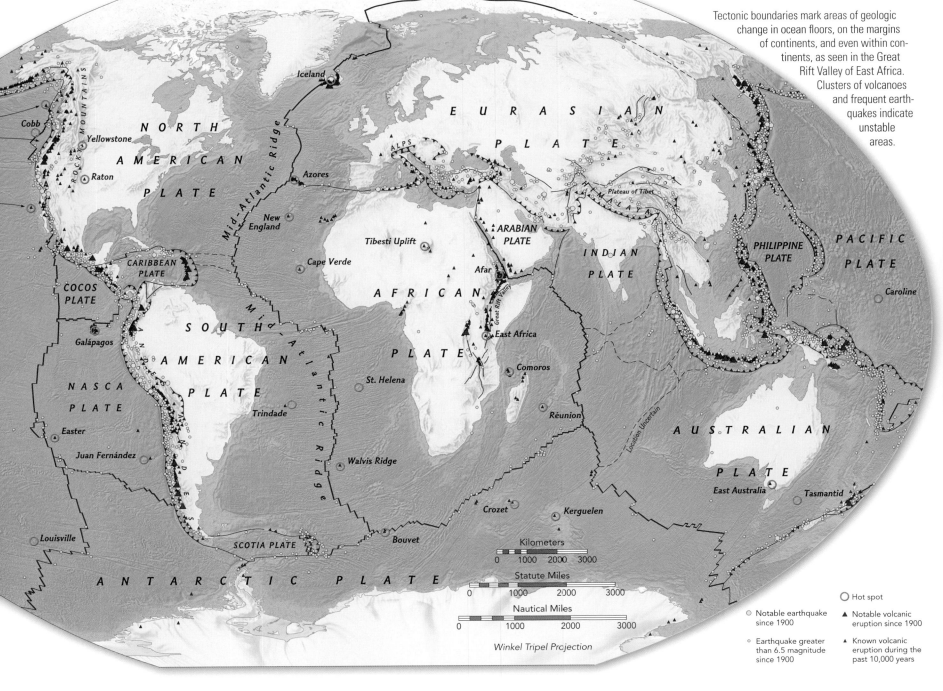

Kilometers
0 1000 2000 3000

Statute Miles
0 1000 2000 3000

Nautical Miles
0 1000 2000 3000

Winkel Tripel Projection

⊙ Notable earthquake since 1900

○ Earthquake greater than 6.5 magnitude since 1900

○ Hot spot

▲ Notable volcanic eruption since 1900

▲ Known volcanic eruption during the past 10,000 years

THE TERM "CLIMATE" describes the average "weather" conditions, as measured over many years, that prevail at any given point around the world at a given time of the year. Daily weather may differ dramatically from that expected on the basis of climatic statistics.

Energy from the sun drives the global climate system. Much of this incoming energy is absorbed in the tropics. Outgoing heat radiation, much of which exits at high latitudes, balances the absorbed incoming solar energy. To achieve a balance across the globe, huge amounts of heat are moved from the tropics to polar regions by both the atmosphere and the oceans.

The tilt of Earth's axis leads to shifting patterns of incoming solar energy throughout the year. More energy is transported to higher latitudes in winter than in summer, and hence the contrast in temperatures between the tropics and polar regions is greatest at this time of year—especially in the Northern Hemisphere.

Scientists present this data in many ways, using climographs (see page 26), which show information about specific places. Alternatively, they produce maps, which show regional and worldwide data.

The effects of the climatic contrasts are seen in the distribution of Earth's life-forms. Temperature, precipitation, and the amount of sunlight all determine what plants can grow in a region and the animals that live there. People are more adaptable, but climate exerts powerful constraints on where we live.

Climatic conditions define planning decisions, such as how much heating oil we need for the winter and the necessary rainfall for agriculture in the summer. Fluctuations from year to year (e.g., cold winters or summer droughts) make planning more difficult.

In the longer term, continued global warming may change climatic conditions around the world, which could dramatically alter temperature and precipitation patterns and lead to more frequent heat waves, floods, and droughts.

JANUARY SOLAR ENERGY

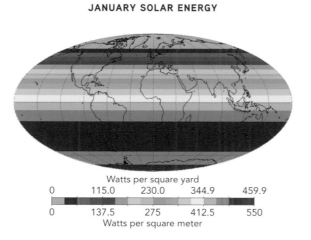

Watts per square yard

| 0 | 115.0 | 230.0 | 344.9 | 459.9 |

| 0 | 137.5 | 275 | 412.5 | 550 |

Watts per square meter

JULY SOLAR ENERGY

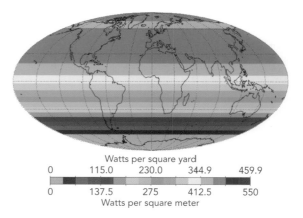

Watts per square yard

| 0 | 115.0 | 230.0 | 344.9 | 459.9 |

| 0 | 137.5 | 275 | 412.5 | 550 |

Watts per square meter

JANUARY AVERAGE TEMPERATURE

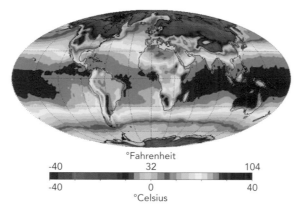

°Fahrenheit

| -40 | 32 | 104 |

| -40 | 0 | 40 |

°Celsius

JULY AVERAGE TEMPERATURE

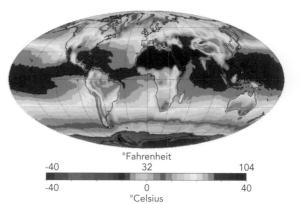

°Fahrenheit

| -40 | 32 | 104 |

| -40 | 0 | 40 |

°Celsius

JANUARY CLOUD COVER

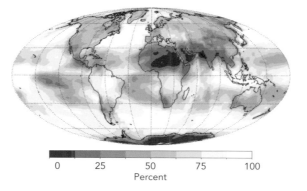

| 0 | 25 | 50 | 75 | 100 |

Percent

JULY CLOUD COVER

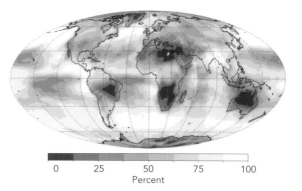

| 0 | 25 | 50 | 75 | 100 |

Percent

JANUARY PRECIPITATION

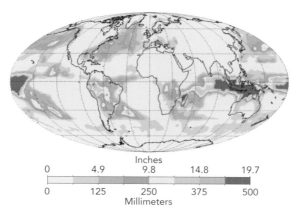

Inches

| 0 | 4.9 | 9.8 | 14.8 | 19.7 |

| 0 | 125 | 250 | 375 | 500 |

Millimeters

JULY PRECIPITATION

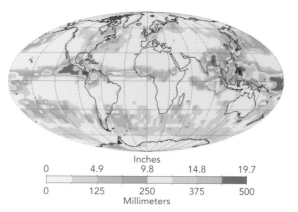

Inches

| 0 | 4.9 | 9.8 | 14.8 | 19.7 |

| 0 | 125 | 250 | 375 | 500 |

Millimeters

10 MILLION YEARS AGO

1 MILLION YEARS AGO

100,000 YEARS AGO

Major Factors That Influence Climate

LATITUDE AND ANGLE OF THE SUN'S RAYS

As Earth circles the sun, the tilt of its axis causes changes in the angle of the sun's rays and in the periods of daylight at different latitudes. Polar regions experience the greatest variation, with long periods of limited or no sunlight in winter and sometimes 24 hours of daylight in the summer.

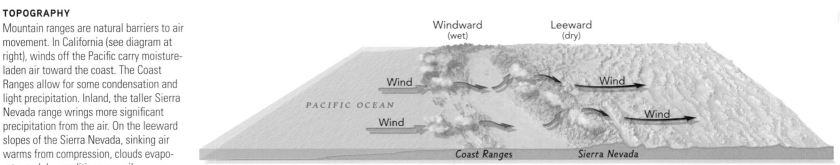

ELEVATION (ALTITUDE)

In general, climatic conditions become colder as elevation increases, just as they do when latitude increases. "Life zones" on a high mountain reflect the changes: Plants at the base are the same as those in surrounding countryside. Farther up, treed vegetation distinctly ends at the tree line; at the highest elevations, snow covers the mountain.

Mount Shasta, California

TOPOGRAPHY

Mountain ranges are natural barriers to air movement. In California (see diagram at right), winds off the Pacific carry moisture-laden air toward the coast. The Coast Ranges allow for some condensation and light precipitation. Inland, the taller Sierra Nevada range wrings more significant precipitation from the air. On the leeward slopes of the Sierra Nevada, sinking air warms from compression, clouds evaporate, and dry conditions prevail.

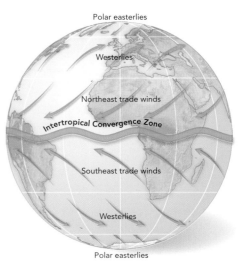

Cool → Warm → Temperature variations as air moves over mountains

EFFECTS OF GEOGRAPHY

The location of a place and its distance from mountains and bodies of water help determine its prevailing wind patterns and what types of air masses affect it. Coastal areas may enjoy refreshing breezes in summer, when cooler ocean air moves ashore. Places south and east of the Great Lakes can expect "lake effect" snow in winter, when cold air travels over relatively warmer waters. In spring and summer, people living in "Tornado Alley" in the central United States watch for thunderstorms. Here, three types of air masses often converge: cold and dry from the north, warm and dry from the southwest, and warm and moist from the Gulf of Mexico. The colliding air masses often spawn tornadic storms.

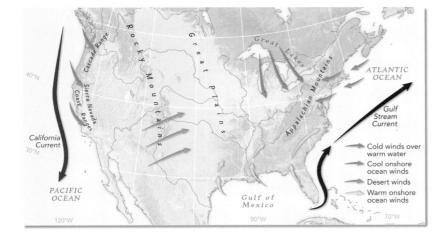

PREVAILING GLOBAL WIND PATTERNS

As shown at right, three large-scale wind patterns are found in the Northern Hemisphere and three are found in the Southern Hemisphere. These are average conditions and do not necessarily reflect conditions on a particular day. As seasons change, the wind patterns shift north or south. So does the intertropical convergence zone, which moves back and forth across the Equator. Sailors called this zone the doldrums because its winds are typically weak.

Polar easterlies
Westerlies
Northeast trade winds
Intertropical Convergence Zone
Southeast trade winds
Westerlies
Polar easterlies

SURFACE OF THE EARTH

Just look at any globe or a world map showing land cover, and you will see another important influence on climate: Earth's surface. The amount of sunlight that is absorbed or reflected by the surface determines how much atmospheric heating occurs. Darker areas, such as heavily vegetated regions, tend to be good absorbers; lighter areas, such as snow- and ice-covered regions, tend to be good reflectors. Oceans absorb a high proportion of the solar energy falling upon them but release it more slowly. Both the oceans and the atmosphere distribute heat around the globe.

Temperature Change over Time

Cold and warm periods punctuate Earth's long history. Some were fairly short (perhaps hundreds of years); others spanned hundreds of thousands of years. In some cold periods, glaciers grew and spread over large regions. In subsequent warm periods, the ice retreated. Each period profoundly affected plant and animal life. The most recent cool period, often called the little ice age, ended in western Europe around the year 1850.

Since the turn of the 20th century, temperatures have been rising steadily throughout the world. But it is not yet clear how much of this warming is due to natural causes and how much derives from human activities, such as the burning of fossil fuels and the clearing of forests.

Global Air Temperature Changes (relative to 1961–1990 average)

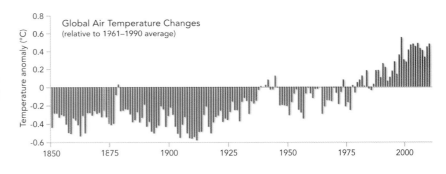

CLIMATE ZONES ARE PRIMARILY CONTROLLED by latitude—which governs the prevailing winds, the angle of the sun's rays, and the length of day throughout the year—and by geographical location with respect to mountains and oceans. Elevation, surface attributes, and other variables modify the primary controlling factors. Latitudinal banding of climate zones is most pronounced over Africa and Asia, where fewer north-south mountain ranges mean less disruption of prevailing winds. In the Western Hemisphere, the high, almost continuous mountain range that extends from western Canada to southern South America helps create dry regions on its leeward slopes. Over the United States, where westerly winds prevail, areas to the east of the range lie in a "rain shadow" and are therefore drier. In northern parts of South America, where easterly trade winds prevail, the rain shadow lies west of the mountains. Ocean effects dominate much of western Europe and southern parts of Australia.

Climographs

The map at right shows the global distribution of climate zones, while the eight climographs (graphs of monthly temperature and precipitation) below provide snapshots of the climate at specific places. Each place has a different climate type, which is described in general terms. Rainfall is shown in a bar graph format (scale on right side of the graph); temperature is expressed with a line graph (scale on left side). Places with highland and upland climates were not included because local changes in elevation can produce significant variations in local conditions.

Climate zones
(based on modified Köppen system)

Humid equatorial climate (A)
- No dry season (Af)
- Short dry season (Am)
- Dry winter (Aw)

Dry climate (B)
- Semiarid (BS) } h = hot
- Arid (BW)   } k = cold

Humid temperate climate (C)
- No dry season (Cf)
- Dry winter (Cw)
- Dry summer (Cs)

Humid cold climate (D)
- No dry season (Df)
- Dry winter (Dw)

Cold polar climate (E)
- Tundra and ice

Highland climate (H)
- Unclassified highlands

Ocean current
- → Cold
- → Warm

a = hot summer
b = cool summer
c = short, cool summer
d = very cold winter

PACIFIC OCEAN

ATLANTIC OCEAN

Beaufort Gyre
Alaska Current
Subarctic Current
North Pacific Drift
California Current
North Equatorial Current
Equatorial Countercurrent
South Equatorial Current
South Subtropical Current
Peru Current
Gulf Stream
North Atlantic Drift
Labrador Current
Brazil Current
Falkland Current
Weddell Gyre

Denver
Buenos Aires

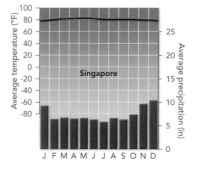

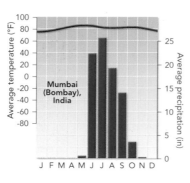

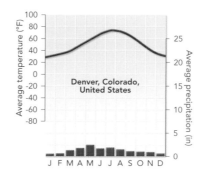

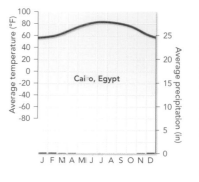

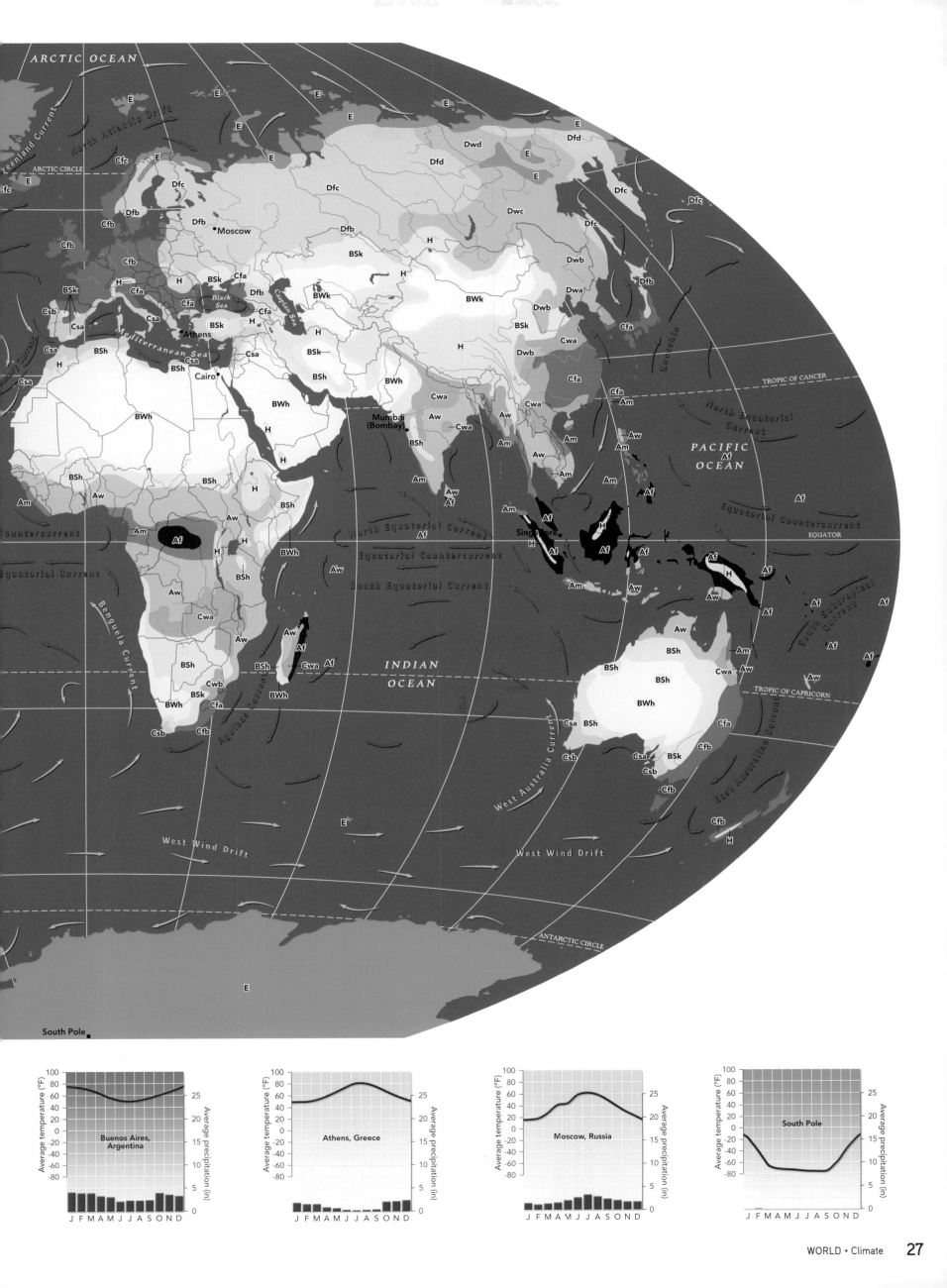

ARCTIC OCEAN

Greenland Current

North Atlantic Drift

ARCTIC CIRCLE

fc

Cfc

Dfc

E E E E E E E E E

Dwd Dfd

Dfc

Dfb
• Moscow

Cfb

Cfb

Dfb

Dfc

Dfd

Dwc

Dfc

Dwb

Dfc

Cfb

BSk

H

Cfa

BSk

H

Cfa

Black
Sea

Dfb

Cfa

Caspian
Sea

BSk

Cfa

BSk

Athens

Mediterranean Sea

Csa

Csa

Csb

BSh

H

Csa

Csa

Csa

Csa

Cairo

BWh

Csa

H

BSh

H

BSh

H

H

BSh

BSk

BWk

BSk

BSh

BWh

BSk

H

Cwa

BWk

H

H

Cwa

Cwa

Aw

Mumbai
(Bombay) •

Aw

Cwa

Cfa

Cfa

Am

Dwb

Dwa

Dwb

Cwa

Dfb

Kuroshio

TROPIC OF CANCER

North Equatorial
Current

BSh

Aw
Af

Aw

Am

Am

Am

Am

Am

Am

PACIFIC
OCEAN

Af

Af

Counter current

Am

Af

North Equatorial Current
Af

Singapore

Af

H

Am

Af

Af

Af

H

Af

Equatorial Counter current

EQUATOR

Af

Af

Af

Equatorial Current

Equatorial Counter current

South Equatorial Current

Aw

Aw

Am

Af

H

Aw

Aw

Af

Af

Af

Af

Af

South Subtropical Current

Af

Af

Benguela Current

Am

Af

Aw

Cwa

Aw

BWh

H

BSh

Aw

Aw

Af

Cwa

Af

INDIAN
OCEAN

Aw

Am

Aw

BSh

BSh

Aw

BSh

BWh

Am

TROPIC OF CAPRICORN

East Australian Current

BSh

Cwa

Aw

BSh

Cwb

BSk

BWh

Cfa

Csb

Cfb

Agulhas Current

BSh

BWh

Csa

BSh

Csb

Csa

BSk

West Australia Current

Cfa

Csb

Cfb

H

E

West Wind Drift

West Wind Drift

ANTARCTIC CIRCLE

E

South Pole •

WORLD • Climate 27

| | Buenos Aires, Argentina | Athens, Greece | Moscow, Russia | South Pole |

WHILE POPULATIONS IN MANY PARTS of the world are expanding, those of Europe—along with some other rich industrial areas such as Japan—show little to no growth, or may actually be shrinking. Many such countries must bring in immigrant workers to keep their economies thriving. A clear correlation exists between wealth and low fertility: the higher the incomes and educational levels, the lower the rates of reproduction.

Many governments keep vital statistics, recording births and deaths, and count their populations regularly to try to plan ahead. The United States has taken a census every ten years since 1790, recording the ages, the occupations, and other important facts about its people. The United Nations helps less developed countries carry out censuses and improve their demographic information.

Governments of some poor countries may find that half their populations are under the age of 20. They are faced with the overwhelming tasks of providing adequate education and jobs while encouraging better family-planning programs. Governments of nations with low birthrates find themselves with growing numbers of elderly people but fewer workers able to provide tax money for health care and pensions.

In the last 150 years, world population has grown more than fivefold, to over seven billion. The industrial revolution helped bring about improvements in food supplies and advances in both medicine and public health, which allowed people to live longer and to have more healthy babies. Today, 367,000 people are born into the world every day, and most of them are in poor African, Asian, and South American countries. This situation concerns planners, who look to demographers (professionals who study all aspects of population) for important data.

Lights of the World

Satellite imagery offers a surprising view of the world at night. Bright lights in Europe, Asia, and the United States give a clear picture of densely populated areas with ample electricity. Reading this map requires great care, however. Some totally dark areas, like most of Australia, do in fact have very small populations, but other light-free areas—in China and Africa, for example—may simply hide dense populations without enough electricity to be seen by a satellite. Wealthy areas with fewer people, such as Florida, may be using their energy wastefully. Ever since the 1970s, demographers have supplemented census data with information from satellite imagery.

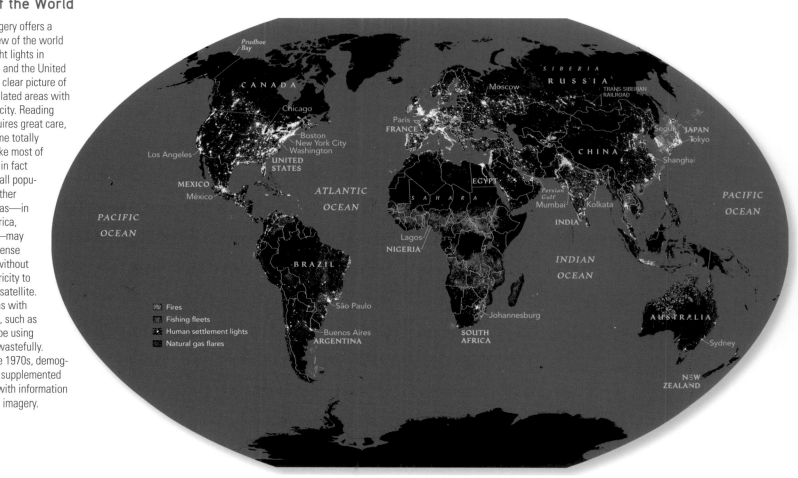

Population Pyramids

A population pyramid shows the number of males and females in every age group of a population. A pyramid for Nigeria reveals that over half—about 54 percent—of the population is under 20, while less than 19 percent of Italy's population is younger than 20.

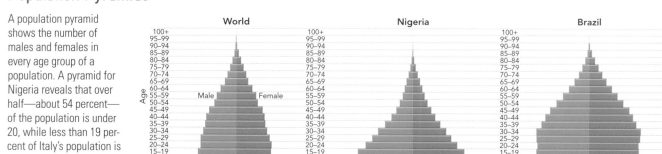

Population Growth

The population of the world is not distributed evenly. In this cartogram, Canada is represented as a narrow strip above the United States, while India looms large. Although Canada has three times India's land area, India's population is 35 times larger than Canada's. In cartograms, the shapes and sizes of countries are distorted to better compare population or other data.

Population sizes are constantly changing, however. In countries that are experiencing many more births than deaths, population totals are ballooning (shown here in red and orange). In others (shown in blue), deaths outnumber births, and populations are shrinking.

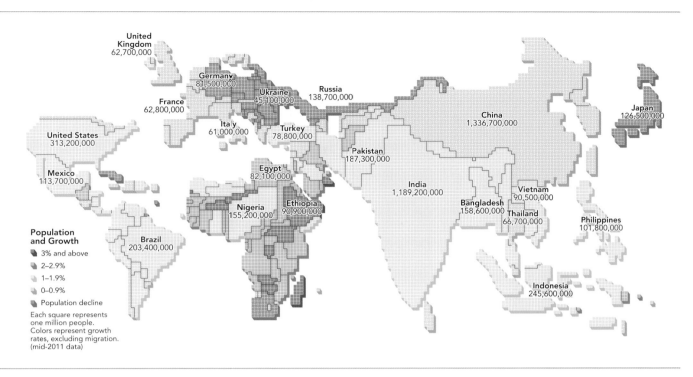

Population and Growth

- 3% and above
- 2–2.9%
- 1–1.9%
- 0–0.9%
- Population decline

Each square represents one million people. Colors represent growth rates, excluding migration. (mid-2011 data)

Population Density

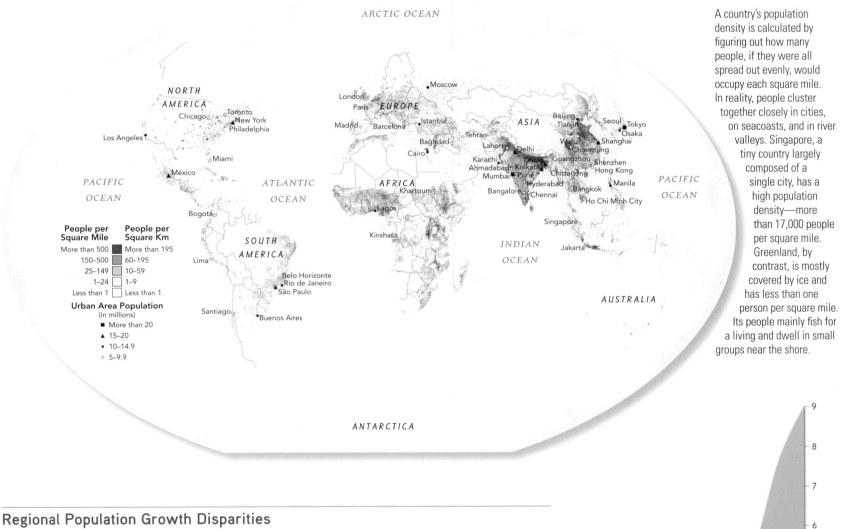

People per Square Mile / People per Square Km

- More than 500 / More than 195
- 150–500 / 60–195
- 25–149 / 10–59
- 1–24 / 1–9
- Less than 1 / Less than 1

Urban Area Population (in millions)
- More than 20
- 15–20
- 10–14.9
- 5–9.9

A country's population density is calculated by figuring out how many people, if they were all spread out evenly, would occupy each square mile. In reality, people cluster together closely in cities, on seacoasts, and in river valleys. Singapore, a tiny country largely composed of a single city, has a high population density—more than 17,000 people per square mile. Greenland, by contrast, is mostly covered by ice and has less than one person per square mile. Its people mainly fish for a living and dwell in small groups near the shore.

Regional Population Growth Disparities

Two centuries ago, the population of the world began a phenomenal expansion. Despite their continued growth, the populations of North America and Australia don't stack up to the population numbers of Asia and Africa. China and India now have more than a billion people each, making Asia the most populous continent. Even Africa, though it has the fastest growth rate, does not yet approach Asia in total numbers. According to some expert predictions, the world's population, now totaling more than seven billion, will start to level off about the year 2050, when it should total more than nine billion. Nearly all the new growth will take place in Asia, Africa, and Latin America; however, Africa's share will be much greater than its present level and China's share will decline.

- Asia
- Africa
- Latin America
- Europe
- North America
- Australia/Oceania

Fertility

Fertility, or birthrate, measures the average number of children born to women in a given population. It can also be expressed as the number of live births per thousand people in a population per year. In low-income countries with limited educational opportunities for girls and women, birthrates reach their highest levels.

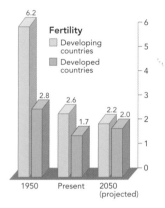

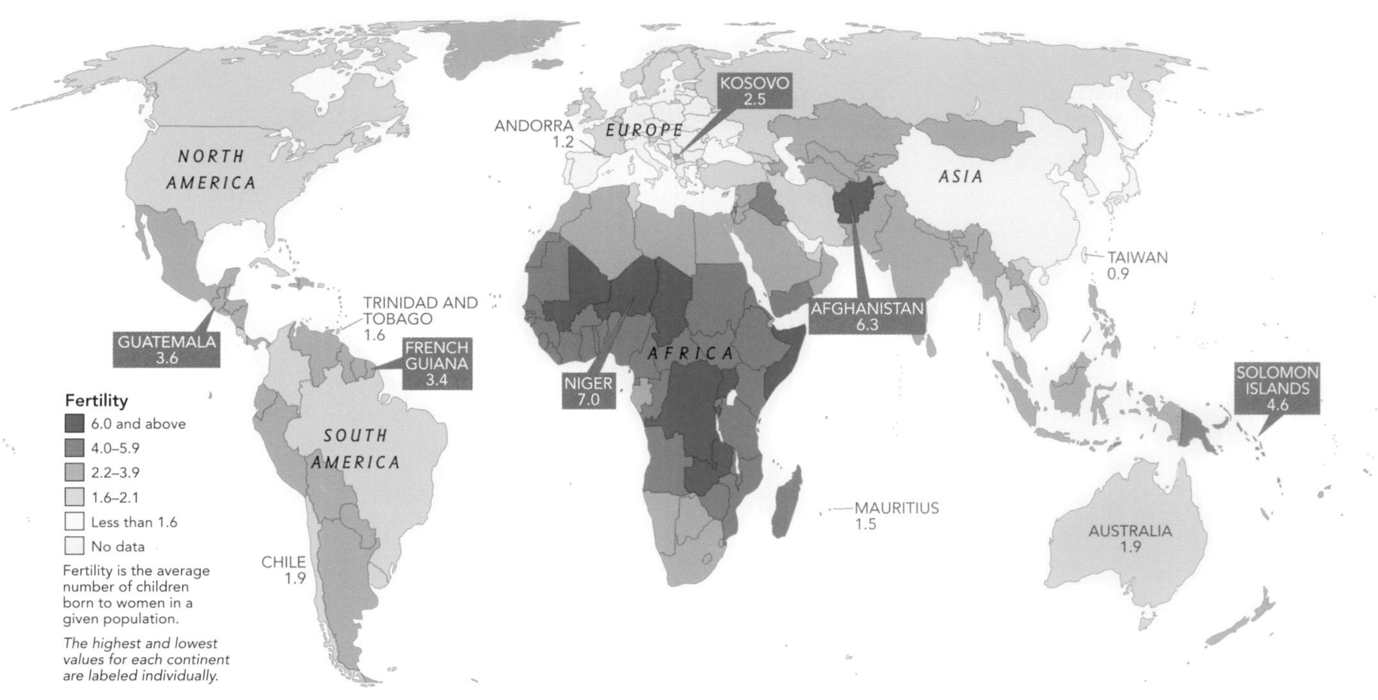

Fertility
- Developing countries
- Developed countries

1950	Present	2050 (projected)
6.2 / 2.8	2.6 / 1.7	2.2 / 2.0

Fertility
- 6.0 and above
- 4.0–5.9
- 2.2–3.9
- 1.6–2.1
- Less than 1.6
- No data

Fertility is the average number of children born to women in a given population.

The highest and lowest values for each continent are labeled individually.

Map labels: NORTH AMERICA; SOUTH AMERICA; EUROPE; ASIA; AFRICA; AUSTRALIA; KOSOVO 2.5; ANDORRA 1.2; TAIWAN 0.9; AFGHANISTAN 6.3; NIGER 7.0; GUATEMALA 3.6; TRINIDAD AND TOBAGO 1.6; FRENCH GUIANA 3.4; CHILE 1.9; MAURITIUS 1.5; SOLOMON ISLANDS 4.6; AUSTRALIA 1.9

Urbanization

People around the world are leaving farms and moving to cities, where jobs and opportunities are better. Since 2008 more than half the world's people live in towns or cities. The shift of population from the countryside to urban centers will probably continue in less developed countries for many years to come.

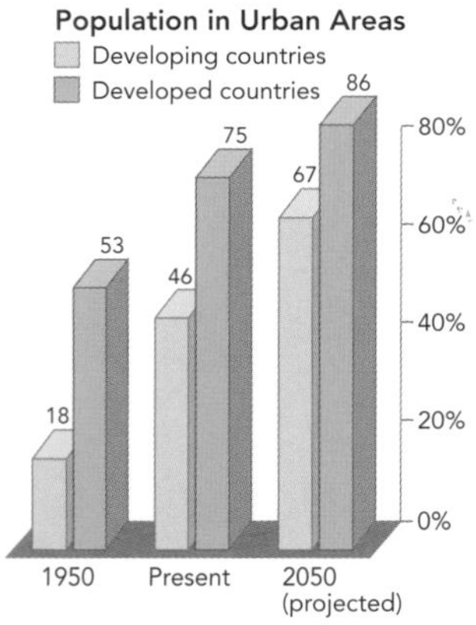

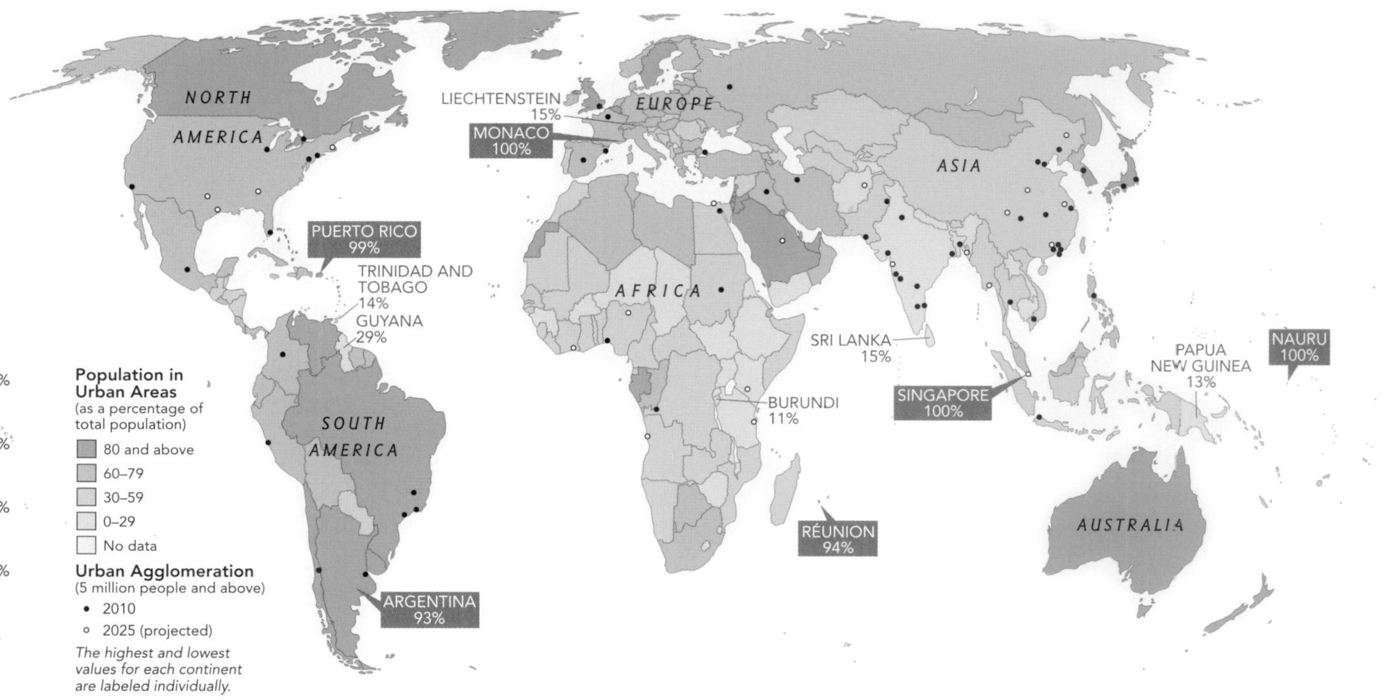

Population in Urban Areas
- Developing countries
- Developed countries

1950	Present	2050 (projected)
18 / 53	46 / 75	67 / 86

Population in Urban Areas (as a percentage of total population)
- 80 and above
- 60–79
- 30–59
- 0–29
- No data

Urban Agglomeration (5 million people and above)
- • 2010
- ○ 2025 (projected)

The highest and lowest values for each continent are labeled individually.

Map labels: NORTH AMERICA; SOUTH AMERICA; EUROPE; ASIA; AFRICA; AUSTRALIA; LIECHTENSTEIN 15%; MONACO 100%; PUERTO RICO 99%; TRINIDAD AND TOBAGO 14%; GUYANA 29%; SRI LANKA 15%; BURUNDI 11%; SINGAPORE 100%; PAPUA NEW GUINEA 13%; NAURU 100%; RÉUNION 94%; ARGENTINA 93%

Urban Population Growth

Urban populations are growing more than twice as fast as populations as a whole. In 2008 the world's city population surpassed its rural population, as rural inhabitants moved to towns, towns became cities and cities merged into megacities with more than ten million people. Globalization speeds the process. Although cities generate wealth and provide better health care along with electricity, clean water, sewage treatment, and other benefits, they can also cause great ecological damage. Squatter settlements and slums may develop if cities cannot keep up with millions of new arrivals. Smog, congestion, pollution, and crime are other dangers. Good city management is a key to future prosperity.

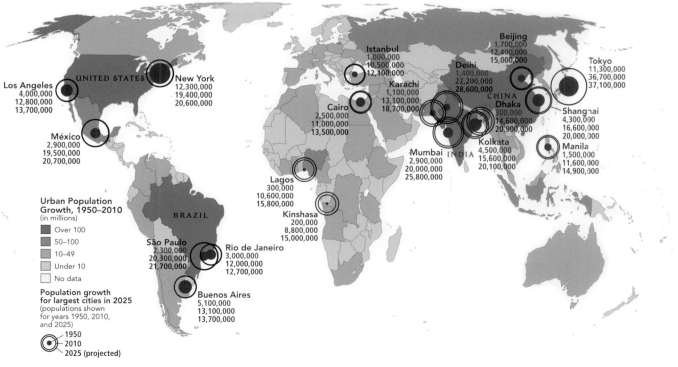

Urban Population Growth, 1950–2010 (in millions)
- Over 100
- 50–100
- 10–49
- Under 10
- No data

Population growth for largest cities in 2025 (populations shown for years 1950, 2010, and 2025)
- 1950
- 2010
- 2025 (projected)

City data:
- Los Angeles: 4,000,000 / 12,800,000 / 13,700,000
- New York: 12,300,000 / 19,400,000 / 20,600,000
- México: 2,900,000 / 19,500,000 / 20,700,000
- São Paulo: 2,300,000 / 20,300,000 / 21,700,000
- Rio de Janeiro: 3,000,000 / 12,000,000 / 12,700,000
- Buenos Aires: 5,100,000 / 13,100,000 / 13,700,000
- Lagos: 300,000 / 10,600,000 / 15,800,000
- Kinshasa: 200,000 / 8,800,000 / 15,000,000
- Cairo: 2,500,000 / 11,000,000 / 13,500,000
- Istanbul: 1,000,000 / 10,500,000 / 12,100,000
- Karachi: 1,100,000 / 13,100,000 / 18,700,000
- Delhi: 1,400,000 / 22,200,000 / 28,600,000
- Beijing: 1,700,000 / 12,400,000 / 15,000,000
- Tokyo: 11,300,000 / 36,700,000 / 37,100,000
- Dhaka: 300,000 / 14,600,000 / 20,900,000
- Shanghai: 4,300,000 / 16,600,000 / 20,000,000
- Mumbai: 2,900,000 / 20,000,000 / 25,800,000
- Kolkata: 4,500,000 / 15,600,000 / 20,100,000
- Manila: 1,500,000 / 11,600,000 / 14,900,000

Map labels: UNITED STATES; BRAZIL; CHINA; INDIA

Life Expectancy

Life expectancy for population groups does not mean that all people die by a certain age. It is an average of death statistics. High infant mortality results in low life expectancy: People who live to adulthood will probably reach old age; there are just fewer of them.

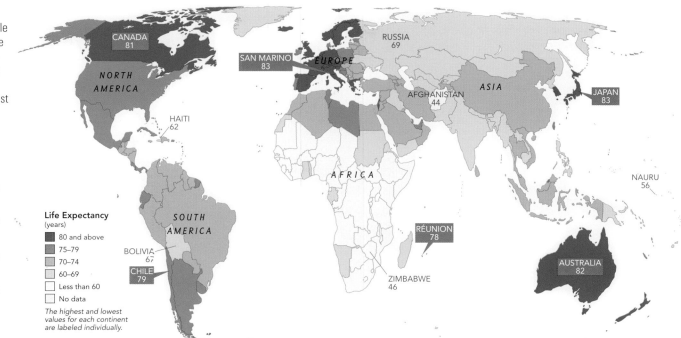

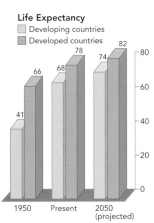

Life Expectancy
- Developing countries
- Developed countries

1950: 41, 66
Present: 68, 78
2050 (projected): 74, 82

Life Expectancy
(years)
- 80 and above
- 75–79
- 70–74
- 60–69
- Less than 60
- No data

The highest and lowest values for each continent are labeled individually.

Migration

International migration has reached its highest level, with foreign workers now providing the labor in several Middle Eastern nations and immigrant workers proving essential to rich countries with low birthrates. Refugees continue to escape grim political and environmental conditions, while businesspeople and tourists keep many economies spinning.

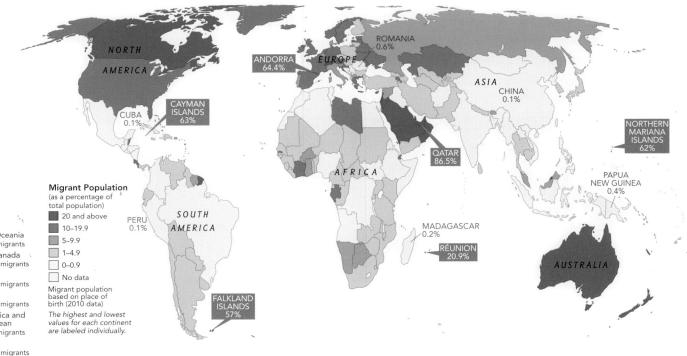

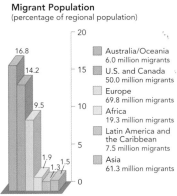

Migrant Population
(percentage of regional population)

- Australia/Oceania 6.0 million migrants — 16.8
- U.S. and Canada 50.0 million migrants — 14.2
- Europe 69.8 million migrants — 9.5
- Africa 19.3 million migrants — 1.9
- Latin America and the Caribbean 7.5 million migrants — 1.3
- Asia 61.3 million migrants — 1.5

Migrant Population
(as a percentage of total population)
- 20 and above
- 10–19.9
- 5–9.9
- 1–4.9
- 0–0.9
- No data

Migrant population based on place of birth (2010 data)

The highest and lowest values for each continent are labeled individually.

Most Populous Places

(MID-2011 DATA)

1. China 1,336,700,000
2. India 1,189,200,000
3. United States 313,200,000
4. Indonesia 245,600,000
5. Brazil 203,400,000
6. Pakistan 187,300,000
7. Bangladesh 158,600,000
8. Nigeria 155,200,000
9. Russia 138,700,000
10. Japan 126,500,000
11. Mexico 113,700,000
12. Philippines 101,800,000
13. Ethiopia 90,900,000
14. Vietnam 90,500,000
15. Egypt 82,100,000
16. Germany 81,500,000
17. Turkey 78,800,000
18. Iran 77,900,000
19. Dem. Rep. of Congo 71,700,000
20. Thailand 66,700,000

Most Crowded Places

DENSITY (POPULATION/SQ. MI.)

1. Monaco 47,350
2. Singapore 19,590
3. Bahrain 4,990
4. Malta 3,380
5. Maldives 2,830
6. Bangladesh 2,710
7. Channel Islands (U.K.) 2,080
8. Palestinian Areas 1,790
9. Taiwan 1,670
10. Barbados 1,650
11. Mauritius 1,630
12. Mayotte (Fr.) 1,460
13. San Marino 1,330
14. South Korea 1,270
15. Nauru 1,260
16. Tuvalu 1,120
17. Puerto Rico (U.S.) 1,080
18. Rwanda 1,070
19. Lebanon 1,060
20. Netherlands 1,040

Demographic Extremes

LIFE EXPECTANCY
LOWEST (FEMALE, IN YEARS):
- 44 Afghanistan
- 45 Zimbabwe
- 48 Lesotho, Swaziland
- 49 Zambia

LOWEST (MALE, IN YEARS):
- 44 Afghanistan
- 46 Zimbabwe
- 47 Dem. Rep. of Congo, Guinea-Bissau
- 48 Central African Republic, Chad

POPULATION AGE STRUCTURE
HIGHEST % POPULATION UNDER AGE 15
- 49% Niger
- 48% Mali, Uganda
- 47% Angola
- 46% Zambia, Dem. Rep. of Congo, Burundi, Mayotte (Fr.)

HIGHEST (FEMALE, IN YEARS):
- 86 Japan, San Marino
- 85 France, Spain
- 84 Australia, Iceland, Israel, Italy, Martinique (Fr.), Singapore, South Korea, Sweden, Switzerland

HIGHEST (MALE, IN YEARS):
- 81 San Marino
- 80 Iceland, Israel, Japan, Sweden, Switzerland
- 79 Australia, Italy, Liechtenstein, Netherlands, New Zealand, Norway, Singapore, Spain

HIGHEST % POPULATION AGE 65 AND OVER
- 24% Monaco
- 23% Japan
- 21% Germany
- 20% Italy
- 19% Greece

Religions

THE GREAT POWER OF RELIGION comes from its ability to speak to the heart of individuals and societies. Since earliest human times, honoring nature spirits or the belief in a supreme being has brought comfort and security in the face of fundamental questions of life and death.

Billions of people are now adherents of Hinduism, Buddhism, Judaism, Christianity, and Islam, all of which began in Asia. Universal elements of these faiths include ritual and prayer, sacred sites and pilgrimage, saints and martyrs, ritual clothing and implements, dietary laws and fasting, festivals and holy days, and special ceremonies for life's major moments. Sometimes otherworldly, most religions have moral and ethical guidelines that attempt to make life better on Earth as well. Their tenets and goals are taught not only at the church, synagogue, mosque, or temple but also through schools, storytelling, parables, painting, sculpture, and even dance and drama.

The world's major religions blossomed from the teachings and revelations of individuals who heeded and transmitted the voice of God or discovered a way to salvation that could be understood by others. Abraham and Moses for Jews, the Buddha for Buddhists, Jesus Christ for Christians, and Muhammad for Muslims fulfilled the roles of divine teachers who experienced essential truths of existence.

Throughout history, priests, rabbis, clergymen, and imams have recited, interpreted, and preached the holy words of sacred texts and writings to the faithful. Today the world's religions, with their guidance here on Earth and some with their hopes and promises for the afterlife, continue to exert an extraordinary force on billions of people.

Dominant Religion

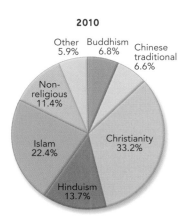

BUDDHISM
Founded about 2,500 years ago by Shakyamuni Buddha (or Gautama Buddha), Buddhism teaches liberation from suffering through the threefold cultivation of morality, meditation, and wisdom. Buddhists revere the Three Jewels: Buddha (the Awakened One), Dharma (the Truth), and Sangha (the community of monks and nuns).

CHRISTIANITY
Christian belief in eternal life is based on the example of Jesus Christ, a Jew born some 2,000 years ago. The New Testament tells of his teaching, persecution, Crucifixion, and resurrection. Today Christianity is found around the world in three main forms: Roman Catholic, Eastern Orthodox, and Protestant.

HINDUISM
Hinduism began in India more than 4,000 years ago and is still flourishing. Sacred texts known as the Vedas form the basis of Hindu faith

Adherents Worldwide

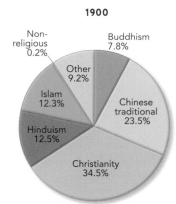

1900
Non-religious 0.2%, Buddhism 7.8%, Other 9.2%, Islam 12.3%, Hinduism 12.5%, Christianity 34.5%, Chinese traditional 23.5%

2010
Other 5.9%, Buddhism 6.8%, Chinese traditional 6.6%, Non-religious 11.4%, Islam 22.4%, Hinduism 13.7%, Christianity 33.2%

The growth of Islam and the decline of Chinese traditional religion stand out as significant changes over the past hundred and ten years. Christianity, the largest of the world's main faiths, has remained fairly stable in its number of adherents. Today more than one in nine people claim to be atheistic or nonreligious.

Adherents by Continent

In terms of the total number of religious adherents, Asia ranks first. This is not only because half the world's people live on that continent but also because three of the five major faiths are practiced there: Hinduism in South Asia; Buddhism in East and Southeast Asia; and Islam from Indonesia to the Central Asian republics to Turkey. Oceania, Europe, North America, and South America are overwhelmingly Christian. Africa, with many millions of Muslims and Christians, also retains large numbers of animists.

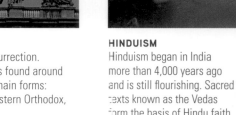
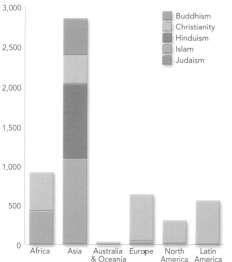

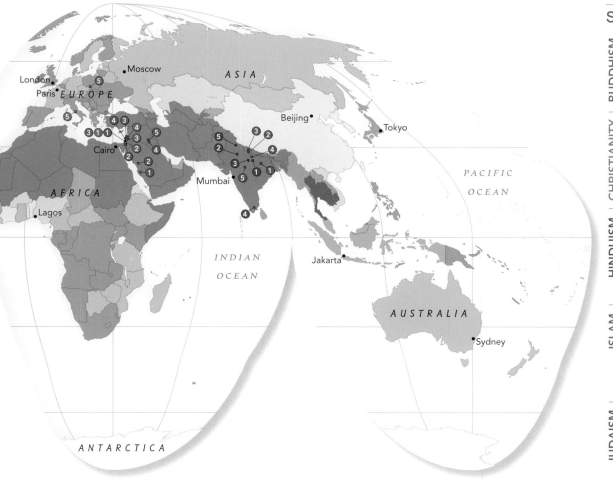

Sacred Places

BUDDHISM
1. Bodhgaya: Where Buddha attained awakening
2. Kusinagara: Where Buddha entered nirvana
3. Lumbini: Place of Buddha's last human birth
4. Sarnath: Place where Buddha delivered his first sermon
5. Sanchi: Location of famous stupa containing relics of Buddha

CHRISTIANITY
1. Jerusalem: Church of the Holy Sepulchre, Jesus' Crucifixion
2. Bethlehem: Jesus' birthplace
3. Nazareth: Where Jesus grew up
4. Shore of the Sea of Galilee: Where Jesus gave the Sermon on the Mount
5. Rome and the Vatican: Tombs of St. Peter and St. Paul

HINDUISM
1. Varanasi (Benares): Most holy Hindu site, home of Shiva
2. Vrindavan: Krishna's birthplace
3. Allahabad: At confluence of Ganges and Yamuna Rivers, purest place to bathe
4. Madurai: Temple of Minakshi, great goddess of the south
5. Badrinath: Vishnu's shrine

ISLAM
1. Mecca: Muhammad's birthplace
2. Medina: City of Muhammad's flight, or Hegira
3. Jerusalem: Dome of the Rock, Muhammad's stepping-stone to heaven
4. Najaf (Shiite): Tomb of Imam Ali
5. Kerbala (Shiite): Tomb of Imam Hoseyn

JUDAISM
1. Jerusalem: Location of the Western Wall and first and second temples
2. Hebron: Tomb of the patriarchs and their wives
3. Safed: Where kabbalah (Jewish mysticism) flourished
4. Tiberias: Where Talmud (source of Jewish law) first composed
5. Auschwitz: Symbol of six million Jews who perished in the Holocaust

and ritual. The main trinity of gods comprises Brahma the creator, Vishnu the preserver, and Shiva the destroyer. Hindus believe in reincarnation.

ISLAM
Muslims believe that the Koran, Islam's sacred book, accurately records the spoken word of God (Allah) as revealed to the Prophet Muhammad, born in Mecca around A.D. 570. Strict adherents pray five times a day, fast during the holy month of Ramadan, and make at least one pilgrimage to Mecca, Islam's holiest city.

JUDAISM
The 4,000-year-old religion of the Jews stands as the oldest of the major faiths that believe in a single God. Judaism's traditions, customs, laws, and beliefs date back to Abraham, the founder, and to the Torah, the first five books of the Old Testament, believed to have been handed down to Moses on Mount Sinai.

Adherents by Country

COUNTRIES WITH THE MOST BUDDHISTS		COUNTRIES WITH THE MOST CHRISTIANS		COUNTRIES WITH THE MOST HINDUS		COUNTRIES WITH THE MOST MUSLIMS		COUNTRIES WITH THE MOST JEWS	
COUNTRY	**BUDDHISTS**	**COUNTRY**	**CHRISTIANS**	**COUNTRY**	**HINDUS**	**COUNTRY**	**MUSLIMS**	**COUNTRY**	**JEWS**
1. China	190,000,000	1. United States	257,311,000	1. India	891,520,000	1. Indonesia	188,164,000	1. Israel	5,295,000
2. Japan	71,562,000	2. Brazil	180,932,000	2. Nepal	20,630,000	2. India	168,250,000	2. United States	5,220,000
3. Thailand	56,497,000	3. Russia	115,120,000	3. Bangladesh	15,600,000	3. Pakistan	166,576,000	3. France	610,000
4. Vietnam	44,383,000	4. China	115,009,000	4. Indonesia	4,550,000	4. Bangladesh	148,078,000	4. Palestine*	510,000
5. Myanmar	36,851,000	5. Mexico	105,583,000	5. Sri Lanka	2,550,000	5. Turkey	75,670,000	5. Argentina	494,000
6. Sri Lanka	13,315,000	6. Philippines	83,151,000	6. Pakistan	2,260,000	6. Iran	73,276,000	6. Canada	435,000
7. Cambodia	12,930,000	7. Nigeria	72,302,000	7. Malaysia	1,750,000	7. Nigeria	72,306,000	7. United Kingdom	280,000
8. India	8,500,000	8. Congo, Dem. Rep.	65,803,000	8. United States	1,445,000	8. Egypt	68,804,000	8. Germany	230,000
9. South Korea	7,325,000	9. India	58,367,000	9. South Africa	1,175,000	9. Algeria	34,712,000	9. Russia	180,000
10. Taiwan*	6,250,000	10. Germany	58,123,000	10. Myanmar	855,000	10. Morocco	31,845,000	10. Ukraine	175,000

*Non-sovereign nation

All figures are estimates based on data for the year 2010.
Countries with the highest reported nonreligious populations include China, Russia, United States, Germany, India, Japan, North Korea, Vietnam, France, and Italy.

A GLOBAL ECONOMIC ACTIVITY MAP (right) reveals striking differences in the composition of output in advanced economies (such as those of the United States, Japan, and Western Europe) compared with less developed countries (such as Nigeria and China). Advanced economies tend to have high proportions of their gross domestic product (GDP) in services, while developing economies have relatively high proportions in agriculture and industry.

There are different ways of looking at the distribution of manufacturing industry activity. When examined by country, the United States leads in production in many industries, but Western European countries are also a major manufacturing force. Western Europe outpaces the U.S. in the production of cars, chemicals, and food.

The world's second largest economy is found in China, and it has been growing quite rapidly. Chinese workers take home only a fraction of the cash pocketed each week by their economic rivals in the West but are quickly catching up to the global economy with their purchase of cell phones and motor vehicles—two basic consumer products of the modern age.

The Middle East—a number of whose countries enjoy relatively high per capita GDP values—produces more fuel than any other region, but it has virtually no other economic output besides that single commodity.

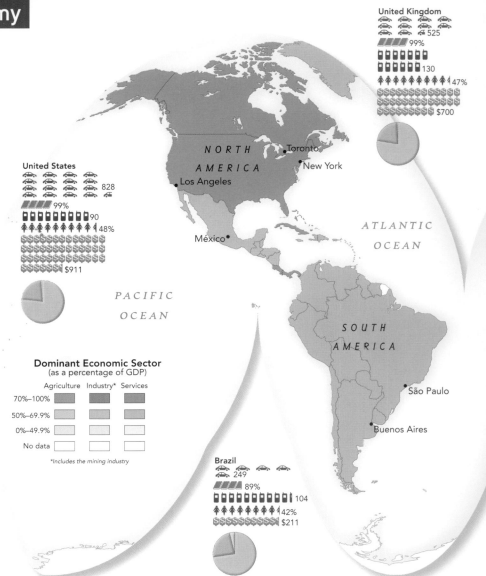

Dominant Economic Sector
(as a percentage of GDP)

Agriculture Industry* Services

70%–100%
50%–69.9%
0%–49.9%
No data

*Includes the mining industry

Labor Migration

People in search of jobs gravitate toward the higher income economies, unless immigration policies prevent them from doing so. Japan, for instance, has one of the world's most restrictive immigration policies and a population that is 99 percent Japanese. Migration is also a major force behind global urbanization. Migrants often choose to move to a particular city, following a migration chain or available jobs. This map shows selected metropolitan areas in terms of foreign-born population. Overall, the largest share of foreign workers in domestic employment is found in the Persian Gulf region.

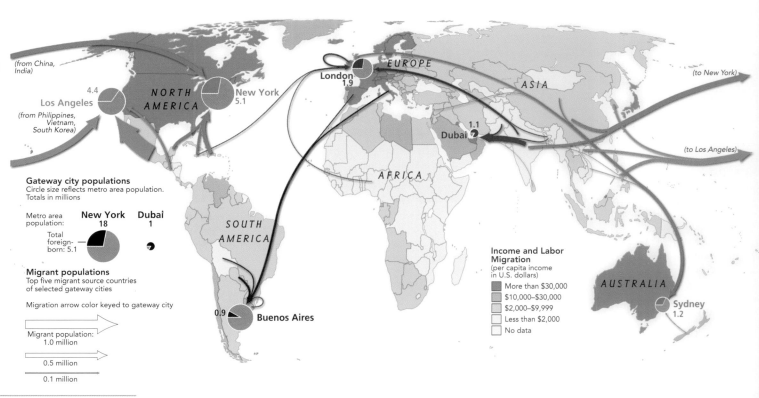

Gateway city populations
Circle size reflects metro area population.
Totals in millions

Metro area population: **New York** 18 **Dubai** 1
Total foreign-born: 5.1

Migrant populations
Top five migrant source countries of selected gateway cities

Migration arrow color keyed to gateway city

Migrant population:
1.0 million
0.5 million
0.1 million

Income and Labor Migration
(per capita income in U.S. dollars)

More than $30,000
$10,000–$30,000
$2,000–$9,999
Less than $2,000
No data

Top GDP Growth Rates
(based on PPP, or purchasing power parity)*

(2010)

1.	Qatar	16%
2.	Paraguay	15%
3.	Singapore	15%
4.	Taiwan	11%
5.	India	10%
6.	China	10%
7.	Turkmenistan	9%
8.	Congo	9%
9.	Sri Lanka	9%
10.	Zimbabwe	9%

The World's Richest and Poorest Countries

RICHEST		GDP PER CAPITA (PPP) (2010)	POOREST		GDP PER CAPITA (PPP) (2010)
1.	Qatar	$88,200	1.	Dem. Rep. of the Congo	$329
2.	Luxembourg	$81,500	2.	Liberia	$396
3.	Singapore	$56,700	3.	Burundi	$412
4.	Norway	$52,000	4.	Zimbabwe	$436
5.	Brunei	$48,300	5.	Somalia	$600
6.	United Arab Emirates	$47,400	6.	Eritrea	$683
7.	United States	$46,900	7.	Central African Republic	$747
8.	Switzerland	$41,900	8.	Niger	$761
9.	Netherlands	$41,000	9.	Sierra Leone	$810
10.	Australia	$39,800	10.	Malawi	$821

*For more information on GDP and PPP, please see maps on page 35.

Figures are listed in U.S. dollars.

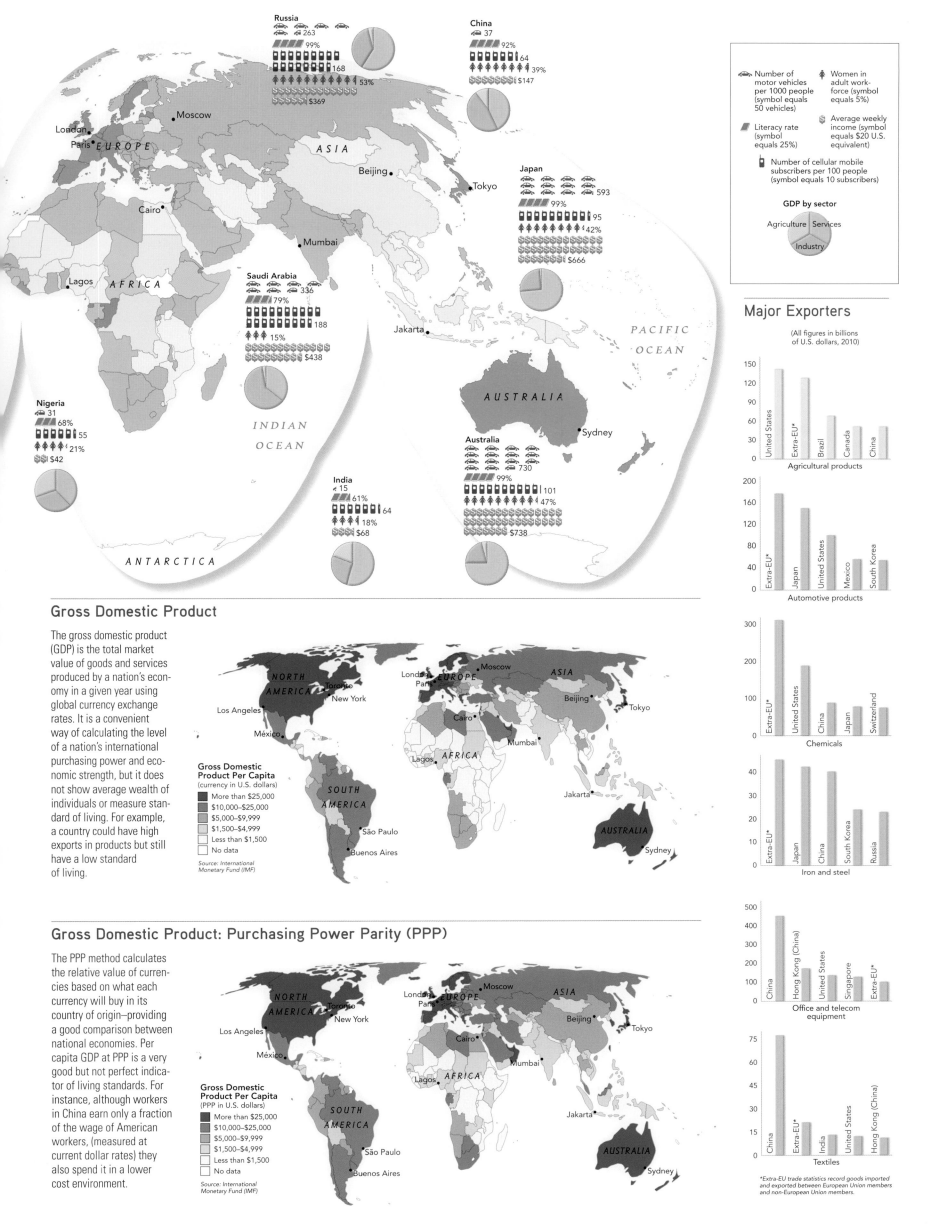

Russia
263
99%
168
53%
$369

China
37
92%
64
39%
$147

Japan
593
99%
95
42%
$666

Saudi Arabia
336
79%
188
15%
$438

Nigeria
31
68%
55
21%
$42

India
15
61%
64
18%
$68

Australia
730
99%
101
47%
$738

London
Paris *EUROPE*
Moscow
ASIA
Cairo
Mumbai
Beijing
Tokyo
Lagos
AFRICA
Jakarta
PACIFIC OCEAN
INDIAN OCEAN
AUSTRALIA
Sydney
ANTARCTICA

Legend:
- Number of motor vehicles per 1000 people (symbol equals 50 vehicles)
- Women in adult work-force (symbol equals 5%)
- Literacy rate (symbol equals 25%)
- Average weekly income (symbol equals $20 U.S. equivalent)
- Number of cellular mobile subscribers per 100 people (symbol equals 10 subscribers)

GDP by sector
Agriculture Services
Industry

Major Exporters

(All figures in billions of U.S. dollars, 2010)

Agricultural products: United States, Extra-EU*, Brazil, Canada, China

Automotive products: Extra-EU*, Japan, United States, Mexico, South Korea

Chemicals: Extra-EU*, United States, China, Japan, Switzerland

Iron and steel: Extra-EU*, Japan, China, South Korea, Russia

Office and telecom equipment: China, Hong Kong (China), United States, Singapore, Extra-EU*

Textiles: China, Extra-EU*, India, United States, Hong Kong (China)

Extra-EU trade statistics record goods imported and exported between European Union members and non-European Union members.

Gross Domestic Product

The gross domestic product (GDP) is the total market value of goods and services produced by a nation's economy in a given year using global currency exchange rates. It is a convenient way of calculating the level of a nation's international purchasing power and economic strength, but it does not show average wealth of individuals or measure standard of living. For example, a country could have high exports in products but still have a low standard of living.

NORTH AMERICA — Toronto, New York, Los Angeles, México
EUROPE — London, Paris, Moscow
ASIA — Beijing, Tokyo
Cairo, Mumbai, Lagos, *AFRICA*, Jakarta
SOUTH AMERICA — São Paulo, Buenos Aires
AUSTRALIA — Sydney

Gross Domestic Product Per Capita
(currency in U.S. dollars)
- More than $25,000
- $10,000–$25,000
- $5,000–$9,999
- $1,500–$4,999
- Less than $1,500
- No data

Source: International Monetary Fund (IMF)

Gross Domestic Product: Purchasing Power Parity (PPP)

The PPP method calculates the relative value of currencies based on what each currency will buy in its country of origin–providing a good comparison between national economies. Per capita GDP at PPP is a very good but not perfect indicator of living standards. For instance, although workers in China earn only a fraction of the wage of American workers, (measured at current dollar rates) they also spend it in a lower cost environment.

NORTH AMERICA — Toronto, New York, Los Angeles, México
EUROPE — London, Paris, Moscow
ASIA — Beijing, Tokyo
Cairo, Mumbai, Lagos, *AFRICA*, Jakarta
SOUTH AMERICA — São Paulo, Buenos Aires
AUSTRALIA — Sydney

Gross Domestic Product Per Capita
(PPP in U.S. dollars)
- More than $25,000
- $10,000–$25,000
- $5,000–$9,999
- $1,500–$4,999
- Less than $1,500
- No data

Source: International Monetary Fund (IMF)

WORLD TRADE HAS EXPANDED at a dizzying pace in the decades following World War II. The dollar value of world merchandise exports rose from $61 billion in 1950 to $15.2 trillion in 2010. Adjusted for price changes, world trade grew 28 times over the last 60 years, much faster than world output. Trade in manufactures expanded much faster than that of mining products (including fuels) and agricultural products. In the last decades many developing countries have become important exporters of manufactures (e.g., China, South Korea, Mexico). However, there are still many less developed countries—primarily in Africa and the Middle East—that are dependent on a few primary commodities for their export earnings. Commercial services exports have expanded rapidly over the past two decades, and amounted to

$3.7 trillion in 2010. While developed countries account for the majority of world services trade, some developing countries now gain most of their export earnings from services exports. Earnings from tourism in the Caribbean and those from software exports in India are prominent examples of developing countries' dynamic services exports.

Capital flows and worker remittances have gained in importance worldwide and are another important aspect of globalization. The stock of worldwide foreign direct investment was estimated to be over $19 trillion in 2010, almost $6 trillion of which was invested in developing countries. Capital markets in many developing countries remain small, fragile, and underdeveloped, which hampers household savings and the funding of local enterprises.

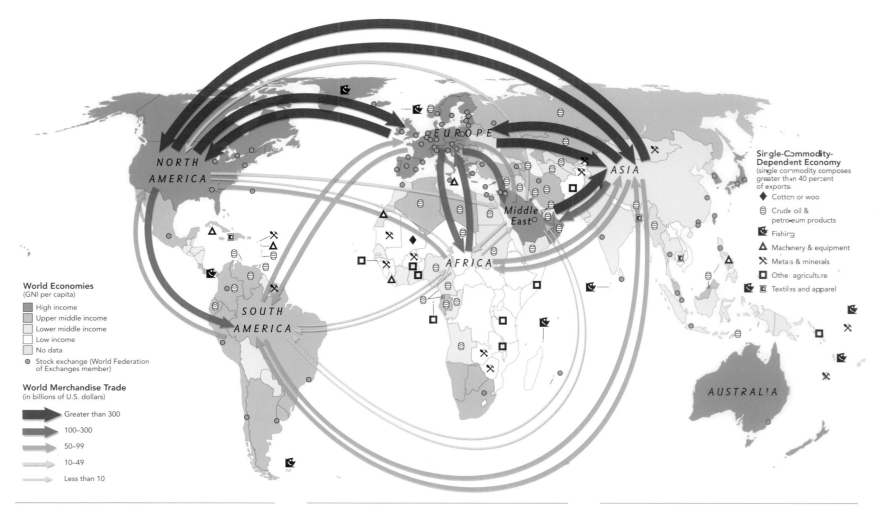

World Economies
(GNI per capita)

- High income
- Upper middle income
- Lower middle income
- Low income
- No data
- ○ Stock exchange (World Federation of Exchanges member)

World Merchandise Trade
(in billions of U.S. dollars)

- Greater than 300
- 100–300
- 50–99
- 10–49
- Less than 10

Single-Commodity-Dependent Economy
(single commodity composes greater than 40 percent of exports)

- ◆ Cotton or wool
- ⚒ Crude oil & petroleum products
- 🐟 Fishing
- △ Machinery & equipment
- ✕ Metals & minerals
- ☐ Other agriculture
- ▨ Textiles and apparel

Growth of World Trade

After World War II the export growth of manufactured goods greatly outstripped other exports. This graph shows the volume growth on a semi-log scale (a straight line represents constant growth) rather than a standard scale (a straight line indicates a constant increase in the absolute values in each year).

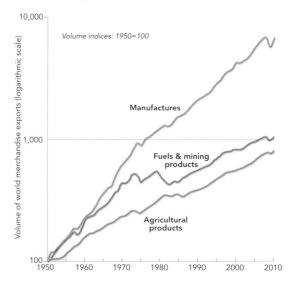

Merchandise Exports

Fuels constitute the fastest growing and largest single category of merchandise exports. Still, manufactured goods dominate, accounting for over two-thirds of world merchandise exports. World exports in chemicals, as well as office and telecom equipment, exceed the export value of all agricultural products.

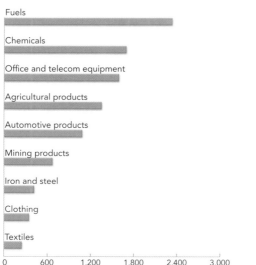

Main Trading Nations

The U.S., Germany, and Japan account for nearly 30 percent of total world merchandise trade. Ongoing negotiations among the 144 member nations of the World Trade Organization are tackling market-access barriers in agriculture, textiles, and clothing—areas where many developing countries hope to compete.

World Debt

Measuring a nation's outstanding foreign debt in relation to its GDP indicates the size of future income needed to pay back the debt; it also shows how much a nation has relied in the past on foreign savings to finance investment and consumption expenditures. A high external debt ratio can pose a financial risk if debt service payments are not assured.

Present Value of External Debt as a Percentage of Gross National Income (GNI), 2006–2010

- More than 80%
- 50%–79%
- 30%–49%
- 15%–29%
- 5%–14%
- Less than 5%
- No data available
- Countries with no IBRD* or IDA* loans or credits

*The World Bank–International Bank for Reconstruction and Development (IBRD) and the International Development Association (IDA)–provide low-interest loans, interest-free credit, and grants to developing countries.

Trade Blocs

Regional trade is on the rise. Agreements between neighboring countries to offer each other trade benefits can create larger markets and improve the economy of the region as a whole. But they can also lead to discrimination, especially when more efficient suppliers outside the regional agreements are prevented from supplying their goods and services.

Major Regional Trade Agreements

- **APEC** - Asia-Pacific Economic Cooperation
- **ASEAN** - Association of Southeast Asian Nations
- **COMESA** - Common Market for Eastern and Southern Africa
- **ECOWAS** - Economic Community of West African States
- **EU** - European Union
- **MERCOSUR** - Southern Common Market
- **SAARC** - South Asian Association for Regional Cooperation
- **APEC & NAFTA** - North American Free Trade Agreement
- **APEC & ASEAN**

Trade Flow: Fuels

The leading exporters of fuel products are countries in the Middle East, Africa, Russia, and central and western Asia; all export more fuel than they consume. But intra-regional energy trade is growing, with some of the key producers—Canada, Indonesia, Norway, and the United Kingdom, for example—located in regions that are net energy importers.

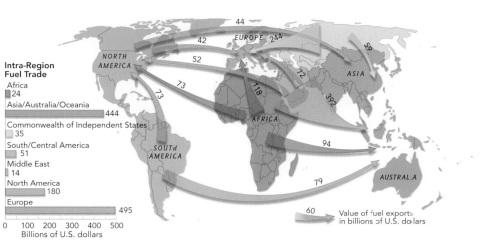

Intra-Region Fuel Trade

- Africa: 24
- Asia/Australia/Oceania: 444
- Commonwealth of Independent States: 35
- South/Central America: 51
- Middle East: 14
- North America: 180
- Europe: 495

0 100 200 300 400 500
Billions of U.S. dollars

60 — Value of fuel exports in billions of U.S. dollars

Trade Flow: Agricultural Products

The world trade in agricultural products is less concentrated than trade in fuels, with processed goods making up the majority. Agricultural products encounter high export barriers, which limit the opportunities for some exporters to expand into foreign markets. Reducing such barriers is a major challenge for governments that are engaged in agricultural trade negotiations.

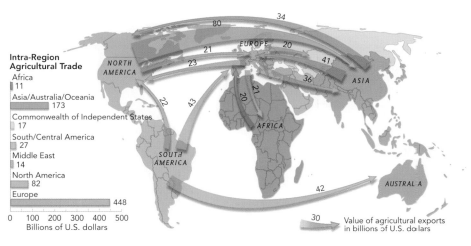

Intra-Region Agricultural Trade

- Africa: 11
- Asia/Australia/Oceania: 173
- Commonwealth of Independent States: 17
- South/Central America: 27
- Middle East: 14
- North America: 82
- Europe: 448

0 100 200 300 400 500
Billions of U.S. dollars

30 — Value of agricultural exports in billions of U.S. dollars

Top Merchandise Exporters and Importers

	PERCENTAGE OF WORLD TOTAL	VALUE (BILLIONS)
TOP EXPORTERS		
China	10.4	$1,578
United States	8.4	$1,278
Germany	8.3	$1,269
Japan	5.1	$770
Netherlands	3.8	$573
France	3.4	$521
South Korea	3.1	$466
Italy	2.9	$448
Belgium	2.7	$412
United Kingdom	2.7	$406
Hong Kong (China)	2.6	$401
Russia	2.6	$400
Canada	2.5	$388
Singapore	2.3	$352
Mexico	2.0	$298
TOP IMPORTERS		
United States	12.8	$1,969
China	9.1	$1,395
Germany	6.9	$1,067
Japan	4.5	$694
France	3.9	$606
United Kingdom	3.6	$560
Netherlands	3.4	$517
Italy	3.1	$484
Hong Kong (China)	2.9	$442
South Korea	2.8	$425
Canada	2.6	$402
Belgium	2.5	$390
India	2.1	$327
Spain	2.0	$314
Singapore	2.0	$311

Top Commercial Services Exporters and Importers

(includes transportation, travel, and other services)

	PERCENTAGE OF WORLD TOTAL	VALUE (BILLIONS)
TOP EXPORTERS		
United States	14.0	$518
Germany	6.3	$232
United Kingdom	6.1	$227
China	4.6	$170
France	3.9	$143
Japan	3.8	$139
India	3.3	$123
Spain	3.3	$123
Netherlands	3.1	$113
Singapore	3.0	$112
Hong Kong (China)	2.9	$106
Ireland	2.6	$97
Italy	2.6	$97
Belgium	2.2	$82
South Korea	2.2	$82
TOP IMPORTERS		
United States	10.2	$358
Germany	7.4	$260
China	5.5	$192
United Kingdom	4.6	$161
Japan	4.4	$156
France	3.7	$129
India	3.3	$116
Ireland	3.1	$108
Italy	3.1	$108
Netherlands	3.0	$106
Singapore	2.7	$96
South Korea	2.6	$93
Canada	2.6	$90
Spain	2.5	$87
Belgium	2.2	$78

IN THE PAST 55 YEARS, health conditions have improved dramatically. With better economic and living conditions and access to immunization and other basic health services, global life expectancy has risen from 40 to 67 years; the death rate for children under five years old has fallen by over 70 percent; and diseases that once killed and disabled millions have been eradicated, eliminated, or greatly reduced in impact. Today, over three-quarters of the world's children benefit from protection against six infectious diseases that were responsible in the past for many millions of infant and child deaths.

Current efforts to improve health face new and daunting challenges, however. Infant and child mortality from infectious diseases remains relatively high in many poor countries. Each year, more than seven million children under five years old die—half of them in sub-Saharan Africa and one-third in South Asia. Improvement in children's health has slowed in the past 20 years, particularly where child death rates have historically been highest.

The HIV/AIDS pandemic has erased decades of steady improvements in sub-Saharan Africa. Worldwide, an estimated 33 million people are HIV-positive, with 23 million of those in Africa. The death toll in Africa has contributed to significant reductions in average life expectancy for many severely affected countries. Recently, however, the overall trend has begun to improve slowly. The annual number of new infections is on the decline, thanks to education and awareness efforts, and treatment is becoming more widely available.

Vast gaps in health outcomes between rich and poor persist. About 99 percent of global childhood deaths occur in poor countries, with the poorest countries having the highest child-mortality rates. In Indonesia, for example, a child born in a poor household is four times as likely to die by her fifth birthday as a child born to a well-off family.

In many high- and middle-income countries, chronic, lifestyle-related diseases such as cardiovascular disease, diabetes, and others are becoming the predominant cause of disability and death. Because the focus of policymakers has been on treatment rather than prevention, the costs of dealing with these ailments contribute to high (and rapidly increasing) health-care spending. Tobacco-related illnesses are major problems worldwide. In developed countries, smoking is the cause of more than one-third of male deaths in middle age, and about one in eight female deaths. It is estimated that due to trends of increasing tobacco use, of all the people aged under 20 alive today in China, 50 million will die prematurely from tobacco use.

Income Levels: Indicators of Health and Literacy

Personal Income
- High income
- Upper middle income
- Lower middle income
- Low income
- No data

Access to Improved Sanitation

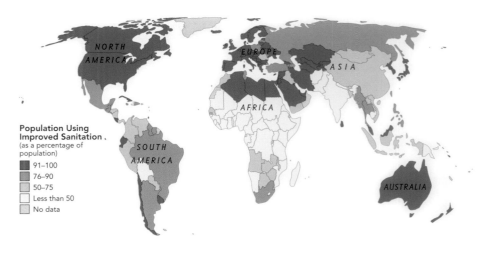

Population Using Improved Sanitation (as a percentage of population)
- 91–100
- 76–90
- 50–75
- Less than 50
- No data

Nutrition

Undernourishment (as a percentage of population)
- 50–75
- 30–49
- 15–29
- 5–14
- No data

Health-Care Availability

Regional differences in health-care resources are striking. While countries in Europe and the Americas have relatively large numbers of physicians and nurses, nations with far higher burdens of disease (particularly African countries) are experiencing severe deficits in both health workers and health facilities.

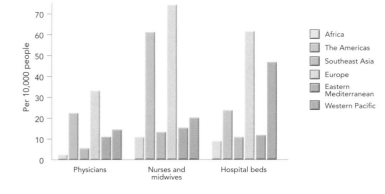

HIV/AIDS

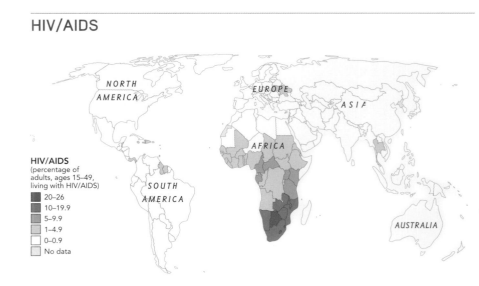

HIV/AIDS (percentage of adults, ages 15–49, living with HIV/AIDS)
- 20–26
- 10–19.9
- 5–9.9
- 1–4.9
- 0–0.9
- No data

Global Disease Burden

Disease Burden
(percentage of deaths attributable to communicable disease or maternal, perinatal, or nutritional conditions)
- 65–100
- 55–64
- 40–54
- 25–39
- 0–24
- No data

Although infectious and parasitic diseases account for nearly one-quarter of total deaths in developing countries, they result in relatively few deaths in wealthier nations. In contrast, cardiovascular diseases and cancer are more significant causes of death in industrialized countries. Over time, as fertility rates fall, social and living conditions improve, the population ages, and further advances are made against infectious diseases in poorer countries, the distribution of causes of death between developed and developing nations may converge.

Causes of Death
- Infectious & parasitic diseases
- Cardiovascular diseases
- Respiratory infections
- Perinatal conditions
- Unintentional injuries
- Cancers
- Respiratory diseases
- Digestive diseases
- Intentional injuries
- Maternal conditions
- Neuropsychiatric disorders
- Other

Low-income Countries   High-income Countries

Under-Five Mortality

Under-Five Mortality Rate
(per 1,000 live births)
- More than 100
- 60–100
- 30–59
- 10–29
- 0–9
- No data

Maternal Mortality

MATERNAL MORTALITY RATIO
PER 100,000 LIVE BIRTHS*

COUNTRIES WITH THE HIGHEST MATERNAL MORTALITY RATES:		COUNTRIES WITH THE LOWEST MATERNAL MORTALITY RATES:	
1. Afghanistan	1,400	1. Greece	2
2. Chad	1,200	2. Ireland	3
3. Somalia	1,200	3. Austria	5
4. Guinea-Bissau	1,000	4. Belgium	5
5. Liberia	990	5. Denmark	5
6. Burundi	970	6. Iceland	5
7. Sierra Leone	970	7. Italy	5
8. Central African Rep.	850	8. Sweden	5
9. Nigeria	840	9. Japan	6
10. Mali	830	10. Spain	6

Adjusted for underreporting and misclassification

Education and Literacy

Adult Literacy
(as a percentage of population)
- More than 94
- 80–94
- 60–79
- 40–59
- 0–39
- No data

Basic education is an investment for the long-term prosperity of a nation, generating individual, household, and social benefits. Some countries (e.g., Eastern and Western Europe, the U.S.) have long traditions of high educational attainment among both genders, and now have well-educated populations of all ages. In contrast, many low-income countries have only recently expanded access to primary education; girls still lag behind boys in enrollment and completion of primary school, and then in making the transition to secondary school. These countries will have to wait many years before most individuals in the productive ages have even minimal levels of reading, writing, and basic arithmetic skills.

The expansion of secondary schooling tends to lag even further behind, so countries with low educational attainment will likely be at a disadvantage for at least a generation. Although no one doubts that the key to long-term economic growth and poverty reduction lies in greater education opportunities for all, many poor countries face the tremendous challenge of paying for schools and teachers today, while having to wait 20 years for the economic return on the investment.

School Enrollment for Girls

Primary Education Enrollment for Girls
(as a percentage of primary school-aged girls)
- More than 93
- 85–93
- 70–84
- 50–69
- 0–49
- No data

Developing Human Capital

In the pyramids below, more red and blue in the bars indicates a higher level of educational attainment, or "human capital," which contributes greatly to a country's potential for future economic growth. These two countries are similar in population size, but their human capital measures are significantly different.

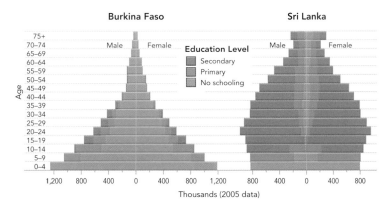

Education Level
- Secondary
- Primary
- No schooling

Burkina Faso   Sri Lanka

Thousands (2005 data)

POLITICAL VIOLENCE, WAR, AND TERROR

continue to plague many areas of the world in the early 21st century, despite dramatic decreases in major armed conflict since 1991. The 20th century is often described as the century of "total war" as modern weapons technologies made every facet of society a potential target in warfare. Whereas the first half of the century was torn by interstate wars among the most powerful states, the latter half was consumed by protracted civil wars in the weakest states. The end of the Cold War emboldened international engagement; concerted efforts toward peace had reduced armed conflicts more than half.

Long-standing wars place enormous burdens on developing countries in the early 21st century; global apprehension is riveted on superpowerful states, super empowered terrorists, and proliferation of "weapons of mass disruption." Globalization brings us closer together and makes us more vulnerable. Though violence is generally subsiding and democracy spreading, tensions are increasing in the world's oil-producing regions. Disengagement with the war in Iraq coincided with political upheavals against autocrats across the Arab Spring countries in 2011. Prospects for a peaceful, globalized future are challenged by drug and arms trafficking and increasing competition over oil supplies.

Political Violence

Political Violence

- Ongoing political violence
- Recently ended political violence
- New outbreaks in 2011
- Major drug-producing country
- ○ Location of terrorist attack(s) resulting in 50 or more deaths, 2000–2011
- → Violent drug-trafficking routes

Length and Magnitude of Conflict

Bar height indicates length of conflict, in years. Bar color conveys magnitude.

46+, 30–45, 20–29, 10–19, 0–9

Total war — Low-level insurgency

State Fragility

The quality of a government's response to rising tensions is the most crucial factor in the management of political conflict. "State fragility" gauges a country's vulnerability to civil disorder and political violence by evaluating government effectiveness and legitimacy in its four functions: security, political, economic, and social. Fragility is most serious when a government cannot provide reasonable levels of security; engages in brutal repression; lacks political accountability and responsiveness; excludes or marginalizes social groups; suffers poverty and inadequate development; fails to manage growth or reinvest; and neglects the well-being and key aspirations of its citizens. State fragility has lessened considerably since the end of the Cold War but remains a serious challenge in many African and Muslim countries.

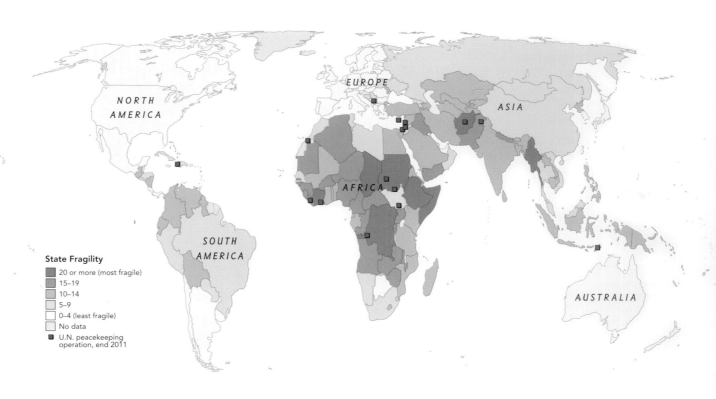

State Fragility
- 20 or more (most fragile)
- 15–19
- 10–14
- 5–9
- 0–4 (least fragile)
- No data
- ■ U.N. peacekeeping operation, end 2011

Change in Magnitude of Ongoing Conflicts

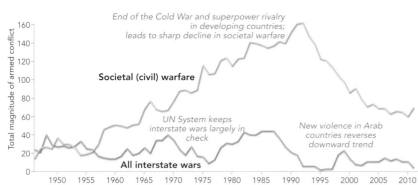

End of the Cold War and superpower rivalry in developing countries; leads to sharp decline in societal warfare

Societal (civil) warfare

UN System keeps interstate wars largely in check

New violence in Arab countries reverses downward trend

All interstate wars

Total magnitude of armed conflict

1950 1955 1960 1965 1970 1975 1980 1985 1990 1995 2000 2005 2010

Global Regimes by Type

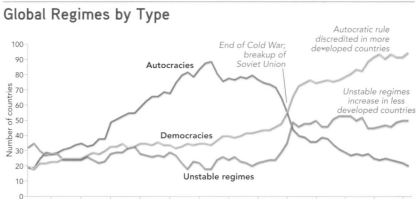

Autocratic rule discredited in more developed countries

Autocracies

End of Cold War; breakup of Soviet Union

Unstable regimes increase in less developed countries

Democracies

Unstable regimes

Number of countries

1950 1955 1960 1965 1970 1975 1980 1985 1990 1995 2000 2005 2010

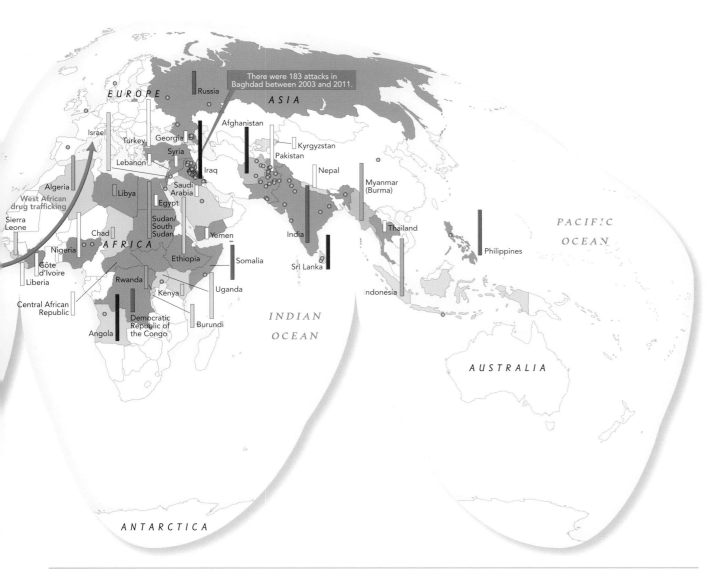

There were 183 attacks in Baghdad between 2003 and 2011.

Terrorist Attacks

The term "terrorism" refers specifically to violent attacks on non-military (political or, especially, civilian) targets. The vast majority of such attacks are domestic; both state and non-state actors can engage in terror tactics. "International terrorism" is a special subset of attacks linked to globalization in which militants go abroad to strike their targets, select domestic targets linked to a foreign state, or attack international transports such as planes or ships. The intentional bombing of civilian targets has become a common tactic in the wars of the early 21st century.

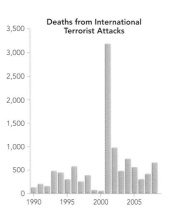

Deaths from International Terrorist Attacks

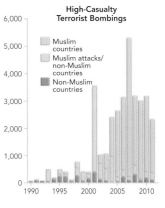

High-Casualty Terrorist Bombings

- Muslim countries
- Muslim attacks/non-Muslim countries
- Non-Muslim countries

Genocides and Politicides Since 1955

Our worst fears are realized when governments are directly involved in killing their own, unarmed citizens. Lethal repression is most often associated with autocratic regimes; its most extreme forms are termed genocide and politicide. These policies involve the intentional destruction, in whole or in part, of a communal or ethnic group (genocide) or opposition group (politicide). "Death squads" and "ethnic cleansing" have brutalized populations in 29 countries at various times since 1955.

Genocides and Politicides
(number of deaths since 1955)
- More than 500,000
- 100,000–500,000
- 50,000–99,999
- 10,000–49,999
- Less than 10,000

Weapons Possessions

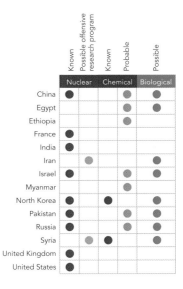

| | Nuclear | | Chemical | Biological |
	Known	Possible offensive research program	Known	Probable	Possible
China	●			●	●
Egypt				●	●
Ethiopia				●	
France	●				
India	●				
Iran		●			●
Israel	●			●	●
Myanmar				●	
North Korea	●		●		●
Pakistan	●			●	●
Russia	●			●	●
Syria		●	●		●
United Kingdom	●				
United States	●				

The proliferation of weapons of mass destruction (WMD) is a principal concern in the 21st century. State fragility and official corruption increase the possibilities that these modern technologies might fall into the wrong hands and be a source of terror, extortion, or war.

Refugees

Refugees are persons who have fled their country of origin due to fear of persecution for reasons of, for example, race, religion, or political opinion. Internally displaced persons (IDPs) are often displaced for the same reasons as refugees, but they still reside in their country of origin. By the end of 2010, the global number of refugees was over 10 million persons; the number of IDPs worldwide was over 22 million.

Refugee Population
(by country of asylum)
- More than 200,000
- 50,000–200,000
- 10,000–49,999
- 1,000–9,999
- Less than 1,000
- No data

Internally Displaced Persons (IDPs)
(countries with greater than 300,000 IDPs)
- More than 2 million
- 1 to 2 million
- 500,000 to 999,999
- 300,000 to 499,999

MOST ENVIRONMENTAL DAMAGE
is caused by human activity. Some harmful
actions are inadvertent—the release, for
example, of chlorofluorocarbons (CFCs), once
thought to be inert gases, into the atmosphere.
Others are deliberate and include such acts as
the disposal of sewage into rivers.

Among the root causes of human-induced
damage are excessive consumption (mainly in
industrialized countries) and rapid population
growth (primarily in the developing nations). So,
even though scientists may develop products
and technologies that have no adverse effects
on the environment, their efforts will be muted
if both population and consumption continue to
increase worldwide.

Socioeconomic and environmental indicators can reveal much about long-term trends;
unfortunately, such data are not collected
routinely in many countries. With respect to
urban environmental quality, suitable indicators
would include electricity consumption, numbers
of automobiles, and rates of land conversion
from rural to urban. The rapid conversion of
countryside to built-up areas during the past 25
to 50 years is a strong indicator that change is
occuring at an ever quickening pace.

Many types of environmental stress are
interrelated and may have far-reaching consequences. Global warming, for one, will likely
increase water scarcity, desertification, deforestation, and coastal flooding (due to rising sea
level)—all of which can have a significant impact
on human populations.

Cities
- ● Megacity, over 10 million
- ○ 5 to 10 million

Pollution
- ✴ Major industrial accident
- ✴ Major oil rig explosion
- → Major oil spill
- ⬂ Dead zone (water persistently oxygen-starved)
- ◗ Areas most sensitive to acid rain
- ━ Frequent pollution from shipping

Desertification
- ▨ Areas at highest risk of desertification

Deforestation
- ▩ Intact forests
- ▨ Other forests
- ▢ Former forest

Global Climate Change

The world's climate is constantly changing—over decades,
centuries, and millennia. Currently, several lines of reason-
ing support the idea that humans are likely to live in a much
warmer world before the end of this century. Atmospheric
concentrations of carbon dioxide and other "greenhouse
gases" are now well above historical levels, and simulation
models predict that these gases will result in a warming of
the lower atmosphere (particularly in polar regions) but a
cooling of the stratosphere. Experimental evidence supports
these predictions.

Indeed, throughout the last decade the globally averaged
annual surface temperature was higher than the hundred-year
mean. Model simulations of the impacts of this warming—
and studies indicating significant reductions already occurring
in polar permafrost and sea ice cover—are so alarming that
most scientists and many policy people believe that immedi-
ate action must be taken to slow the changes.

Depletion of the Ozone Layer

Beginning in the 1950s, increasing amounts of CFCs and
other gases with similar properties were released into the
atmosphere. CFCs are chemically inert in the lower atmosphere but decompose in the stratosphere, subsequently
destroying ozone. This understanding provided the basis for
successful United Nations actions (Vienna Convention, 1985;
Montréal Protocol, 1987) to phase out these gases.

First noted in the mid-1980s, the springtime "ozone hole"
over the Antarctic reached its maximum in 2006. With
sustained efforts to restrict CFCs and other ozone-depleting
chemicals, scientists have begun to see the beginning of a
long-term recovery of the ozone layer. Stratospheric ozone
shields the Earth from the sun's ultraviolet radiation. Thin-
ning of this protective layer puts people at risk for skin cancer and cataracts. It can also have devastating effects on the
Earth's biological functions.

Pollution

People know that water is not always pure and that
beaches may be closed to bathers due to raw sewage. An
example of serious contamination is the Minamata, Japan,
disaster of the 1950s. More than a hundred people died
and thousands were paralyzed after they ate fish containing mercury discharged from a local factory. Examples of
water and soil pollution also include the contamination
of groundwater, salinization of irrigated lands in semiarid
regions, and the so-called chemical time bomb issue,
where accumulated toxins are suddenly mobilized following
a change in external conditions. Preventing and mitigating
such problems requires the modernization of industrial
plants, additional staff training, a better understanding of
the problems, the development of more effective policies,
and greater public support.

Urban air quality remains a serious problem, particularly
in developing countries. In some developed countries, successful control measures have improved air quality over the
past 50 years; in others, trends have actually reversed, with
brown haze often hanging over metropolitan areas.

Solid-and hazardous-waste disposal is a universal urban
problem, and the issue is on many political agendas. In
the world's poorest countries, "garbage pickers" (usually
women and children) are symbols of abject poverty. In
North America, toxic wastes are frequently transported
long distances. But transport introduces the risk of highway
and rail accidents, causing serious local contamination.

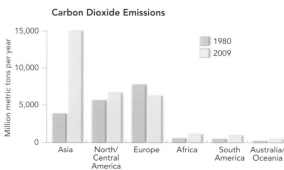

Carbon Dioxide Emissions

(bar chart, Million metric tons per year; legend: 1980, 2009; categories: Asia, North/Central America, Europe, Africa, South America, Australia/Oceania)

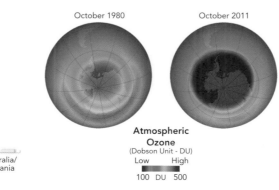

October 1980   October 2011

Atmospheric Ozone
(Dobson Unit - DU)
Low   High
100   DU   500

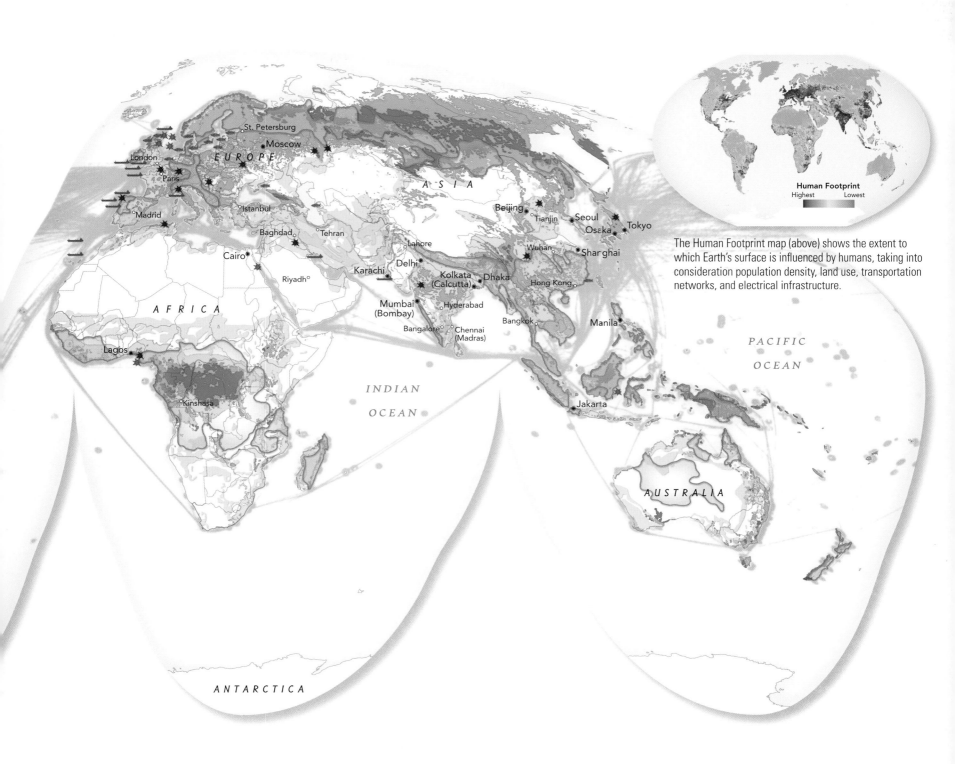

The Human Footprint map (above) shows the extent to which Earth's surface is influenced by humans, taking into consideration population density, land use, transportation networks, and electrical infrastructure.

Human Footprint
Highest   Lowest

Water Scarcity

Shortages of drinking water are increasing in many parts of the world, and studies indicate that by the year 2025, one billion people in northern China, Afghanistan, Pakistan, Iraq, Egypt, Tunisia, and other areas will face "absolute drinking water scarcity." But water is also needed by industry and agriculture, in hydroelectric-power production, and for transport. With increasing population, industrialization, and global warming, the situation can only worsen.

Water scarcity has already applied a major brake on development in many countries, including Poland, Singapore, and parts of North America. In countries where artesian wells are pumping groundwater more rapidly than it can be replaced, water is actually being mined. In river basins where water is shared by several jurisdictions, social tensions will increase. This is particularly so in the Middle East, North Africa, and East Africa, where the availability of fresh water is less than 1,300 cubic yards (1,000 cu m) per capita per annum; water-rich countries such as Iceland, New Zealand, and Canada enjoy more than a hundred times as much.

Irrigation can be a particularly wasteful use of water. Some citrus-growing nations, for example, are exporting not only fruit but also so-called virtual water, which includes the water inside the fruit as well as the wasted irrigation water that drains away from the orchards. Many individuals and organizations believe that water scarcity is the major environmental issue of the 21st century.

Soil Degradation and Desertification

Deserts exist where rainfall is too scarce to support significant nonirrigated agriculture, except in a few favored localities. Even in these "oases," occasional sandstorms may inhibit agricultural activity. In semiarid zones, lands can easily become degraded or barren if they are overused or subject to long or frequent drought. The Sahel of Africa faced this situation in the 1970s and early 1980s, but rainfall subsequently returned to normal, and some of the land recovered.

Often, an extended drought over a wide area can trigger desertification if the land has already been degraded by human actions. Causes of degradation include overgrazing, overcultivation, deforestation, soil erosion, overconsumption of groundwater, and the salinization/waterlogging of irrigated lands.

An emerging issue is the effect of climate change on desertification. Warming will probably lead to more drought in more parts of the world. Glaciers would begin to disappear, and the meltwater flowing through semiarid downstream areas would diminish.

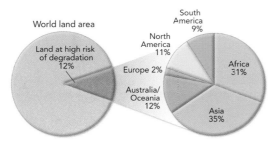

World land area

Land at high risk of degradation 12%

North America 11%

South America 9%

Europe 2%

Africa 31%

Australia/Oceania 12%

Asia 35%

Deforestation

Widespread deforestation in the wet tropics is largely the result of short-term and unsustainable uses. In El Salvador, Rwanda, and the Philippines, only 14, 18, and 26 percent (respectively) of the total land still has a closed forest cover. International agencies such as FAO, UNEP, UNESCO, WWF/IUCN, and others are working to improve the situation through education, restoration, and land protection. Panama enjoys a very high level of forest protection (65 percent); by contrast, Russia protects just 2 percent.

The loss of forests has contributed to the atmospheric buildup of carbon dioxide (a greenhouse gas), changes in rainfall patterns (in Brazil at least), soil erosion, and soil nutrient losses. Deforestation in the wet tropics, where more than half of the world's species live, is the main cause of biodiversity loss.

In contrast to the tropics, the forest cover in the temperate zones has increased slightly in the past 50 years because of the adoption of conservation practices and because abandoned farmland has been replaced by forest.

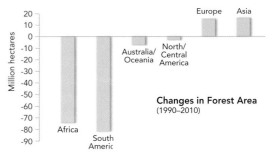

Changes in Forest Area
(1990–2010)

Million hectares

Europe   Asia

Australia/Oceania   North/Central America

Africa

South America

THE EARTH

Mass: 5,973,600,000,000,000,000,000,000 (5.9736 sextillion) metric tons

Total Area: 510,066,000 sq km (196,938,000 sq mi)

Land Area: 148,647,000 sq km (57,393,000 sq mi), 29.1% of total

Water Area: 361,419,000 sq km (139,545,000 sq mi), 70.9% of total

Population: 7,047,265,000

THE EARTH'S EXTREMES

Hottest Place: Dalol, Danakil Depression, Ethiopia, annual average temperature 34°C (93°F)

Coldest Place: Ridge A, Antarctica, annual average temperature -74°C (-94°F)

Hottest Recorded Temperature: Al Aziziyah, Libya 58°C (136.4°F), September 3, 1922

Coldest Recorded Temperature: Vostok, Antarctica -89.2°C (-128.6°F), July 21, 1983

Wettest Place: Mawsynram, Meghalaya, India, annual average rainfall 1,187 cm (467 in)

Driest Place: Arica, Atacama Desert, Chile, rainfall barely measurable

Highest Waterfall: Angel Falls, Venezuela 979 m (3,212 ft)

Largest Hot Desert: Sahara, Africa 9,000,000 sq km (3,475,000 sq mi)

Largest Ice Desert: Antarctica 13,209,000 sq km (5,100,000 sq mi)

Largest Canyon: Grand Canyon, Colorado River, Arizona 446 km (277 mi) long along river, 180 m (600 ft) to 29 km (18 mi) wide, about 1.8 km (1.1 mi) deep

Largest Cave Chamber: Sarawak Cave, Gunung Mulu National Park, Malaysia 16 hectares and 79 meters high (40.2 acres and 260 feet)

Largest Cave System: Mammoth Cave, Kentucky, over 591 km (367 mi) of passageways mapped

Most Predictable Geyser: Old Faithful, Wyoming, annual average interval 66 to 80 minutes

Longest Reef: Great Barrier Reef, Australia 2,300 km (1,429 mi)

Greatest Tidal Range: Bay of Fundy, Canadian Atlantic Coast 16 m (52 ft)

LOWEST SURFACE POINT ON EACH CONTINENT

	METERS	FEET
Dead Sea, Asia	-422	-1,385
Lake Assal, Africa	-156	-512
Laguna del Carbón, South America	-105	-344
Death Valley, North America	-86	-282
Caspian Sea, Europe	-28	-92
Lake Eyre, Australia	-16	-52
Bentley Subglacial Trench, Antarctica	-2,555	-8,383

AREA OF EACH CONTINENT

	SQ KM	SQ MI	PERCENT OF EARTH'S LAND
Asia	44,570,000	17,208,000	30.0
Africa	30,065,000	11,608,000	20.2
North America	24,474,000	9,449,000	16.5
South America	17,819,000	6,880,000	12.0
Antarctica	13,209,000	5,100,000	8.9
Europe	9,947,000	3,841,000	6.7
Australia	7,687,000	2,968,000	5.2

HIGHEST POINT ON EACH CONTINENT

	METERS	FEET
Mount Everest, Asia	8,850	29,035
Cerro Aconcagua, South America	6,959	22,831
Mount McKinley (Denali), N. America	6,194	20,320
Kilimanjaro, Africa	5,895	19,340
El'brus, Europe	5,642	18,510
Vinson Massif, Antarctica	4,897	16,066
Mount Kosciuszko, Australia	2,228	7,310

LARGEST ISLANDS

		AREA	
		SQ KM	SQ MI
1	**Greenland**	2,166,000	836,000
2	**New Guinea**	792,500	306,000
3	**Borneo**	725,500	280,100
4	**Madagascar**	587,000	226,600
5	**Baffin Island**	507,500	196,000
6	**Sumatra**	427,300	165,000
7	**Honshu**	227,400	87,800
8	**Great Britain**	218,100	84,200
9	**Victoria Island**	217,300	83,900
10	**Ellesmere Island**	196,200	75,800
11	**Sulawesi (Celebes)**	178,700	69,000
12	**South Island (New Zealand)**	150,400	58,100
13	**Java**	126,700	48,900
14	**North Island (New Zealand)**	113,700	43,900
15	**Island of Newfoundland**	108,900	42,000

LARGEST DRAINAGE BASINS

		AREA	
		SQ KM	SQ MI
1	**Amazon, South America**	7,050,000	2,722,000
2	**Congo, Africa**	3,700,000	1,429,000
3	**Mississippi-Missouri, North America**	3,250,000	1,255,000
4	**Paraná, South America**	3,100,000	1,197,000
5	**Yenisey-Angara, Asia**	2,700,000	1,042,000
6	**Ob-Irtysh, Asia**	2,430,000	938,000
7	**Lena, Asia**	2,420,000	934,000
8	**Nile, Africa**	1,900,000	734,000
9	**Amur, Asia**	1,840,000	710,000
10	**Mackenzie-Peace, North America**	1,765,000	681,000
11	**Ganges-Brahmaputra, Asia**	1,730,000	668,000
12	**Volga, Europe**	1,380,000	533,000
13	**Zambezi, Africa**	1,330,000	513,000
14	**Niger, Africa**	1,200,000	463,000
15	**Chang Jiang (Yangtze), Asia**	1,175,000	454,000

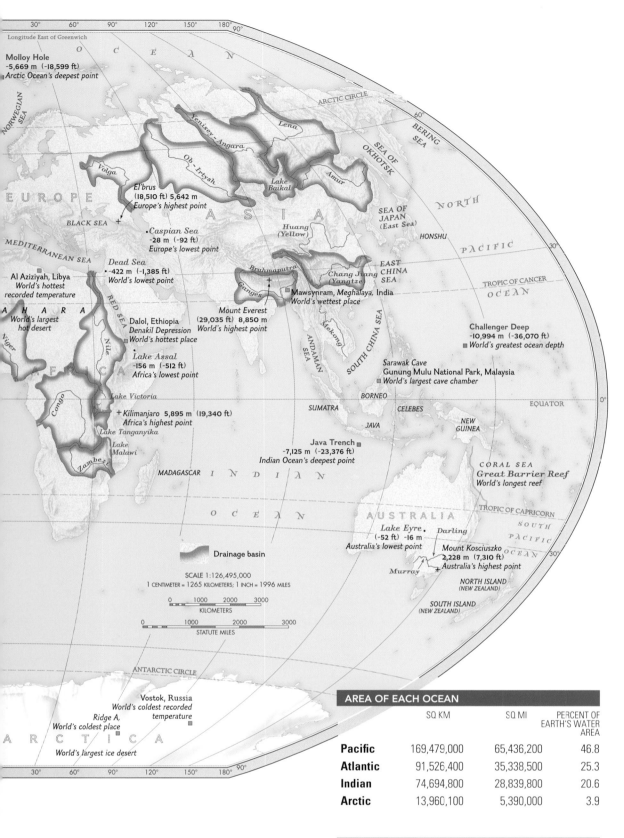

Molloy Hole
-5,669 m (-18,599 ft)
Arctic Ocean's deepest point

El'brus
(18,510 ft) 5,642 m
Europe's highest point

Caspian Sea
-28 m (-92 ft)
Europe's lowest point

Dead Sea
-422 m (-1,385 ft)
World's lowest point

Mawsynram, Meghalaya, India
World's wettest place

Al Aziziyah, Libya
World's hottest recorded temperature

Dalol, Ethiopia
Denakil Depression
World's hottest place

Mount Everest
(29,035 ft) 8,850 m
World's highest point

Challenger Deep
-10,994 m (-36,070 ft)
■ *World's greatest ocean depth*

World's largest hot desert

Lake Assal
-156 m (-512 ft)
Africa's lowest point

Sarawak Cave
Gunung Mulu National Park, Malaysia
■ *World's largest cave chamber*

Kilimanjaro 5,895 m (19,340 ft)
Africa's highest point

Java Trench
-7,125 m (-23,376 ft)
Indian Ocean's deepest point

Great Barrier Reef
World's longest reef

Lake Eyre
(-52 ft) -16 m
Australia's lowest point

Mount Kosciuszko
2,228 m (7,310 ft)
Australia's highest point

Drainage basin

SCALE 1:126,495,000
1 CENTIMETER = 1265 KILOMETERS; 1 INCH = 1996 MILES

KILOMETERS

STATUTE MILES

Vostok, Russia
World's coldest recorded temperature

Ridge A,
World's coldest place

World's largest ice desert

GEOPOLITICAL EXTREMES

Largest Country: Russia 17,075,400 sq km (6,592,850 sq mi)

Smallest Country: Vatican City 0.4 sq km (0.2 sq mi)

Most Populous Country: China 1,336,720,000 people

Least Populous Country: Vatican City 830 people

Most Crowded Country: Monaco 15,270 per sq km (38,173 per sq mi)

Least Crowded Country: Mongolia 2.0 per sq km (5.2 per sq mi)

Largest Metropolitan Area: Tokyo 36,669,000 people

Country with the Greatest Number of Bordering Countries: China 14, Russia 14

ENGINEERING WONDERS

Tallest Office Building: Taipei 101, Taipei, Taiwan 508 m (1,667 ft)

Tallest Tower (Freestanding): Tokyo Sky Tree, Tokyo, Japan 634 m (2,080 ft)

Tallest Manmade Structure: Burj Khalifa, Dubai, United Arab Emirates 828 m (2,716 ft)

Longest Wall: Great Wall of China, approx. 3,460 km (2,150 mi)

Longest Road: Pan-American highway (not including gap in Panama and Colombia), more than 24,140 km (15,000 mi)

Longest Railroad: Trans-Siberian Railroad, Russia 9,288 km (5,772 mi)

Longest Road Tunnel: Laerdal Tunnel, Laerdal, Norway 24.5 km (15.2 mi)

Longest Rail Tunnel: Seikan submarine rail tunnel, Honshu to Hokkaido, Japan 53.9 km (33.5 mi)

Highest Bridge: Millau Viaduct, France 343 m (1,125 ft)

Longest Highway Bridge: Qingdao Haiwan Bridge, Shandong, China 42.6 km (26.4 mi)

Longest Suspension Bridge: Akashi-Kaikyo Bridge, Japan 3,911 m (12,831 ft)

Longest Boat Canal: Grand Canal, China, over 1,770 km (1,100 mi)

Longest Irrigation Canal: Garagum Canal, Turkmenistan, nearly 1,100 km (700 mi)

Largest Artificial Lake: Lake Volta, Volta River, Ghana 9,065 sq km (3,500 sq mi)

Tallest Dam: Nurek Dam, Vakhsh River, Tajikistan 300 m (984 ft)

Tallest Pyramid: Great Pyramid of Khufu, Egypt 138 m (455 ft)

Deepest Mine: TauTona Gold Mine, South Africa 3902 m (12,802 ft) deep

Longest Submarine Cable: Sea-Me-We 3 cable, connects 33 countries on four continents, 39,000 km (24,200 mi) long

AREA OF EACH OCEAN

	SQ KM	SQ MI	PERCENT OF EARTH'S WATER AREA
Pacific	169,479,000	65,436,200	46.8
Atlantic	91,526,400	35,338,500	25.3
Indian	74,694,800	28,839,800	20.6
Arctic	13,960,100	5,390,000	3.9

DEEPEST POINT IN EACH OCEAN

	METERS	FEET
Challenger Deep, Pacific Ocean	-10,971	-35,994
Puerto Rico Trench, Atlantic Ocean	-8,605	-28,232
Java Trench, Indian Ocean	-7,125	-23,376
Molloy Hole, Arctic Ocean	-5,669	-18,599

LARGEST LAKES BY AREA

	AREA SQ KM	AREA SQ MI	MAXIMUM DEPTH METERS	DEPTH FEET
1 Caspian Sea	371,000	143,200	1,025	3,363
2 Lake Superior	82,100	31,700	406	1,332
3 Lake Victoria	69,500	26,800	82	269
4 Lake Huron	59,600	23,000	229	751
5 Lake Michigan	57,800	22,300	281	922
6 Lake Tanganyika	32,600	12,600	1,470	4,823
7 Lake Baikal	31,500	12,200	1,637	5,371
8 Great Bear Lake	31,300	12,100	446	1,463
9 Lake Malawi	28,900	11,200	695	2,280
10 Great Slave Lake	28,600	11,000	614	2,014

LONGEST RIVERS

		KM	MI
1	Nile, Africa	6,695	4,160
2	Amazon, South America	6,679	4,150
3	Chang Jiang (Yangtze), Asia	6,244	3,880
4	Mississippi-Missouri, North America	5,970	3,710
5	Yenisey-Angara, Asia	5,810	3,610
6	Huang (Yellow), Asia	5,778	3,590
7	Ob-Irtysh, Asia	5,410	3,362
8	Congo, Africa	4,700	2,900
9	Paraná-Río de la Plata, S. America	4,695	2,917
10	Amur, Asia	4,416	2,744
11	Lena, Asia	4,400	2,734
12	Mackenzie-Peace, North America	4,241	2,635
13	Mekong, Asia	4,184	2,600
14	Niger, Africa	4,170	2,591
15	Murray-Darling, Australia	3,718	2,310
16	Volga, Europe	3,685	2,290
17	Purus, South America	3,400	2,113

LARGEST SEAS BY AREA

		AREA SQ KM	AREA SQ MI	AVGERAGE DEPTH METERS	DEPTH FEET
1	Coral Sea	4,183,510	1,615,260	2,471	8,107
2	South China Sea	3,596,390	1,388,570	1,180	3,871
3	Caribbean Sea	2,834,290	1,094,330	2,596	8,517
4	Bering Sea	2,519,580	972,810	1,832	6,010
5	Mediterranean Sea	2,469,100	953,320	1,572	5,157
6	Sea of Okhotsk	1,625,190	627,490	814	2,671
7	Gulf of Mexico	1,531,810	591,430	1,544	5,066
8	Norwegian Sea	1,425,280	550,300	1,768	5,801
9	Greenland Sea	1,157,850	447,050	1,443	4,734
10	Sea of Japan	1,008,260	389,290	1,647	5,404
11	Hudson Bay	1,005,510	388,230	119	390
12	East China Sea	785,990	303,470	374	1,227
13	Andaman Sea	605,760	233,890	1,061	3,481
14	Red Sea	436,280	168,450	494	1,621
15	Black Sea	410,150	158,360	1,336	4,383

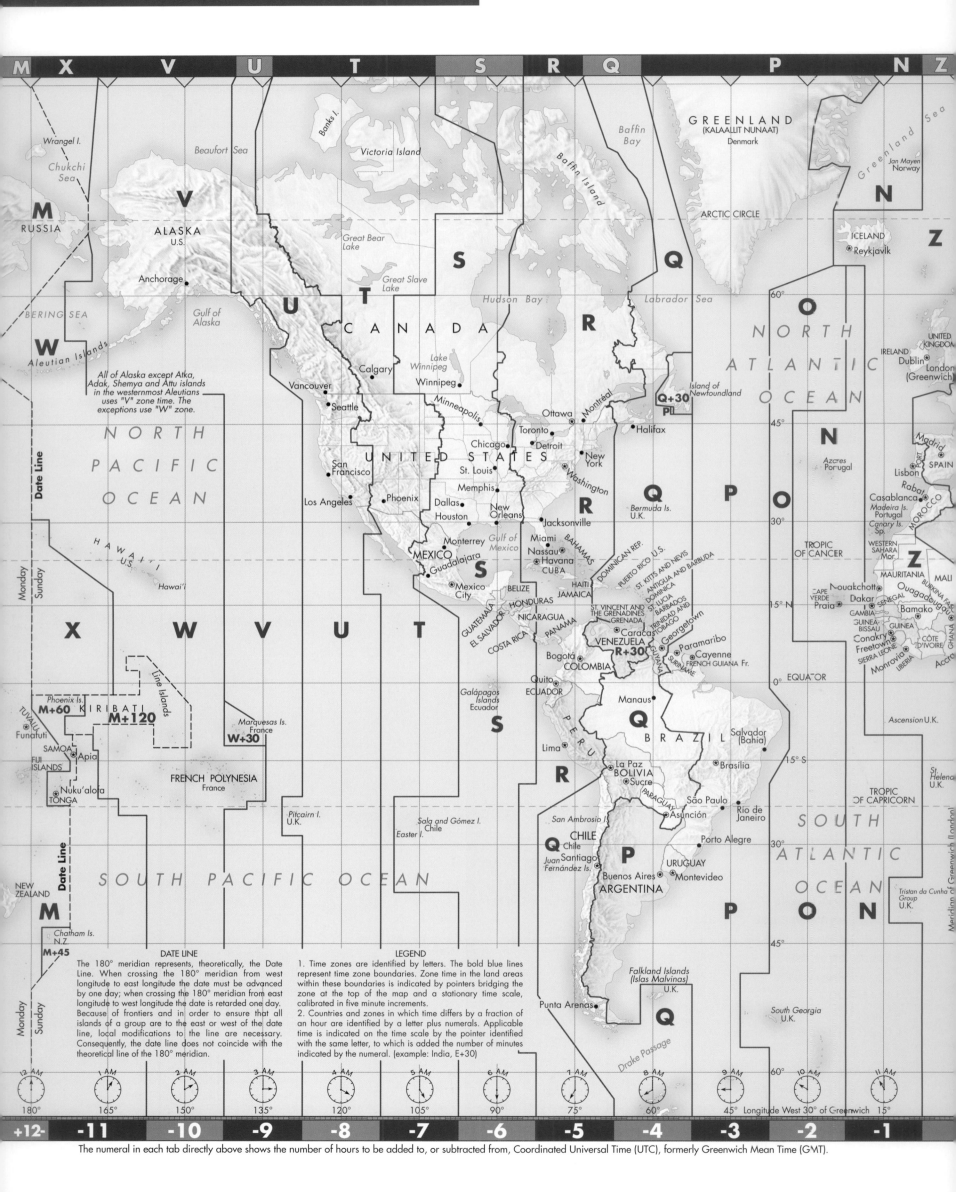

DATE LINE
The 180° meridian represents, theoretically, the Date Line. When crossing the 180° meridian from west longitude to east longitude the date must be advanced by one day; when crossing the 180° meridian from east longitude to west longitude the date is retarded one day. Because of frontiers and in order to ensure that all islands of a group are to the east or west of the date line, local modifications to the line are necessary. Consequently, the date line does not coincide with the theoretical line of the 180° meridian.

LEGEND
1. Time zones are identified by letters. The bold blue lines represent time zone boundaries. Zone time in the land areas within these boundaries is indicated by pointers bridging the zone at the top of the map and a stationary time scale, calibrated in five minute increments.
2. Countries and zones in which time differs by a fraction of an hour are identified by a letter plus numerals. Applicable time is indicated on the time scale by the pointer identified with the same letter, to which is added the number of minutes indicated by the numeral. (example: India, E+30)

The numeral in each tab directly above shows the number of hours to be added to, or subtracted from, Coordinated Universal Time (UTC), formerly Greenwich Mean Time (GMT).

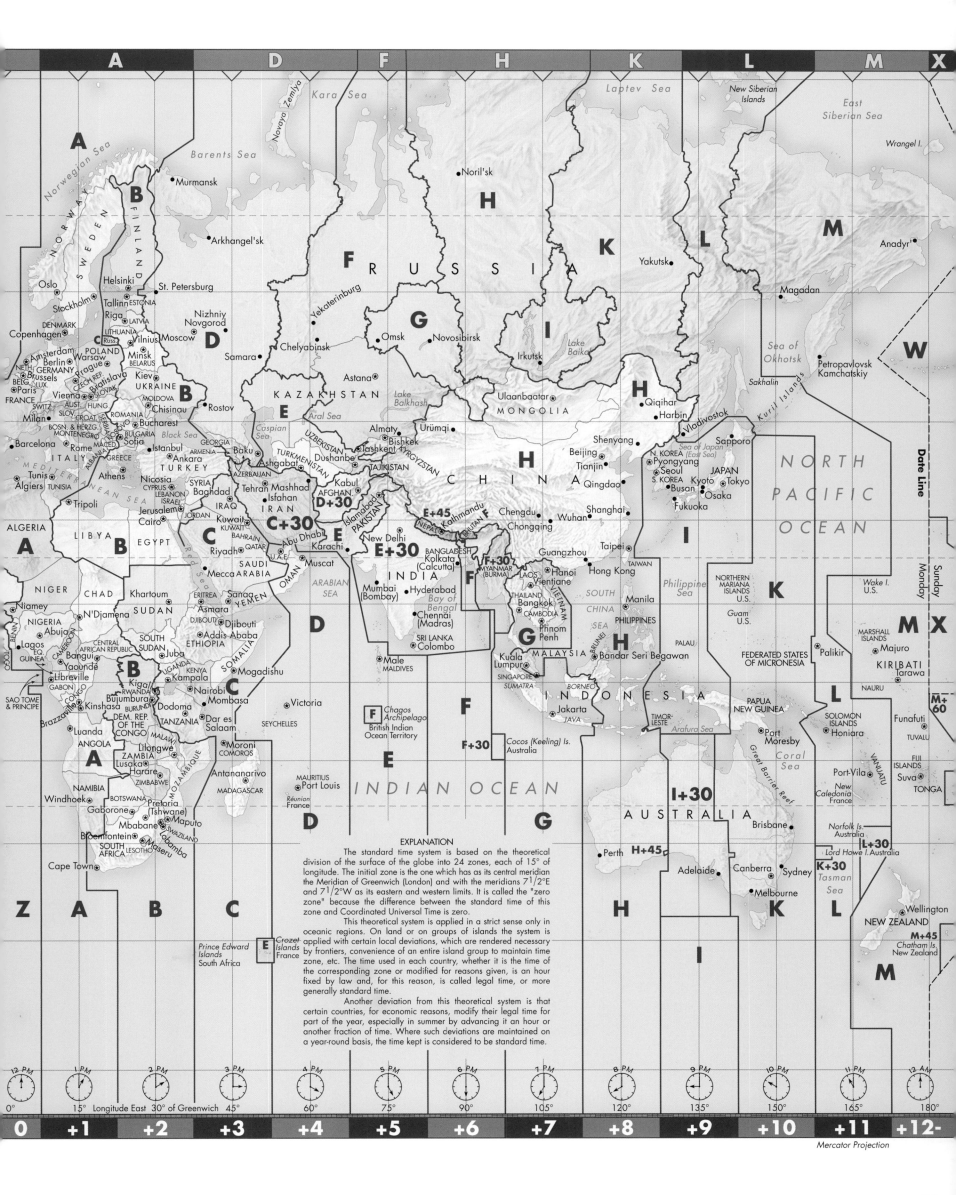

EXPLANATION

The standard time system is based on the theoretical division of the surface of the globe into 24 zones, each of 15° of longitude. The initial zone is the one which has as its central meridian the Meridian of Greenwich (London) and with the meridians 7 1/2°E and 7 1/2°W as its eastern and western limits. It is called the "zero zone" because the difference between the standard time of this zone and Coordinated Universal Time is zero.

This theoretical system is applied in a strict sense only in oceanic regions. On land or on groups of islands the system is applied with certain local deviations, which are rendered necessary by frontiers, convenience of an entire island group to maintain time zone, etc. The time used in each country, whether it is the time of the corresponding zone or modified for reasons given, is an hour fixed by law and, for this reason, is called legal time, or more generally standard time.

Another deviation from this theoretical system is that certain countries, for economic reasons, modify their legal time for part of the year, especially in summer by advancing it an hour or another fraction of time. Where such deviations are maintained on a year-round basis, the time kept is considered to be standard time.

Mercator Projection

North America

LOCATED BETWEEN THE ATLANTIC, Pacific, and Arctic Oceans, North America is almost an island unto itself, connected to the rest of the world only by the tenuous thread running through the Isthmus of Panama. Geologically old in some places, young in others, and diverse throughout, the continent sweeps from Arctic tundra in the north through the plains, prairies, and deserts of the interior to the tropical rain forests of Central America. Its eastern coastal plain is furrowed by broad rivers that drain worn and ancient mountain ranges, while in the West younger and more robust ranges thrust their still growing high peaks skyward. Though humans have peopled the continent for perhaps as long as 40,000 years, political boundaries were unknown there until some 400 years ago when European settlers imprinted the land with their ideas of ownership. Despite, or perhaps because of, its relative youth—and its geographic location—most of North America has remained remarkably stable. In the past century, when country borders throughout much of the rest of the world have altered dramatically, they have changed little in North America, while the system of government by democratic rule, first rooted in this continent's soil in the 18th century, has spread to many corners of the globe.

Third largest of the Earth's continents, North America seems made for human habitation. Its waterways—the inland seas of Hudson Bay and the Great Lakes, the enormous Mississippi system draining its midsection, and the countless navigable rivers of the East—have long provided natural corridors for human commerce. In its vast interior, the nurturing soils of plains and prairies have offered up bountiful harvests, while rich deposits of oil and gas have fueled industrial growth, making this continent's mainland one of the world's economic powerhouses.

Just in the past couple of centuries, North America has experienced dramatic changes in its population, landscapes, and environment, an incredible transformation brought about by waves of immigration, booming economies, and relentless development. During the 20th century, the United States and Canada managed to propel themselves into the ranks of the world's richest nations. But success has brought a host of concerns, not least of which is the continued exploitation of natural resources. North America is home to roughly 8 percent of the planet's people, yet its per capita consumption of energy is almost six times as great as the average for all other continents.

The United States ended the 20th century as the only true superpower, with a military presence and political, economic, and cultural influences that extend around the globe. But the rest of the continent south of the U.S. failed to keep pace, plagued by poverty, despotic governments, and social unrest. Poverty has spurred millions of Mexicans, Central Americans, and Caribbean islanders to migrate northward (legally and illegally) in search of better lives. Finding ways to integrate these disenfranchised masses into the continent's economic miracle is one of the greatest challenges facing North America in the 21st century.

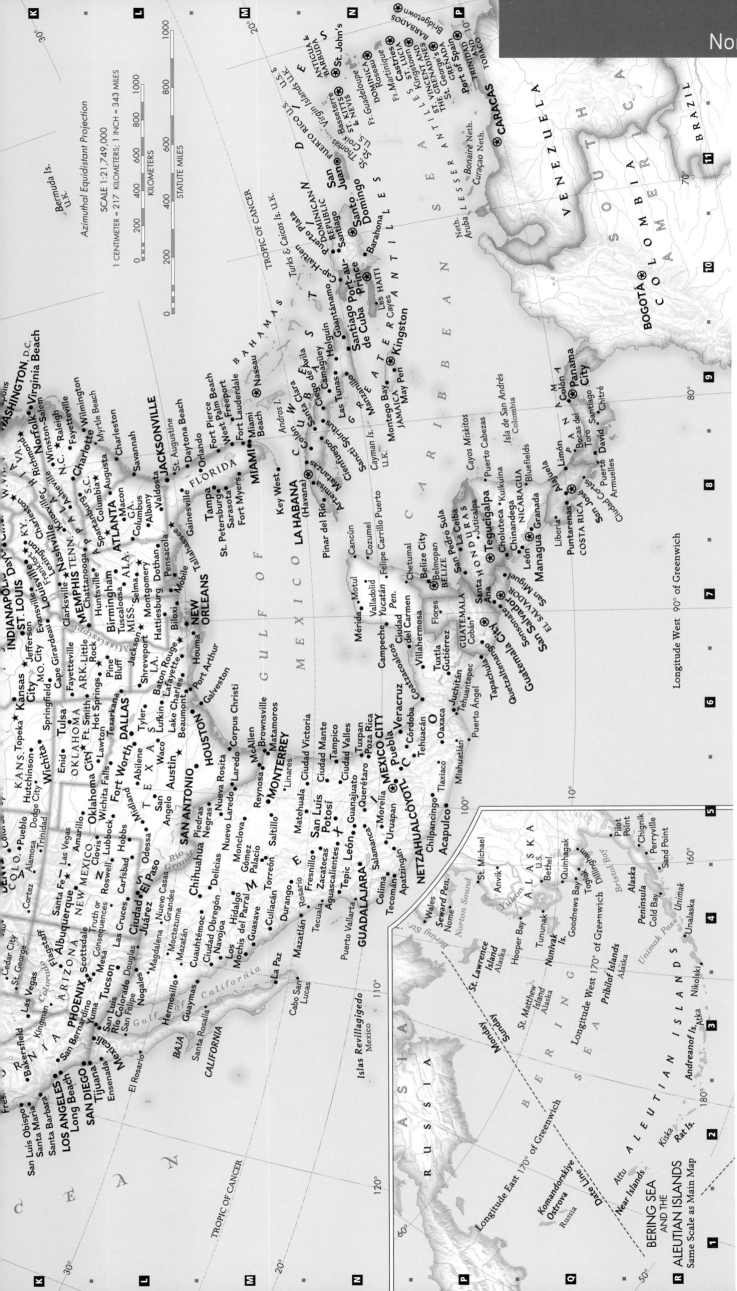

CONTINENTAL DATA

TOTAL NUMBER OF COUNTRIES: 23

FIRST INDEPENDENT COUNTRY:
United States, July 4, 1776

"YOUNGEST" COUNTRY:
St. Kitts and Nevis, Sept. 19, 1983

LARGEST COUNTRY BY AREA:
Canada 9,984,670 sq km
(3,855,081 sq mi)

SMALLEST COUNTRY BY AREA:
St. Kitts and Nevis 261 sq km
(101 sq mi)

PERCENT URBAN POPULATION: 75%

MOST POPULOUS COUNTRY:
United States 313,847,000

LEAST POPULOUS COUNTRY:
St. Kitts and Nevis 50,700

MOST DENSELY POPULATED COUNTRY:
Barbados 670 per sq km
(1,735 per sq mi)

LEAST DENSELY POPULATED COUNTRY:
Canada 3.4 per sq km (8.9 per sq mi)

LARGEST CITY BY POPULATION:
Mexico City, Mexico 19,460,000

HIGHEST GDP PER CAPITA:
United States $48,100

LOWEST GDP PER CAPITA:
Haiti $1,200

AVERAGE LIFE EXPECTANCY IN
NORTH AMERICA: 76 years

AVERAGE LITERACY RATE IN
NORTH AMERICA: 96%

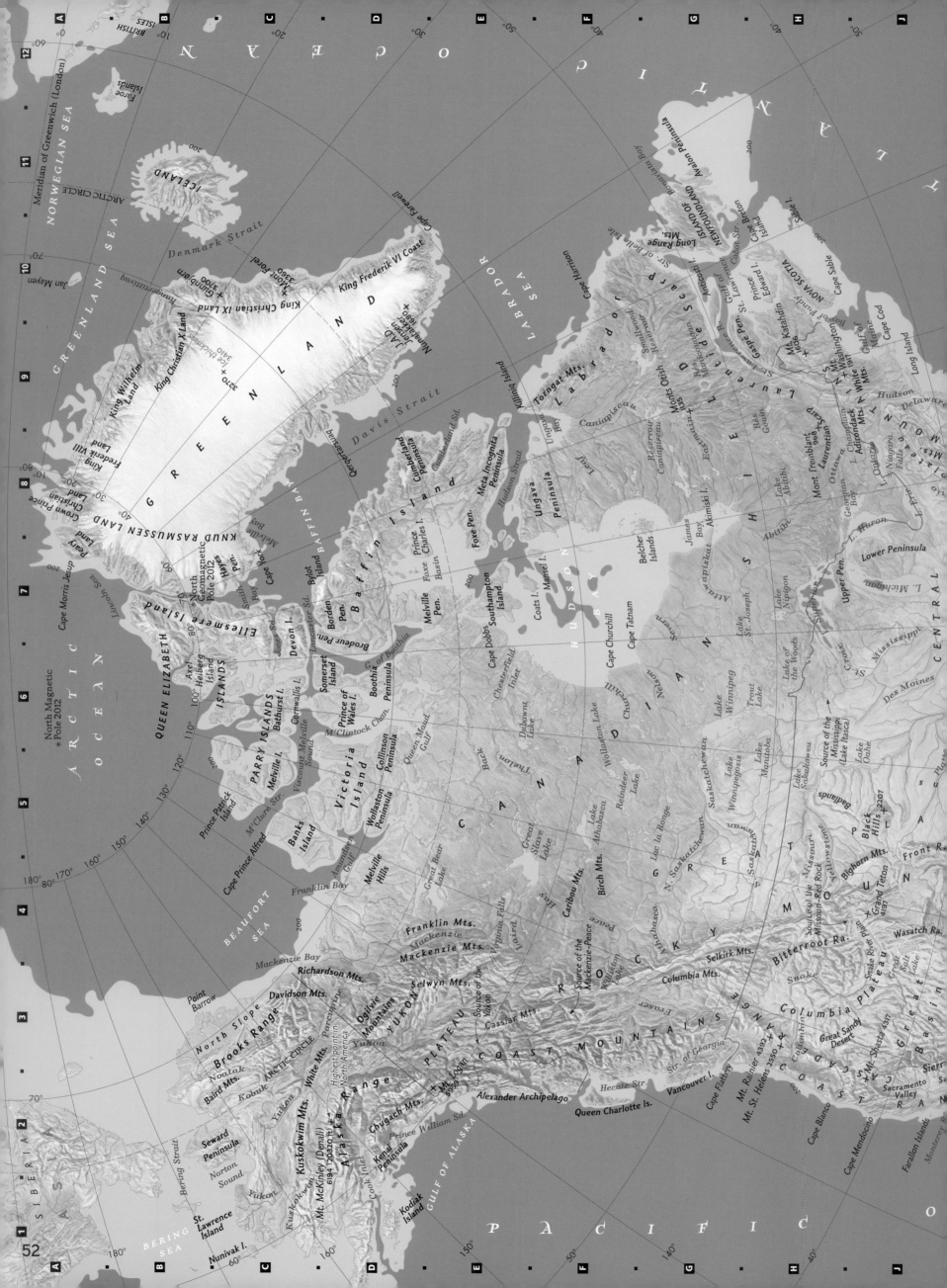

ARCTIC OCEAN

ATLANTIC OCEAN

PACIFIC OCEAN

GREENLAND

NORWEGIAN SEA

GREENLAND SEA

BAFFIN BAY

LABRADOR SEA

HUDSON BAY

BEAUFORT SEA

BERING SEA

GULF OF ALASKA

PACIFIC

SIBERIA

ASIA

British Isles
Faroe Islands
Iceland
Jan Mayen

Meridian of Greenwich (London)
ARCTIC CIRCLE

Denmark Strait
Cape Farewell

Mont Forel +3360
+Gunnbjørn 3700
Jætten +
Nunatakket 3410
Ice thickness
3270 +

King Frederik VI Coast
King Christian IX Land
King Christian X Land
King Wilhelm Land
King Frederik VIII Land
Crown Prince Christian Land
Peary Land

KNUD RASMUSSEN LAND
QUEEN ELIZABETH ISLANDS
Ellesmere Island
North Geomagnetic Pole 2012
Axel Heiberg Island
Hayes Pen.
Smith Sd.
Cape York

Lincoln Sea
Cape Morris Jesup
North Magnetic Pole 2012

ARCTIC OCEAN

Prince Patrick Island
Cape Prince Alfred
M'Clure Str.
Banks Island
Melville I.
Bathurst I.
PARRY ISLANDS
Cornwallis I.
Somerset Island
Boothia Peninsula
Prince of Wales I.
Devon I.
Jones Sd.
Lancaster Sd.
Bylot Island
Borden Pen.
Brodeur Pen.
Baffin Island
BAFFIN Island

Davis Strait
Cumberland Pen.
Cumberland Peninsula
Meta Incognita Peninsula
Hudson Strait
Killiniq Island

Victoria Island
Collinson Peninsula
Wollaston Peninsula
Queen Maud Gulf
M'Clintock Chan.
Viscount Melville Sound
G. of Boothia
Amundsen Gulf

Melville Hills
Franklin Bay
Mackenzie Bay
Point Barrow
North Slope
Brooks Range
Baird Mts.
Noatak
Kobuk
Davidson Mts.
Richardson Mts.
Ogilvie Mountains
Porcupine
White Mts.
ARCTIC CIRCLE
Yukon

Seward Peninsula
Norton Sound
St. Lawrence Island
Nunivak I.
Kuskokwim
Kuskokwim Mts.
Mt. McKinley (Denali) 6194 *20320 ft
Highest point in North America
Alaska Range
Chugach Mts.
Kenai Peninsula
Cook Inlet
Prince William Sd.
Kodiak Island
Bering Strait

Mt. Logan 5959 +
Selwyn Mts.
Cassiar Mts.
Source of the Yukon
YUKON PLATEAU
COAST MOUNTAINS
Alexander Archipelago
Queen Charlotte Is.
Hecate Str.
Vancouver I.
Str. of Georgia
Cape Flattery

Franklin Mts.
Mackenzie
Mackenzie Mts.
Virginia Falls
Liard
Great Bear Lake
Great Slave Lake
Birch Mts.
Caribou Mts.
Peace
Source of the Mackenzie-Peace
Athabasca
Lake Athabasca
Williston Lake
Fraser
Selkirk Mts.
Columbia Mts.
Columbia
COAST RANGE
Mt. Rainier 4392 *
Mt. St. Helens 2550 +
Cape Blanco
Cape Mendocino
Farallon Is.

CANADIAN SHIELD

Back
Thelon
Dubawnt Lake
Chesterfield Inlet
Cape Dobbs
Cape Kendall
Southampton Island
Coats I.
Mansel I.
Foxe Pen.
Foxe Basin
Prince Charles I.
Melville Pen.

Cape Churchill
Cape Tatnam
Churchill
Nelson
Severn
Wollaston Lake
Reindeer Lake
Lake Athabasca
Loc la Ronge
Saskatchewan
N. Saskatchewan
S. Saskatchewan
Lake Winnipeg
Lake Winnipegosis
Lake Manitoba
Lake Sakatchewan
Lake of the Woods
Trout Lake
Lake Nipigon
Badlands
Black Hills + 2207
Lake Oahe
Des Moines
Mississippi
Source of the Mississippi (Lake Itasca)
St. Croix
Lake Superior
L. Michigan
Lake Huron
Upper Pen.
Lower Peninsula
Georgian Bay
GREAT PLAINS
ROCKY MOUNTAINS
Source of the Missouri-Red Rock
Missouri
Yellowstone
Bighorn Mts.
Grand Teton 4197 +
Wasatch Ra.
Great Salt Lake
Bitterroot Ra.
Snake
Columbia Plateau
Great Sandy Desert
Mt. Shasta 4317 +
Sacramento Valley
Front R.
Sierra
GREAT BASIN

LABRADOR
Torngat Mts.
Ungava Bay
Ungava Peninsula
Caniapiscau
Leaf
Caniapiscau
Réservoir Caniapiscau
Monts Otish 1135
Rés. Gouin
Réservoir Manicouagan
Smallwood Reservoir
Cape Harrison

Str. of Belle Isle
Long Range Mts.
NEWFOUNDLAND
ISLAND OF NEWFOUNDLAND
Avalon Peninsula
Bonavista Bay
Cabot Str.
Cape Breton Island
Sable I.
Gulf of St. Lawrence
Gaspé Pen.
Prince Edward I.
NOVA SCOTIA
Cape Sable
Bay of Fundy
Gulf of Maine
Mt. Katahdin 1606
Mt. Washington 1917
White Mts.
Adirondack Mts.
Cape Cod
Long Island
Delaware
Hudson
L. Champlain
Niagara Falls
Lake Ontario
Lake Erie
L. St. Clair
APPALACHIAN MOUNTAINS
Anticosti I.
LAURENTIDE SCARP
Laurentian Scarp
Mont Tremblant 968
Ottawa
Abitibi
Lake Abitibi
Akimiski I.
Attawapiskat
James Bay
Belcher Islands
Lake St. Joseph

CANADA

CENTRAL

52

A B C D E F G H J

12 11 10 9 8 7 6 5 4 3 2 1

CONTINENTAL DATA

Area:
24,474,000 sq km (9,449,000 sq mi)

Greatest north-south extent:
7,200 km (4,470 mi)

Greatest east-west extent:
6,400 km (3,980 mi)

Highest point:
Mount McKinley (Denali), Alaska, United States 6,194 m (20,320 ft)

Lowest point:
Death Valley, California, United States -86 m (-282 ft)

Lowest recorded temperature:
Snag, Yukon Territory, Canada -63°C (-81.4°F), February 3, 1947

Highest recorded temperature:
Death Valley, California, United States 56.6°C (134°F), July 10, 1913

Longest rivers:
• Mississippi-Missouri
5,970 km (3,710 mi)
• Mackenzie-Peace
4,241 km (2,635 mi)
• Yukon
3,220 km (2,000 mi)

Largest natural lakes:
• Lake Superior
82,100 sq km (31,700 sq mi)
• Lake Huron
59,600 sq km (23,000 sq mi)
• Lake Michigan
57,800 sq km (22,300 sq mi)

Earth's extremes located

in North America:
• Largest Cave System:
Mammoth Cave, Kentucky, United States; over 530 km (330 mi) of mapped passageways

• **Most Predictable Geyser:**
Old Faithful, Wyoming, United States; annual average interval 75 to 79 minutes

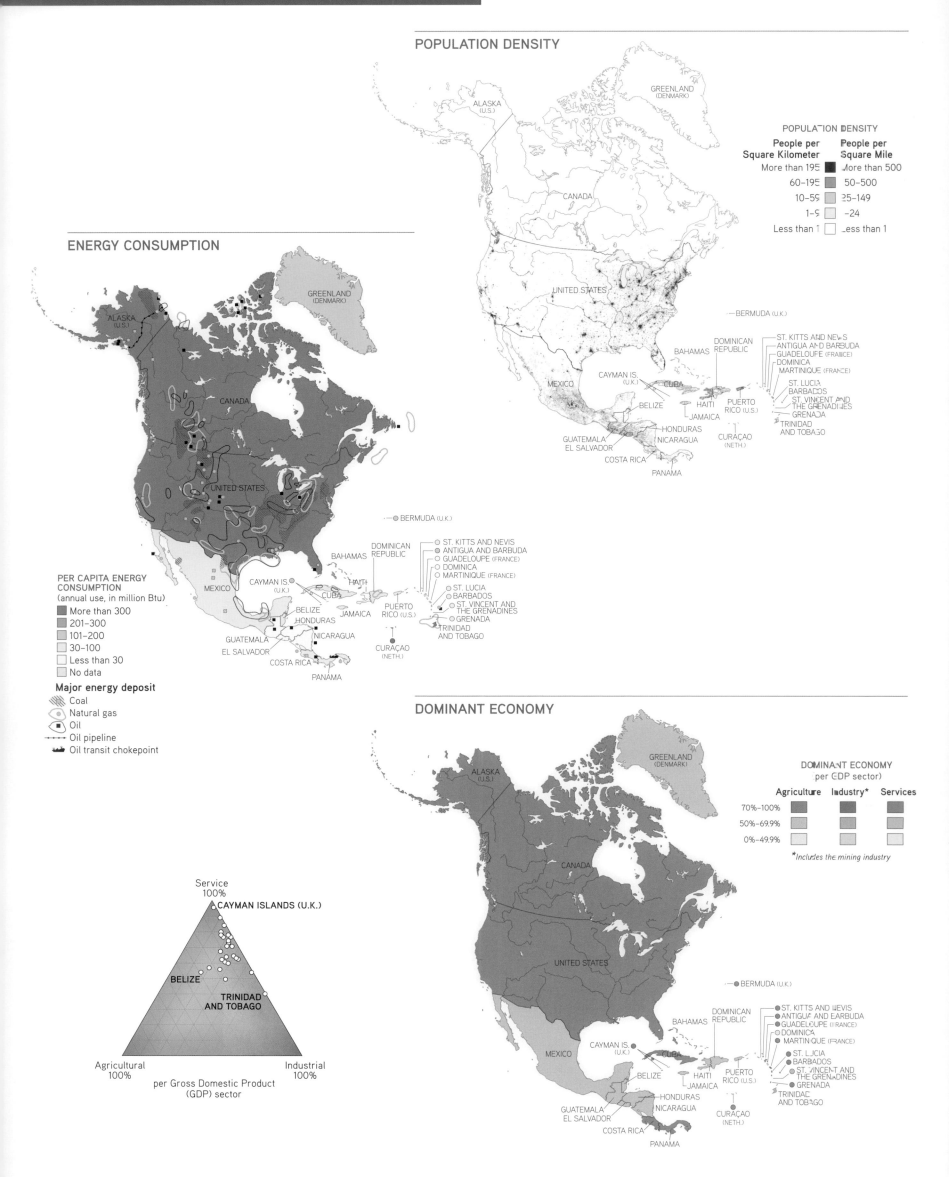

POPULATION DENSITY

POPULATION DENSITY

People per Square Kilometer	People per Square Mile
More than 195	More than 500
60–195	50–500
10–59	25–149
1–9	–24
Less than 1	Less than 1

GREENLAND (DENMARK)

ALASKA (U.S.)

CANADA

UNITED STATES

BERMUDA (U.K.)

MEXICO

BAHAMAS

CAYMAN IS. (U.K.)

CUBA

BELIZE

HAITI

JAMAICA

DOMINICAN REPUBLIC

PUERTO RICO (U.S.)

ST. KITTS AND NEVIS
ANTIGUA AND BARBUDA
GUADELOUPE (FRANCE)
DOMINICA
MARTINIQUE (FRANCE)
ST. LUCIA
BARBADOS
ST. VINCENT AND THE GRENADINES
GRENADA
TRINIDAD AND TOBAGO

GUATEMALA
EL SALVADOR

HONDURAS
NICARAGUA

COSTA RICA

PANAMA

CURAÇAO (NETH.)

ENERGY CONSUMPTION

ALASKA (U.S.)

GREENLAND (DENMARK)

CANADA

UNITED STATES

BERMUDA (U.K.)

MEXICO

BAHAMAS

CAYMAN IS. (U.K.)

CUBA

BELIZE
HONDURAS

HAITI

JAMAICA

DOMINICAN REPUBLIC

PUERTO RICO (U.S.)

ST. KITTS AND NEVIS
ANTIGUA AND BARBUDA
GUADELOUPE (FRANCE)
DOMINICA
MARTINIQUE (FRANCE)
ST. LUCIA
BARBADOS
ST. VINCENT AND THE GRENADINES
GRENADA
TRINIDAD AND TOBAGO

GUATEMALA
EL SALVADOR

NICARAGUA

COSTA RICA

PANAMA

CURAÇAO (NETH.)

PER CAPITA ENERGY CONSUMPTION
(annual use, in million Btu)

- More than 300
- 201–300
- 101–200
- 30–100
- Less than 30
- No data

Major energy deposit

- Coal
- Natural gas
- Oil
- Oil pipeline
- Oil transit chokepoint

Service 100%

CAYMAN ISLANDS (U.K.)

BELIZE

TRINIDAD AND TOBAGO

Agricultural 100%

Industrial 100%

per Gross Domestic Product (GDP) sector

DOMINANT ECONOMY

DOMINANT ECONOMY
(per GDP sector)

	Agriculture	Industry*	Services
70%–100%			
50%–69.9%			
0%–49.9%			

*Includes the mining industry

GREENLAND (DENMARK)

ALASKA (U.S.)

CANADA

UNITED STATES

BERMUDA (U.K.)

MEXICO

CAYMAN IS. (U.K.)

CUBA

BELIZE

HAITI

JAMAICA

DOMINICAN REPUBLIC

BAHAMAS

PUERTO RICO (U.S.)

ST. KITTS AND NEVIS
ANTIGUA AND BARBUDA
GUADELOUPE (FRANCE)
DOMINICA
MARTINIQUE (FRANCE)
ST. LUCIA
BARBADOS
ST. VINCENT AND THE GRENADINES
GRENADA
TRINIDAD AND TOBAGO

GUATEMALA
EL SALVADOR

HONDURAS
NICARAGUA

COSTA RICA

PANAMA

CURAÇAO (NETH.)

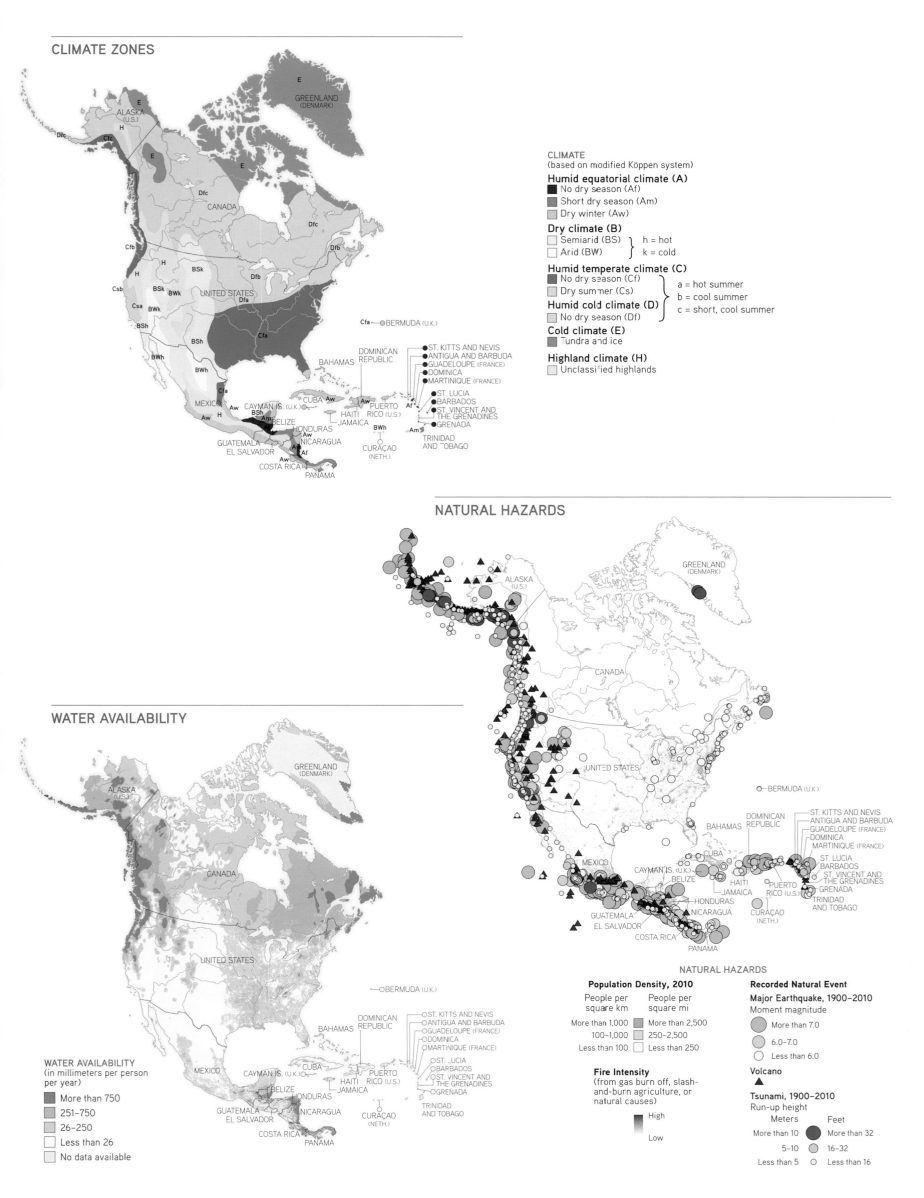

CLIMATE ZONES

CLIMATE
(based on modified Köppen system)

Humid equatorial climate (A)
- No dry season (Af)
- Short dry season (Am)
- Dry winter (Aw)

Dry climate (B)
- Semiarid (BS)   } h = hot
- Arid (BW)   } k = cold

Humid temperate climate (C)
- No dry season (Cf)
- Dry summer (Cs)

Humid cold climate (D)
- No dry season (Df)

a = hot summer
b = cool summer
c = short, cool summer

Cold climate (E)
- Tundra and ice

Highland climate (H)
- Unclassified highlands

NATURAL HAZARDS

WATER AVAILABILITY

WATER AVAILABILITY
(in millimeters per person per year)
- More than 750
- 251–750
- 26–250
- Less than 26
- No data available

NATURAL HAZARDS

Population Density, 2010

People per square km	People per square mi
More than 1,000	More than 2,500
100–1,000	250–2,500
Less than 100	Less than 250

Fire Intensity
(from gas burn off, slash-and-burn agriculture, or natural causes)
High
Low

Recorded Natural Event

Major Earthquake, 1900–2010
Moment magnitude
- More than 7.0
- 6.0–7.0
- Less than 6.0

Volcano

Tsunami, 1900–2010
Run-up height

Meters	Feet
More than 10	More than 32
5–10	16–32
Less than 5	Less than 16

C A N A D A

O N T A R I O

Q U E B E C

NEW BRUNSWICK

PRINCE EDWARD ISLAND

NOVA SCOTIA

Lake of the Woods

International Falls
Big Falls
Bemidji
Hibbing
Ely
Grand Marais
Isle Royale
...roit Lakes
Duluth
Hancock
Superior
Ironwood
Ishpeming
Marquette
Escanaba
Sault Ste. Marie
Drummond I.

Lake Superior

MICHIGAN

Presque Isle
Houlton
Mt. Katahdin 5268
Bingham
Danforth
Calais
MAINE
Bangor
Bay of Fundy

GULF OF MAINE

Brainerd
Moose Lake
Spooner
Rhinelander
Tomahawk
Petoskey
Alpena
Oscoda

MINNESOTA
.. Cloud
St. Paul
Minneapolis
Faribault
Mankato
Rochester
Albert Lea
Austin
Mason City

Eau Claire
Wausau
WISCONSIN
Appleton
Oshkosh
Green Bay
Madison
La Crosse
Sheboygan

Cadillac
Bay City
Saginaw
Flint
Pontiac
Grand Rapids
Lansing
Muskegon

Lake Huron
Georgian Bay

Lake Ontario

Watertown
Saranac Lake
Mt. Marcy 5344
Burlington
Montpelier
VERMONT
NEW HAMPSHIRE
Mt. Washington 6288
Concord
Manchester
Nashua
Lowell
Augusta
Lewiston
Portland

Waterbury
Saultawa

MILWAUKEE
Racine
Kenosha
Waukegan

Rochester
Syracuse
NEW YORK
Utica
Schenectady
Albany
Springfield
MASSACHUSETTS
Worcester
BOSTON
Cape Cod
New Bedford
Nantucket I.

IOWA
rt Dodge
Ames
Waterloo
Cedar Rapids
Dubuque

Madison
Racine
Kenosha
Rockford
Evanston
CHICAGO
Aurora
Joliet

Grand Rapids
Kalamazoo
Ann Arbor
DETROIT
Lake Erie
CLEVELAND
Toledo
Sandusky

Niagara Falls
Buffalo
Cheektowaga
Jamestown
Binghamton
Ithaca
Elmira
Scranton
Wilkes-Barre
Bradford
Williamsport
Hartford
CONN.
New Haven
Bridgeport
Long Island
NEW YORK
Jersey City
Newark
NEW JERSEY
Trenton
RHODE ISLAND
Providence

ATLANTIC OCEAN

Des Moines
...ouncil Bluffs
...maha
Burlington

Rock Island
Peoria
Bloomington
ILLINOIS
Springfield
Decatur

South Bend
Elkhart
Gary
Fort Wayne
Kokomo
Muncie
INDIANA
Dayton
Lima
Marion

Akron
Canton
Youngstown
OHIO
Springfield
COLUMBUS
PITTSBURGH
Wheeling
Altoona
Harrisburg
Reading
Johnstown
PENNSYLVANIA

Newburgh
Philadelphia
Atlantic City

Kirksville
St. Joseph
Quincy
Springfield

Terre Haute
INDIANAPOLIS
Covington
Frankfort

Cincinnati
Portsmouth
Parkersburg
Clarksburg
WEST VIRGINIA
Cumberland
Hagerstown
BALTIMORE
Annapolis
MARYLAND
WASHINGTON, D.C.
DELAWARE
Dover
Wilmington
Delaware Bay

Kansas City
Jefferson City
ST. LOUIS
East St. Louis
Belleville
MISSOURI
Rolla
Lebanon

Alton
New Albany
Louisville
Lexington
KENTUCKY
Owensboro

Huntington
Ashland
Charleston
Staunton
Charlottesville
VIRGINIA
Richmond
Petersburg
Alexandria
Chesapeake Bay
Newport News
Norfolk
Virginia Beach

...awrence
...peka

Evansville
Madisonville
Bowling Green
Hazard
Beckley
Bluefield
Roanoke
Lynchburg
Martinsville
Kitty Hawk
Albemarle Sound

Cape Girardeau
Cairo
Paducah
Bristol
Kingsport
Knoxville
Greensboro
Durham
Raleigh
Goldsboro
Pamlico Sound

Parsons
...offeyville
...tlesville
...lsa
Joplin

Poplar Bluff
Clarksville
Nashville
TENNESSEE
Oak Ridge
Winston-Salem
NORTH CAROLINA
New Bern

Fayetteville
Jonesboro
Paragould
Dyersburg
Jackson
Columbia
Murfreesboro
Chattanooga
6684 +
Asheville
Greensboro
Gastonia
Charlotte
Fayetteville
Lumberton
Wilmington

Muskogee
Fort Smith
...mulgee
W. Memphis
MEMPHIS
Florence
Decatur
Huntsville
Rome
Greenville
Spartanburg
Anderson
Athens
Columbia
SOUTH CAROLINA
Florence
Myrtle Beach

McAlester
ARKANSAS
Little Rock
Hot Springs
Pine Bluff
Arkadelphia
Clarksdale
Tupelo
Gadsden
Marietta
ATLANTA
Augusta
Aiken
Orangeburg
Charleston
Georgetown

Hope
Camden
El Dorado
Greenville
Columbus
Birmingham
Bessemer
La Grange
Macon
Walterboro
Beaufort
Port Royal Sound

Texarkana
MISSISSIPPI
Tuscaloosa
ALABAMA
GEORGIA
Americus
Fitzgerald
Savannah

...ngview
...er
Shreveport
Natchitoches
...acogdoches
Monroe
Tallulah
Vicksburg
Jackson
Meridian
Laurel
Selma
Montgomery
Phenix City
Columbus
Albany
Dublin
Douglas
Brunswick

LOUISIANA
Natchez
Hattiesburg
Prichard
Enterprise
Dothan
Thomasville
Valdosta
Waycross
JACKSONVILLE

Lufkin
Alexandria
Bogalusa
Biloxi
Mobile
Pensacola
Panama City
Tallahassee
Lake City
Perry
St. Augustine

...untsville
Lake Charles
Lafayette
Opelousas
Baton Rouge
Gulfport
Pascagoula
Mobile Bay
Apalachicola
Gainesville
Ocala
Palatka
Daytona Beach
De Land

...OUSTON
Beaumont
Orange
New Iberia
Houma
NEW ORLEANS
Grand Isle
Pilottown
FLORIDA
Leesburg
Sanford
Orlando
Cocoa
Titusville
Merritt Island
Melbourne

...adena
...ytown
...as City
Galveston
Freeport
Bay City

GULF OF MEXICO

Clearwater
Tampa
Lakeland
St. Petersburg
Tampa Bay
Bradenton
Sarasota
Sebring
L. Okeechobee
Vero Beach
Fort Pierce
West Palm Beach

Fort Myers
Fort Lauderdale
Hollywood
MIAMI
Miami Beach
Coral Gables
Homestead

Florida Keys
Key West
Straits of Florida

BAHAMAS

TROPIC OF CANCER

CUBA

HAITI

Albers Conic Equal-Area Projection
SCALE 1:10,824,000
1 CENTIMETER = 108 KILOMETERS; 1 INCH = 171 MILES

0 100 200 300 400 500
KILOMETERS

0 100 200 300 400 500
STATUTE MILES

PRINCIPAL HAWAIIAN ISLANDS

Longitude West 90° of Greenwich
Longitude West 159° of Greenwich
156°

PACIFIC OCEAN

Kīlauea
Kapa'a
KAUA'I
Līhu'e
Pu'uwai
Ni'ihau
Ka'ula
Waimea
Kaulakahi Channel
Kaua'i Channel

Hale'iwa
Wahiawā
O'AHU
Kāne'ohe
Waipahu
Pearl Harbor
Honolulu
Kaiwi Channel
MOLOKA'I
Kaunakakai
Nalulu

Lahaina
Lāna'i City
LĀNA'I
Kaho'olawe
Maunaloa
Kahului
MAUI
Hāna
'Upolu Point
10023
'Alenuihāhā Channel

Waimea (Kamuela)
Hawi
Honoka'a
Pa'auilo
HAWAI'I
13796
Kailua
Hilo
Mauna Loa 13679
Kea'au
Pāhoa
Kīlauea 4077
Pāhala
Na'ālehu
Kalae (South Point)

0 100 km
0 100 statute mi

ATLANTIC OCEAN

GULF OF MEXICO

PACIFIC OCEAN

PRINCIPAL HAWAIIAN ISLANDS

Albers Conic Equal-Area Projection
SCALE 1:10,824,000
1 CENTIMETER = 108 KILOMETERS; 1 INCH = 171 MILES

elevations in feet

10,000
9,000
8,000
7,000
6,000
5,000
4,000
3,000
2,000
1,000
250
0 (sea level)

POPULATION DENSITY

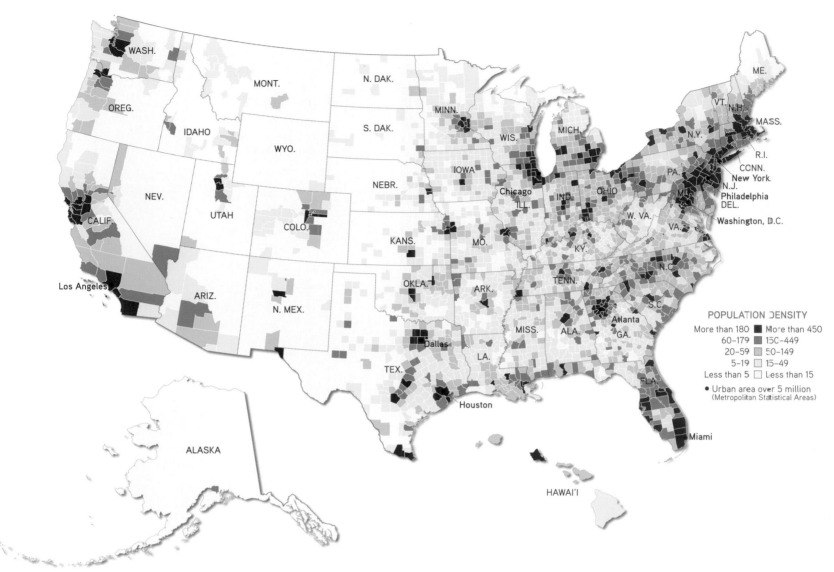

WASH.

MONT.

N. DAK.

ME.

OREG.

IDAHO

MINN.

VT. N.H.

S. DAK.

WIS.

MICH.

N.Y.

MASS.

R.I.

CONN.

New York

N.J.

Philadelphia

DEL.

Washington, D.C.

WYO.

NEBR.

IOWA

Chicago

IND.

OHIO

ILL.

PA.

W. VA.

VA.

NEV.

UTAH

COLO.

CALIF.

KANS.

MO.

KY.

N.C.

TENN.

Los Angeles

ARIZ.

N. MEX.

OKLA.

ARK.

S.C.

Atlanta

GA.

Dallas

MISS.

ALA.

TEX.

LA.

FLA.

Houston

Miami

ALASKA

HAWAI'I

POPULATION DENSITY

More than 180	More than 450
60–179	150–449
20–59	50–149
5–19	15–49
Less than 5	Less than 15

• Urban area over 5 million
(Metropolitan Statistical Areas)

POPULATION CHANGE

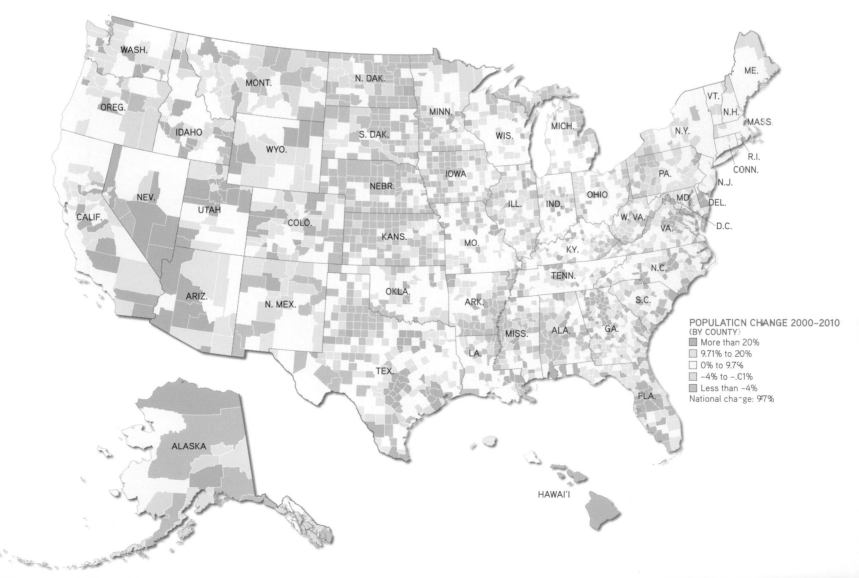

WASH.

MONT.

N. DAK.

ME.

OREG.

IDAHO

MINN.

VT.

N.H.

MASS.

WYO.

S. DAK.

WIS.

MICH.

N.Y.

R.I.

CONN.

NEBR.

IOWA

PA.

N.J.

NEV.

UTAH

COLO.

ILL.

IND.

OHIO

MD.

DEL.

D.C.

CALIF.

KANS.

MO.

W. VA.

VA.

KY.

ARIZ.

N. MEX.

OKLA.

ARK.

TENN.

N.C.

S.C.

MISS.

ALA.

GA.

TEX.

LA.

FLA.

ALASKA

HAWAI'I

POPULATION CHANGE 2000–2010
(BY COUNTY)

	More than 20%
	9.71% to 20%
	0% to 9.7%
	–4% to –.01%
	Less than –4%

National change: 9.7%

WATERSHEDS

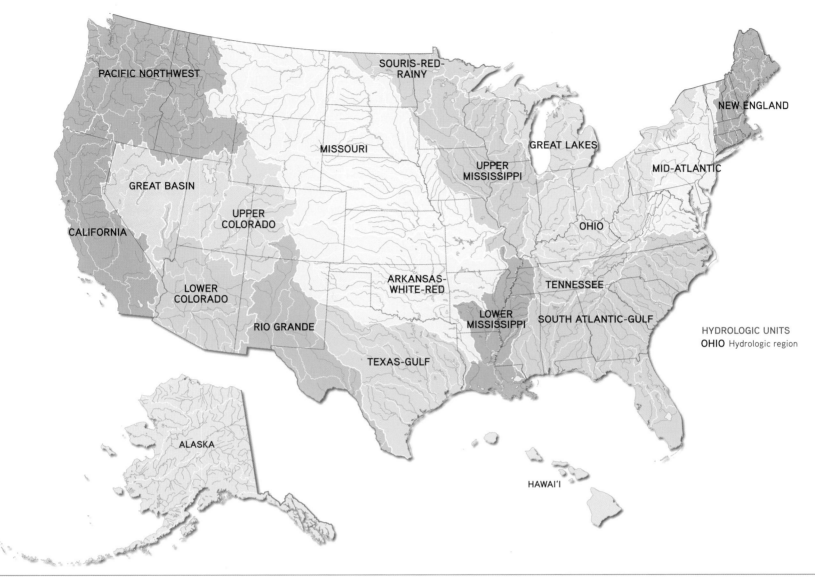

PACIFIC NORTHWEST

SOURIS-RED-RAINY

NEW ENGLAND

MISSOURI

GREAT LAKES

MID-ATLANTIC

GREAT BASIN

UPPER MISSISSIPPI

UPPER COLORADO

OHIO

CALIFORNIA

LOWER COLORADO

ARKANSAS-WHITE-RED

TENNESSEE

RIO GRANDE

LOWER MISSISSIPPI

SOUTH ATLANTIC-GULF

TEXAS-GULF

HYDROLOGIC UNITS
OHIO Hydrologic region

ALASKA

HAWAI'I

FEDERAL LANDS

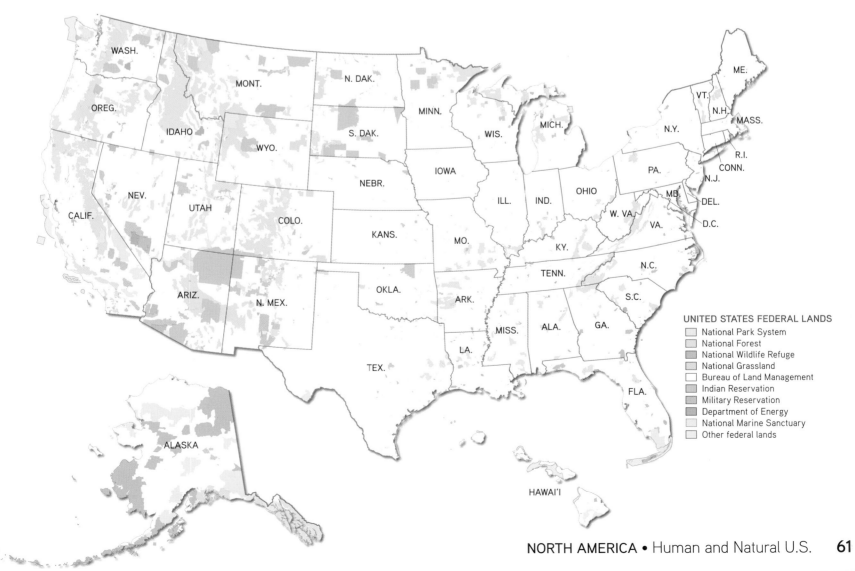

WASH.

MONT.

N. DAK.

ME.

OREG.

IDAHO

WYO.

S. DAK.

MINN.

VT.
N.H.

MASS.

N.Y.

R.I.
CONN.

NEV.

UTAH

COLO.

NEBR.

IOWA

WIS.

MICH.

PA.

N.J.

CALIF.

KANS.

ILL.

IND.

OHIO

MD.

DEL.

W. VA.

VA.

D.C.

ARIZ.

N. MEX.

OKLA.

MO.

KY.

TENN.

N.C.

ARK.

S.C.

MISS.

ALA.

GA.

LA.

TEX.

FLA.

ALASKA

HAWAI'I

UNITED STATES FEDERAL LANDS
- National Park System
- National Forest
- National Wildlife Refuge
- National Grassland
- Bureau of Land Management
- Indian Reservation
- Military Reservation
- Department of Energy
- National Marine Sanctuary
- Other federal lands

COUNTRIES

Antigua and Barbuda
ANTIGUA AND BARBUDA

AREA	443 sq km (171 sq mi)
POPULATION	89,000
CAPITAL	Saint John's 27,000
RELIGION	Protestant, Roman Catholic
LANGUAGE	English, local dialects
LITERACY	86%
LIFE EXPECTANCY	76 years
GDP PER CAPITA	$22,100

ECONOMY IND: tourism, construction, light manufacturing (clothing, alcohol, household appliances) AGR: cotton, fruits, vegetables, bananas, coconuts, cucumbers, mangoes, sugarcane, livestock EXP: petroleum products, bedding, handicrafts, electronic components, transport equipment, food and live animals

Bahamas
COMMONWEALTH OF THE BAHAMAS

AREA	13,880 sq km (5,359 sq mi)
POPULATION	316,000
CAPITAL	Nassau 248,000
RELIGION	Protestant, other Christian, Roman Catholic
LANGUAGE	English, Creole
LITERACY	96%
LIFE EXPECTANCY	71 years
GDP PER CAPITA	$30,900

ECONOMY IND: tourism, banking, cement, oil transshipment, salt, rum, aragonite, pharmaceuticals, spiral-welded steel pipe AGR: citrus, vegetables, poultry EXP: mineral products and salt, animal products, rum, chemicals, fruit and vegetables

Barbados
BARBADOS

AREA	430 sq km (166 sq mi)
POPULATION	288,000
CAPITAL	Bridgetown 112,000
RELIGION	Protestant, none
LANGUAGE	English
LITERACY	100%
LIFE EXPECTANCY	75 years
GDP PER CAPITA	$23,600

ECONOMY IND: tourism, sugar, light manufacturing, component assembly for export AGR: sugarcane, vegetables, cotton EXP: manufactures, sugar and molasses, rum, other foods and beverages, chemicals, electrical components

Belize
BELIZE

AREA	22,966 sq km (8,867 sq mi)
POPULATION	328,000
CAPITAL	Belmopan 20,000
RELIGION	Roman Catholic, Protestant, none
LANGUAGE	Spanish, Creole
LITERACY	77%
LIFE EXPECTANCY	68 years
GDP PER CAPITA	$8,300

ECONOMY IND: garment production, food processing, tourism, construction, oil AGR: bananas, cacao, citrus, sugar, fish, cultured shrimp, lumber EXP: sugar, bananas, citrus, clothing, fish products, molasses, wood, crude oil

Canada
CANADA

AREA	9,984,670 sq km (3,855,081 sq mi)
POPULATION	34,300,000
CAPITAL	Ottawa 1,170,000
RELIGION	Roman Catholic, Protestant, none
LANGUAGE	English, French
LITERACY	99%
LIFE EXPECTANCY	81 years
GDP PER CAPITA	$40,300

ECONOMY IND: transportation equipment, chemicals, processed and unprocessed minerals, food products, wood and paper products, fish products, petroleum and natural gas AGR: wheat, barley, oilseed, tobacco, fruits, vegetables, dairy products, forest products, fish EXP: motor vehicles and parts, industrial machinery, aircraft, telecommunications equipment, chemicals, plastics, fertilizers, wood pulp, timber, crude petroleum, natural gas, electricity, aluminum

Costa Rica
REPUBLIC OF COSTA RICA

AREA	51,100 sq km (19,730 sq mi)
POPULATION	4,636,000
CAPITAL	San José 1,416,000
RELIGION	Roman Catholic, Evangelical
LANGUAGE	Spanish, English
LITERACY	95%
LIFE EXPECTANCY	78 years
GDP PER CAPITA	$11,500

ECONOMY IND: microprocessors, food processing, medical equipment, textiles and clothing, construction materials, fertilizer, plastic products AGR: bananas, pineapples, coffee, melons, ornamental plants, sugar, corn, rice, beans, potatoes, beef, poultry, dairy, timber EXP: bananas, pineapples, coffee, melons, ornamental plants, sugar, beef, seafood, electronic components, medical equipment

Cuba
REPUBLIC OF CUBA

AREA	110,860 sq km (42,803 sq mi)
POPULATION	11,075,000
CAPITAL	Havana 2,140,000
RELIGION	Roman Catholic
LANGUAGE	Spanish
LITERACY	100%
LIFE EXPECTANCY	78 years
GDP PER CAPITA	$9,900

ECONOMY IND: sugar, petroleum, tobacco, construction, nickel, steel, cement, agricultural machinery, pharmaceuticals AGR: sugar, tobacco, citrus, coffee, rice, potatoes, beans, livestock EXP: sugar, nickel, tobacco, fish, medical products, citrus, coffee

Dominica
COMMONWEALTH OF DOMINICA

AREA	751 sq km (290 sq mi)
POPULATION	73,000
CAPITAL	Roseau 14,000
RELIGION	Roman Catholic, Protestant
LANGUAGE	English, French patois
LITERACY	94%
LIFE EXPECTANCY	76 years
GDP PER CAPITA	$13,600

ECONOMY IND: soap, coconut oil, tourism, copra, furniture, cement blocks, shoes AGR: bananas, citrus, mangos, root crops, coconuts, cocoa EXP: bananas, soap, bay oil, vegetables, grapefruit, oranges

Dominican Republic
DOMINICAN REPUBLIC

AREA	48,670 sq km (18,791 sq mi)
POPULATION	10,089,000
CAPITAL	Santo Domingo 2,138,000
RELIGION	Roman Catholic
LANGUAGE	Spanish
LITERACY	87%
LIFE EXPECTANCY	77 years
GDP PER CAPITA	$9,300

ECONOMY IND: tourism, sugar processing, ferronickel and gold mining, textiles, cement, tobacco AGR: sugarcane, coffee, cotton, cocoa, tobacco, rice, beans, potatoes, corn, bananas, cattle, pigs, dairy products, beef, eggs EXP: ferronickel, sugar, gold, silver, coffee, cocoa, tobacco, meats, consumer goods

El Salvador
REPUBLIC OF EL SALVADOR

AREA	21,041 sq km (8,124 sq mi)
POPULATION	6,091,000
CAPITAL	San Salvador 1,534,000
RELIGION	Roman Catholic, Protestant, none
LANGUAGE	Spanish, Nahua
LITERACY	81%
LIFE EXPECTANCY	74 years
GDP PER CAPITA	$7,600

ECONOMY IND: food processing, beverages, petroleum, chemicals, fertilizer, textiles, furniture, light metals AGR: coffee, sugar, corn, rice, beans, oilseed, cotton, sorghum, beef, dairy products EXP: offshore assembly exports, coffee, sugar, textiles and apparel, gold, ethanol, chemicals, electricity, iron and steel manufactures

Grenada
GRENADA

AREA	344 sq km (133 sq mi)
POPULATION	109,000
CAPITAL	Saint George's 40,000
RELIGION	Roman Catholic, Anglican, other Protestant
LANGUAGE	English, French patois
LITERACY	96%
LIFE EXPECTANCY	73 years
GDP PER CAPITA	$13,300

ECONOMY IND: food and beverages, textiles, light assembly operations, tourism, construction AGR: bananas, cocoa, nutmeg, mace, citrus, avocados, root crops, sugarcane, corn, vegetables EXP: bananas, cocoa, nutmeg, fruit and vegetables, clothing, mace

Guatemala
REPUBLIC OF GUATEMALA

AREA	108,889 sq km (42,042 sq mi)
POPULATION	14,099,000
CAPITAL	Guatemala 1,075,000
RELIGION	Roman Catholic, Protestant, indigenous Mayan beliefs
LANGUAGE	Spanish, Amerindian languages
LITERACY	69%
LIFE EXPECTANCY	71 years
GDP PER CAPITA	$5,000

ECONOMY IND: sugar, textiles and clothing, furniture, chemicals, petroleum, metals, rubber, tourism AGR: sugarcane, corn, bananas, coffee, beans, cardamom, cattle, sheep, pigs, chickens EXP: coffee, sugar, petroleum, apparel, bananas, fruits and vegetables, cardamom

Haiti
REPUBLIC OF HAITI

AREA	27,750 sq km (10,714 sq mi)
POPULATION	9,802,000
CAPITAL	Port-au-Prince 2,643,000
RELIGION	Roman Catholic, Protestant
LANGUAGE	French, Creole
LITERACY	53%
LIFE EXPECTANCY	63 years
GDP PER CAPITA	$1,200

ECONOMY IND: textiles, sugar refining, flour milling, cement, light assembly based on imported parts AGR: coffee, mangoes, sugarcane, rice, corn, sorghum, wood EXP: apparel, manufactures, oils, cocoa, mangoes, coffee

Honduras
REPUBLIC OF HONDURAS

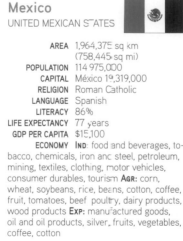

AREA	112,090 sq km (43,278 sq mi)
POPULATION	8,297,000
CAPITAL	Tegucigalpa 1,000,000
RELIGION	Roman Catholic
LANGUAGE	Spanish, Amerindian dialects
LITERACY	80%
LIFE EXPECTANCY	71 years
GDP PER CAPITA	$4,300

ECONOMY IND: sugar, coffee, woven and knit apparel, wood products, cigars AGR: bananas, coffee, citrus, corn, African palm, beef, timber, shrimp, tilapia, lobster EXP: apparel, coffee, shrimp, wire harnesses, cigars, bananas, gold, palm oil, fruit, lobster, lumber

Jamaica
JAMAICA

AREA	10,991 sq km (4,244 sq mi)
POPULATION	2,889,000
CAPITAL	Kingston 580,000
RELIGION	Protestant, none
LANGUAGE	English, English patois
LITERACY	88%
LIFE EXPECTANCY	73 years
GDP PER CAPITA	$9,000

ECONOMY IND: tourism, bauxite/alumina, agro processing, light manufactures, rum, cement, metal, paper, chemical products, telecommunications AGR: sugarcane, bananas, coffee, citrus, yams, ackees, vegetables, poultry, goats, milk, crustaceans, mollusks EXP: alumina, bauxite, sugar, rum, coffee, yams, beverages, chemicals, wearing apparel, mineral fuels

Mexico
UNITED MEXICAN STATES

AREA	1,964,375 sq km (758,445 sq mi)
POPULATION	114,975,000
CAPITAL	México 19,319,000
RELIGION	Roman Catholic
LANGUAGE	Spanish
LITERACY	86%
LIFE EXPECTANCY	77 years
GDP PER CAPITA	$15,100

ECONOMY IND: food and beverages, tobacco, chemicals, iron and steel, petroleum, mining, textiles, clothing, motor vehicles, consumer durables, tourism AGR: corn, wheat, soybeans, rice, beans, cotton, coffee, fruit, tomatoes, beef, poultry, dairy products, wood products EXP: manufactured goods, oil and oil products, silver, fruits, vegetables, coffee, cotton

Nicaragua
REPUBLIC OF NICARAGUA

AREA 130,370 sq km
(50,336 sq mi)
POPULATION 5,728,000
CAPITAL Managua 934,000
RELIGION Roman Catholic, Protestant, none
LANGUAGE Spanish
LITERACY 68%
LIFE EXPECTANCY 72 years
GDP PER CAPITA $3,200
ECONOMY **IND:** food processing, chemicals, machinery and metal products, knit and woven apparel, petroleum refining and distribution, beverages, footwear, wood **AGR:** coffee, bananas, sugarcane, cotton, rice, corn, tobacco, sesame, soya, beans, beef, veal, pork, poultry, dairy products, shrimp, lobsters **EXP:** coffee, beef, shrimp and lobster, tobacco, sugar, gold, peanuts, textiles and apparel

Panama
REPUBLIC OF PANAMA

AREA 75,420 sq km
(29,120 sq mi)
POPULATION 3,510,000
CAPITAL Panamá 1,346,000
RELIGION Roman Catholic, Protestant
LANGUAGE Spanish, English
LITERACY 92%
LIFE EXPECTANCY 78 years
GDP PER CAPITA $13,600
ECONOMY **IND:** construction, brewing, cement and other construction materials, sugar milling **AGR:** bananas, rice, corn, coffee, sugarcane, vegetables, livestock, shrimp **EXP:** bananas, shrimp, sugar, coffee, clothing

St. Kitts and Nevis
FEDERATION OF SAINT KITTS AND NEVIS

AREA 261 sq km (101 sq mi)
POPULATION 50,700
CAPITAL Basseterre 13,000
RELIGION Anglican, other Protestant, Roman Catholic
LANGUAGE English
LITERACY 98%
LIFE EXPECTANCY 75 years
GDP PER CAPITA $16,400
ECONOMY **IND:** tourism, cotton, salt, copra, clothing, footwear, beverages **AGR:** sugarcane, rice, yams, vegetables, bananas, fish **EXP:** machinery, food, electronics, beverages, tobacco

St. Lucia
SAINT LUCIA

AREA 616 sq km (238 sq mi)
POPULATION 162,000
CAPITAL Castries 15,000
RELIGION Roman Catholic, Protestant
LANGUAGE English, French patois
LITERACY 90%
LIFE EXPECTANCY 77 years
GDP PER CAPITA $12,900
ECONOMY **IND:** clothing, assembly of electronic components, beverages, corrugated cardboard boxes, tourism, lime processing, coconut processing **AGR:** bananas, coconuts, vegetables, citrus, root crops, cocoa **EXP:** bananas, clothing, cocoa, vegetables, fruits, coconut oil

St. Vincent and the Grenadines
SAINT VINCENT AND THE GRENADINES

AREA 389 sq km (150 sq mi)
POPULATION 104,000
CAPITAL Kingstown 28,000
RELIGION Protestant, Roman Catholic
LANGUAGE English, French patois
LITERACY 96%
LIFE EXPECTANCY 74 years
GDP PER CAPITA $11,700
ECONOMY **IND:** food processing, cement, furniture, clothing, starch **AGR:** bananas, coconuts, sweet potatoes, spices, small numbers of cattle, sheep, pigs, goats, fish **EXP:** bananas, eddoes and dasheen (taro), arrowroot starch, tennis racquets

Trinidad and Tobago
REPUBLIC OF TRINIDAD AND TOBAGO

AREA 5,128 sq km (1,980 sq mi)
POPULATION 1,227,000
CAPITAL Port of Spain 57,000
RELIGION Roman Catholic, Protestant, Hindu
LANGUAGE English, Caribbean Hindustani, French, Spanish
LITERACY 99%
LIFE EXPECTANCY 72 years
GDP PER CAPITA $20,300
ECONOMY **IND:** petroleum and petroleum products, liquefied natural gas (LNG), methanol, ammonia, urea, steel products, beverages, food processing, cement, cotton textiles **AGR:** cocoa, rice, citrus, coffee, vegetables, poultry **EXP:** petroleum and petroleum products, liquefied natural gas (LNG), methanol, ammonia, urea, steel products, beverages, cereal and cereal products, sugar, cocoa, coffee, citrus fruit, vegetables, flowers

United States
UNITED STATES OF AMERICA

AREA 9,826,675 sq km
(3,794,079 sq mi)
POPULATION 313,847,000
CAPITAL Washington 4,421,000
RELIGION Protestant, Roman Catholic, unaffiliated
LANGUAGE English, Spanish
LITERACY 99%
LIFE EXPECTANCY 78 years
GDP PER CAPITA $48,100
ECONOMY **IND:** petroleum, steel, motor vehicles, aerospace, telecommunications, chemicals, electronics, food processing, consumer goods, lumber, mining **AGR:** wheat, corn, other grains, fruits, vegetables, cotton, beef, pork, poultry, dairy products, fish, forest products **EXP:** agricultural products, industrial supplies, capital goods, consumer goods

DEPENDENCIES

Anguilla
(U.K.)
ANGUILLA

AREA 91 sq km (35 sq mi)
POPULATION 15,400
CAPITAL The Valley 2,000
RELIGION Protestant
LANGUAGE English
LITERACY 95%
LIFE EXPECTANCY 81 years
GDP PER CAPITA $12,200
ECONOMY **IND:** tourism, boat building, offshore financial services **AGR:** small quantities of tobacco, vegetables, cattle raising **EXP:** lobster, fish, livestock, salt, concrete blocks, rum

Aruba
(NETHERLANDS)
ARUBA

AREA 180 sq km (69 sq mi)
POPULATION 108,000
CAPITAL Oranjestad 33,000
RELIGION Roman Catholic
LANGUAGE Papiamento, Spanish, English, Dutch
LITERACY 97%
LIFE EXPECTANCY 76 years
GDP PER CAPITA $21,800
ECONOMY **IND:** tourism, transshipment facilities **AGR:** aloes, livestock, fish **EXP:** live animals and animal products, art and collectibles, machinery and electrical equipment, transport equipment

Bermuda
(U.K.)
BERMUDA

AREA 54 sq km (21 sq mi)
POPULATION 69,100
CAPITAL Hamilton 12,000
RELIGION Protestant, Roman Catholic, none
LANGUAGE English, Portuguese
LITERACY 98%
LIFE EXPECTANCY 81 years
GDP PER CAPITA $69,900
ECONOMY **IND:** international business, tourism, light manufacturing **AGR:** bananas, vegetables, citrus, flowers, dairy products, honey **EXP:** reexports of pharmaceuticals

British Virgin Islands
(U.K.)
BRITISH VIRGIN ISLANDS

AREA 151 sq km (58 sq mi)
POPULATION 31,100
CAPITAL Road Town 9,000
RELIGION Protestant, Roman Catholic
LANGUAGE English
LITERACY 98%
LIFE EXPECTANCY 78 years
GDP PER CAPITA $38,500
ECONOMY **IND:** tourism, light industry, construction, rum, concrete block, offshore financial center **AGR:** fruits, vegetables, livestock, poultry, fish **EXP:** rum, fresh fish, fruits, animals, gravel, sand

Cayman Islands
(U.K.)
CAYMAN ISLANDS

AREA 264 sq km (102 sq mi)
POPULATION 52,600
CAPITAL George Town 32,000
RELIGION Protestant, Roman Catholic
LANGUAGE English
LITERACY 98%
LIFE EXPECTANCY 81 years
GDP PER CAPITA $43,800
ECONOMY **IND:** tourism, banking, insurance and finance, construction, construction materials, furniture **AGR:** vegetables, fruit, livestock, turtle farming **EXP:** turtle products, manufactured consumer goods

Curaçao
(NETHERLANDS)
LAND CURAÇAO

AREA 444 sq km (171 sq mi)
POPULATION 142,000
CAPITAL Willemstad 123,000
RELIGION Roman Catholic, Protestant
LANGUAGE Papiamento, Dutch
LITERACY NA
LIFE EXPECTANCY NA
GDP PER CAPITA $15,000
ECONOMY **IND:** tourism, petroleum refining, petroleum transshipment facilities, light manufacturing **AGR:** aloe, sorghum, peanuts, vegetables, tropical fruit **EXP:** petroleum products

Greenland
(DENMARK)
GREENLAND

AREA 2,166,086 sq km
(836,326 sq mi)
POPULATION 57,700
CAPITAL Nuuk 15,000
RELIGION Evangelical Lutheran, traditional Inuit spiritual beliefs
LANGUAGE Greenlandic, Danish, English
LITERACY 100%
LIFE EXPECTANCY 71 years
GDP PER CAPITA $36,500
ECONOMY **IND:** fish processing, gold, niobium, tantalite, uranium, iron and diamond mining, handicrafts, hides and skins, small shipyards **AGR:** forage crops, garden and greenhouse vegetables, sheep, reindeer, fish **EXP:** fish and fish products, metals

Guadeloupe, Martinique
(FRANCE)

Guadeloupe and Martinique are now recognized as French regions, having equal status to the 22 metropolitan regions that make up European France. Please see "France" for facts about Guadeloupe and Martinique.

Montserrat
(U.K.)
MONTSERRAT

AREA 102 sq km (39 sq mi)
POPULATION 5,160
CAPITAL Plymouth (abandoned), Brades (interim) 1,000
RELIGION Protestant, Roman Catholic
LANGUAGE English
LITERACY 97%
LIFE EXPECTANCY 73 years
GDP PER CAPITA $3,400
ECONOMY **IND:** tourism, rum, textiles, electronic appliances **AGR:** cabbages, carrots, cucumbers, tomatoes, onions, peppers, livestock products **EXP:** electronic components, plastic bags, apparel, hot peppers, limes, live plants, cattle

Puerto Rico
(U.S.)
COMMONWEALTH OF PUERTO RICO

AREA 13,790 sq km (5,324 sq mi)
POPULATION 3,999,000
CAPITAL San Juan 2,730,000
RELIGION Roman Catholic, Protestant
LANGUAGE Spanish, English
LITERACY 94%
LIFE EXPECTANCY 79 years
GDP PER CAPITA $16,300
ECONOMY **IND:** pharmaceuticals, electronics, apparel, food products, tourism **AGR:** sugarcane, coffee, pineapples, bananas, livestock products, chickens **EXP:** chemicals, electronics, apparel, canned tuna, rum, beverage concentrates, medical equipment

St.-Barthélemy
(FRANCE)
OVERSEAS COLLECTIVITY OF SAINT BARTHÉLEMY

AREA 21 sq km (8 sq mi)
POPULATION 7,300
CAPITAL Gustavia 2,000
RELIGION Roman Catholic, Protestant, Jehovah's Witnesses
LANGUAGE French, English
LITERACY NA
LIFE EXPECTANCY NA
GDP PER CAPITA NA
ECONOMY **IND:** NA **AGR:** NA **EXP:** NA

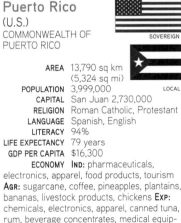

St.-Martin

(FRANCE)
OVERSEAS COLLECTIVITY
OF SAINT MARTIN

AREA	54 sq km (21 sq mi)
POPULATION	31,000
CAPITAL	Marigot 6,000
RELIGION	Roman Catholic, Jehovah's Witnesses, Protestant
LANGUAGE	French, English, Dutch, French patois, Spanish, Papiamento
LITERACY	NA
LIFE EXPECTANCY	NA
GDP PER CAPITA	NA
ECONOMY	IND: tourism, light industry and manufacturing, heavy industry AGR: NA EXP: NA

St.-Pierre and Miquelon

(FRANCE)
TERRITORIAL COLLECTIVITY OF
SAINT PIERRE AND MIQUELON

AREA	242 sq km (93 sq mi)
POPULATION	5,800
CAPITAL	Saint-Pierre 5,000
RELIGION	Roman Catholic
LANGUAGE	French
LITERACY	99%
LIFE EXPECTANCY	80 years
GDP PER CAPITA	$7,000
ECONOMY	IND: fish processing and supply base for fishing fleets, tourism AGR: vegetables, poultry, cattle, sheep, pigs, fish EXP: fish and fish products, soybeans, animal feed, mollusks and crustaceans, fox and mink pelts

Sint Maarten

(NETHERLANDS)
COUNTRY OF SINT MAARTEN

AREA	34 sq km (13 sq mi)
POPULATION	37,400
CAPITAL	Philipsburg 1,000
RELIGION	Protestant, Roman Catholic
LANGUAGE	English, Spanish, Dutch, Papiamento
LITERACY	NA
LIFE EXPECTANCY	NA
GDP PER CAPITA	$15,400
ECONOMY	IND: tourism, light industry, and manufacturing AGR: sugar EXP: sugar

Turks and Caicos Islands

(U.K.)
TURKS AND CAICOS
ISLANDS

AREA	948 sq km (366 sq mi)
POPULATION	46,300
CAPITAL	Cockburn Town 6,000
RELIGION	Protestant, Roman Catholic
LANGUAGE	English
LITERACY	98%
LIFE EXPECTANCY	79 years
GDP PER CAPITA	$11,500
ECONOMY	IND: tourism, offshore financial services AGR: corn, beans, cassava (tapioca), citrus fruits, fish EXP: lobster, dried and fresh conch, conch shells

Virgin Islands

(U.S.)
UNITED STATES
VIRGIN ISLANDS

AREA	1,910 sq km (737 sq mi)
POPULATION	109,600
CAPITAL	Charlotte Amalie 54,000
RELIGION	Protestant, Roman Catholic
LANGUAGE	English, Spanish, Spanish Creole
LITERACY	90-95%
LIFE EXPECTANCY	79 years
GDP PER CAPITA	$14,500
ECONOMY	IND: tourism, petroleum refining, watch assembly, rum distilling, construction, pharmaceuticals, textiles, electronics AGR: fruit, vegetables, sorghum, Senepol cattle EXP: refined petroleum products

UNITED STATES' STATE FLAGS

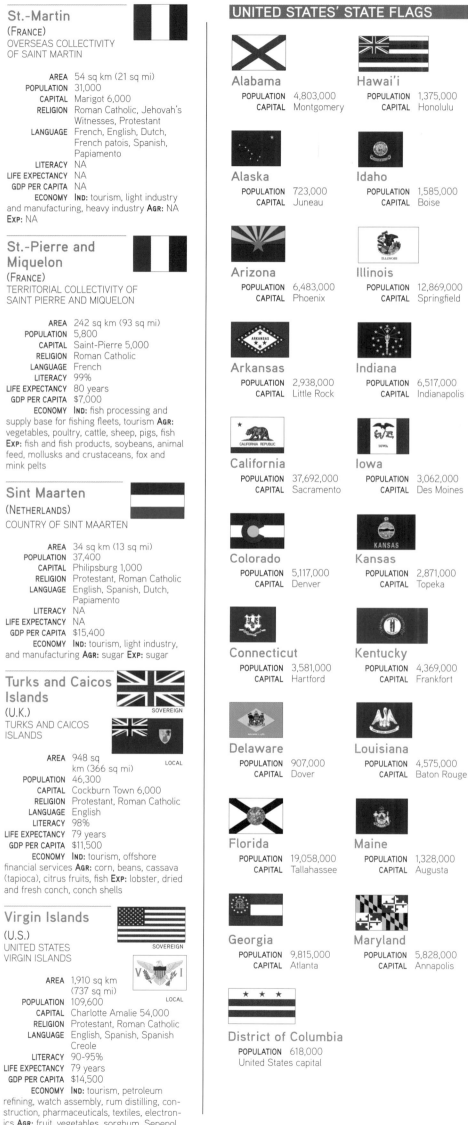

State	Population	Capital
Alabama	4,803,000	Montgomery
Hawai'i	1,375,000	Honolulu
Massachusetts	6,588,000	Boston
New Mexico	2,082,000	Santa Fe
South Dakota	842,000	Pierre
Alaska	723,000	Juneau
Idaho	1,585,000	Boise
Michigan	9,876,000	Lansing
New York	19,465,000	Albany
Tennessee	6,403,000	Nashville
Arizona	6,483,000	Phoenix
Illinois	12,869,000	Springfield
Minnesota	5,345,000	St. Paul
North Carolina	9,656,000	Raleigh
Texas	25,675,000	Austin
Arkansas	2,938,000	Little Rock
Indiana	6,517,000	Indianapolis
Mississippi	2,979,000	Jackson
North Dakota	684,000	Bismarck
Utah	2,817,000	Salt Lake City
California	37,692,000	Sacramento
Iowa	3,062,000	Des Moines
Missouri	6,011,000	Jefferson City
Ohio	11,545,000	Columbus
Vermont	626,000	Montpelier
Colorado	5,117,000	Denver
Kansas	2,871,000	Topeka
Montana	999,000	Helena
Oklahoma	3,792,000	Oklahoma City
Virginia	8,097,000	Richmond
Connecticut	3,581,000	Hartford
Kentucky	4,369,000	Frankfort
Nebraska	1,843,000	Lincoln
Oregon	3,872,000	Salem
Washington	6,830,000	Olympia
Delaware	907,000	Dover
Louisiana	4,575,000	Baton Rouge
Nevada	2,723,000	Carson City
Pennsylvania	12,743,000	Harrisburg
West Virginia	1,855,000	Charleston
Florida	19,058,000	Tallahassee
Maine	1,328,000	Augusta
New Hampshire	1,318,000	Concord
Rhode Island	1,051,000	Providence
Wisconsin	5,712,000	Madison
Georgia	9,815,000	Atlanta
Maryland	5,828,000	Annapolis
New Jersey	8,821,000	Trenton
South Carolina	4,679,000	Columbia
Wyoming	568,000	Cheyenne

District of Columbia

POPULATION 618,000
United States capital

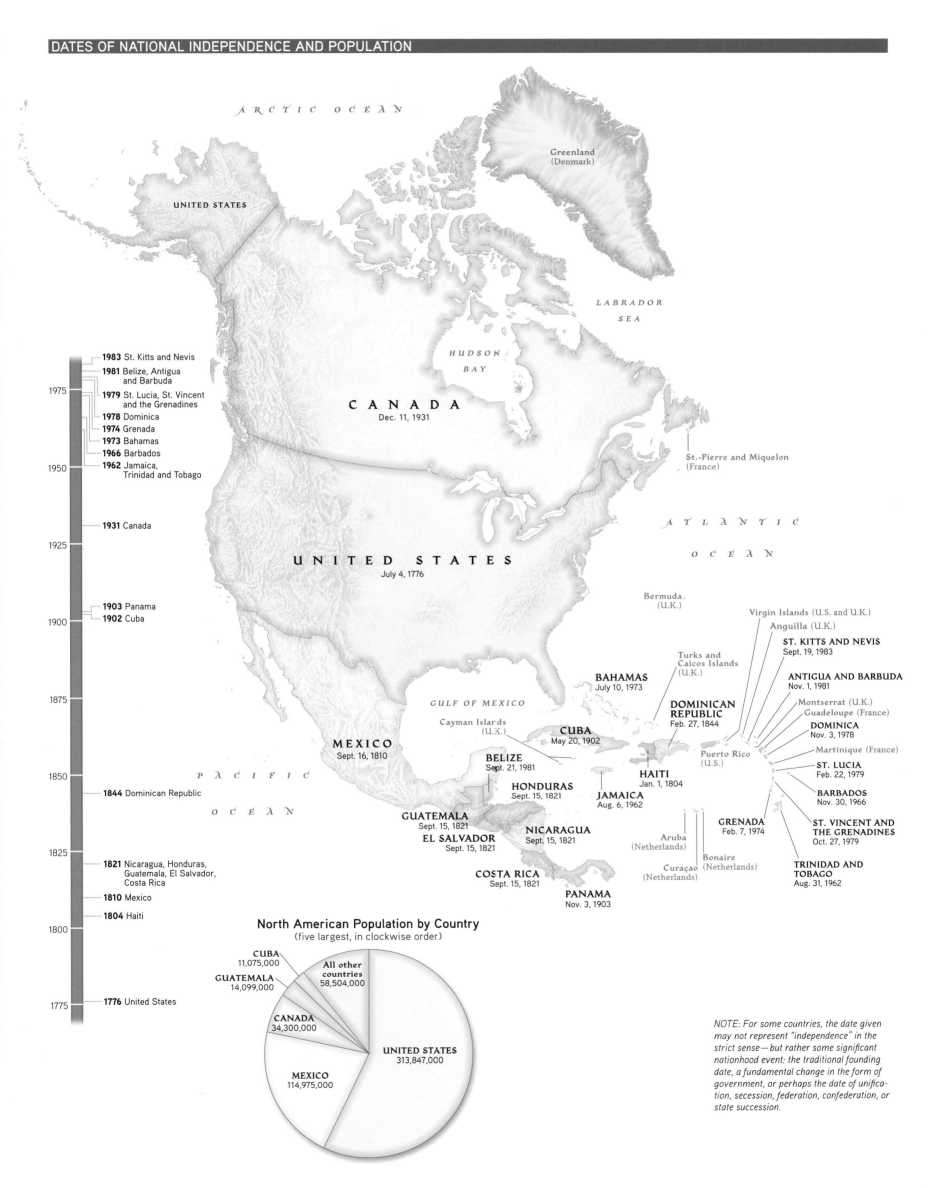

ARCTIC OCEAN

Greenland
(Denmark)

UNITED STATES

LABRADOR
SEA

HUDSON
BAY

CANADA
Dec. 11, 1931

St.-Pierre and Miquelon
(France)

ATLANTIC

OCEAN

UNITED STATES
July 4, 1776

Bermuda
(U.K.)

Virgin Islands (U.S. and U.K.)
Anguilla (U.K.)

ST. KITTS AND NEVIS
Sept. 19, 1983

Turks and
Caicos Islands
(U.K.)

ANTIGUA AND BARBUDA
Nov. 1, 1981

BAHAMAS
July 10, 1973

Montserrat (U.K.)
Guadeloupe (France)

DOMINICAN
REPUBLIC
Feb. 27, 1844

DOMINICA
Nov. 3, 1978

GULF OF MEXICO

CUBA
May 20, 1902

Cayman Islands
(U.K.)

Puerto Rico
(U.S.)

Martinique (France)

MEXICO
Sept. 16, 1810

BELIZE
Sept. 21, 1981

HAITI
Jan. 1, 1804

ST. LUCIA
Feb. 22, 1979

PACIFIC

HONDURAS
Sept. 15, 1821

JAMAICA
Aug. 6, 1962

BARBADOS
Nov. 30, 1966

OCEAN

GUATEMALA
Sept. 15, 1821

EL SALVADOR
Sept. 15, 1821

NICARAGUA
Sept. 15, 1821

Aruba
(Netherlands)

GRENADA
Feb. 7, 1974

ST. VINCENT AND
THE GRENADINES
Oct. 27, 1979

COSTA RICA
Sept. 15, 1821

Bonaire
(Netherlands)

Curaçao
(Netherlands)

TRINIDAD AND
TOBAGO
Aug. 31, 1962

PANAMA
Nov. 3, 1903

1983 St. Kitts and Nevis
1981 Belize, Antigua
and Barbuda
1979 St. Lucia, St. Vincent
and the Grenadines
1978 Dominica
1974 Grenada
1973 Bahamas
1966 Barbados
1962 Jamaica,
Trinidad and Tobago

1975

1950

1931 Canada

1925

1903 Panama
1902 Cuba

1900

1875

1850

1844 Dominican Republic

1821 Nicaragua, Honduras,
Guatemala, El Salvador,
Costa Rica
1810 Mexico
1804 Haiti

1825

1800

1776 United States

1775

North American Population by Country
(five largest, in clockwise order)

CUBA
11,075,000

GUATEMALA
14,099,000

All other
countries
58,504,000

CANADA
34,300,000

UNITED STATES
313,847,000

MEXICO
114,975,000

*NOTE: For some countries, the date given
may not represent "independence" in the
strict sense—but rather some significant
nationhood event: the traditional founding
date, a fundamental change in the form of
government, or perhaps the date of unification, secession, federation, confederation, or
state succession.*

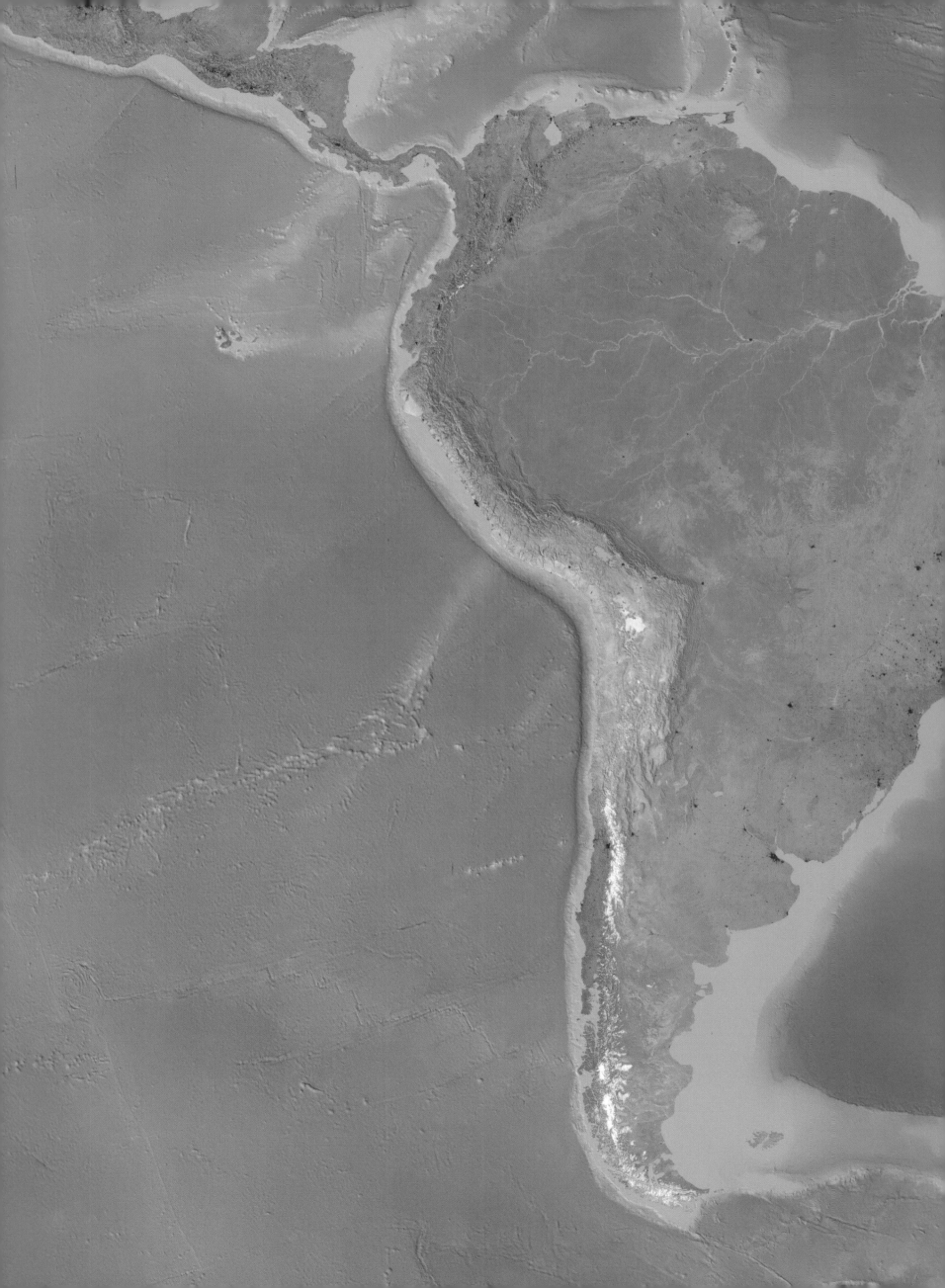

South America

CONTINENT OF EXTREMES, South America extends from the Isthmus of Panama, in the Northern Hemisphere, to a ragged tail less than 700 miles (1,130 kilometers) from Antarctica. There the Andes, a continuous continental rampart that forms the world's second highest range, finally dives undersea to continue as a submarine ridge. Occupying nearly half the continent, the world's largest and biologically richest rain forest spans the Equator, drained by the Amazon River, second longest river but largest by volume anywhere.

These formidable natural barriers shaped lopsided patterns of settlement in South America, the fourth largest continent. As early as 1531, when Spaniard Francisco Pizarro began his conquest of the Inca Empire, Iberians were pouring into coastal settlements that now hold most of the continent's burgeoning population. Meanwhile, Portuguese planters imported millions of African slaves to work vast sugar estates on Brazil's littoral. There and elsewhere, wealth and power coalesced in family oligarchies and in the Roman Catholic Church, building a system that 19th-century liberal revolutions failed to dismantle.

But eventual independence did not necessarily bring regional unity: Boundary wars dragged on into the 20th century before yielding the present-day borders of 12 nations. French Guiana remains an overseas department ruled from Paris; the Falkland Islands are a dependent territory of the United Kingdom. Natural riches still dominate economies, in the form of processed agricultural goods and minerals, as manufacturing matures. Privatization of nationalized industries in the 1990s followed free-market policies instituted by military regimes in the '70s and '80s, sometimes adding tumult to nations troubled by debt and inflation. By the end of the century, however, democracy had flowered across the continent, spurring an era of relative prosperity.

A rich blend of Iberian, African, and Amerindian traditions, South America has one of the world's liveliest and most distinctive cultures. Although the majority of people can still trace their ancestors back to Spain or Portugal, waves of immigration have transformed South America into an ethnic smorgasbord. This blend has produced a vibrant modern culture with influence far beyond the bounds of its South American cradle.

The vast majority of South Americans live in cities rather than the rain forest or mountains. A massive rural exodus since the 1950s has transformed South America into the second most urbanized continent (after Australia), a region that now boasts 3 of the world's 15 largest cities—São Paulo, Buenos Aires, and Rio de Janeiro. Ninety percent of the people live within 200 miles (320 kilometers) of the coast, leaving huge expanses of the interior virtually unpopulated. Despite protests from indigenous tribes and environmental groups, South American governments have tried to spur growth by opening up the Amazon region to economic exploitation, thereby wreaking ecological havoc. The Amazon could very well be the key to the region's economic future—not by the exploitation of the world's richest forest, but by the sustainable management and commercial development of its largely untapped biodiversity into medical, chemical, and nutritional products.

Longitude West 55° of Greenwich
EQUATOR
TROPIC OF CAPRICORN
COLOMBIA
VENEZUELA
GUYANA
SURINAME
FRENCH GUIANA
France
ECUADOR
PERU
BOLIVIA
PARAGUAY
BRAZIL
TRINIDAD AND TOBAGO
Port of Spain
Tobago
Trinidad
I. de San Andrés
Colombia
Isla de Malpelo
Colombia
Golfo de Venezuela
Golfo de Panamá
Golfo de Guayaquil
PANAMA CANAL
Panama City
BARRANQUILLA
CARTAGENA
MARACAIBO
Barquisimeto
CARACAS
VALENCIA
MEDELLÍN
BOGOTÁ
CALI
Cúcuta
Bucaramanga
Georgetown
Paramaribo
Cayenne
Boundary claimed by Suriname
QUITO
GUAYAQUIL
Cuenca
Iquitos
MANAUS
Santarém
Macapá
BELÉM
São Luís
Teresina
FORTALEZA
Natal
João Pessoa
RECIFE
Maceió
Aracaju
SALVADOR (Bahia)
Arquipélago de Fernando de Noronha
Brazil
Atol das Rocas
Brazil
TRUJILLO
Chiclayo
LIMA
Callao
Arequipa
Cusco
Lago Titicaca
LA PAZ (administrative)
Sucre (legal)
COCHABAMBA
Santa Cruz
Porto Velho
Rio Branco
Ji-Paraná (Rondônia)
Cuiabá
Campo Grande
Corumbá
BRASÍLIA
GOIÂNIA
Anápolis
Uberlândia
BELO HORIZONTE
RIO DE JANEIRO
Niterói
Duque de Caxias
NOVA IGUAÇU
SÃO PAULO
Santo André
Santos
Campinas
CURITIBA
Asunción
Antofagasta
Iquique
Arica
Tacna
Amazonas (Amazon)
Solimoes (Amazonas)
Negro
Branco
Madeira
Purus
Tapajós
Xingu
Tocantins
Araguaia
São Francisco
Paraguay
Paranaíba
Orinoco
Teles Pires (São Manuel)
Represa de Sobradinho
Represa da Balbina
Ilha de Marajó

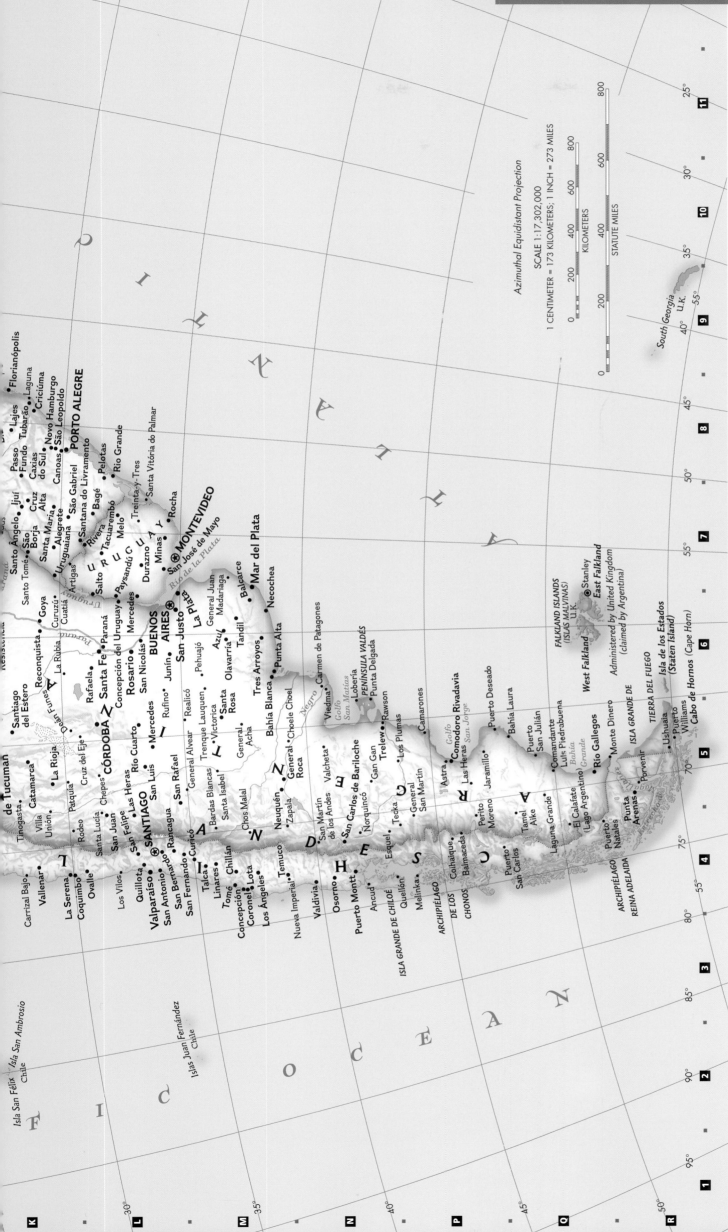

CONTINENTAL DATA

TOTAL NUMBER OF COUNTRIES: 12

FIRST INDEPENDENT COUNTRY:
Colombia, July 20, 1810

"YOUNGEST" COUNTRY:
Suriname, Nov. 25, 1975

LARGEST COUNTRY BY AREA:
Brazil 8,514,877 sq km
(3,287,594 sq mi)

SMALLEST COUNTRY BY AREA:
Suriname 163,820 sq km
(63,251 sq mi)

PERCENT URBAN POPULATION: 80%

MOST POPULOUS COUNTRY:
Brazil 205,717,000

LEAST POPULOUS COUNTRY:
Suriname 560,000

**MOST DENSELY POPULATED
COUNTRY:**
Ecuador 53.7 per sq km
(139.1 per sq mi)

**LEAST DENSELY POPULATED
COUNTRY:**
Suriname 3.4 per sq km
(8.9 per sq mi)

LARGEST CITY BY POPULATION:
São Paulo, Brazil 20,260,000

HIGHEST GDP PER CAPITA:
Argentina $17,400

LOWEST GDP PER CAPITA:
Bolivia $4,800

**AVERAGE LIFE EXPECTANCY
IN SOUTH AMERICA:** 72 years

**AVERAGE LITERACY RATE
IN SOUTH AMERICA:** 91%

Azimuthal Equidistant Projection

SCALE 1:17,302,000

1 CENTIMETER = 173 KILOMETERS; 1 INCH = 273 MILES

CONTINENTAL DATA

AREA: 17,819,000 sq km
(6,880,000 sq mi)

GREATEST NORTH-SOUTH EXTENT:
7,645 km (4,750 mi)

GREATEST EAST-WEST EXTENT:
5,150 km (3,200 mi)

HIGHEST POINT:
Cerro Aconcagua, Argentina
6,959 m (22,831 ft)

LOWEST POINT:
Laguna del Carbón, Argentina
-105 m (-344 ft)

LOWEST RECORDED TEMPERATURE:
Sarmiento, Argentina -33°C
(-27°F), June 1, 1907

HIGHEST RECORDED TEMPERATURE:
Rivadavia, Argentina 49°C (120°F),
December 11, 1905

LONGEST RIVERS:
• Amazon 6,437 km (4,000 mi)
• Paraná-Río de la Plata
4,000 km (2,485 mi)
• Purus 3,380 km (2,100 mi)

LARGEST NATURAL LAKES:
• Lake Maracaibo *(recognized by some as a lake)* 13,280 sq km
(5,127 sq mi)
• Lake Titicaca 8,372 sq km
(3,232 sq mi)
• Lake Poopó, 2,499 SQ KM
(965 SQ MI)

EARTH'S EXTREMES LOCATED

IN SOUTH AMERICA:
• Driest Place:
Arica, Atacama Desert, Chile;
rainfall barely measurable
• Highest Waterfall:
Angel Falls, Venezuela 979 m (3,212 ft)

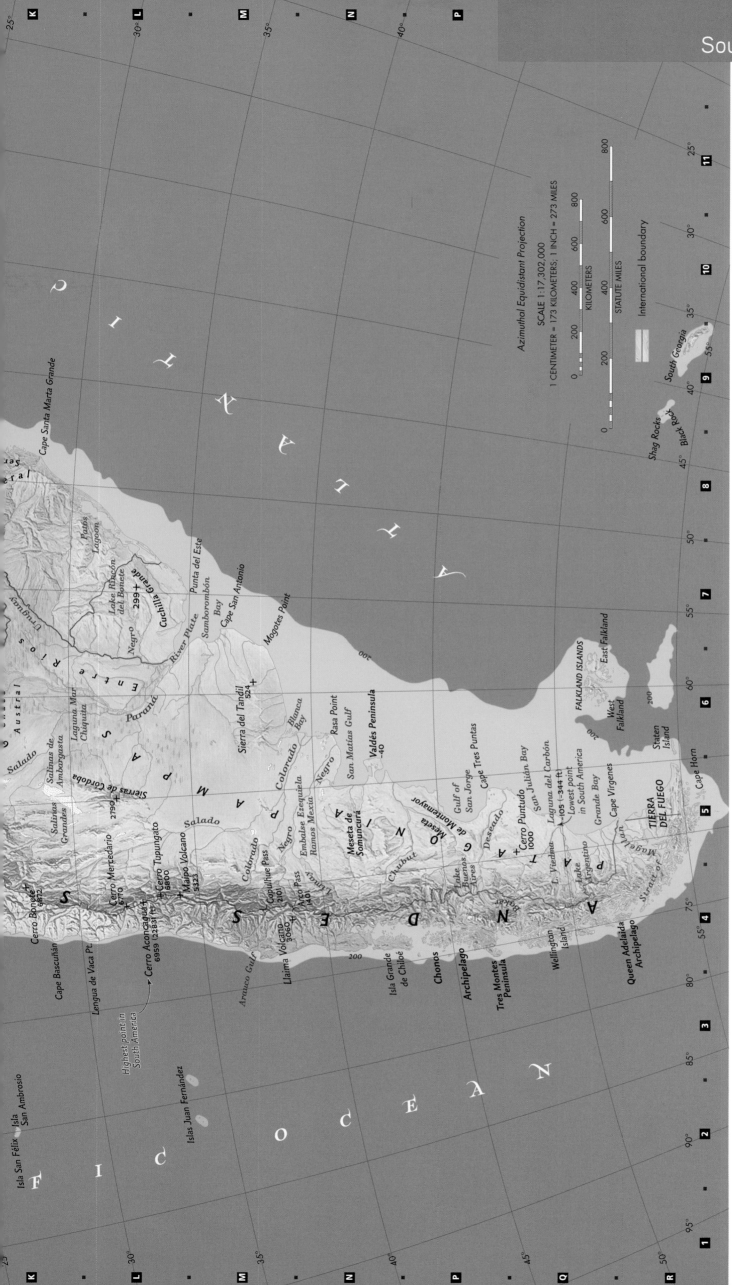

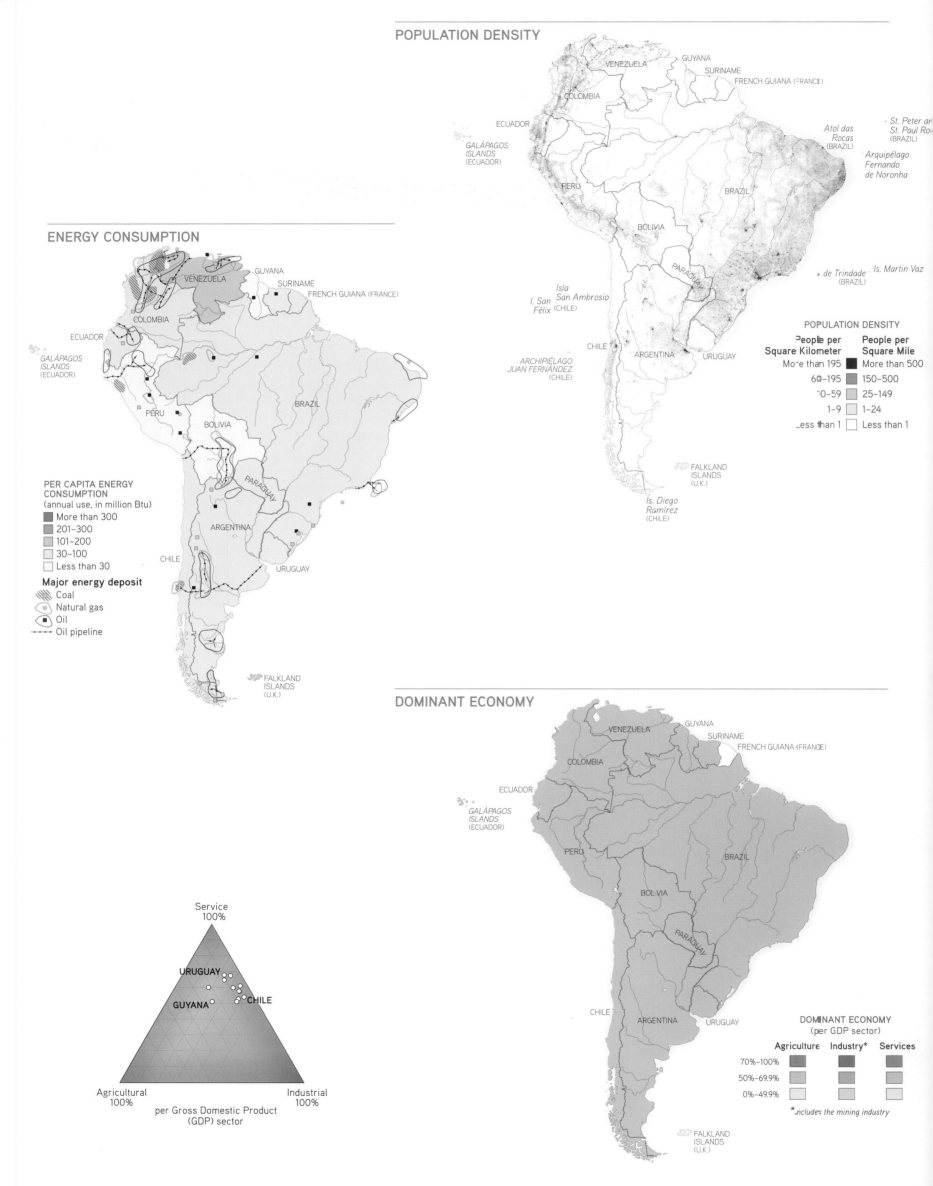

POPULATION DENSITY

POPULATION DENSITY

People per Square Kilometer	People per Square Mile
More than 195	More than 500
60–195	150–500
10–59	25–149
1–9	1–24
Less than 1	Less than 1

ENERGY CONSUMPTION

PER CAPITA ENERGY CONSUMPTION
(annual use, in million Btu)
- More than 300
- 201–300
- 101–200
- 30–100
- Less than 30

Major energy deposit
- Coal
- Natural gas
- Oil
- Oil pipeline

DOMINANT ECONOMY

Service 100%

URUGUAY

GUYANA

CHILE

Agricultural 100%

Industrial 100%

per Gross Domestic Product (GDP) sector

DOMINANT ECONOMY
(per GDP sector)

	Agriculture	Industry*	Services
70%–100%			
50%–69.9%			
0%–49.9%			

*includes the mining industry

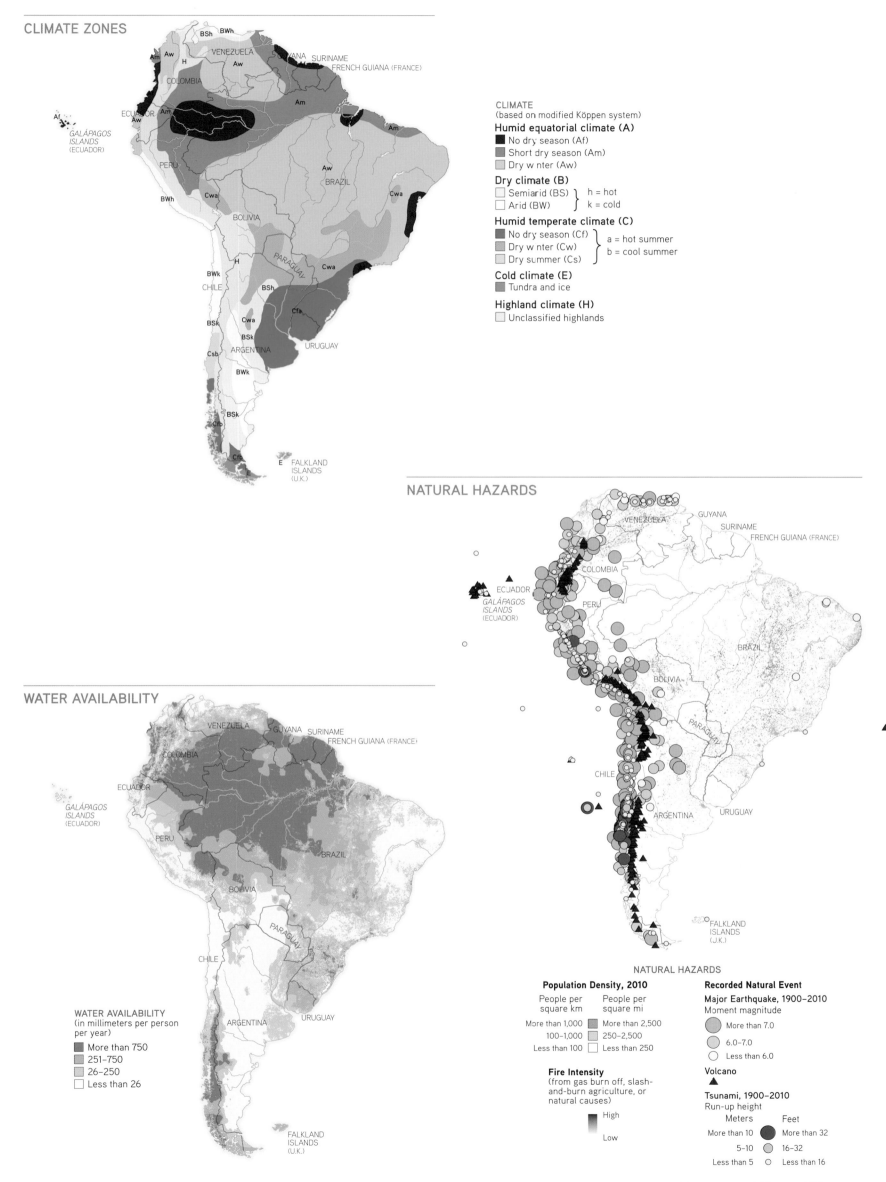

CLIMATE ZONES

BSh BWh
VENEZUELA
GUYANA SURINAME
FRENCH GUIANA (FRANCE)
Aw
H
Am Aw
COLOMBIA
Af
GALÁPAGOS
ISLANDS
(ECUADOR)
ECUADOR
Aw Am
Am
PERU
Am
BWh
Aw
BRAZIL
Cwa
BOLIVIA
Cwa
PARAGUAY
H
Cwa
BWk
CHILE
BSh
BSk
Cwa
BSk
Csb
ARGENTINA
BWk
URUGUAY
BSk
Cfb
Cfa
Cfb
E
E FALKLAND
ISLANDS
(U.K.)

CLIMATE
(based on modified Köppen system)

Humid equatorial climate (A)
No dry season (Af)
Short dry season (Am)
Dry winter (Aw)

Dry climate (B)
Semiarid (BS)   h = hot
Arid (BW)   k = cold

Humid temperate climate (C)
No dry season (Cf)   a = hot summer
Dry winter (Cw)   b = cool summer
Dry summer (Cs)

Cold climate (E)
Tundra and ice

Highland climate (H)
Unclassified highlands

NATURAL HAZARDS

VENEZUELA
GUYANA
SURINAME
FRENCH GUIANA (FRANCE)
COLOMBIA
ECUADOR
GALÁPAGOS
ISLANDS
(ECUADOR)
PERU
BRAZIL
BOLIVIA
PARAGUAY
CHILE
ARGENTINA
URUGUAY
FALKLAND
ISLANDS
(U.K.)

WATER AVAILABILITY

VENEZUELA
GUYANA
SURINAME
FRENCH GUIANA (FRANCE)
COLOMBIA
ECUADOR
GALÁPAGOS
ISLANDS
(ECUADOR)
PERU
BRAZIL
BOLIVIA
PARAGUAY
CHILE
ARGENTINA
URUGUAY
FALKLAND
ISLANDS
(U.K.)

WATER AVAILABILITY
(in millimeters per person
per year)
More than 750
251–750
26–250
Less than 26

NATURAL HAZARDS

Population Density, 2010

People per square km	People per square mi
More than 1,000	More than 2,500
100–1,000	250–2,500
Less than 100	Less than 250

Fire Intensity
(from gas burn off, slash-
and-burn agriculture, or
natural causes)
High
Low

Recorded Natural Event

Major Earthquake, 1900–2010
Moment magnitude
More than 7.0
6.0–7.0
Less than 6.0

Volcano

Tsunami, 1900–2010
Run-up height

Meters	Feet
More than 10	More than 32
5–10	16–32
Less than 5	Less than 16

COUNTRIES

Argentina
ARGENTINE REPUBLIC

AREA	2,780,400 sq km (1,073,512 sq mi)
POPULATION	42,192,000
CAPITAL	Buenos Aires 13,074,000
RELIGION	Roman Catholic
LANGUAGE	Spanish, Italian, English, German, French
LITERACY	97%
LIFE EXPECTANCY	77 years
GDP PER CAPITA	$17,400

ECONOMY IND: food processing, motor vehicles, consumer durables, textiles, chemicals and petrochemicals, printing, metallurgy, steel AGR: sunflower seeds, lemons, soybeans, grapes, corn, tobacco, peanuts, tea, wheat, livestock EXP: soybeans and derivatives, petroleum and gas, vehicles, corn, wheat

Bolivia
PLURINATIONAL STATE OF BOLIVIA

AREA	1,098,591 sq km (424,162 sq mi)
POPULATION	10,290,000
CAPITAL	La Paz (administrative) 1,673,000, Sucre (constitutional) 1,649,000
RELIGION	Roman Catholic
LANGUAGE	Spanish, Quechua, Aymara
LITERACY	87%
LIFE EXPECTANCY	68 years
GDP PER CAPITA	$4,800

ECONOMY IND: mining, smelting, petroleum, food and beverages, tobacco, handicrafts, clothing AGR: soybeans, coffee, coca, cotton, corn, sugarcane, rice, potatoes, timber EXP: natural gas, soybeans and soy products, crude petroleum, zinc ore, tin

Brazil
FEDERATIVE REPUBLIC OF BRAZIL

AREA	8,514,877 sq km (3,287,594 sq mi)
POPULATION	205,717,000
CAPITAL	Brasília 3,905,000
RELIGION	Roman Catholic, Protestant
LANGUAGE	Portuguese
LITERACY	89%
LIFE EXPECTANCY	73 years
GDP PER CAPITA	$11,600

ECONOMY IND: textiles, shoes, chemicals, cement, lumber, iron ore, tin, steel, aircraft, motor vehicles and parts, other machinery and equipment AGR: coffee, soybeans, wheat, rice, corn, sugarcane, cocoa, citrus, beef EXP: transport equipment, iron ore, soybeans, footwear, coffee, autos

Chile
REPUBLIC OF CHILE

AREA	756,102 sq km (291,931 sq mi)
POPULATION	17,067,000
CAPITAL	Santiago 5,952,000
RELIGION	Roman Catholic, Evangelical
LANGUAGE	Spanish, Mapudungun, German, English
LITERACY	96%
LIFE EXPECTANCY	78 years
GDP PER CAPITA	$16,100

ECONOMY IND: copper, lithium, other minerals, foodstuffs, fish processing, iron and steel, wood and wood products, transport equipment, cement, textiles AGR: grapes, apples, pears, onions, wheat, corn, oats, peaches, garlic, asparagus, beans, beef, poultry, wool, fish, timber EXP: copper, fruit, fish products, paper and pulp, chemicals, wine

Colombia
REPUBLIC OF COLOMBIA

AREA	1,138,910 sq km (439,733 sq mi)
POPULATION	45,239,000
CAPITAL	Bogotá 8,500,000
RELIGION	Roman Catholic
LANGUAGE	Spanish
LITERACY	90%
LIFE EXPECTANCY	75 years
GDP PER CAPITA	$10,100

ECONOMY IND: textiles, food processing, oil, clothing and footwear, beverages, chemicals, cement, gold, coal, emeralds AGR: coffee, cut flowers, bananas, rice, tobacco, corn, sugarcane, cocoa beans, oilseed, vegetables, forest products, shrimp EXP: petroleum, coffee, coal, nickel, emeralds, apparel, bananas, cut flowers

Ecuador
REPUBLIC OF ECUADOR

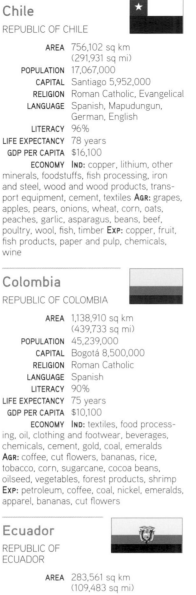

AREA	283,561 sq km (109,483 sq mi)
POPULATION	15,224,000
CAPITAL	Quito 1,846,000
RELIGION	Roman Catholic
LANGUAGE	Spanish, Quechua
LITERACY	91%
LIFE EXPECTANCY	76 years
GDP PER CAPITA	$8,300

ECONOMY IND: petroleum, food processing, textiles, wood products, chemicals AGR: bananas, coffee, cocoa, rice, potatoes, manioc (tapioca), plantains, sugarcane, cattle, sheep, pigs, beef, pork, dairy products, balsa wood, fish, shrimp EXP: petroleum, bananas, cut flowers, shrimp, cacao, coffee, wood, fish

Guyana
COOPERATIVE REPUBLIC OF GUYANA

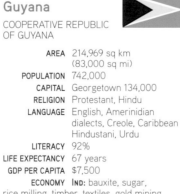

AREA	214,969 sq km (83,000 sq mi)
POPULATION	742,000
CAPITAL	Georgetown 134,000
RELIGION	Protestant, Hindu
LANGUAGE	English, Amerinidian dialects, Creole, Caribbean Hindustani, Urdu
LITERACY	92%
LIFE EXPECTANCY	67 years
GDP PER CAPITA	$7,500

ECONOMY IND: bauxite, sugar, rice milling, timber, textiles, gold mining AGR: sugarcane, rice, edible oils, shrimp, fish, beef, pork, poultry EXP: sugar, gold, bauxite, alumina, rice, shrimp, molasses, rum, timber

Paraguay
REPUBLIC OF PARAGUAY

AREA	406,752 sq km (157,047 sq mi)
POPULATION	6,542,000
CAPITAL	Asunción 2,030,000
RELIGION	Roman Catholic
LANGUAGE	Spanish, Guarani
LITERACY	94%
LIFE EXPECTANCY	76 years
GDP PER CAPITA	$5,500

ECONOMY IND: sugar, cement, textiles, beverages, wood products, steel, metallurgy, electric power AGR: cotton, sugarcane, soybeans, corn, wheat, tobacco, cassava (tapioca), fruits, vegetables, beef, pork, eggs, milk, timber EXP: soybeans, feed, cotton, meat, edible oils, electricity, wood, leather

Peru
REPUBLIC OF PERU

AREA	1,285,216 sq km (496,222 sq mi)
POPULATION	29,550,000
CAPITAL	Lima 8,941,000
RELIGION	Roman Catholic, Evangelical
LANGUAGE	Spanish, Quechua, Aymara, Ashaninka
LITERACY	93%
LIFE EXPECTANCY	73 years
GDP PER CAPITA	$10,000

ECONOMY IND: mining and refining of minerals, steel, metal fabrication, petroleum extraction and refining, natural gas and natural gas liquefaction, fishing and fish processing, cement, textiles, clothing, food processing AGR: asparagus, coffee, cocoa, cotton, sugarcane, rice, potatoes, corn, plantains, grapes, oranges, pineapples, guavas, bananas, apples, lemons, pears, coca, tomatoes, mango, barley, medicinal plants, palm oil, marigolds, onions, wheat, dry beans, poultry, beef, dairy products, fish, guinea pigs EXP: copper, gold, zinc, tin, iron ore, molybdenum, crude petroleum and petroleum products, natural gas, coffee, potatoes, asparagus and other vegetables, fruit, apparel and textiles, fishmeal

Suriname
REPUBLIC OF SURINAME

AREA	163,820 sq km (63,251 sq mi)
POPULATION	560,000
CAPITAL	Paramaribo 214,000
RELIGION	Hindu, Protestant, Roman Catholic, Muslim
LANGUAGE	Dutch, English, Sranang Tongo, Caribbean Hindustani, Javanese
LITERACY	90%
LIFE EXPECTANCY	71 years
GDP PER CAPITA	$9,500

ECONOMY IND: bauxite and gold mining, alumina production, oil, lumbering, food processing, fishing AGR: paddy rice, bananas, palm kernels, coconuts, plantains, peanuts, beef, chickens, shrimp, forest products EXP: alumina, gold, crude oil, lumber, shrimp and fish, rice, bananas

Uruguay
ORIENTAL REPUBLIC OF URUGUAY

AREA	176,215 sq km (68,037 sq mi)
POPULATION	3,316,000
CAPITAL	Montevideo 1,635,000
RELIGION	Roman Catholic, none
LANGUAGE	Spanish, Portunol, Brazilero
LITERACY	98%
LIFE EXPECTANCY	76 years
GDP PER CAPITA	$15,400

ECONOMY IND: food processing, electrical machinery, transportation equipment, petroleum products, textiles, chemicals, beverages AGR: beef, soybeans, cellulose, rice, wheat, lumber, dairy products, fish EXP: beef, soybeans, cellulose, rice, wheat, wood, dairy products, wool

Venezuela
BOLIVARIAN REPUBLIC OF VENEZUELA

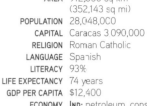

AREA	912,050 sq km (352,143 sq mi)
POPULATION	28,048,000
CAPITAL	Caracas 3,090,000
RELIGION	Roman Catholic
LANGUAGE	Spanish
LITERACY	93%
LIFE EXPECTANCY	74 years
GDP PER CAPITA	$12,400

ECONOMY IND: petroleum, construction materials, food processing, textiles, iron ore mining, steel, aluminum, motor vehicle assembly AGR: corn, sorghum, sugarcane, rice, bananas, vegetables, coffee, beef, pork, milk, eggs, fish EXP: petroleum, bauxite and aluminum, minerals, chemicals, agricultural products, basic manufactures

DEPENDENCIES

Falkland Islands
(U.K.)
FALKLAND ISLANDS

SOVEREIGN

LOCAL

AREA	12,173 sq km (4,700 sq mi)
POPULATION	3,140
CAPITAL	Stanley 2,000
RELIGION	Christian
LANGUAGE	English
LITERACY	NA
LIFE EXPECTANCY	NA
GDP PER CAPITA	$35,400

ECONOMY IND: fish and wool processing, tourism AGR: fodder and vegetable crops, sheep, dairy products, fish, squid EXP: wool, hides, meat, fish, squid

French Guiana
(FRANCE)

French Guiana is now recognized as a French region, having equal status to the 22 metropolitan regions that make up European France. Please see "France" for facts about French Guiana.

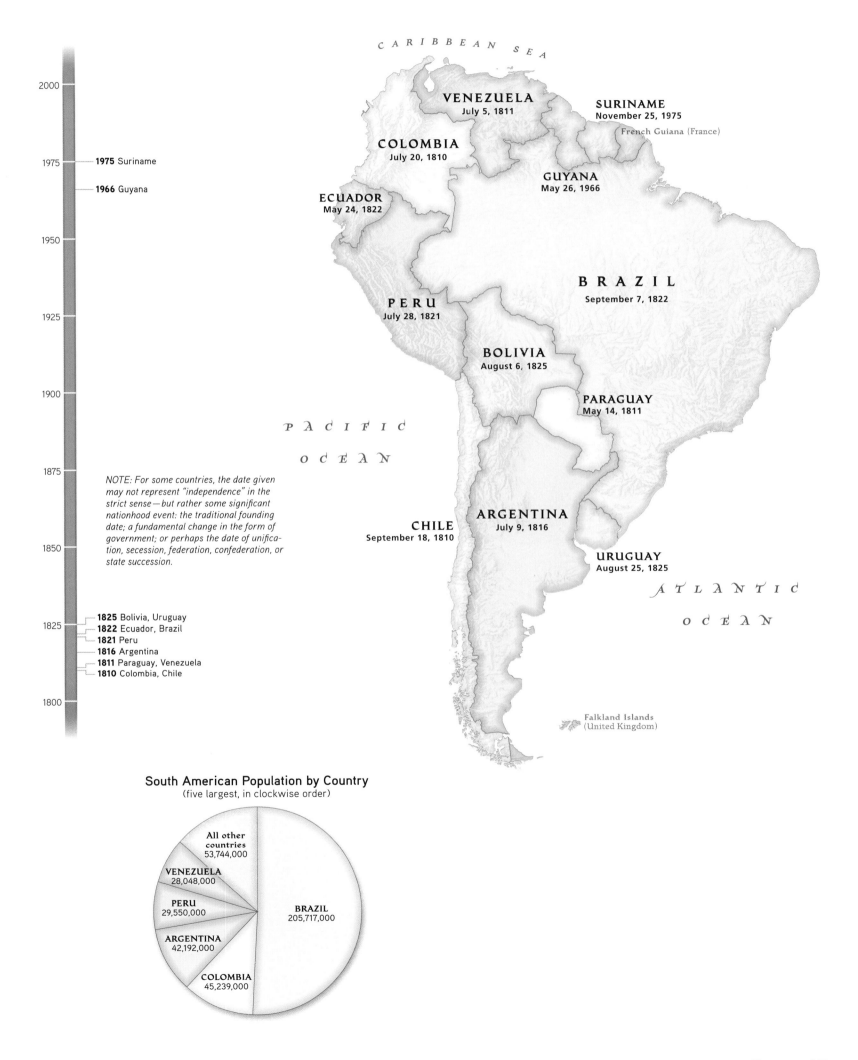

2000

1975 — **1975** Suriname

— **1966** Guyana

1950

1925

1900

1875

NOTE: For some countries, the date given may not represent "independence" in the strict sense—but rather some significant nationhood event: the traditional founding date; a fundamental change in the form of government; or perhaps the date of unification, secession, federation, confederation, or state succession.

1850

1825 — **1825** Bolivia, Uruguay
— **1822** Ecuador, Brazil
— **1821** Peru
— **1816** Argentina
— **1811** Paraguay, Venezuela
— **1810** Colombia, Chile

1800

VENEZUELA
July 5, 1811

SURINAME
November 25, 1975

French Guiana (France)

COLOMBIA
July 20, 1810

GUYANA
May 26, 1966

ECUADOR
May 24, 1822

BRAZIL
September 7, 1822

PERU
July 28, 1821

BOLIVIA
August 6, 1825

PARAGUAY
May 14, 1811

CHILE
September 18, 1810

ARGENTINA
July 9, 1816

URUGUAY
August 25, 1825

Falkland Islands
(United Kingdom)

South American Population by Country
(five largest, in clockwise order)

All other countries
53,744,000

VENEZUELA
28,048,000

PERU
29,550,000

BRAZIL
205,717,000

ARGENTINA
42,192,000

COLOMBIA
45,239,000

Europe

EUROPE APPEARS FROM SPACE as a cluster of peninsulas and islands thrusting westward from Asia into the Atlantic Ocean. The smallest continent except Australia, Europe nonetheless has a population density second only to Asia's. Colliding tectonic plates and retreating Ice Age glaciers continue to shape Europe's fertile plains and rugged mountains, and the North Atlantic's Gulf Stream tempers the continent's climate. Europe's highly irregular coastline measures more than one and a half times the length of the Equator, leaving only 14 out of 45 counties landlocked.

Europe has been inhabited for some 40,000 years. During the last millennium Europeans explored the planet and established far-flung empires, leaving their imprint on every corner of the Earth. Europe led the world in science and invention, and launched the industrial revolution. Great periods of creativity in the arts have occurred at various times all over the continent and shape its collective culture. By the end of the 19th century Europe dominated world commerce, spreading European ideas, languages, legal systems, and political patterns around the globe. But the Europeans who explored, colonized, and knitted together the world's regions knew themselves only as Portuguese, Spanish, Dutch, British, French, German, and Russian. After centuries of rivalry and war the two devastating world wars launched from its soil in the 20th century ended Europe's world dominance. By the 1960s nearly all its colonies had gained independence.

European countries divided into two blocs, playing out the new superpowers' Cold War—the west allied to North America and the east bound to the Soviet Union, with Germany split between them. From small beginnings in the 1950s, Western Europe began to unify. Germany's unification and the Soviet Union's unexpected breakup in the early 1990s sped the movement. Led by former enemies France and Germany, 25 countries of Western Europe now form the European Union (EU), with common European citizenship. Several Eastern European countries clamor to join. In 1999, 12 of the EU members adopted a common currency, the euro, creating a single economic market, one of the largest in the world. Political union will come harder. A countercurrent of nationalism and ethnic identity has splintered the Balkan Peninsula, and the future of Russia is impossible to predict.

Scores of distinct ethnic groups, speaking some 40 languages, inhabit more than 40 countries, which vary in size from European Russia to tiny Luxembourg, each with its own history and traditions. Yet Europe has a more uniform culture than any other continent. Its population is overwhelmingly of one race, Caucasian, despite the recent arrival of immigrants from Africa and Asia. Most of its languages fall into three groups with Indo-European roots: Germanic, Romance, or Slavic. One religion, Christianity, predominates in various forms, and social structures nearly everywhere are based on economic classes. However, immigrant groups established as legitimate and illegal workers, refugees, and asylum seekers cling to their own habits, religions, and languages. Every European society is becoming more multicultural, with political as well as cultural consequences.

CONTINENTAL DATA

TOTAL NUMBER OF COUNTRIES: 46

FIRST INDEPENDENT COUNTRY:
San Marino, September 3, 301

"YOUNGEST" COUNTRY:
Kosovo, February 17, 2008

LARGEST COUNTRY BY AREA:
Russia 17,098,242 sq km
(6,601,631 sq mi)

SMALLEST COUNTRY BY AREA:
Vatican City 0.4 sq km (0.2 sq mi)

PERCENT URBAN POPULATION: 75%

MOST POPULOUS COUNTRY:
Russia 138,082,000

LEAST POPULOUS COUNTRY:
Vatican City 836

MOST DENSELY POPULATED COUNTRY:
Monaco 15,250 per sq km
(38,125 per sq mi)

LEAST DENSELY POPULATED COUNTRY:
Iceland 3.0 per sq km
(7.9 per sq mi)

LARGEST CITY BY POPULATION:
Moscow, Russia 10,550,000

HIGHEST GDP PER CAPITA:
Luxembourg $84,700

LOWEST GDP PER CAPITA:
Moldova $3,400

**AVERAGE LIFE EXPECTANCY
IN EUROPE:** 75 years

**AVERAGE LITERACY RATE
IN EUROPE:** 99%

A commonly accepted division between Asia and Europe—here marked with a green line—is formed by the Ural Mountains, Ural River, Caspian Sea, Caucasus Mountains, and the Black Sea with its outlets, the Bosporus and Dardanelles.

TRANSDNIESTRIA
Since the break-up of the Soviet Union, Ukrainian and Russian minorities have been struggling for independence from Moldova.

A commonly accepted division between Asia and Europe—here marked by a green line—is formed by the Ural Mountains, Ural River, Caspian Sea, Caucasus Mountains, and the Black Sea with its outlets, the Bosporus and Dardanelles.

Azimuthal Equidistant Projection

SCALE 1:13,664,000
1 CENTIMETER = 137 KILOMETERS; 1 INCH = 215 MILES

0 100 200 300 400 500
KILOMETERS

0 100 200 300 400 500
STATUTE MILES

International boundary

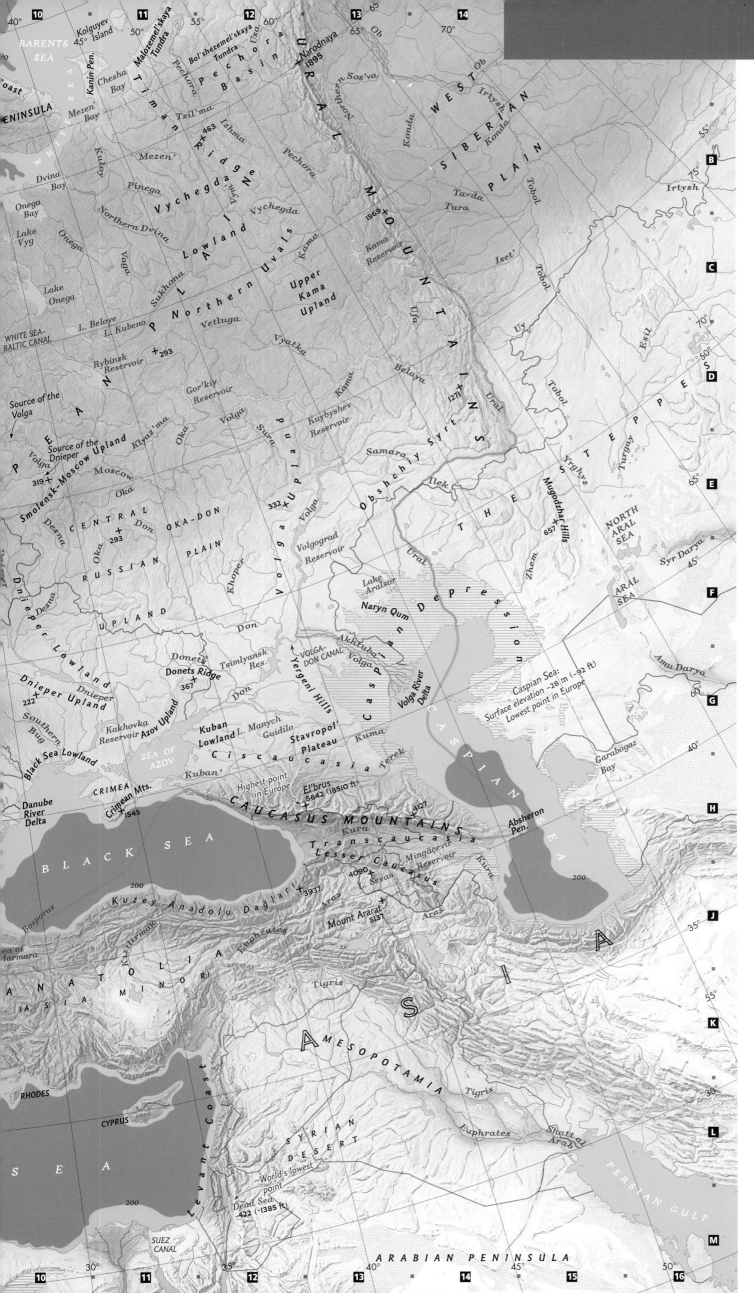

CONTINENTAL DATA

AREA: 9,947,000 sq km
(3,841,000 sq mi)

GREATEST NORTH-SOUTH EXTENT:
4,800 km (2,980 mi)

GREATEST EAST-WEST EXTENT:
6,400 km (3,980 mi)

HIGHEST POINT: El'brus, Russia
5,642 m (18,510 ft)

LOWEST POINT: Caspian Sea
-28 m (-92 ft)

LOWEST RECORDED TEMPERATURE:
Ust'Shchugor, Russia -55°C
(-67°F), Date unknown

HIGHEST RECORDED TEMPERATURE:
Seville, Spain 50°C (122°F),
August 4, 1881

LONGEST RIVERS:
•Volga 3,685 km (2,290 mi)
•Danube 2,848 km (1,770 mi)
•Dnieper 2,285 km (1,420 mi)

LARGEST NATURAL LAKES:
•Caspian Sea 371,000 sq km
(143,200 sq mi)
•Lake Ladoga 17,872 sq km
(6,900 sq mi)
•Lake Onega 9,842 sq km
(3,800 sq mi)

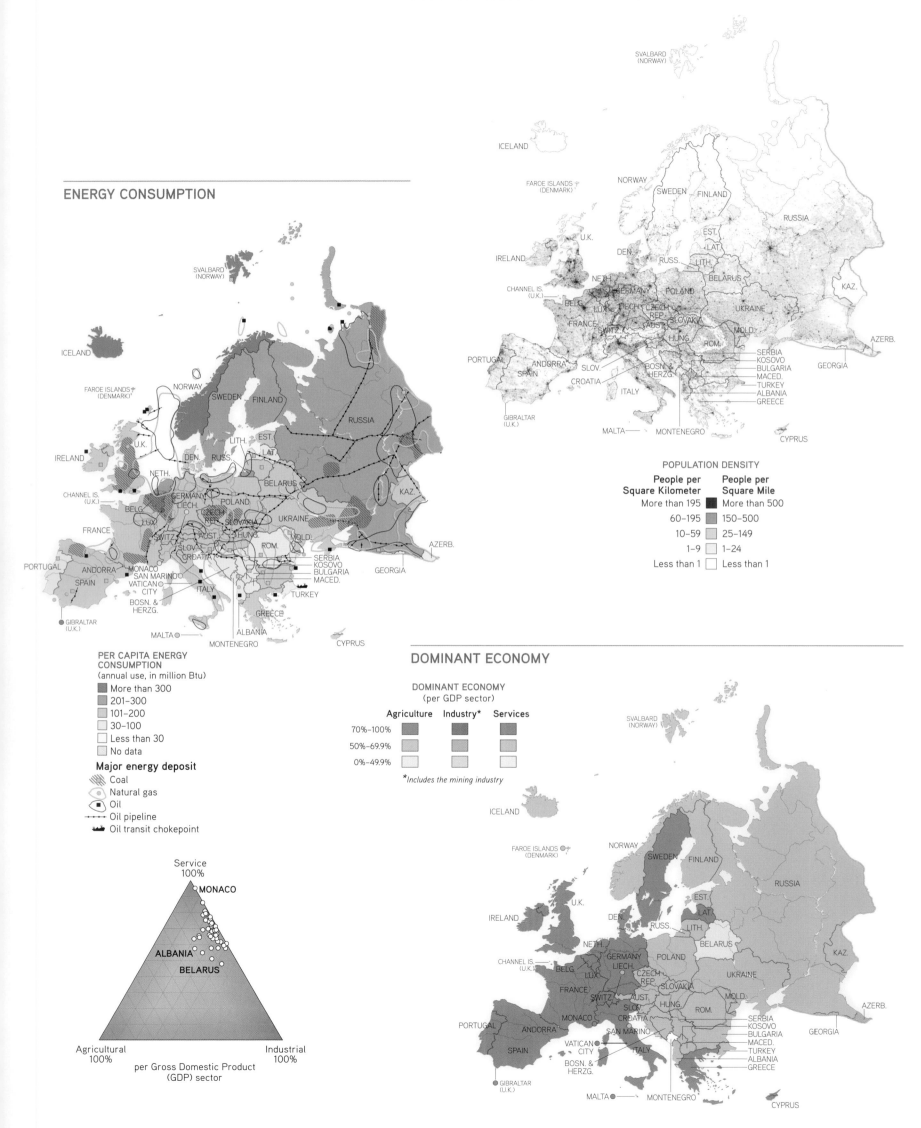

POPULATION DENSITY

ENERGY CONSUMPTION

PER CAPITA ENERGY
CONSUMPTION
(annual use, in million Btu)

- More than 300
- 201–300
- 101–200
- 30–100
- Less than 30
- No data

Major energy deposit

- Coal
- Natural gas
- Oil
- Oil pipeline
- Oil transit chokepoint

POPULATION DENSITY

People per Square Kilometer	People per Square Mile
More than 195	More than 500
60–195	150–500
10–59	25–149
1–9	1–24
Less than 1	Less than 1

DOMINANT ECONOMY

DOMINANT ECONOMY
(per GDP sector)

	Agriculture	Industry*	Services
70%–100%			
50%–69.9%			
0%–49.9%			

*Includes the mining industry

Service
100%

MONACO

ALBANIA

BELARUS

Agricultural
100%

Industrial
100%

per Gross Domestic Product
(GDP) sector

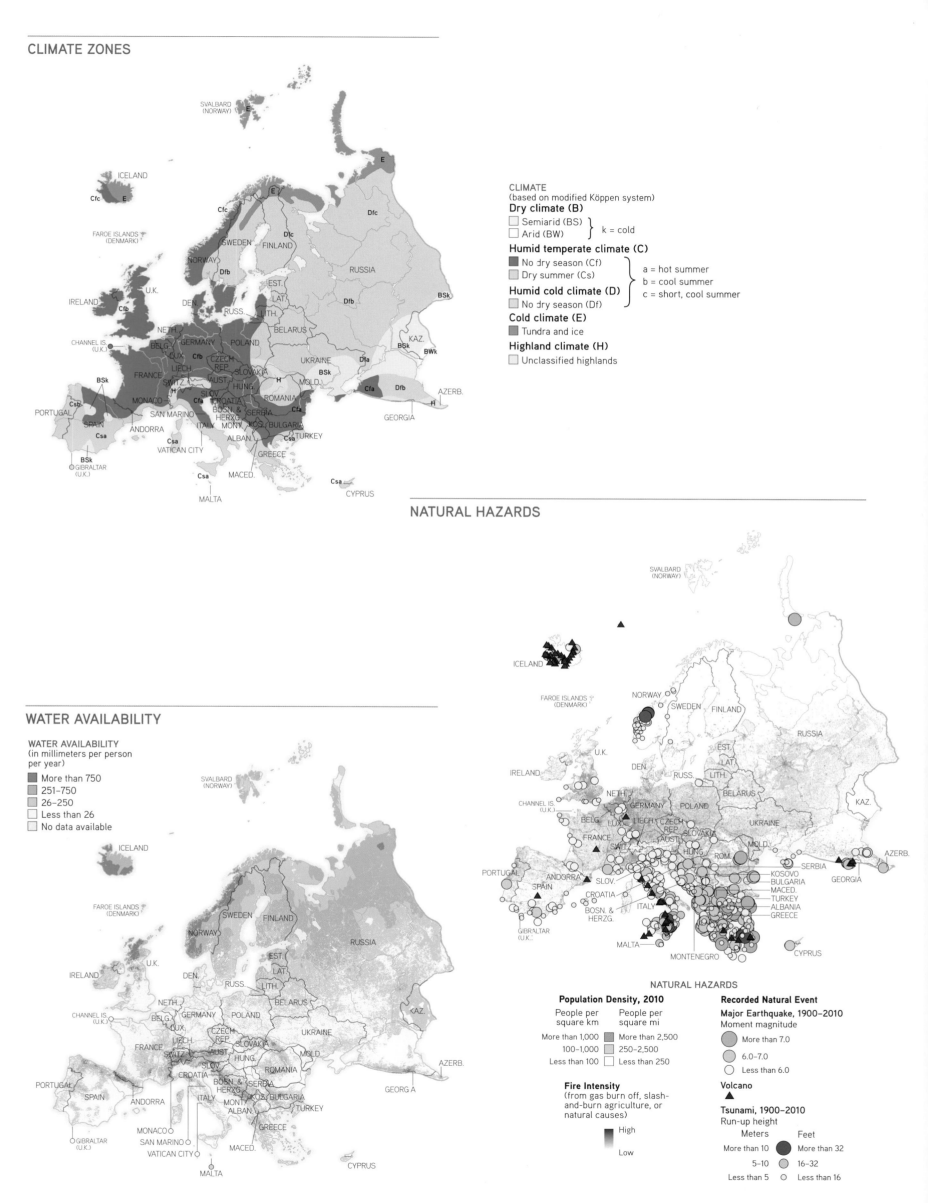

CLIMATE ZONES

NATURAL HAZARDS

WATER AVAILABILITY

CLIMATE
(based on modified Köppen system)

Dry climate (B)
- Semiarid (BS)
- Arid (BW) } k = cold

Humid temperate climate (C)
- No dry season (Cf)
- Dry summer (Cs) } a = hot summer b = cool summer

Humid cold climate (D)
- No dry season (Df) } c = short, cool summer

Cold climate (E)
- Tundra and ice

Highland climate (H)
- Unclassified highlands

WATER AVAILABILITY
(in millimeters per person per year)
- More than 750
- 251–750
- 26–250
- Less than 26
- No data available

NATURAL HAZARDS

Population Density, 2010

People per square km	People per square mi
More than 1,000	More than 2,500
100–1,000	250–2,500
Less than 100	Less than 250

Fire Intensity
(from gas burn off, slash-and-burn agriculture, or natural causes)
- High
- Low

Recorded Natural Event

Major Earthquake, 1900–2010
Moment magnitude
- More than 7.0
- 6.0–7.0
- Less than 6.0

Volcano

Tsunami, 1900–2010
Run-up height

Meters	Feet
More than 10	More than 32
5–10	16–32
Less than 5	Less than 16

COUNTRIES

Albania
REPUBLIC OF ALBANIA

AREA	28,748 sq km (11,100 sq mi)
POPULATION	3,003,000
CAPITAL	Tirana 433,000
RELIGION	Muslim, Albanian Orthodox, Roman Catholic
LANGUAGE	Albanian, Greek, Vlach, Romani, Slavic dialects
LITERACY	99%
LIFE EXPECTANCY	78 years
GDP PER CAPITA	$7,800

ECONOMY **IND:** food processing, textiles and clothing, lumber, oil, cement, chemicals, mining, basic metals, hydropower **AGR:** wheat, corn, potatoes, vegetables, fruits, sugar beets, grapes, meat, dairy products **EXP:** textiles and footwear, asphalt, metals and metallic ores, crude oil, vegetables, fruits, tobacco

Andorra
PRINCIPALITY OF ANDORRA

AREA	468 sq km (181 sq mi)
POPULATION	85,100
CAPITAL	Andorra la Vella 25,000
RELIGION	Roman Catholic
LANGUAGE	Catalan, French, Castilian, Portuguese
LITERACY	100%
LIFE EXPECTANCY	83 years
GDP PER CAPITA	$37,200

ECONOMY **IND:** tourism (particularly skiing), cattle raising, timber, banking, tobacco, furniture **AGR:** small quantities of rye, wheat, barley, oats, vegetables, sheep **EXP:** tobacco products, furniture

Austria
REPUBLIC OF AUSTRIA

AREA	83,871 sq km (32,383 sq mi)
POPULATION	8,220,000
CAPITAL	Vienna 1,693,000
RELIGION	Roman Catholic
LANGUAGE	German
LITERACY	98%
LIFE EXPECTANCY	80 years
GDP PER CAPITA	$41,700

ECONOMY **IND:** construction, machinery, vehicles and parts, food, metals, chemicals, lumber and wood processing, paper and paperboard, communications equipment, tourism **AGR:** grains, potatoes, wine, fruit, dairy products, cattle, pigs, poultry, lumber **EXP:** machinery and equipment, motor vehicles and parts, paper and paperboard, metal goods, chemicals, iron and steel, textiles, foodstuffs

Belarus
REPUBLIC OF BELARUS

AREA	207,600 sq km (80,154 sq mi)
POPULATION	9,543,000
CAPITAL	Minsk 1,837,000
RELIGION	Eastern Orthodox
LANGUAGE	Belarusian, Russian
LITERACY	100%
LIFE EXPECTANCY	71 years
GDP PER CAPITA	$14,900

ECONOMY **IND:** metal-cutting machine tools, tractors, trucks, earthmovers, motorcycles, televisions, synthetic fibers, fertilizer, textiles, radios, refrigerators **AGR:** grain, potatoes, vegetables, sugar beets, flax, beef, milk **EXP:** machinery and equipment, mineral products, chemicals, metals, textiles, foodstuffs

Belgium
KINGDOM OF BELGIUM

AREA	30,528 sq km (11,787 sq mi)
POPULATION	10,438,000
CAPITAL	Brussels 1,892,000
RELIGION	Roman Catholic
LANGUAGE	Dutch, French
LITERACY	99%
LIFE EXPECTANCY	80 years
GDP PER CAPITA	$37,600

ECONOMY **IND:** engineering and metal products, motor vehicle assembly, transportation equipment, scientific instruments, processed food and beverages, chemicals, basic metals, textiles, glass, petroleum **AGR:** sugar beets, fresh vegetables, fruits, grain, tobacco, beef, veal, pork, milk **EXP:** machinery and equipment, chemicals, finished diamonds, metals and metal products, foodstuffs

Bosnia and Herzegovina
BOSNIA AND HERZEGOVINA

AREA	51,197 sq km (19,767 sq mi)
POPULATION	4,622,000
CAPITAL	Sarajevo 392,000
RELIGION	Muslim, Orthodox, Roman Catholic
LANGUAGE	Bosnian, Croatian, Serbian
LITERACY	97%
LIFE EXPECTANCY	79 years
GDP PER CAPITA	$8,200

ECONOMY **IND:** steel, coal, iron ore, lead, zinc, manganese, bauxite, aluminum, vehicle assembly, textiles, tobacco products, wooden furniture, ammunition, domestic appliances, oil refining **AGR:** wheat, corn, fruits, vegetables, livestock **EXP:** metals, clothing, wood products

Bulgaria
REPUBLIC OF BULGARIA

AREA	110,879 sq km (42,810 sq mi)
POPULATION	7,038,000
CAPITAL	Sofia 1,192,000
RELIGION	Bulgarian Orthodox, Muslim
LANGUAGE	Bulgarian
LITERACY	98%
LIFE EXPECTANCY	74 years
GDP PER CAPITA	$13,500

ECONOMY **IND:** electricity, gas, water, food, beverages, tobacco, machinery and equipment, base metals, chemical products, coke, refined petroleum, nuclear fuel **AGR:** vegetables, fruits, tobacco, wine, wheat, barley, sunflowers, sugar beets, livestock **EXP:** clothing, footwear, iron and steel, machinery and equipment, fuels

Croatia
REPUBLIC OF CROATIA

AREA	56,594 sq km (21,851 sq mi)
POPULATION	4,480,000
CAPITAL	Zagreb 685,000
RELIGION	Roman Catholic
LANGUAGE	Croatian
LITERACY	98%
LIFE EXPECTANCY	76 years
GDP PER CAPITA	$18,300

ECONOMY **IND:** chemicals and plastics, machine tools, fabricated metal, electronics, pig iron and rolled steel products, aluminum, paper, wood products, construction materials, textiles, shipbuilding, petroleum and petroleum refining, food and beverages, tourism **AGR:** arable crops, vegetables, fruits, grapes for wine, livestock, dairy products **EXP:** transport equipment, machinery, textiles, chemicals, foodstuffs, fuels

Cyprus
REPUBLIC OF CYPRUS

AREA	9,251 sq km (3,572 sq mi)
POPULATION	1,138,000
CAPITAL	Nicosia 240,000
RELIGION	Greek Orthodox, Muslim
LANGUAGE	Greek, Turkish, English
LITERACY	98%
LIFE EXPECTANCY	78 years
GDP PER CAPITA	$29,100

ECONOMY **IND:** tourism, food and beverage processing, cement and gypsum production, ship repair and refurbishment, textiles, light chemicals, metal products, wood, paper, stone, and clay products **AGR:** citrus, vegetables, barley, grapes, olives, vegetables, poultry, pork, lamb, dairy, cheese **EXP:** citrus, potatoes, pharmaceuticals, cement, clothing

Czech Republic
CZECH REPUBLIC

AREA	78,867 sq km (30,451 sq mi)
POPULATION	10,177,000
CAPITAL	Prague 1,162,000
RELIGION	Roman Catholic
LANGUAGE	Czech
LITERACY	99%
LIFE EXPECTANCY	77 years
GDP PER CAPITA	$25,900

ECONOMY **IND:** motor vehicles, metallurgy, machinery and equipment, glass, armaments **AGR:** wheat, potatoes, sugar beets, hops, fruit, pigs, poultry **EXP:** machinery and transport equipment, raw materials and fuel, chemicals

Denmark
KINGDOM OF DENMARK

AREA	43,094 sq km (16,639 sq mi)
POPULATION	5,543,000
CAPITAL	Copenhagen 1,174,000
RELIGION	Evangelical Lutheran
LANGUAGE	Danish
LITERACY	99%
LIFE EXPECTANCY	79 years
GDP PER CAPITA	$40,200

ECONOMY **IND:** iron, steel, nonferrous metals, chemicals, food processing, machinery and transportation equipment, textiles and clothing, electronics, construction, furniture and other wood products, shipbuilding and refurbishment, windmills, pharmaceuticals, medical equipment **AGR:** barley, wheat, potatoes, sugar beets, pork, dairy products, fish **EXP:** machinery and instruments, meat and meat products, dairy products, fish, pharmaceuticals, furniture, windmills

Estonia
REPUBLIC OF ESTONIA

AREA	45,228 sq km (17,463 sq mi)
POPULATION	1,275,000
CAPITAL	Tallinn 399,000
RELIGION	Evangelica Lutheran, Orthodox
LANGUAGE	Estonian, Russian
LITERACY	100%
LIFE EXPECTANCY	74 years
GDP PER CAPITA	$20,200

ECONOMY **IND:** engineering, electronics, wood and wood products, textiles, information technology, telecommunications **AGR:** grain, potatoes, vegetables, livestock and dairy products, fish **EXP:** machinery and electrical equipment, wood and wood products, metals, furniture, vehicles and parts, food products and beverages, textiles, plastics

Finland
REPUBLIC OF FINLAND

AREA	338,145 sq km (130,558 sq mi)
POPULATION	5,263,000
CAPITAL	Helsinki 1,107,000
RELIGION	Lutheran Church of Finland
LANGUAGE	Finnish
LITERACY	100%
LIFE EXPECTANCY	79 years
GDP PER CAPITA	$38,300

ECONOMY **IND:** metals and metal products, electronics, machinery and scientific instruments, shipbuilding, pulp and paper, foodstuffs, chemicals, textiles, clothing **AGR:** barley, wheat, sugar beets, potatoes, dairy cattle, fish **EXP:** electrical and optical equipment, machinery, transport equipment, paper and pulp, chemicals, basic metals, timber

France
FRENCH REPUBLIC

AREA	643,801 sq km (248,572 sq mi)
POPULATION	65,631,000
CAPITAL	Paris 10,410,000
RELIGION	Roman Catholic, Muslim
LANGUAGE	French
LITERACY	99%
LIFE EXPECTANCY	81 years
GDP PER CAPITA	$35,000

ECONOMY **IND:** machinery, chemicals, automobiles, metallurgy, aircraft, electronics, textiles, food processing, tourism **AGR:** wheat, cereals, sugar beets, potatoes, wine grapes, beef, dairy products, fish **EXP:** machinery and transportation equipment, aircraft, plastics, chemicals, pharmaceutical products, iron and steel, beverages

Germany
FEDERAL REPUBLIC OF GERMANY

AREA	357,022 sq km (137,846 sq mi)
POPULATION	81,306,000
CAPITAL	Berlin 3,438,000
RELIGION	Protestant, Roman Catholic
LANGUAGE	German
LITERACY	99%
LIFE EXPECTANCY	80 years
GDP PER CAPITA	$37,900

ECONOMY **IND:** iron, steel, coal, cement, chemicals, machinery, vehicles, machine tools, electronics, food and beverages, shipbuilding, textiles **AGR:** potatoes, wheat, barley, sugar beets, fruit, cabbages, cattle, pigs, poultry **EXP:** motor vehicles, machinery, chemicals, computer and electronic products, electrical equipment, pharmaceuticals, metals, transport equipment, foodstuffs, textiles, rubber and plastic products

Greece
HELLENIC REPUBLIC

AREA	131,957 sq km (50,949 sq mi)
POPULATION	10,767,827
CAPITAL	Athens 3,252,000
RELIGION	Greek Orthodox
LANGUAGE	Greek
LITERACY	96%
LIFE EXPECTANCY	80 years
GDP PER CAPITA	$27,600

ECONOMY **IND:** tourism, food and tobacco processing, textiles, chemicals, metal products, mining, petroleum **AGR:** wheat, corn, barley, sugar beets, olives, tomatoes, wine, tobacco, potatoes, beef, dairy products **EXP:** food and beverages, manufactured goods, petroleum products, chemicals, textiles

Hungary
HUNGARY

AREA	93,028 sq km (35,918 sq mi)
POPULATION	9,958,000
CAPITAL	Budapest 1,705,000
RELIGION	Roman Catholic, Calvinist
LANGUAGE	Hungarian
LITERACY	99%
LIFE EXPECTANCY	75 years
GDP PER CAPITA	$19,600

ECONOMY **IND:** mining, metallurgy, construction materials, processed foods, textiles, chemicals (especially pharmaceuticals), motor vehicles **AGR:** wheat, corn, sunflower seed, potatoes, sugar beets, pigs, cattle, poultry, dairy products **EXP:** machinery and equipment, other manufactures, food products, raw materials, fuels and electricity

Iceland
REPUBLIC OF ICELAND

AREA	103,000 sq km (39,768 sq mi)
POPULATION	313,000
CAPITAL	Reykjavík 198,000
RELIGION	Lutheran Church of Iceland
LANGUAGE	Icelandic, English, Nordic languages
LITERACY	99%
LIFE EXPECTANCY	81 years
GDP PER CAPITA	$38,000

ECONOMY **IND:** fish processing, aluminum smelting, ferrosilicon production, geothermal power, hydropower, tourism **AGR:** potatoes, green vegetables, mutton, chicken, pork, beef, dairy products, fish **EXP:** fish and fish products, aluminum, animal products, ferrosilicon, diatomite

Ireland
REPUBLIC OF IRELAND

AREA	70,273 sq km (27,132 sq mi)
POPULATION	4,722,000
CAPITAL	Dublin 5,751,000
RELIGION	Roman Catholic
LANGUAGE	English, Irish
LITERACY	99%
LIFE EXPECTANCY	80 years
GDP PER CAPITA	$39,500

ECONOMY **IND:** pharmaceuticals, chemicals, computer hardware and software, food products, beverages and brewing, medical devices **AGR:** beef, dairy products, barley, potatoes, wheat **EXP:** machinery and equipment, computers, chemicals, medical devices, pharmaceuticals, food products, animal products

Italy
ITALIAN REPUBLIC

AREA	301,340 sq km (116,347 sq mi)
POPULATION	61,261,000
CAPITAL	Rome 3,357,000
RELIGION	Roman Catholic
LANGUAGE	Italian, German, French, Slovene
LITERACY	98%
LIFE EXPECTANCY	82 years
GDP PER CAPITA	$30,100

ECONOMY **IND:** tourism, machinery, iron and steel, chemicals, food processing, textiles, motor vehicles, clothing, footwear, ceramics **AGR:** fruits, vegetables, grapes, potatoes, sugar beets, grain, olives, beef, dairy products, fish **EXP:** engineering products, textiles and clothing, production machinery, motor vehicles, transport equipment, chemicals, food, beverages and tobacco, minerals, and nonferrous metals

Kosovo
REPUBLIC OF KOSOVO

AREA	10,887 sq km (4,203 sq mi)
POPULATION	1,837,000
CAPITAL	Prishtina 172,000
RELIGION	Muslim, Serbian Orthodox, Roman Catholic
LANGUAGE	Albanian, Serbian, Bosnian, Turkish, Roma
LITERACY	92%
LIFE EXPECTANCY	70 years
GDP PER CAPITA	$6,400

ECONOMY **IND:** mineral mining, construction materials, base metals, leather, machinery, appliances **AGR:** wheat, corn, berries, potatoes, peppers **EXP:** mining and processed metal products, scrap metals, leather products, machinery, appliances

Latvia
REPUBLIC OF LATVIA

AREA	64,589 sq km (24,938 sq mi)
POPULATION	2,192,000
CAPITAL	Riga 711,000
RELIGION	Lutheran, Orthodox
LANGUAGE	Latvian, Russian
LITERACY	100%
LIFE EXPECTANCY	73 years
GDP PER CAPITA	$15,400

ECONOMY **IND:** processed foods, processed wood products, textiles, processed metals, pharmaceuticals, railroad cars, synthetic fibers, electronics **AGR:** grain, rapeseed, potatoes, vegetables, pork, poultry, milk, eggs, fish **EXP:** food products, wood and wood products, metals, machinery and equipment, textiles

Liechtenstein
PRINCIPALITY OF LIECHTENSTEIN

AREA	160 sq km (62 sq mi)
POPULATION	36,700
CAPITAL	Vaduz 5,000
RELIGION	Roman Catholic
LANGUAGE	German, Alemannic dialect
LITERACY	100%
LIFE EXPECTANCY	82 years
GDP PER CAPITA	$141,100

ECONOMY **IND:** electronics, metal manufacturing, dental products, ceramics, pharmaceuticals, food products, precision instruments, tourism, optical instruments **AGR:** wheat, barley, corn, potatoes, livestock, dairy products **EXP:** small specialty machinery, connectors for audio and video, parts for motor vehicles, dental products, hardware, prepared foodstuffs, electronic equipment, optical products

Lithuania
REPUBLIC OF LITHUANIA

AREA	65,300 sq km (25,212 sq mi)
POPULATION	3,526,000
CAPITAL	Vilnius 546,000
RELIGION	Roman Catholic
LANGUAGE	Lithuanian
LITERACY	100%
LIFE EXPECTANCY	76 years
GDP PER CAPITA	$18,700

ECONOMY **IND:** metal-cutting machine tools, electric motors, television sets, refrigerators and freezers, petroleum refining, shipbuilding (small ships), furniture making, textiles, food processing, fertilizers, agricultural machinery, optical equipment, electronic components, computers, amber jewelry **AGR:** grain, potatoes, sugar beets, flax, vegetables, beef, milk, eggs, fish **EXP:** mineral products, machinery and equipment, chemicals, textiles, foodstuffs, plastics

Luxembourg
GRAND DUCHY OF LUXEMBOURG

AREA	2,586 sq km (998 sq mi)
POPULATION	509,000
CAPITAL	Luxembourg 90,000
RELIGION	Roman Catholic
LANGUAGE	Luxembourgish, German, French
LITERACY	100%
LIFE EXPECTANCY	80 years
GDP PER CAPITA	$84,700

ECONOMY **IND:** banking and financial services, iron and steel, information technology, telecommunications, cargo transportation, food processing, chemicals, metal products, engineering, tires, glass, aluminum, tourism **AGR:** grapes, barley, oats, potatoes, wheat, fruits, dairy and livestock products **EXP:** machinery and equipment, steel products, chemicals, rubber products, glass

Macedonia
REPUBLIC OF MACEDONIA

AREA	25,713 sq km (9,928 sq mi)
POPULATION	2,082,000
CAPITAL	Skopje 480,000
RELIGION	Macedonian Orthodox, Muslim
LANGUAGE	Macedonian, Albanian
LITERACY	96%
LIFE EXPECTANCY	75 years
GDP PER CAPITA	$10,400

ECONOMY **IND:** food processing, beverages, textiles, chemicals, iron, steel, cement, energy, pharmaceuticals **AGR:** grapes, tobacco, vegetables, fruits, milk, eggs **EXP:** food, beverages, tobacco, textiles, miscellaneous manufactures, iron and steel

Malta
REPUBLIC OF MALTA

AREA	316 sq km (122 sq mi)
POPULATION	410,000
CAPITAL	Valletta 199,000
RELIGION	Roman Catholic
LANGUAGE	Maltese
LITERACY	93%
LIFE EXPECTANCY	80 years
GDP PER CAPITA	$25,700

ECONOMY **IND:** tourism, electronics, ship building and repair, construction, food and beverages, pharmaceuticals, footwear, clothing, tobacco, aviation services, financial services, information technology services **AGR:** potatoes, cauliflower, grapes, wheat, barley, tomatoes, citrus, cut flowers, green peppers, pork, milk, poultry, eggs **EXP:** electrical machinery, mechanical appliances, fish and crustaceans, pharmaceutical products, printed material

Moldova
REPUBLIC OF MOLDOVA

AREA	33,851 sq km (13,070 sq mi)
POPULATION	3,657,000
CAPITAL	Chişinău 650,000
RELIGION	Eastern Orthodox
LANGUAGE	Moldovan, Russian, Gagauz
LITERACY	99%
LIFE EXPECTANCY	70 years
GDP PER CAPITA	$3,400

ECONOMY **IND:** sugar, vegetable oil, food processing, agricultural machinery, foundry equipment, refrigerators and freezers, washing machines, hosiery, shoes, textiles **AGR:** vegetables, fruits, grapes, grain, sugar beets, sunflower seed, tobacco, beef, milk, wine **EXP:** foodstuffs, textiles, machinery

Monaco
PRINCIPALITY OF MONACO

AREA	2 sq km (1 sq mi)
POPULATION	30,500
CAPITAL	Monaco 30,500
RELIGION	Roman Catholic
LANGUAGE	French, English, Italian, Monegasque
LITERACY	99%
LIFE EXPECTANCY	90 years
GDP PER CAPITA	$63,400

ECONOMY **IND:** tourism, construction, small-scale industrial and consumer products **AGR:** none **EXP:** NA

Montenegro
MONTENEGRO

AREA	13,812 sq km (5,333 sq mi)
POPULATION	657,000
CAPITAL	Podgorica 144,000
RELIGION	Orthodox, Muslim
LANGUAGE	Serbian, Montenegrin
LITERACY	96%
LIFE EXPECTANCY	74 years
GDP PER CAPITA	$11,200

ECONOMY **IND:** steelmaking, aluminum, agricultural processing, consumer goods, tourism **AGR:** tobacco, potatoes, citrus fruits, olives, grapes, sheep **EXP:** NA

Netherlands
KINGDOM OF THE NETHERLANDS

AREA	41,543 sq km (16,040 sq mi)
POPULATION	16,731,000
CAPITAL	Amsterdam 1,044,000 (seat of government is The Hague)
RELIGION	Roman Catholic, Protestant
LANGUAGE	Dutch, Frisian
LITERACY	99%
LIFE EXPECTANCY	81 years
GDP PER CAPITA	$42,300

ECONOMY **IND:** agroindustries, metal and engineering products, electrical machinery and equipment, chemicals, petroleum, construction, microelectronics, fishing **AGR:** grains, potatoes, sugar beets, fruits, vegetables, livestock **EXP:** machinery and equipment, chemicals, fuels, foodstuffs

Norway
KINGDOM OF NORWAY

AREA	323,802 sq km (125,020 sq mi)
POPULATION	4,707,000
CAPITAL	Oslo 875,000
RELIGION	Church of Norway
LANGUAGE	Norwegian, Sami
LITERACY	100%
LIFE EXPECTANCY	80 years
GDP PER CAPITA	$53,300

ECONOMY **IND:** petroleum and gas, food processing, shipbuilding, pulp and paper products, metals, chemicals, timber, mining, textiles, fishing **AGR:** barley, wheat, potatoes, pork, beef, veal, milk, fish **EXP:** petroleum and petroleum products, machinery and equipment, metals, chemicals, ships, fish

Poland
REPUBLIC OF POLAND

AREA	312,685 sq km (120,728 sq mi)
POPULATION	38,415,000
CAPITAL	Warsaw 1,710,000
RELIGION	Roman Catholic
LANGUAGE	Polish
LITERACY	100%
LIFE EXPECTANCY	76 years
GDP PER CAPITA	$20,100

ECONOMY **IND**: machine building, iron and steel, coal mining, chemicals, shipbuilding, food processing, glass, beverages, textiles **AGR**: potatoes, fruits, vegetables, wheat, poultry, eggs, pork, dairy **EXP**: machinery and transport equipment, intermediate manufactured goods, miscellaneous manufactured goods, food and live animals

Portugal
PORTUGUESE REPUBLIC

AREA	92,090 sq km (35,556 sq mi)
POPULATION	10,781,000
CAPITAL	Lisbon 2,808,000
RELIGION	Roman Catholic
LANGUAGE	Portuguese, Mirandese
LITERACY	93%
LIFE EXPECTANCY	79 years
GDP PER CAPITA	$23,200

ECONOMY **IND**: textiles, clothing, footwear, wood and cork, paper, chemicals, auto-parts manufacturing, base metals, dairy products, wine and other foods, porcelain and ceramics, glassware, technology, telecommunications, ship construction and refurbishment, tourism **AGR**: grain, potatoes, tomatoes, olives, grapes, sheep, cattle, goats, pigs, poultry, dairy products, fish **EXP**: agricultural products, food products, wine, oil products, chemical products, plastics and rubber, hides, leather, wood and cork, wood pulp and paper, textile materials, clothing, footwear, machinery and tools, base metals

Romania
ROMANIA

AREA	238,391 sq km (92,043 sq mi)
POPULATION	21,849,000
CAPITAL	Bucharest 1,933,000
RELIGION	Eastern Orthodox
LANGUAGE	Romanian
LITERACY	97%
LIFE EXPECTANCY	74 years
GDP PER CAPITA	$12,300

ECONOMY **IND**: electric machinery and equipment, textiles and footwear, light machinery and auto assembly, mining, timber, construction materials, metallurgy, chemicals, food processing, petroleum refining **AGR**: wheat, corn, barley, sugar beets, sunflower seed, potatoes, grapes, eggs, sheep **EXP**: machinery and equipment, metals and metal products, textiles and footwear, chemicals, agricultural products, minerals and fuels

Russia
RUSSIAN FEDERATION

AREA	17,098,242 sq km (6,601,631 sq mi)
POPULATION	138,082,000
CAPITAL	Moscow 10,523,000
RELIGION	Russian Orthodox, Muslim
LANGUAGE	Russian
LITERACY	99%
LIFE EXPECTANCY	66 years
GDP PER CAPITA	$16,700

ECONOMY **IND**: coal, oil, gas, chemicals and metals, machine building, radar, missile production, advanced electronic components, shipbuilding, road and rail transportation equipment, communications equipment, agricultural machinery, tractors, construction equipment, electric power generating and transmitting equipment, medical and scientific instruments, consumer durables, textiles, foodstuffs, handicrafts **AGR**: grain, sugar beets, sunflower seed, vegetables, fruits, beef, milk **EXP**: petroleum and petroleum products, natural gas, metals, wood and wood products, chemicals, a wide variety of civilian and military manufactures

San Marino
REPUBLIC OF SAN MARINO

AREA	61 sq km (24 sq mi)
POPULATION	32,100
CAPITAL	San Marino 4,000
RELIGION	Roman Catholic
LANGUAGE	Italian
LITERACY	96%
LIFE EXPECTANCY	83 years
GDP PER CAPITA	$36,200

ECONOMY **IND**: tourism, banking, textiles, electronics, ceramics, cement, wine **AGR**: wheat, grapes, corn, olives, cattle, pigs, horses, beef, cheese, hides **EXP**: building stone, lime, wood, chestnuts, wheat, wine, baked goods, hides, ceramics

Serbia
REPUBLIC OF SERBIA

AREA	77,474 sq km (29,913 sq mi)
POPULATION	7,277,000
CAPITAL	Belgrade 1,115,000
RELIGION	Serbian Orthodox
LANGUAGE	Serbian
LITERACY	96%
LIFE EXPECTANCY	75 years
GDP PER CAPITA	$10,700

ECONOMY **IND**: base metals, furniture, food processing, machinery, chemicals, sugar, tires, clothes, pharmaceuticals **AGR**: wheat, maize, sugar beets, sunflower, raspberries, beef, pork, milk **EXP**: iron and steel, rubber, clothes, wheat, fruit and vegetables, nonferrous metals, electric appliances, metal products, weapons and ammunition

Slovakia
SLOVAK REPUBLIC

AREA	49,035 sq km (18,932 sq mi)
POPULATION	5,483,000
CAPITAL	Bratislava 428,000
RELIGION	Roman Catholic, Protestant
LANGUAGE	Slovak, Hungarian
LITERACY	100%
LIFE EXPECTANCY	76 years
GDP PER CAPITA	$23,400

ECONOMY **IND**: metal and metal products, food and beverages, electricity, gas, coke, oil, nuclear fuel, chemicals and manmade fibers, machinery, paper and printing, earthenware and ceramics, transport vehicles, textiles, electrical and optical apparatus, rubber products **AGR**: grains, potatoes, sugar beets, hops, fruit, pigs, cattle, poultry, forest products **EXP**: machinery and electrical equipment, vehicles, base metals, chemicals and minerals, plastics

Slovenia
REPUBLIC OF SLOVENIA

AREA	20,273 sq km (7,827 sq mi)
POPULATION	1,997,000
CAPITAL	Ljubljana 260,000
RELIGION	Catholic
LANGUAGE	Slovenian
LITERACY	100%
LIFE EXPECTANCY	77 years
GDP PER CAPITA	$29,100

ECONOMY **IND**: ferrous metallurgy and aluminum products, lead and zinc smelting, electronics (including military electronics), trucks, automobiles, electric power equipment, wood products, textiles, chemicals, machine tools **AGR**: potatoes, hops, wheat, sugar beets, corn, grapes, cattle, sheep, poultry **EXP**: manufactured goods, machinery and transport equipment, chemicals, food

Spain
KINGDOM OF SPAIN

AREA	505,370 sq km (195,123 sq mi)
POPULATION	47,043,000
CAPITAL	Madrid 5,762,000
RELIGION	Roman Catholic
LANGUAGE	Castilian Spanish, Catalan
LITERACY	98%
LIFE EXPECTANCY	81 years
GDP PER CAPITA	$30,600

ECONOMY **IND**: textiles and apparel (including footwear), food and beverages, metals and metal manufactures, chemicals, shipbuilding, automobiles, machine tools, tourism, clay and refractory products, footwear, pharmaceuticals, medical equipment **AGR**: grain, vegetables, olives, wine grapes, sugar beets, citrus, beef, pork, poultry, dairy products, fish **EXP**: machinery, motor vehicles, foodstuffs, pharmaceuticals, medicines, other consumer goods

Sweden
KINGDOM OF SWEDEN

AREA	450,295 sq km (173,859 sq mi)
POPULATION	9,104,000
CAPITAL	Stockholm 1,279,000
RELIGION	Lutheran
LANGUAGE	Swedish
LITERACY	99%
LIFE EXPECTANCY	81 years
GDP PER CAPITA	$40,600

ECONOMY **IND**: iron and steel, precision equipment (bearings, radio and telephone parts, armaments), wood pulp and paper products, processed foods, motor vehicles **AGR**: barley, wheat, sugar beets, meat, milk **EXP**: machinery, motor vehicles, paper products, pulp and wood, iron and steel products, chemicals

Switzerland
SWISS CONFEDERATION

AREA	41,277 sq km (15,937 sq mi)
POPULATION	7,656,000
CAPITAL	Bern 346,000
RELIGION	Roman Catholic, Protestant
LANGUAGE	German, French
LITERACY	99%
LIFE EXPECTANCY	81 years
GDP PER CAPITA	$43,400

ECONOMY **IND**: machinery, chemicals, watches, textiles, precision instruments, tourism, banking, and insurance **AGR**: grains, fruits, vegetables, meat, eggs **EXP**: machinery, chemicals, metals, watches, agricultural products

Ukraine
UKRAINE

AREA	603,550 sq km (233,031 sq mi)
POPULATION	44,854,000
CAPITAL	Kiev 2,779,000
RELIGION	Ukrainian Orthodox
LANGUAGE	Ukrainian, Russian
LITERACY	99%
LIFE EXPECTANCY	69 years
GDP PER CAPITA	$7,200

ECONOMY **IND**: coal, electric power, ferrous and nonferrous metals, machinery and transport equipment, chemicals, food processing **AGR**: grain, sugar beets, sunflower seeds, vegetables, beef, milk **EXP**: ferrous and nonferrous metals, fuel and petroleum products, chemicals, machinery and transport equipment, food products

United Kingdom
UNITED KINGDOM OF GREAT BRITAIN AND NORTHERN IRELAND

AREA	243,510 sq km (94,058 sq mi)
POPULATION	63,047,000
CAPITAL	London 8,615,000
RELIGION	Christian
LANGUAGE	English
LITERACY	99%
LIFE EXPECTANCY	80 years
GDP PER CAPITA	$35,900

ECONOMY **IND**: machine tools, electric power equipment, automation equipment, railroad equipment, shipbuilding, aircraft, motor vehicles and parts, electronics and communications equipment, metals, chemicals, coal, petroleum, paper and paper products, food processing, textiles, clothing, other consumer goods **AGR**: cereals, oilseed, potatoes, vegetables, cattle, sheep, poultry, fish **EXP**: manufactured goods, fuels, chemicals, food, beverages, tobacco

Vatican City
THE HOLY SEE (VATICAN CITY STATE)

AREA	0.4 sq km (0.2 sq mi)
POPULATION	836
CAPITAL	Vatican City 836
RELIGION	Roman Catholic
LANGUAGE	Italian, Latin, French
LITERACY	100%
LIFE EXPECTANCY	NA
GDP PER CAPITA	NA

ECONOMY **IND**: printing, production of coins, medals, postage stamps, mosaics and staff uniforms, worldwide banking and financial activities **AGR**: NA **EXP**: NA

DEPENDENCIES

Faroe Islands
(DENMARK)

FAROE ISLANDS
SOVEREIGN

LOCAL

AREA	1,393 sq km (538 sq mi)
POPULATION	49,500
CAPITAL	Tórshavn 20,000
RELIGION	Evangelical Lutheran
LANGUAGE	Faroese, Danish
LITERACY	99%
LIFE EXPECTANCY	80 years
GDP PER CAPITA	$30,300

ECONOMY **IND**: fishing, fish processing, small ship repair and refurbishment, handicrafts **AGR**: milk, potatoes, vegetables, sheep, salmon, other fish **EXP**: fish and fish products, stamps, ships

Gibraltar
(U.K.)

GIBRALTAR
SOVEREIGN

LOCAL

AREA	7 sq km (3 sq mi)
POPULATION	29,000
CAPITAL	Gibraltar 29,000
RELIGION	Roman Catholic
LANGUAGE	English, Spanish, Italian, Portuguese
LITERACY	80%
LIFE EXPECTANCY	79 years
GDP PER CAPITA	$43,000

ECONOMY **IND**: tourism, banking and finance, ship repairing, tobacco **AGR**: none **EXP**: (principally reexports) petroleum, manufactured goods

Guernsey
(U.K.)

BAILIWICK OF GUERNSEY

AREA	78 sq km (30 sq mi)
POPULATION	65,300
CAPITAL	Saint Peter Port 17,000
RELIGION	Protestant, Roman Catholic
LANGUAGE	English, French, Norman
LITERACY	NA
LIFE EXPECTANCY	82 years
GDP PER CAPITA	$44,600
ECONOMY	IND: tourism, banking

AGR: tomatoes, greenhouse flowers, sweet peppers, eggplant, fruit, Guernsey cattle
EXP: tomatoes, flowers and ferns, sweet peppers, eggplant, other vegetables

Isle of Man
(U.K.)

ISLE OF MAN

AREA	572 sq km (221 sq mi)
POPULATION	85,400
CAPITAL	Douglas 26,000
RELIGION	Protestant, Roman Catholic
LANGUAGE	English, Manx Gaelic
LITERACY	NA
LIFE EXPECTANCY	81 years
GDP PER CAPITA	$35,000
ECONOMY	IND: financial services,

light manufacturing, tourism AGR: cereals, vegetables, cattle, sheep, pigs, poultry
EXP: tweeds, herring, processed shellfish, beef, lamb

Jersey
(U.K.)

BAILIWICK OF JERSEY

AREA	116 sq km (45 sq mi)
POPULATION	94,900
CAPITAL	Saint Helier 30,000
RELIGION	Protestant, Roman Catholic
LANGUAGE	English
LITERACY	NA
LIFE EXPECTANCY	81 years
GDP PER CAPITA	$57,000
ECONOMY	IND: tourism, banking and

finance, dairy, electronics AGR: potatoes, cauliflower, tomatoes, beef, dairy products
EXP: light industrial and electrical goods, dairy cattle, foodstuffs, textiles, flowers

Svalbard
(NORWAY)

SVALBARD

AREA	62,045 sq km (23,956 sq mi)
POPULATION	1,970
CAPITAL	Longyearbyen 1,000
RELIGION	NA
LANGUAGE	Norwegian, Russian
LITERACY	NA
LIFE EXPECTANCY	NA
GDP PER CAPITA	NA
ECONOMY	IND: NA AGR: NA EXP: NA

2008 Kosovo
2006 Montenegro
1993 Czech Republic, Slovakia
1992 Bosnia and Herzegovina, Serbia
1991 Croatia, Slovenia, Russia, Ukraine, Belarus, Moldova, Macedonia

1964 Malta
1960 Cyprus
1944 Iceland

1929 Vatican City
1922 Ireland
1919 Lithuania, Estonia, Latvia
1918 Poland
1917 Finland
1912 Albania
1905 Norway
1881 Romania
1878 Bulgaria
1871 Germany

1861 Italy

1839 Luxembourg
1831 Belgium
1829 Greece

1719 Liechtenstein

1579 Netherlands

1523 Sweden
1492 Spain

1419 Monaco

1291 Switzerland
1278 Andorra

1156 Austria

1140 Portugal

1001 Hungary

10th Century Denmark
10th Century United Kingdom

486 France

301 A.D. San Marino

NOTE: For some countries, the date given may not represent "independence" in the strict sense—but rather some significant nationhood event: the traditional founding date; a fundamental change in the form of government; or perhaps the date of unification, secession, federation, confederation, or state succession.

European Population by Country
(ten largest, in clockwise order)

RUSSIA 138,082,000
GERMANY 81,306,000
FRANCE 65,631,000
UNITED KINGDOM 63,047,000
ITALY 61,261,000
SPAIN 47,043,000
UKRAINE 44,854,000
POLAND 38,415,000
ROMANIA 21,849,000
NETHERLANDS 16,731,000
All other countries 158,887,000

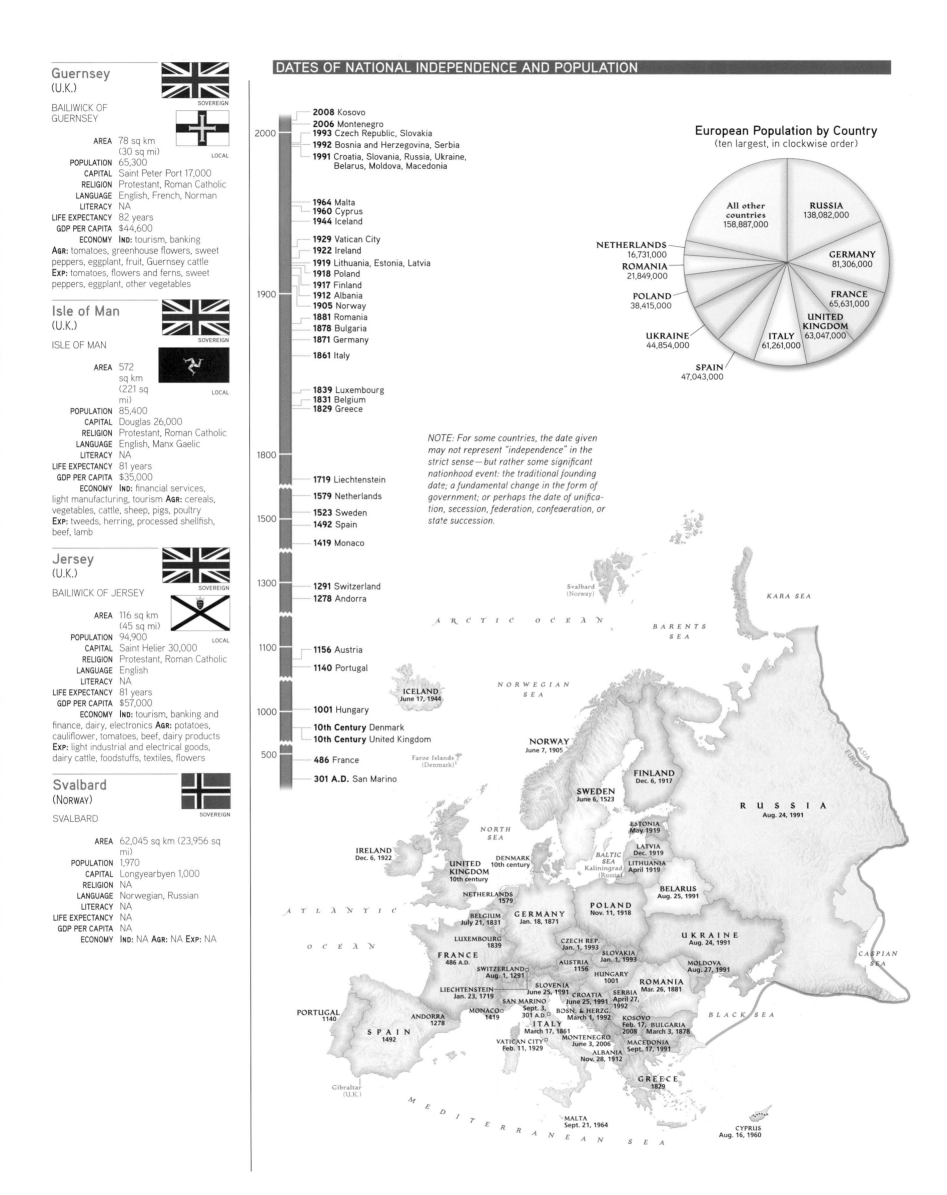

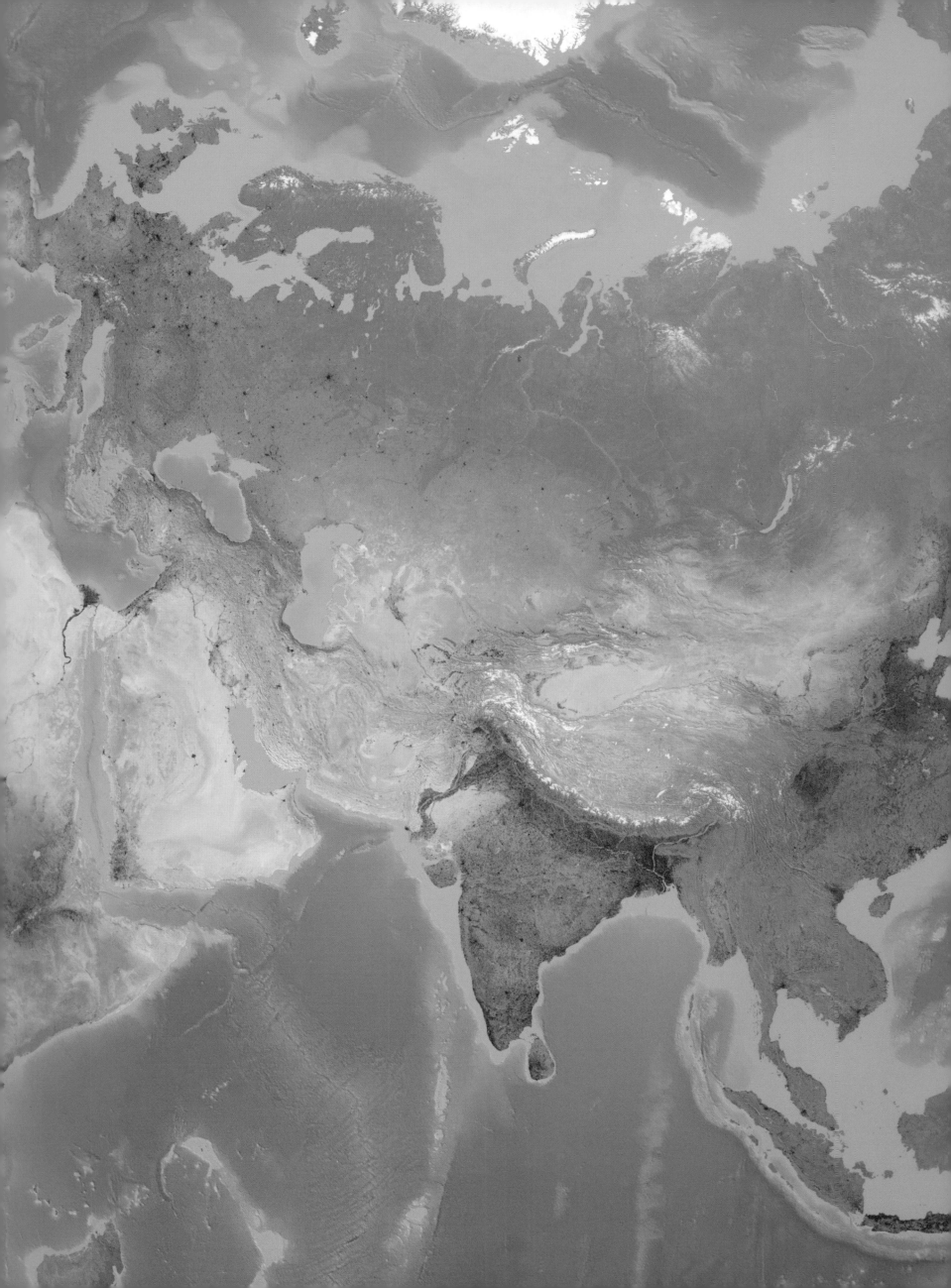

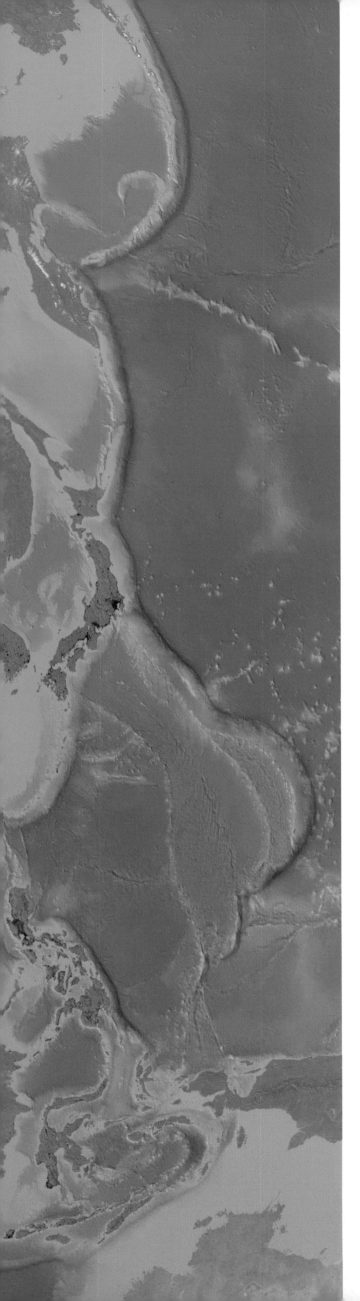

Asia

THE CONTINENT OF ASIA, occupying four-fifths of the giant Eurasian landmass, stretches across ten time zones, from the Pacific Ocean in the east to the Ural Mountains and Black Sea in the west. It is the largest of the continents, with dazzling geographic diversity and 30 percent of the Earth's land surface. Asia includes numerous island nations, such as Japan, the Philippines, Indonesia, and Sri Lanka, as well as many of the world's major islands: Borneo, Sumatra, Honshu, Celebes, Java, and half of New Guinea. Siberia, the huge Asian section of Russia, reaches deep inside the Arctic Circle and fills the continent's northern quarter. To its south lie the large countries of Kazakhstan, Mongolia, and China. Within its 46 countries, Asia holds 60 percent of humanity, yet deserts, mountains, jungles, and inhospitable zones render much of the continent empty or underpopulated.

Great river systems allowed the growth of the world's first civilizations in the Middle East, the Indian subcontinent, and northern China. Numerous cultural forces, each linked to these broad geographical areas, have formed and influenced Asia's rich civilizations and hundreds of ethnic groups. The two oldest are the cultural milieus of India and China. India's culture still reverberates throughout countries as varied as Sri Lanka, Pakistan, Nepal, Burma, Cambodia, and Indonesia. The world religions of Hinduism and Buddhism originated in India and spread as traders, scholars, and priests sought distant footholds. China's ancient civilization has profoundly influenced the development of all of East Asia, much of Southeast Asia, and parts of Central Asia. Most influential of all Chinese institutions were the Chinese written language, a complex script with thousands of characters, and Confucianism, an ethical worldview that affected philosophy, politics, and relations within society. Islam, a third great influence in Asia, proved formidable in its energy and creative genius. Arabs from the seventh century onward, spurred on by faith, moved rapidly into Southwest Asia. Their religion and culture, particularly Arabic writing, spread through Iran and Afghanistan to the Indian subcontinent.

Today nearly all of Asia's people continue to live beside rivers or along coastal zones. Dense concentrations of population fill Japan, China's eastern half, Java, parts of Southeast Asia, and much of the Indian subcontinent. China and India, acting as demographic, political, and cultural counterweights, hold nearly half of Asia's population. India, with a billion people, expects to surpass China as the world's most populous nation by 2050. As China seeks to take center stage, flexing economic muscle and pushing steadily into the oil-rich South China Sea, many Asian neighbors grow concerned. The development of nuclear weapons by India and Pakistan complicates international relations. Economic recovery after the financial turmoil of the late 1990s preoccupies many countries, while others yearn to escape dire poverty. Religious, ethnic, and territorial conflicts continue to beset the continent, from the Middle East to Korea, from Cambodia to Uzbekistan. Asians also face the threats of overpopulation, resource depletion, pollution, and the growth of megacities. Yet if vibrant Asia meets the challenges of rebuilding and reconciliation, overcoming age-old habits of rivalry, corruption, and cronyism, it may yet fulfill the promise to claim the first hundred years of the new millennium as Asia's century.

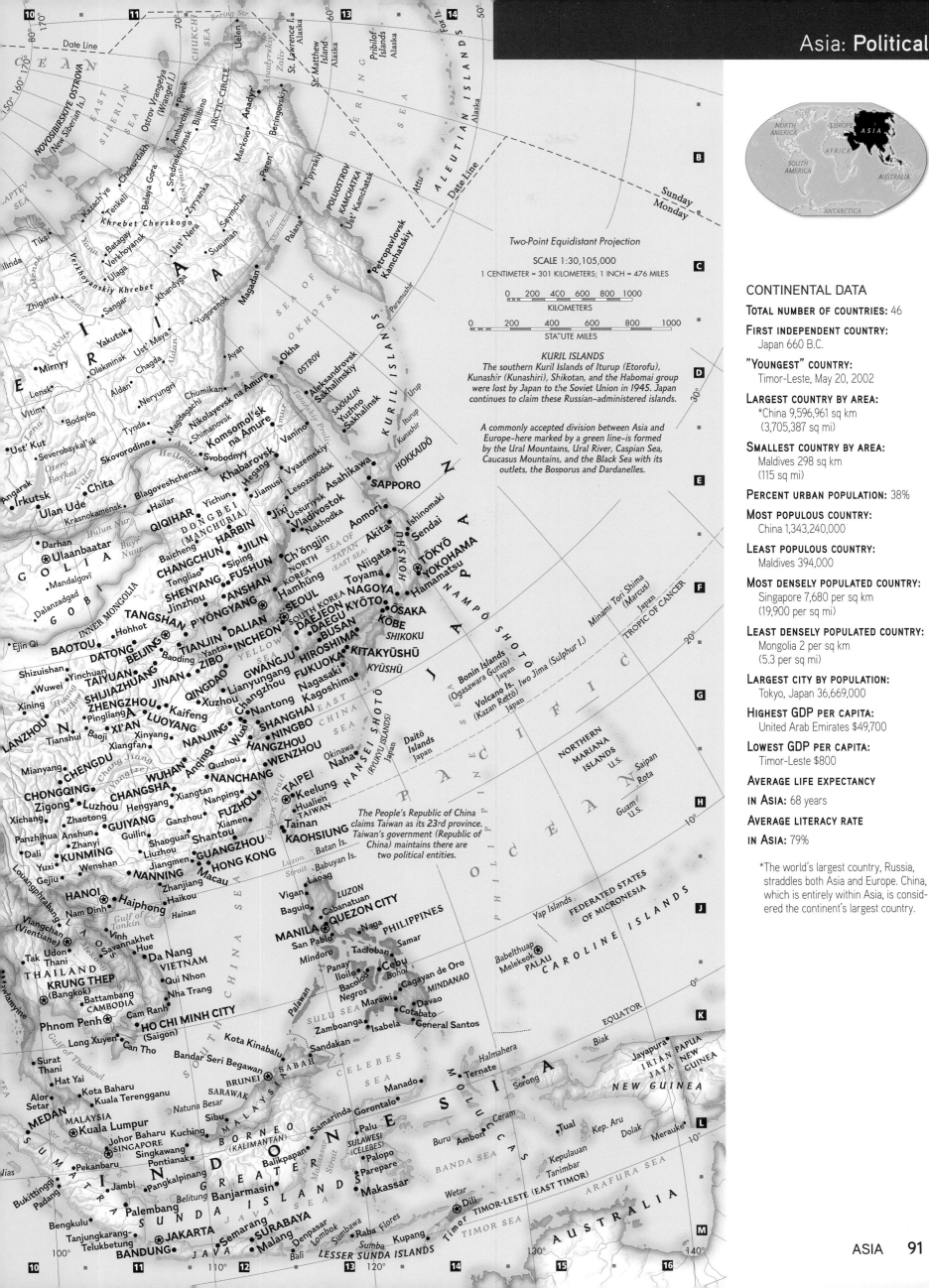

CONTINENTAL DATA

TOTAL NUMBER OF COUNTRIES: 46

FIRST INDEPENDENT COUNTRY:
Japan 660 B.C.

"YOUNGEST" COUNTRY:
Timor-Leste, May 20, 2002

LARGEST COUNTRY BY AREA:
*China 9,596,961 sq km
(3,705,387 sq mi)

SMALLEST COUNTRY BY AREA:
Maldives 298 sq km
(115 sq mi)

PERCENT URBAN POPULATION: 38%

MOST POPULOUS COUNTRY:
China 1,343,240,000

LEAST POPULOUS COUNTRY:
Maldives 394,000

MOST DENSELY POPULATED COUNTRY:
Singapore 7,680 per sq km
(19,900 per sq mi)

LEAST DENSELY POPULATED COUNTRY:
Mongolia 2 per sq km
(5.3 per sq mi)

LARGEST CITY BY POPULATION:
Tokyo, Japan 36,669,000

HIGHEST GDP PER CAPITA:
United Arab Emirates $49,700

LOWEST GDP PER CAPITA:
Timor-Leste $800

AVERAGE LIFE EXPECTANCY

IN ASIA: 68 years

AVERAGE LITERACY RATE

IN ASIA: 79%

*The world's largest country, Russia, straddles both Asia and Europe. China, which is entirely within Asia, is considered the continent's largest country.

ASIA   91

CONTINENTAL DATA

AREA: 44,570,000 sq km
(17,208,000 sq mi)

GREATEST NORTH-SOUTH EXTENT:
8,690 km (5,400 mi)

GREATEST EAST-WEST EXTENT:
9,700 km (6,030 mi)

HIGHEST POINT:
Mount Everest, China-Nepal
8,850 m (29,035 ft)

LOWEST POINT:
Dead Sea, Israel-Jordan
-422 m (-1,385 ft)

LOWEST RECORDED TEMPERATURE:
• Oymyakon, Russia -68°C
(-90°F), February 6, 1933
• Verkhoyansk, Russia
-68°C (-90°F), February 7, 1892

HIGHEST RECORDED TEMPERATURE:
Tirat Zevi, Israel 54°C (129°F),
June 21, 1942

LONGEST RIVERS:
• Chang Jiang (Yangtze)
6,244 km (3,880 mi)
• Yenisey-Angara 5,810 km (3,610 mi)
• Huang (Yellow) 5,778 km (3,590 mi)

LARGEST NATURAL LAKES:
• Caspian Sea 371,000 sq km
(143,200 sq mi)
• Lake Baikal 31,500 sq km
(12,200 sq mi)
• Aral Sea 18,000 sq km
(6,900 sq mi)

EARTH'S EXTREMES LOCATED IN ASIA:
• Wettest Place:
Mawsynram, India; annual
average rainfall 1,187 cm (467 in)
• Largest Cave Chamber:
Sarawak Cave, Gunung Mulu
National Park, Malaysia;
16 hectares and 79 m high
(40 acres, 260 ft)

Two-Point Equidistant Projection

SCALE 1:30,105,000
1 CENTIMETER = 301 KILOMETERS; 1 INCH = 476 MILES

KILOMETERS

STATUTE MILES

International boundary

Disputed or undefined boundary

*A commonly accepted division between Asia and
Europe–here marked by a green line–is formed
by the Ural Mountains, Ural River, Caspian Sea,
Caucasus Mountains, and the Black Sea with its
outlets, the Bosporus and Dardanelles.*

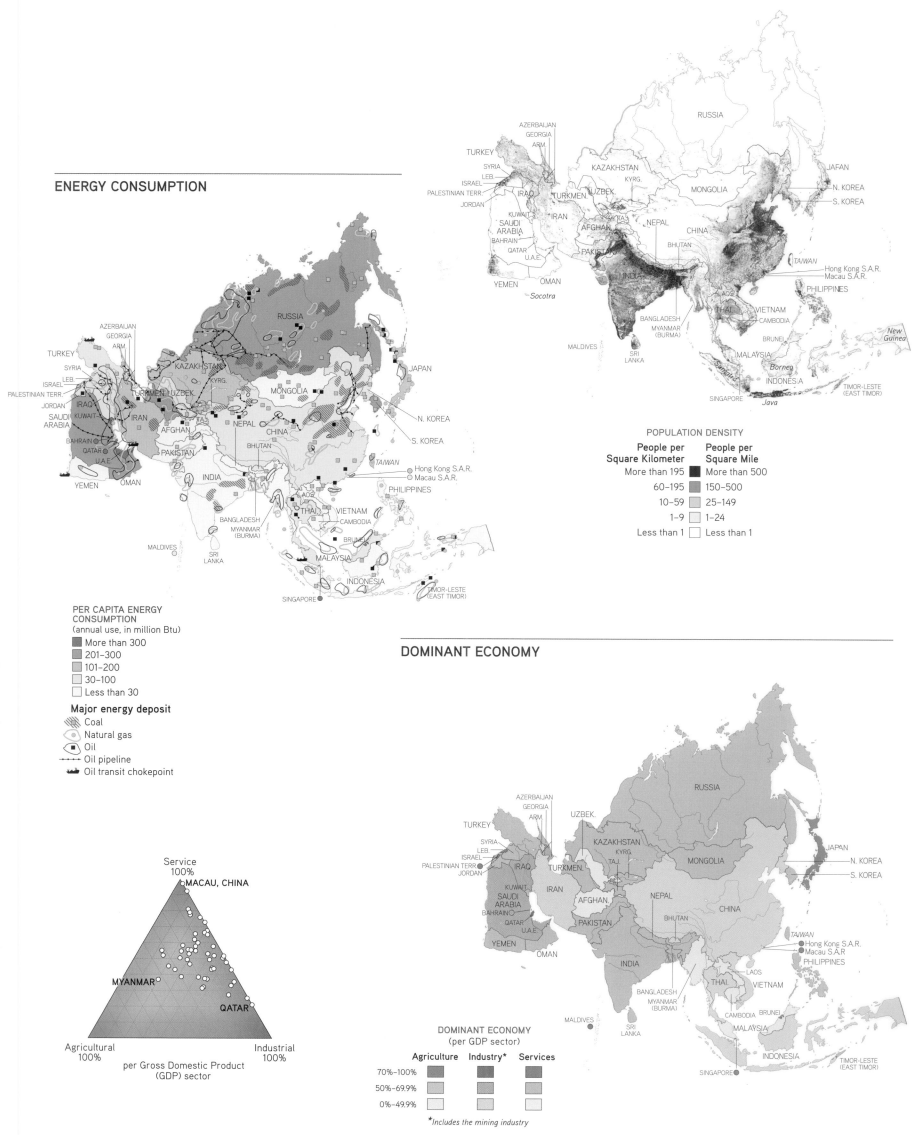

POPULATION DENSITY

POPULATION DENSITY

People per Square Kilometer	People per Square Mile
More than 195	More than 500
60–195	150–500
10–59	25–149
1–9	1–24
Less than 1	Less than 1

ENERGY CONSUMPTION

PER CAPITA ENERGY CONSUMPTION
(annual use, in million Btu)

- More than 300
- 201–300
- 101–200
- 30–100
- Less than 30

Major energy deposit

- Coal
- Natural gas
- Oil
- Oil pipeline
- Oil transit chokepoint

Service 100%

MACAU, CHINA

MYANMAR

QATAR

Agricultural 100%

Industrial 100%

per Gross Domestic Product (GDP) sector

DOMINANT ECONOMY

DOMINANT ECONOMY
(per GDP sector)

	Agriculture	Industry*	Services
70%–100%			
50%–69.9%			
0%–49.9%			

*Includes the mining industry

CLIMATE ZONES

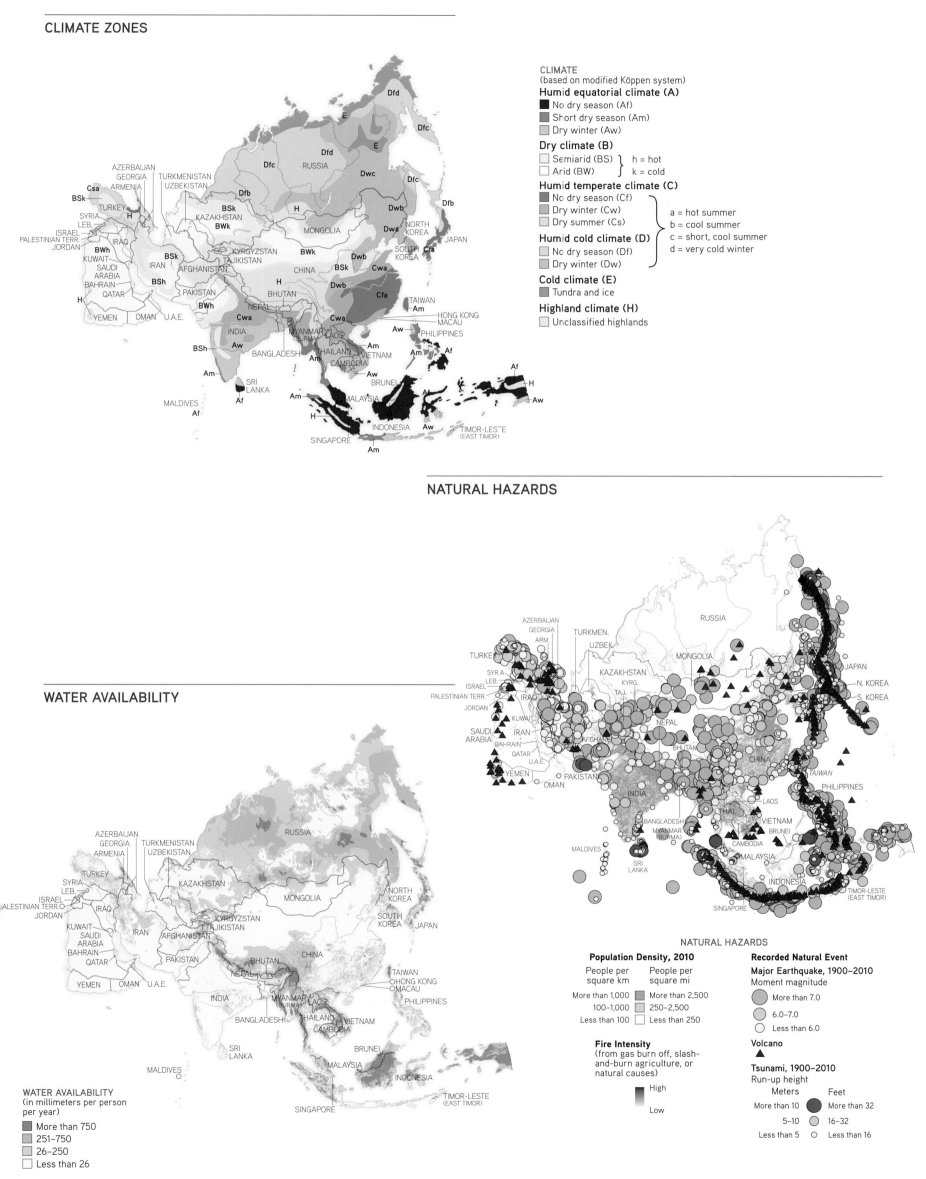

CLIMATE
(based on modified Köppen system)

Humid equatorial climate (A)
- No dry season (Af)
- Short dry season (Am)
- Dry winter (Aw)

Dry climate (B)
- Semiarid (BS) } h = hot
- Arid (BW)   } k = cold

Humid temperate climate (C)
- No dry season (Cf) ⎫
- Dry winter (Cw)   ⎬ a = hot summer
- Dry summer (Cs)   ⎭ b = cool summer
                              c = short, cool summer
Humid cold climate (D)   d = very cold winter
- No dry season (Df) ⎫
- Dry winter (Dw)   ⎭

Cold climate (E)
- Tundra and ice

Highland climate (H)
- Unclassified highlands

NATURAL HAZARDS

NATURAL HAZARDS

Population Density, 2010

People per square km	People per square mi
More than 1,000	More than 2,500
100–1,000	250–2,500
Less than 100	Less than 250

Fire Intensity
(from gas burn off, slash-and-burn agriculture, or natural causes)
- High
- Low

Recorded Natural Event

Major Earthquake, 1900–2010
Moment magnitude
- More than 7.0
- 6.0–7.0
- Less than 6.0

Volcano
▲

Tsunami, 1900–2010
Run-up height

Meters	Feet
More than 10	More than 32
5–10	16–32
Less than 5	Less than 16

WATER AVAILABILITY

WATER AVAILABILITY
(in millimeters per person per year)
- More than 750
- 251–750
- 26–250
- Less than 26

COUNTRIES

Afghanistan
ISLAMIC REPUBLIC OF AFGHANISTAN

AREA	652,230 sq km (251,826 sq mi)
POPULATION	30,420,000
CAPITAL	Kabul 3,573,000
RELIGION	Sunni Muslim, Shia Muslim
LANGUAGE	Afghan Persian or Dari, Pashto, Turkic languages
LITERACY	28%
LIFE EXPECTANCY	50 years
GDP PER CAPITA	$1,000

ECONOMY IND: small-scale production of textiles, soap, furniture, shoes, fertilizer, apparel, food-products, non-alcoholic beverages, mineral water, cement, handwoven carpets, natural gas, coal, copper AGR: opium, wheat, fruits, nuts, wool, mutton, sheepskins, lambskins EXP: opium, fruits and nuts, handwoven carpets, wool, cotton, hides and pelts, precious and semi-precious gems

Armenia
REPUBLIC OF ARMENIA

AREA	29,743 sq km (11,484 sq mi)
POPULATION	2,970,000
CAPITAL	Yerevan 1,110,000
RELIGION	Armenian Apostolic
LANGUAGE	Armenian
LITERACY	99%
LIFE EXPECTANCY	73 years
GDP PER CAPITA	$5,400

ECONOMY IND: diamond-processing, metal-cutting machine tools, forging-pressing machines, electric motors, tires, knitted wear, hosiery, shoes, silk fabric, chemicals, trucks, instruments, microelectronics, jewelry manufacturing, software development, food processing, brandy, mining AGR: fruit (especially grapes), vegetables, livestock EXP: pig iron, unwrought copper, nonferrous metals, diamonds, mineral products, foodstuffs, energy

Azerbaijan
REPUBLIC OF AZERBAIJAN

AREA	86,600 sq km (33,436 sq mi)
POPULATION	9,494,000
CAPITAL	Baku 1,950,000
RELIGION	Muslim
LANGUAGE	Azerbaijani (Azeri)
LITERACY	99%
LIFE EXPECTANCY	71 years
GDP PER CAPITA	$10,200

ECONOMY IND: petroleum and natural gas, petroleum products, oilfield equipment, steel, iron ore, cement, chemicals and petrochemicals, textiles AGR: cotton, grain, rice, grapes, fruit, vegetables, tea, tobacco, cattle, pigs, sheep, goats EXP: oil and gas, machinery, cotton, foodstuffs

Bahrain
KINGDOM OF BAHRAIN

AREA	760 sq km (293 sq mi)
POPULATION	1,248,000
CAPITAL	Manama 163,000
RELIGION	Muslim
LANGUAGE	Arabic, English, Farsi, Urdu
LITERACY	87%
LIFE EXPECTANCY	78 years
GDP PER CAPITA	$27,300

ECONOMY IND: petroleum processing and refining, aluminum smelting, iron pelletization, fertilizers, Islamic and offshore banking, insurance, ship repairing, tourism AGR: fruit, vegetables, poultry, dairy products, shrimp, fish EXP: petroleum and petroleum products, aluminum, textiles

Bangladesh
PEOPLE'S REPUBLIC OF BANGLADESH

AREA	143,998 sq km (55,598 sq mi)
POPULATION	161,084,000
CAPITAL	Dhaka 14,251,000
RELIGION	Muslim, Hindu
LANGUAGE	Bangla, English
LITERACY	48%
LIFE EXPECTANCY	70 years
GDP PER CAPITA	$1,700

ECONOMY IND: cotton textiles, jute, garments, tea processing, paper newsprint, cement, chemical fertilizer, light engineering, sugar AGR: rice, jute, tea, wheat, sugarcane, potatoes, tobacco, pulses, oilseeds, spices, fruit, beef, milk, poultry EXP: garments, frozen fish and seafood, jute and jute goods, leather

Bhutan
KINGDOM OF BHUTAN

AREA	38,394 sq km (14,824 sq mi)
POPULATION	717,000
CAPITAL	Thimphu 89,000
RELIGION	Lamaistic Buddhist, Indian- and Nepalese-influenced Hinduism
LANGUAGE	Sharchhopka, Dzongkha, Lhotshamkha
LITERACY	47%
LIFE EXPECTANCY	68 years
GDP PER CAPITA	$6,000

ECONOMY IND: cement, wood products, processed fruits, alcoholic beverages, calcium carbide, tourism AGR: rice, corn, root crops, citrus, foodgrains, dairy products, eggs EXP: electricity (to India), ferrosilicon, cement, calcium carbide, copper wire, manganese, vegetable oil

Brunei
BRUNEI DARUSSALAM

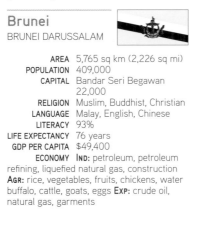

AREA	5,765 sq km (2,226 sq mi)
POPULATION	409,000
CAPITAL	Bandar Seri Begawan 22,000
RELIGION	Muslim, Buddhist, Christian
LANGUAGE	Malay, English, Chinese
LITERACY	93%
LIFE EXPECTANCY	76 years
GDP PER CAPITA	$49,400

ECONOMY IND: petroleum, petroleum refining, liquefied natural gas, construction AGR: rice, vegetables, fruits, chickens, water buffalo, cattle, goats, eggs EXP: crude oil, natural gas, garments

Cambodia
KINGDOM OF CAMBODIA

AREA	181,035 sq km (69,898 sq mi)
POPULATION	14,953,000
CAPITAL	Phnom Penh 1,519,000
RELIGION	Buddhist
LANGUAGE	Khmer, French, English
LITERACY	74%
LIFE EXPECTANCY	63 years
GDP PER CAPITA	$2,300

ECONOMY IND: tourism, garments, construction, rice milling, fishing, wood and wood products, rubber, cement, gem mining, textiles AGR: rice, rubber, corn, vegetables, cashews, tapioca, silk EXP: clothing, timber, rubber, rice, fish, tobacco, footwear

China
PEOPLE'S REPUBLIC OF CHINA

AREA	9,596,961 sq km (3,705,387 sq mi)
POPULATION	1,343,240,000
CAPITAL	Beijing 12,214,000
RELIGION	Daoist, Buddhist, Atheist
LANGUAGE	Mandarin, Yue, Wu, Minbei, Minnan, Xiang, Gan, Hakka, Mongolian, Uighur, Tibetan
LITERACY	92%
LIFE EXPECTANCY	75 years
GDP PER CAPITA	$8,400

ECONOMY IND: mining and ore processing, iron, steel, aluminum, and other metals, coal, machine building, armaments, textiles and apparel, petroleum, cement, chemicals, fertilizers, consumer products, footwear, toys, and electronics, food processing, transportation equipment, automobiles, rail cars and locomotives, ships, aircraft, telecommunications equipment, commercial space launch vehicles, satellites AGR: rice, wheat, potatoes, corn, peanuts, tea, millet, barley, apples, cotton, oilseed, pork, fish EXP: electrical and other machinery, data processing equipment, apparel, textiles, iron and steel, optical and medical equipment

Georgia
GEORGIA

AREA	69,700 sq km (26,911 sq mi)
POPULATION	4,571,000
CAPITAL	T'bilisi 1,115,000
RELIGION	Orthodox Christian, Muslim
LANGUAGE	Georgian, Abkhaz
LITERACY	100%
LIFE EXPECTANCY	77 years
GDP PER CAPITA	$5,400

ECONOMY IND: steel, aircraft, machine tools, electrical appliances, mining (manganese and copper), chemicals, wood products, wine AGR: citrus, grapes, tea, hazelnuts, vegetables, livestock EXP: scrap metal, wine, mineral water, ores, vehicles, fruits and nuts

India
REPUBLIC OF INDIA

AREA	3,287,263 sq km (1,269,212 sq mi)
POPULATION	1,205,074,000
CAPITAL	New Delhi 21,720,000
RELIGION	Hindu, Muslim
LANGUAGE	Hindi, Bengali, English, 13 other official languages
LITERACY	61%
LIFE EXPECTANCY	67 years
GDP PER CAPITA	$3,700

ECONOMY IND: textiles, chemicals, food processing, steel, transportation equipment, cement, mining, petroleum, machinery, software, pharmaceuticals AGR: rice, wheat, oilseed, cotton, jute, tea, sugarcane, lentils, onions, potatoes, dairy products, sheep, goats, poultry, fish EXP: petroleum products, precious stones, machinery, iron and steel, chemicals, vehicles, apparel

Indonesia
REPUBLIC OF INDONESIA

AREA	1,904,569 sq km (735,354 sq mi)
POPULATION	248,216,000
CAPITAL	Jakarta 9,121,000
RELIGION	Muslim
LANGUAGE	Bahasa Indonesia, English, Dutch, Javanese
LITERACY	90%
LIFE EXPECTANCY	72 years
GDP PER CAPITA	$4,700

ECONOMY IND: petroleum and natural gas, textiles, apparel, footwear, mining, cement, chemical fertilizers, plywood, rubber, food, tourism AGR: rice, cassava (tapioca), peanuts, rubber, cocoa, coffee, palm oil, copra, poultry, beef, pork, eggs EXP: oil and gas, electrical appliances, plywood, textiles, rubber

Iran
ISLAMIC REPUBLIC OF IRAN

AREA	1,648,195 sq km (636,368 sq mi)
POPULATION	78,869,000
CAPITAL	Tehran 7,190,000
RELIGION	Shia Muslim, Sunni Muslim
LANGUAGE	Persian, Azeri Turkic, Kurdish
LITERACY	77%
LIFE EXPECTANCY	70 years
GDP PER CAPITA	$12,200

ECONOMY IND: petroleum, petrochemicals, fertilizers, caustic soda, textiles, cement and other construction materials, food processing (particularly sugar refining and vegetable oil production), ferrous and non-ferrous metal fabrication, armaments AGR: wheat, rice, other grains, sugar beets, sugar cane, fruits, nuts, cotton, dairy products, wool, caviar EXP: petroleum, chemical and petrochemical products, fruits and nuts, carpets

Iraq
REPUBLIC OF IRAQ

AREA	438,317 sq km (169,234 sq mi)
POPULATION	31,129,000
CAPITAL	Baghdad 5,751,000
RELIGION	Shia Muslim, Sunni Muslim
LANGUAGE	Arabic, Kurdish, Turkoman, Assyrian, Armenian
LITERACY	74%
LIFE EXPECTANCY	71 years
GDP PER CAPITA	$3,900

ECONOMY IND: petroleum, chemicals, textiles, leather, construction materials, food processing, fertilizer, metal fabrication/processing AGR: wheat, barley, rice, vegetables, dates, cotton, cattle, sheep, poultry EXP: crude oil, crude materials excluding fuels, food and live animals

Israel
STATE OF ISRAEL

AREA	20,770 sq km (8,019 sq mi)
POPULATION	7,591,000
CAPITAL	Jerusalem 768,000
RELIGION	Jewish, Muslim
LANGUAGE	Hebrew, Arabic, English
LITERACY	97%
LIFE EXPECTANCY	81 years
GDP PER CAPITA	$31,000

ECONOMY IND: high-technology products, wood and paper products, potash and phosphates, food, beverages, and tobacco, caustic soda, cement, construction, metals products, chemical products, plastics, diamond cutting, textiles, footwear AGR: citrus, vegetables, cotton, beef, poultry, dairy products EXP: machinery and equipment, software, cut diamonds, agricultural products, chemicals, textiles and apparel

Japan
JAPAN

AREA	377,915 sq km (145,913 sq mi)
POPULATION	127,368,000
CAPITAL	Tokyo 36,507,000
RELIGION	Shintoism, Buddhism
LANGUAGE	Japanese
LITERACY	99%
LIFE EXPECTANCY	84 years
GDP PER CAPITA	$34,300

ECONOMY **IND:** motor vehicles, electronic equipment, machine tools, steel and nonferrous metals, ships, chemicals, textiles, processed foods **AGR:** rice, sugar beets, vegetables, fruit, pork, poultry, dairy products, eggs, fish **EXP:** motor vehicles, semiconductors, iron and steel products, auto parts, plastic materials, power generating machinery

Jordan
HASHEMITE KINGDOM OF JORDAN

AREA	89,342 sq km (34,495 sq mi)
POPULATION	6,509,000
CAPITAL	Amman 1,088,000
RELIGION	Sunni Muslim
LANGUAGE	Arabic, English
LITERACY	90%
LIFE EXPECTANCY	80 years
GDP PER CAPITA	$5,900

ECONOMY **IND:** clothing, fertilizers, potash, phosphate mining, pharmaceuticals, petroleum refining, cement, inorganic chemicals, light manufacturing, tourism **AGR:** citrus, tomatoes, cucumbers, olives, strawberries, stone fruits, sheep, poultry, dairy **EXP:** clothing, fertilizers, potash, phosphates, vegetables, pharmaceuticals

Kazakhstan
REPUBLIC OF KAZAKHSTAN

AREA	2,724,900 sq km (1,052,084 sq mi)
POPULATION	17,522,000
CAPITAL	Astana 650,000
RELIGION	Muslim, Russian Orthodox
LANGUAGE	Kazakh, Russian
LITERACY	100%
LIFE EXPECTANCY	70 years
GDP PER CAPITA	$13,000

ECONOMY **IND:** oil, coal, iron ore, manganese, chromite, lead, zinc, copper, titanium, bauxite, gold, silver, phosphates, sulfur, uranium, iron and steel, tractors and other agricultural machinery, electric motors, construction materials **AGR:** grain (mostly spring wheat), cotton, livestock **EXP:** oil and oil products, ferrous metals, chemicals, machinery, grain, wool, meat, coal

Kuwait
STATE OF KUWAIT

AREA	17,818 sq km (6,880 sq mi)
POPULATION	2,646,000
CAPITAL	Kuwait 2,230,000
RELIGION	Sunni Muslim, Shia Muslim
LANGUAGE	Arabic, English
LITERACY	93%
LIFE EXPECTANCY	77 years
GDP PER CAPITA	$40,700

ECONOMY **IND:** petroleum, petrochemicals, cement, shipbuilding and repair, water desalination, food processing, construction materials **AGR:** fish **EXP:** oil and refined products, fertilizers

Kyrgyzstan
KYRGYZ REPUBLIC

AREA	199,951 sq km (77,201 sq mi)
POPULATION	5,497,000
CAPITAL	Bishkek 854,000
RELIGION	Muslim, Russian Orthodox
LANGUAGE	Kyrgyz, Uzbek, Russian
LITERACY	99%
LIFE EXPECTANCY	69 years
GDP PER CAPITA	$2,400

ECONOMY **IND:** small machinery, textiles, food processing, cement, shoes, sawn logs, refrigerators, furniture, electric motors, gold, rare earth metals **AGR:** tobacco, cotton, potatoes, vegetables, grapes, fruits and berries, sheep, goats, cattle, wool **EXP:** gold, cotton, wool, garments, meat, tobacco, mercury, uranium, hydropower, machinery, shoes

Laos
LAO PEOPLE'S DEMOCRATIC REPUBLIC

AREA	236,800 sq km (91,428 sq mi)
POPULATION	6,586,000
CAPITAL	Vientiane 799,000
RELIGION	Buddhist
LANGUAGE	Lao, French, English
LITERACY	73%
LIFE EXPECTANCY	63 years
GDP PER CAPITA	$2,700

ECONOMY **IND:** copper, tin, gold, and gypsum mining, timber, electric power, agricultural processing, construction, garments, cement, tourism **AGR:** sweet potatoes, vegetables, corn, coffee, sugarcane, tobacco, cotton, tea, peanuts, rice, water buffalo, pigs, cattle, poultry **EXP:** wood products, coffee, electricity, tin, copper, gold

Lebanon
LEBANESE REPUBLIC

AREA	10,400 sq km (4,015 sq mi)
POPULATION	4,140,000
CAPITAL	Beirut 1,909,000
RELIGION	Muslim, Christian
LANGUAGE	Arabic, French, English, Armenian
LITERACY	87%
LIFE EXPECTANCY	75 years
GDP PER CAPITA	$15,600

ECONOMY **IND:** banking, tourism, food processing, wine, jewelry, cement, textiles, mineral and chemical products, wood and furniture products, oil refining, metal fabricating **AGR:** citrus, grapes, tomatoes, apples, vegetables, potatoes, olives, tobacco, sheep, goats **EXP:** jewelry, base metals, chemicals, miscellaneous consumer goods, fruit and vegetables, tobacco, construction minerals, electric power machinery and switchgear, textile fibers, paper

Malaysia
MALAYSIA

AREA	329,847 sq km (127,354 sq mi)
POPULATION	29,180,000
CAPITAL	Kuala Lumpur 1,494,000
RELIGION	Muslim, Buddhist
LANGUAGE	Bahasa Malaysia, English, Chinese, Tamil, Telugu, Malayalam, Panjabi, Thai
LITERACY	89%
LIFE EXPECTANCY	74 years
GDP PER CAPITA	$15,600

ECONOMY **IND:** rubber and oil palm processing and manufacturing, light manufacturing, pharmaceuticals, medical technology, electronics, tin mining and smelting, logging, timber processing, petroleum production, agriculture processing **AGR:** palm oil, rubber, cocoa, rice, subsistence crops, timber, pepper **EXP:** electronic equipment, petroleum and liquefied natural gas, wood and wood products, palm oil, rubber, textiles, chemicals

Maldives
REPUBLIC OF MALDIVES

AREA	298 sq km (115 sq mi)
POPULATION	394,000
CAPITAL	Male 120,000
RELIGION	Sunni Muslim
LANGUAGE	Dhivehi, English
LITERACY	94%
LIFE EXPECTANCY	75 years
GDP PER CAPITA	$8,400

ECONOMY **IND:** tourism, fish processing, shipping, boat building, coconut processing, garments, woven mats, rope, handicrafts, coral and sand mining **AGR:** coconuts, corn, sweet potatoes, fish **EXP:** fish

Mongolia
MONGOLIA

AREA	1,564,116 sq km (603,905 sq mi)
POPULATION	3,180,000
CAPITAL	Ulaanbaatar 949,000
RELIGION	Buddhist Lamaist, none
LANGUAGE	Khalkha Mongol, Turkic, Russian
LITERACY	98%
LIFE EXPECTANCY	69 years
GDP PER CAPITA	$4,500

ECONOMY **IND:** construction and construction materials, mining (coal, copper, molybdenum, fluorspar, tin, tungsten, and gold), oil, food and beverages, processing of animal products, cashmere and natural fiber manufacturing **AGR:** wheat, barley, vegetables, forage crops, sheep, goats, cattle, camels, horses **EXP:** copper, apparel, livestock, animal products, cashmere, wool, hides, fluorspar, other nonferrous metals, coal, crude oil

Myanmar (Burma)
REPUBLIC OF THE UNION OF MYANMAR

AREA	676,578 sq km (261,227 sq mi)
POPULATION	54,585,000
CAPITAL	Nay Pyi Taw (administrative), Yangon (legislative) 992,000, 4,350,000
RELIGION	Buddhist
LANGUAGE	Burmese
LITERACY	90%
LIFE EXPECTANCY	65 years
GDP PER CAPITA	$1,300

ECONOMY **IND:** agricultural processing, wood and wood products, copper, tin, tungsten, iron, cement, construction materials, pharmaceuticals, fertilizer, oil and natural gas, garments, jade and gems **AGR:** rice, pulses, beans, sesame, groundnuts, sugarcane, hardwood, fish and fish products **EXP:** natural gas, wood products, pulses, beans, fish, rice, clothing, jade and gems

Nepal
FEDERAL DEMOCRATIC REPUBLIC OF NEPAL

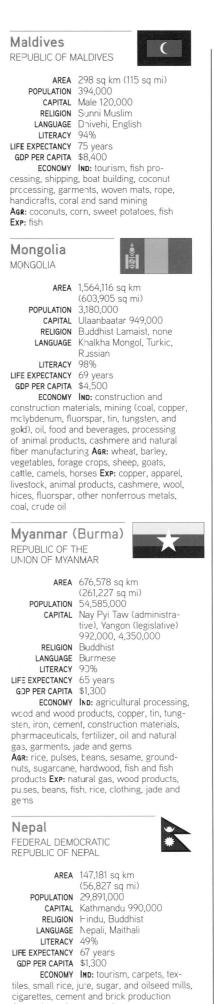

AREA	147,181 sq km (56,827 sq mi)
POPULATION	29,891,000
CAPITAL	Kathmandu 990,000
RELIGION	Hindu, Buddhist
LANGUAGE	Nepali, Maithali
LITERACY	49%
LIFE EXPECTANCY	67 years
GDP PER CAPITA	$1,300

ECONOMY **IND:** tourism, carpets, textiles, small rice, jute, sugar, and oilseed mills, cigarettes, cement and brick production **AGR:** pulses, rice, corn, wheat, sugarcane, jute, root crops, milk, water buffalo meat **EXP:** clothing, pulses, carpets, textiles, juice, pashima, jute goods

North Korea
DEMOCRATIC PEOPLE'S REPUBLIC OF KOREA

AREA	120,538 sq km (46,540 sq mi)
POPULATION	24,589,000
CAPITAL	Pyongyang 2,828,000
RELIGION	None, Buddhist, Confucianist
LANGUAGE	Korean
LITERACY	99%
LIFE EXPECTANCY	69 years
GDP PER CAPITA	$1,800

ECONOMY **IND:** military products, machine building, electric power, chemicals, mining (coal, iron ore, limestone, magnesite, graphite, copper, zinc, lead, and precious metals), metallurgy, textiles, food processing, tourism **AGR:** rice, corn, potatoes, soybeans, pulses, cattle, pigs, pork, eggs **EXP:** minerals, metallurgical products, manufactures (including armaments), textiles, agricultural and fishery products

Oman
SULTANATE OF OMAN

AREA	309,500 sq km (119,498 sq mi)
POPULATION	3,090,000
CAPITAL	Muscat 634,000
RELIGION	Ibadhi Muslim
LANGUAGE	Arabic, English, Baluchi, Urdu
LITERACY	81%
LIFE EXPECTANCY	74 years
GDP PER CAPITA	$26,200

ECONOMY **IND:** crude oil production and refining, natural and liquefied natural gas production, construction, cement, copper, steel, chemicals, optic fiber **AGR:** dates, limes, bananas, alfalfa, vegetables, camels, cattle, fish **EXP:** petroleum, reexports, fish, metals, textiles

Pakistan
ISLAMIC REPUBLIC OF PAKISTAN

AREA	796,095 sq km (307,372 sq mi)
POPULATION	190,291,000
CAPITAL	Islamabad 832,000
RELIGION	Sunni Muslim, Shia Muslim
LANGUAGE	Punjabi, Sindhi, Saraiki, English, Urdu
LITERACY	50%
LIFE EXPECTANCY	66 years
GDP PER CAPITA	$2,800

ECONOMY **IND:** textiles and apparel, food processing, pharmaceuticals, construction materials, paper products, fertilizer, shrimp **AGR:** cotton, wheat, rice, sugarcane, fruits, vegetables, milk, beef, mutton, eggs **EXP:** textiles (garments, bed linen, cotton cloth, yarn), rice, leather goods, sports goods, chemicals, manufactures, carpets and rugs

Philippines
REPUBLIC OF THE PHILIPPINES

AREA	300,000 sq km (115,830 sq mi)
POPULATION	103,775,000
CAPITAL	Manila 11,449,000
RELIGION	Catholic
LANGUAGE	Filipino, English, Tagalog
LITERACY	93%
LIFE EXPECTANCY	72 years
GDP PER CAPITA	$4,100

ECONOMY **IND:** electronics assembly, garments, footwear, pharmaceuticals, chemicals, wood products, food processing, petroleum refining, fishing **AGR:** sugarcane, coconuts, rice, corn, bananas, cassavas, pineapples, mangoes, pork, eggs, beef, fish **EXP:** semiconductors and electronic products, transport equipment, garments, copper products, petroleum products, coconut oil, fruits

Qatar
STATE OF QATAR

AREA	11,586 sq km (4,473 sq mi)
POPULATION	1,952,000
CAPITAL	Doha 427,000
RELIGION	Muslim
LANGUAGE	Arabic, English
LITERACY	89%
LIFE EXPECTANCY	78 years
GDP PER CAPITA	$102,700

ECONOMY **IND:** liquefied natural gas, crude oil production and refining, ammonia, fertilizers, petrochemicals, steel reinforcing bars, cement, commercial ship repair **AGR:** fruits, vegetables, poultry, dairy products, beef, fish **EXP:** liquefied natural gas, petroleum products, fertilizers, steel

Saudi Arabia
KINGDOM OF SAUDI ARABIA

AREA	2,149,690 sq km (829,995 sq mi)
POPULATION	26,535,000
CAPITAL	Riyadh 4,725,000
RELIGION	Muslim
LANGUAGE	Arabic
LITERACY	79%
LIFE EXPECTANCY	74 years
GDP PER CAPITA	$24,000

ECONOMY **IND:** crude oil production, petroleum refining, basic petrochemicals, ammonia, industrial gases, sodium hydroxide (caustic soda), cement, fertilizer, plastics, metals, commercial ship repair, commercial aircraft repair, construction **AGR:** wheat, barley, tomatoes, melons, dates, citrus, mutton, chickens, eggs, milk **EXP:** petroleum and petroleum products

Singapore
REPUBLIC OF SINGAPORE

AREA	697 sq km (269 sq mi)
POPULATION	5,353,000
CAPITAL	Singapore 4,737,000
RELIGION	Buddhist, Muslim, none
LANGUAGE	Mandarin, English, Malay, Hokkien, Tamil
LITERACY	93%
LIFE EXPECTANCY	84 years
GDP PER CAPITA	$59,900

ECONOMY **IND:** electronics, chemicals, financial services, oil drilling equipment, petroleum refining, rubber processing and rubber products, processed food and beverages, ship repair, offshore platform construction, life sciences, entrepot trade **AGR:** orchids, vegetables, poultry, eggs, fish, ornamental fish **EXP:** machinery and equipment (including electronics and telecommunications), pharmaceuticals and other chemicals, refined petroleum products

South Korea
REPUBLIC OF KOREA

AREA	99,720 sq km (38,502 sq mi)
POPULATION	48,861,000
CAPITAL	Seoul 9,778,000
RELIGION	None, Christian, Buddhist
LANGUAGE	Korean, English
LITERACY	98%
LIFE EXPECTANCY	79 years
GDP PER CAPITA	$31,700

ECONOMY **IND:** electronics, telecommunications, automobile production, chemicals, shipbuilding, steel **AGR:** rice, root crops, barley, vegetables, fruit, cattle, pigs, chickens, milk, eggs, fish **EXP:** semiconductors, wireless telecommunications equipment, motor vehicles, computers, steel, ships, petrochemicals

Sri Lanka
DEMOCRATIC SOCIALIST REPUBLIC OF SRI LANKA

AREA	65,610 sq km (25,332 sq mi)
POPULATION	21,481,000
CAPITAL	Colombo (administrative) 681,000, Sri Jayewardenepura Kotte (legislative) 123,000
RELIGION	Buddhist
LANGUAGE	Sinhala, Tamil, English
LITERACY	91%
LIFE EXPECTANCY	76 years
GDP PER CAPITA	$5,600

ECONOMY **IND:** processing of rubber, tea, coconuts, tobacco and other agricultural commodities, telecommunications, insurance, banking, tourism, shipping, clothing, textiles, cement, petroleum refining, information technology services, construction **AGR:** rice, sugarcane, grains, pulses, oilseed, spices, vegetables, fruit, tea, rubber, coconuts, milk, eggs, hides, beef, fish **EXP:** textiles and apparel, tea and spices, rubber manufactures, precious stones, coconut products, fish

Syria
SYRIAN ARAB REPUBLIC

AREA	185,180 sq km (71,498 sq mi)
POPULATION	22,531,000
CAPITAL	Damascus 2,527,000
RELIGION	Sunni Muslim, other Muslim, Christian
LANGUAGE	Arabic, Kurdish, Armenian, Aramaic, Circassian, French, English
LITERACY	80%
LIFE EXPECTANCY	75 years
GDP PER CAPITA	$5,100

ECONOMY **IND:** petroleum, textiles, food processing, beverages, tobacco, phosphate rock mining, cement, oil seeds crushing, car assembly **AGR:** wheat, barley, cotton, lentils, chickpeas, olives, sugar beets, beef, mutton, eggs, poultry, milk **EXP:** crude oil, minerals, petroleum products, fruits and vegetables, cotton fiber, textiles, clothing, meat and live animals, wheat

Tajikistan
REPUBLIC OF TAJIKISTAN

AREA	143,100 sq km (55,251 sq mi)
POPULATION	7,768,000
CAPITAL	Dushanbe 704,000
RELIGION	Sunni Muslim
LANGUAGE	Tajik, Russian
LITERACY	100%
LIFE EXPECTANCY	66 years
GDP PER CAPITA	$2,000

ECONOMY **IND:** aluminum, cement, vegetable oil **AGR:** cotton, grain, fruits, grapes, vegetables, cattle, sheep, goats **EXP:** aluminum, electricity, cotton, fruits, vegetable oil, textiles

Thailand
KINGDOM OF THAILAND

AREA	513,120 sq km (198,116 sq mi)
POPULATION	67,091,000
CAPITAL	Bangkok 6,902,000
RELIGION	Buddhist
LANGUAGE	Thai, English
LITERACY	93%
LIFE EXPECTANCY	74 years
GDP PER CAPITA	$9,700

ECONOMY **IND:** tourism, textiles and garments, agricultural processing, beverages, tobacco, cement, light manufacturing such as jewelry and electric appliances, computers and parts, integrated circuits, furniture, plastics, automobiles and automotive parts, tungsten, tin **AGR:** rice, cassava (tapioca), rubber, corn, sugarcane, coconuts, soybeans **EXP:** textiles and footwear, fishery products, rice, rubber, jewelry, automobiles, computers and electrical appliances

Timor-Leste (East Timor)
DEMOCRATIC REPUBLIC OF TIMOR-LESTE

AREA	14,874 sq km (5,743 sq mi)
POPULATION	1,201,000
CAPITAL	Dili 166,000
RELIGION	Roman Catholic
LANGUAGE	Tetum, Portuguese, Indonesian, English
LITERACY	59%
LIFE EXPECTANCY	68 years
GDP PER CAPITA	$3,100

ECONOMY **IND:** printing, soap manufacturing, handicrafts, woven cloth **AGR:** coffee, rice, corn, cassava, sweet potatoes, soybeans, cabbage, mangoes, bananas, vanilla **EXP:** coffee, sandalwood, marble

Turkey
REPUBLIC OF TURKEY

AREA	783,562 sq km (302,533 sq mi)
POPULATION	79,749,000
CAPITAL	Ankara 3,846,000
RELIGION	Sunni Muslim
LANGUAGE	Turkish, Kurdish
LITERACY	87%
LIFE EXPECTANCY	73 years
GDP PER CAPITA	$14,600

ECONOMY **IND:** textiles, food processing, autos, electronics, mining (coal, chromate, copper, boron), steel, petroleum, construction, lumber, paper **AGR:** tobacco, cotton, grain, olives, sugar beets, hazelnuts, pulse, citrus, livestock **EXP:** apparel, foodstuffs, textiles, metal manufactures, transport equipment

Turkmenistan
TURKMENISTAN

AREA	488,100 sq km (188,455 sq mi)
POPULATION	5,055,000
CAPITAL	Ashgabat 637,000
RELIGION	Muslim
LANGUAGE	Turkmen, Russian, Uzbek
LITERACY	99%
LIFE EXPECTANCY	69 years
GDP PER CAPITA	$7,500

ECONOMY **IND:** natural gas, oil, petroleum products, textiles, food processing **AGR:** cotton, grain, livestock **EXP:** gas, crude oil, petrochemicals, textiles, cotton fiber

United Arab Emirates
UNITED ARAB EMIRATES

AREA	83,600 sq km (32,278 sq mi)
POPULATION	5,314,000
CAPITAL	Abu Dhabi 666,000
RELIGION	Muslim
LANGUAGE	Arabic, Persian, English, Hindi, Urdu
LITERACY	78%
LIFE EXPECTANCY	77 years
GDP PER CAPITA	$48,500

ECONOMY **IND:** petroleum and petrochemicals, fishing, aluminum, cement, fertilizers, commercial ship repair, construction materials, some boat building, handicrafts, textiles **AGR:** dates, vegetables, watermelons, poultry, eggs, dairy products, fish **EXP:** crude oil, natural gas, reexports, dried fish, dates

Uzbekistan
REPUBLIC OF UZBEKISTAN

AREA	447,400 sq km (172,741 sq mi)
POPULATION	28,394,000
CAPITAL	Tashkent 2,201,000
RELIGION	Sunni Muslim
LANGUAGE	Uzbek, Russian
LITERACY	99%
LIFE EXPECTANCY	73 years
GDP PER CAPITA	$3,300

ECONOMY **IND:** textiles, food processing, machine building, metallurgy, mining, hydrocarbon extraction, chemicals **AGR:** cotton, vegetables, fruits, grain, livestock **EXP:** energy products, cotton, gold, mineral fertilizers, ferrous and nonferrous metals, textiles, food products, machinery, automobiles

Vietnam
SOCIALIST REPUBLIC OF VIETNAM

AREA	331,210 sq km (127,880 sq mi)
POPULATION	91,519,000
CAPITAL	Hanoi 2,668,000
RELIGION	None, Buddhist
LANGUAGE	Vietnamese, English
LITERACY	94%
LIFE EXPECTANCY	72 years
GDP PER CAPITA	$3,300

ECONOMY **IND:** food processing, garments, shoes, machine-building, mining, coal, steel, cement, chemical fertilizer, glass, tires, oil, mobile phones **AGR:** paddy rice, coffee, rubber, tea, pepper, soybeans, cashews, sugar cane, peanuts, bananas, poultry, fish, seafood **EXP:** clothes, shoes, marine products, crude oil, electronics, wooden products, rice, machinery

Yemen
REPUBLIC OF YEMEN

AREA	527,968 sq km (203,848 sq mi)
POPULATION	24,772,000
CAPITAL	Sanaa 2,229,000
RELIGION	Muslim
LANGUAGE	Arabic
LITERACY	50%
LIFE EXPECTANCY	64 years
GDP PER CAPITA	$2,500

ECONOMY **IND:** crude oil production and petroleum refining, small-scale production of cotton textiles and leather goods, food processing, handicrafts, small aluminum products factory, cement, commercial ship repair, natural gas production **AGR:** grain, fruits, vegetables, pulses, qat, coffee, cotton, dairy products, livestock (sheep, goats, cattle, camels), poultry, fish **EXP:** crude oil, coffee, dried and salted fish, liquefied natural gas

AREAS OF SPECIAL STATUS

Gaza Strip
GAZA STRIP

AREA	360 sq km (139 sq mi)
POPULATION	1,710,000
CAPITAL	none
RELIGION	Sunni Muslim
LANGUAGE	Arabic, Hebrew, English
LITERACY	92%
LIFE EXPECTANCY	74 years
GDP PER CAPITA	$2,900

ECONOMY **IND:** textiles, food processing, furniture **AGR:** olives, fruit, vegetables, flowers, beef, dairy products **EXP:** strawberries, carnations, vegetables

Taiwan

TAIWAN

AREA	35,980 sq km (13,892 sq mi)
POPULATION	23,114,000
CAPITAL	Taipei 2,633,000
RELIGION	mixture of Buddhist and Taoist
LANGUAGE	Mandarin, Taiwanese, Hakka
LITERACY	96%
LIFE EXPECTANCY	78 years
GDP PER CAPITA	$37,900
ECONOMY	IND: electronics, communications and information technology products, petroleum refining, armaments, chemicals, textiles, iron and steel, machinery, cement, food processing, vehicles, consumer products, pharmaceuticals AGR: rice, vegetables, fruit, tea, flowers, pigs, poultry, fish EXP: electronics, flat panels, machinery, metals, textiles, plastics, chemicals, optical, photographic, measuring, and medical instruments

West Bank

WEST BANK

AREA	5,860 sq km (2,263 sq mi)
POPULATION	2,623,000
CAPITAL	none
RELIGION	Muslim, Jewish
LANGUAGE	Arabic, Hebrew, English
LITERACY	92%
LIFE EXPECTANCY	75 years
GDP PER CAPITA	$2,900
ECONOMY	IND: small-scale manufacturing, quarrying, textiles, soap, olive-wood carvings, and mother-of-pearl souvenirs AGR: olives, citrus fruit, vegetables, beef, dairy products EXP: stone, olives, fruit, vegetables, limestone

DATES OF NATIONAL INDEPENDENCE AND POPULATION

Asian Population by Country
(ten largest, in clockwise order)

IRAN 78,869,000
TURKEY 79,749,000
VIETNAM 91,519,000
PHILIPPINES 103,775,000
JAPAN 127,368,000
BANGLADESH 161,084,000
PAKISTAN 190,291,000
INDONESIA 248,216,000

All other countries 585,066,000
CHINA 1,343,240,000
INDIA 1,205,074,000

2002 Timor-Leste
1991 Georgia, Azerbaijan, Kyrgyzstan, Uzbekistan, Tajikistan, Armenia, Turkmenistan, Kazakhstan
1990 Yemen
1984 Brunei
1979 Iran
1971 Bangladesh, Bahrain, Qatar, United Arab Emirates
1965 Maldives, Singapore
1961 Kuwait
1957 Malaysia
1953 Cambodia
1949 Laos, Bhutan
1948 Myanmar, Sri Lanka, Israel
1947 India, Pakistan
1946 Syria, Jordan, Philippines
1945 North Korea, South Korea, Indonesia, Vietnam
1943 Lebanon
1932 Saudi Arabia, Iraq
1923 Turkey
1921 Mongolia
1919 Afghanistan

1768 Nepal
1650 Oman
1238 Thailand
221 B.C. China
660 B.C. Japan

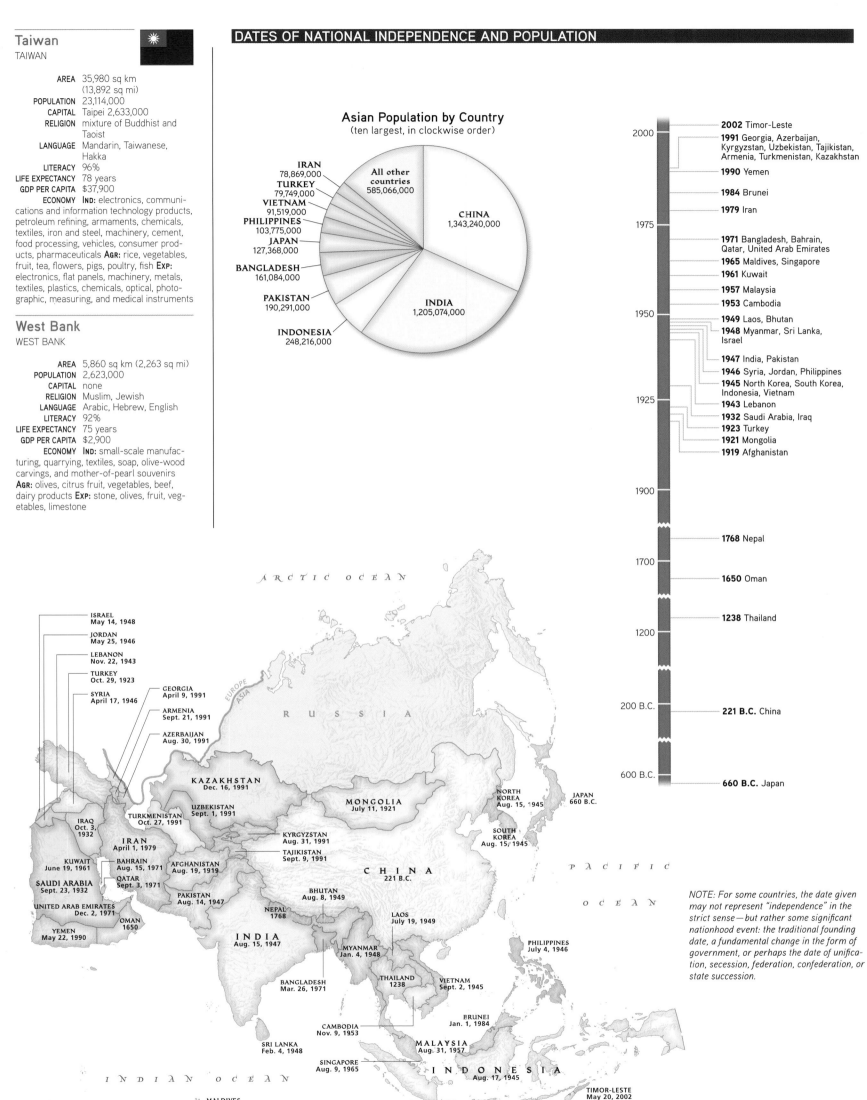

ISRAEL May 14, 1948
JORDAN May 25, 1946
LEBANON Nov. 22, 1943
TURKEY Oct. 29, 1923
SYRIA April 17, 1946
GEORGIA April 9, 1991
ARMENIA Sept. 21, 1991
AZERBAIJAN Aug. 30, 1991
IRAQ Oct. 3, 1932
KUWAIT June 19, 1961
SAUDI ARABIA Sept. 23, 1932
UNITED ARAB EMIRATES Dec. 2, 1971
YEMEN May 22, 1990
BAHRAIN Aug. 15, 1971
QATAR Sept. 3, 1971
OMAN 1650
IRAN April 1, 1979
TURKMENISTAN Oct. 27, 1991
UZBEKISTAN Sept. 1, 1991
KAZAKHSTAN Dec. 16, 1991
KYRGYZSTAN Aug. 31, 1991
TAJIKISTAN Sept. 9, 1991
AFGHANISTAN Aug. 19, 1919
PAKISTAN Aug. 14, 1947
NEPAL 1768
BHUTAN Aug. 8, 1949
INDIA Aug. 15, 1947
BANGLADESH Mar. 26, 1971
MYANMAR Jan. 4, 1948
SRI LANKA Feb. 4, 1948
MALDIVES July 26, 1965
MONGOLIA July 11, 1921
CHINA 221 B.C.
NORTH KOREA Aug. 15, 1945
SOUTH KOREA Aug. 15, 1945
JAPAN 660 B.C.
LAOS July 19, 1949
THAILAND 1238
VIETNAM Sept. 2, 1945
CAMBODIA Nov. 9, 1953
SINGAPORE Aug. 9, 1965
MALAYSIA Aug. 31, 1957
PHILIPPINES July 4, 1946
BRUNEI Jan. 1, 1984
INDONESIA Aug. 17, 1945
TIMOR-LESTE May 20, 2002

ARCTIC OCEAN
RUSSIA
EUROPE ASIA
PACIFIC OCEAN
INDIAN OCEAN

NOTE: For some countries, the date given may not represent "independence" in the strict sense—but rather some significant nationhood event: the traditional founding date, a fundamental change in the form of government, or perhaps the date of unification, secession, federation, confederation, or state succession.

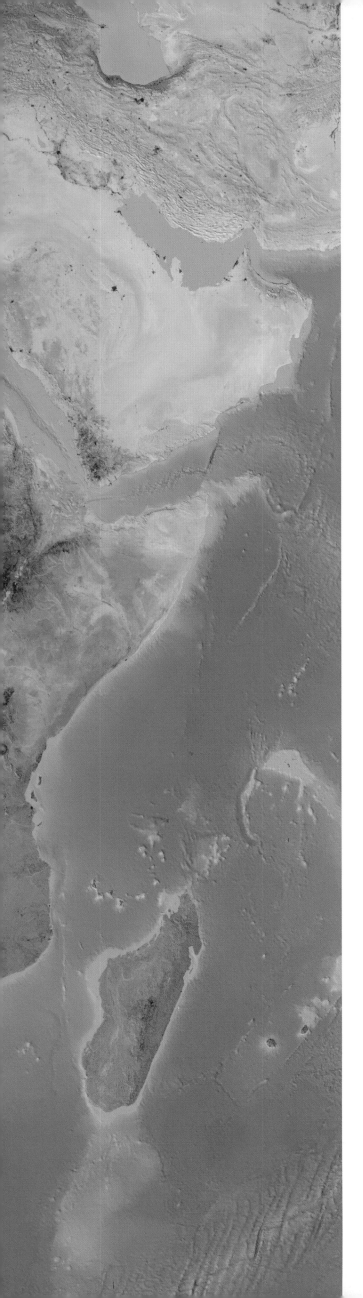

Africa

ELEMENTAL AND UNCONQUERABLE, AFRICA remains something of a paradox among continents. Birthplace of humankind and of the great early civilizations of Egypt and Kush, also called Nubia, the continent has since thwarted human efforts to exploit many of its resources. The forbidding sweep of the Sahara, largest desert in the world, holds the northern third of Africa in thrall, while the bordering Sahel sands alternately advance and recede in unpredictable, drought-invoking rhythms. In contrast to the long, life-giving thread of the Nile, the lake district in the east, and the Congo drainage in central Africa, few major waterways provide irrigation and commercial navigation to large, arid segments of the continent.

Africa's unforgettable form, bulging to the west, lies surrounded by oceans and seas. The East African Rift System is the continent's most dramatic geologic feature. This great rent actually begins in the Red Sea, then cuts southward to form the stunning landscape of lakes, volcanoes, and deep valleys that finally ends near the mouth of the Zambezi River. Caused by the Earth's crust pulling apart, the rift may one day separate East Africa from the rest of the continent.

Most of Africa is made up of savannah—high, rolling, grassy plains. These savannahs have been home since earliest times to people often called Bantu, a reference to both social groupings and their languages. Other distinct physical types exist around the continent as well: BaMbuti (Pygmies), San (Bushmen), Nilo-Saharans, and Hamito-Semitics (Berbers and Cushites). Africa's astonishing 1,600 spoken languages—more than any other continent—reflect the great diversity of ethnic and social groups.

Africa ranks among the richest regions in the world in natural resources; it contains vast reserves of fossil fuels, precious metals, ores, and gems, including almost all of the world's chromium, much uranium, copper, enormous underground gold reserves, and diamonds. Yet Africa accounts for a mere one percent of world economic output. South Africa's economy alone nearly equals that of all other sub-Saharan countries. Many obstacles complicate the way forward. African countries experience great gaps in wealth between city and country, and many face growing slums around megacities such as Lagos and Cairo. Nearly 40 other African cities have populations over a million. Lack of clean water and the spread of diseases—malaria, tuberculosis, cholera, and AIDS—undermine people's health. Nearly 24 million Africans are now infected with HIV/AIDS, which killed 1.9 million Africans in 2005. AIDS has shortened life expectancy to 47 years in parts of Africa, destroyed families, and erased decades of social progress and economic activity by killing people in their prime working years. In addition, war and huge concentrations of refugees displaced by fighting, persecution, and famine deter any chance of growth and stability.

Africa's undeveloped natural beauty—along with its wealth of animal life, despite a vast dimunition in their numbers due to poaching and habitat loss—has engendered a booming tourist industry. Names such as "Serengeti Plain," "Kalahari Desert," "Okavango Delta," and "Victoria Falls" still evoke images of an Africa unspoiled, unconquerable, and, throughout the Earth, unsurpassed.

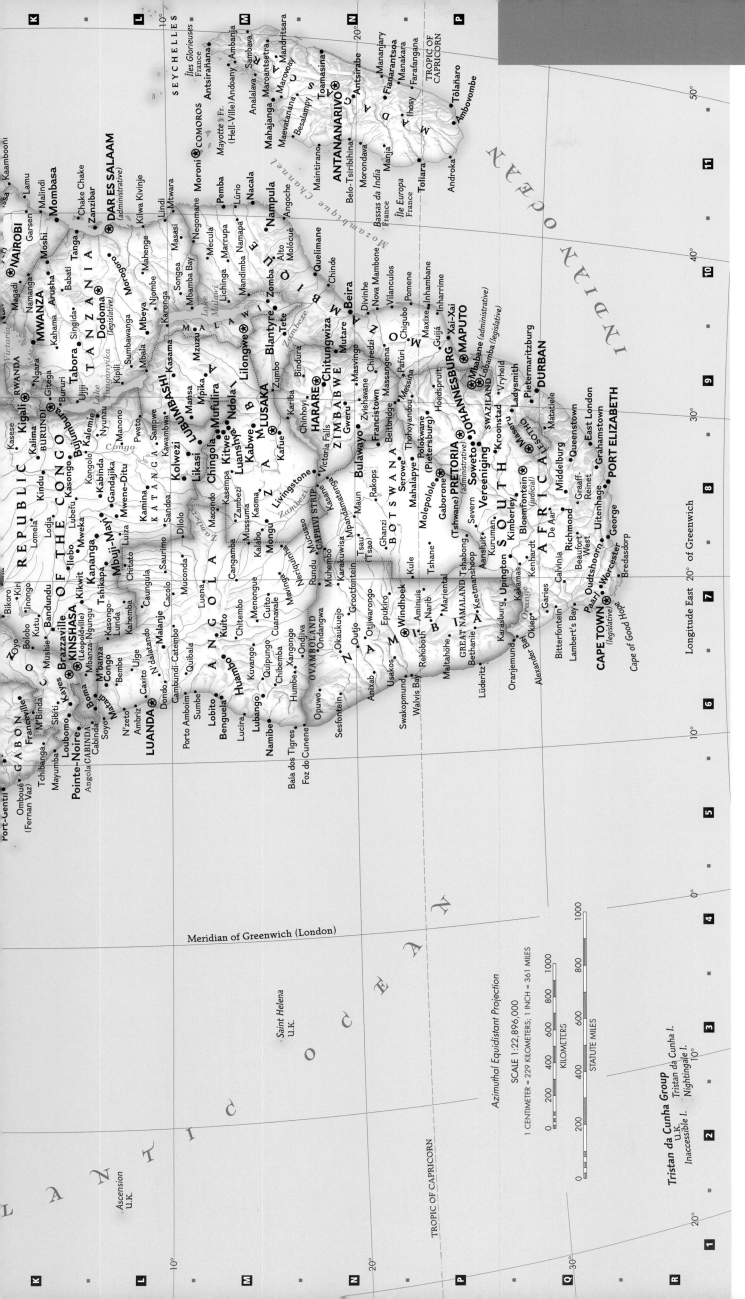

CONTINENTAL DATA

TOTAL NUMBER OF COUNTRIES: 54

FIRST INDEPENDENT COUNTRY:
Ethiopia, over 2,000 years old

"YOUNGEST" COUNTRY:
South Sudan, July 9, 2011

LARGEST COUNTRY IN AREA:
Algeria 2,381,741 sq km
(919,590 sq mi)

SMALLEST COUNTRY IN AREA:
Seychelles 455 sq km (176 sq mi)

PERCENT URBAN POPULATION: 37%

MOST POPULOUS COUNTRY:
Nigeria 170,124,000

LEAST POPULOUS COUNTRY:
Seychelles 90,000

MOST DENSELY POPULATED COUNTRY:
Mauritius 643.6 per sq km
(1,666.2 per sq mi)

LEAST DENSELY POPULATED COUNTRY:
Namibia 2.6 per sq km
(6.8 per sq mi)

LARGEST CITY BY POPULATION:
Cairo, Egypt 11,000,000

HIGHEST GDP PER CAPITA:
Equatorial Guinea $50,200

LOWEST GDP PER CAPITA:
Comoros, Malawi, Somalia $600

AVERAGE LIFE EXPECTANCY IN AFRICA:
52 years

AVERAGE LITERACY RATE IN AFRICA:
63%

Tropic of Cancer
Equator   AFRICA
Tropic of Capricorn

CONTINENTAL DATA

AREA: 30,065,000 sq km
(11,608,000 sq mi)

GREATEST NORTH-SOUTH EXTENT:
8,047 km (5,000 mi)

GREATEST EAST-WEST EXTENT:
7,564 km (4,700 mi)

HIGHEST POINT:
Kilimanjaro, Tanzania
5,895 m (19,340 ft)

LOWEST POINT:
Lake Assal, Djibouti
-156 m (-512 ft)

LOWEST RECORDED TEMPERATURE:
Ifrane, Morocco -24°C (-11°F),
February 11, 1935

HIGHEST RECORDED TEMPERATURE:
Al Aziziyah, Libya 58°C (136.4°F)
September 13, 1922

LONGEST RIVERS:
• Nile 6,695 km (4,160 mi)
• Congo 4,700 km (2,900 mi)
• Niger 4,170 km (2,591 mi)

LARGEST NATURAL LAKES:
• Lake Victoria 69,500 sq km
(26,800 sq mi)
• Lake Tanganyika 32,600 sq km
(12,600 sq mi)
• Lake Malawi (Lake Nyasa)
28,900 sq km
(11,200 sq MI)

EARTH'S EXTREMES IN AFRICA:
• Largest Desert on Earth:
Sahara 9,000,000 sq km
(3,475,000 sq mi)
• Hottest Place on Earth:
Dalol, Danakil Desert,
Ethiopia; annual average
temperature 34°C (93°F)

Africa: Human and Natural Themes

POPULATION DENSITY

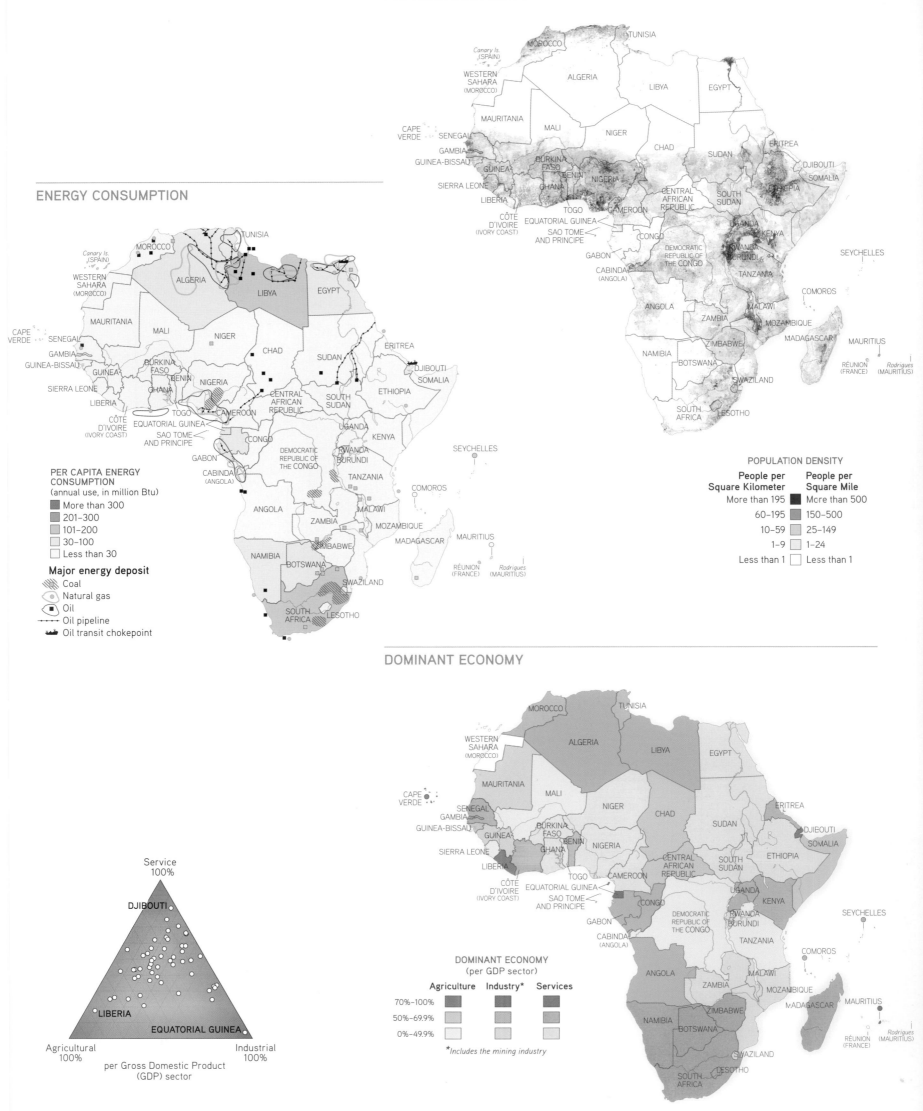

POPULATION DENSITY

People per Square Kilometer	People per Square Mile
More than 195	More than 500
60–195	150–500
10–59	25–149
1–9	1–24
Less than 1	Less than 1

ENERGY CONSUMPTION

PER CAPITA ENERGY CONSUMPTION
(annual use, in million Btu)

- More than 300
- 201–300
- 101–200
- 30–100
- Less than 30

Major energy deposit

- Coal
- Natural gas
- Oil
- Oil pipeline
- Oil transit chokepoint

DOMINANT ECONOMY

Service 100%

DJIBOUTI

LIBERIA

EQUATORIAL GUINEA

Agricultural 100%

Industrial 100%

per Gross Domestic Product (GDP) sector

DOMINANT ECONOMY
(per GDP sector)

	Agriculture	Industry*	Services
70%–100%			
50%–69.9%			
0%–49.9%			

*Includes the mining industry

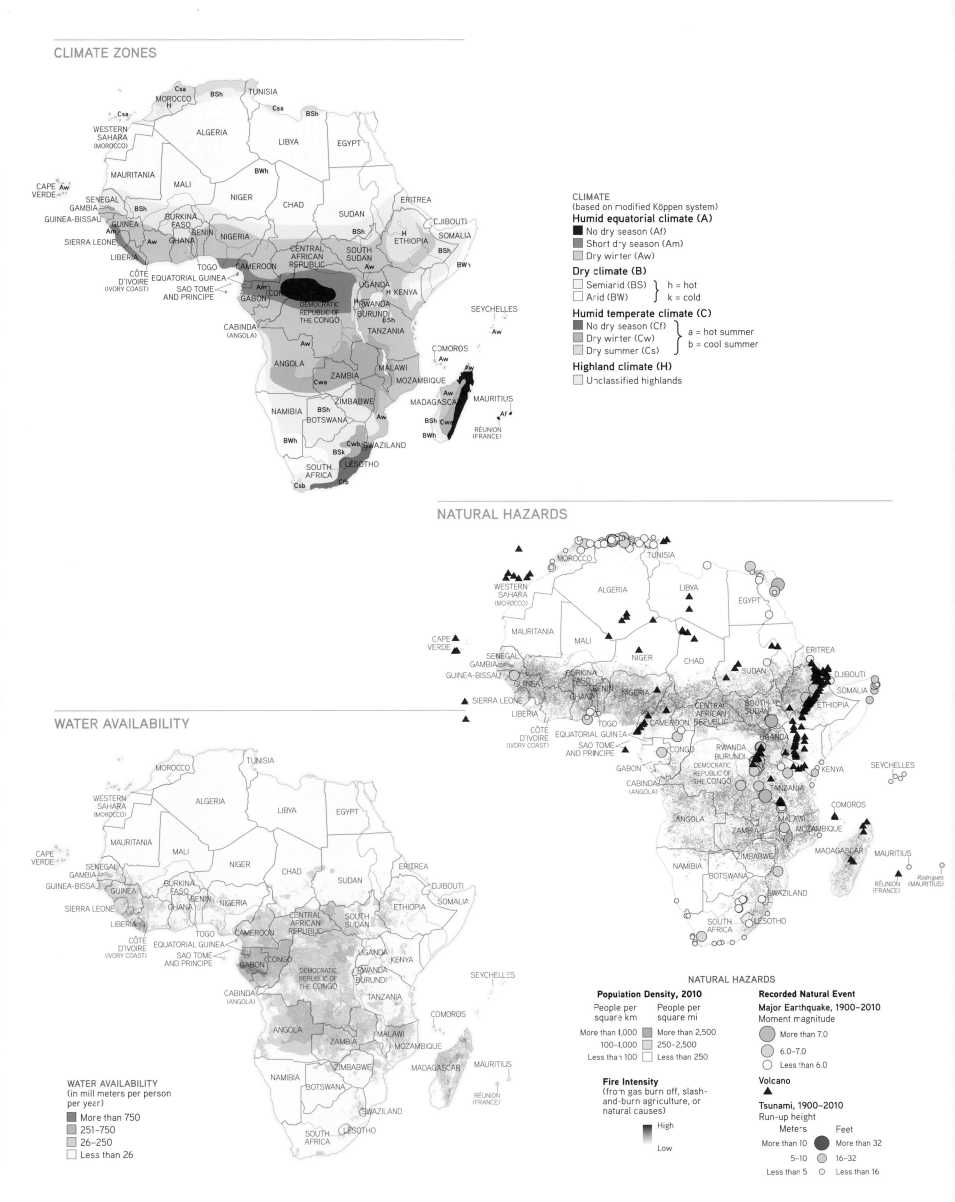

CLIMATE ZONES

CLIMATE
(based on modified Köppen system)

Humid equatorial climate (A)
- No dry season (Af)
- Short dry season (Am)
- Dry winter (Aw)

Dry climate (B)
- Semiarid (BS) } h = hot
- Arid (BW) } k = cold

Humid temperate climate (C)
- No dry season (Cf)
- Dry winter (Cw) } a = hot summer
- Dry summer (Cs) } b = cool summer

Highland climate (H)
- Unclassified highlands

NATURAL HAZARDS

WATER AVAILABILITY

WATER AVAILABILITY
(in mill meters per person per year)
- More than 750
- 251–750
- 26–250
- Less than 26

NATURAL HAZARDS

Population Density, 2010

People per square km	People per square mi
More than 1,000	More than 2,500
100–1,000	250–2,500
Less than 100	Less than 250

Fire Intensity
(from gas burn off, slash-and-burn agriculture, or natural causes)

High
Low

Recorded Natural Event

Major Earthquake, 1900–2010
Moment magnitude
- More than 7.0
- 6.0–7.0
- Less than 6.0

Volcano

Tsunami, 1900–2010
Run-up height

Meters	Feet
More than 10	More than 32
5–10	16–32
Less than 5	Less than 16

COUNTRIES

Algeria
PEOPLE'S DEMOCRATIC
REPUBLIC OF ALGERIA

AREA	2,381,741 sq km
	(919,590 sq mi)
POPULATION	35,406,000
CAPITAL	Algiers 2,800,000
RELIGION	Sunni Muslim
LANGUAGE	Arabic, French, Berber
	dialects
LITERACY	70%
LIFE EXPECTANCY	75 years
GDP PER CAPITA	$7,200

ECONOMY **IND:** petroleum, natural gas, light industries, mining, electrical, petrochemical, food processing **AGR:** wheat, barley, oats, grapes, olives, citrus, fruits, sheep, cattle **EXP:** petroleum, natural gas, petroleum products

Angola
REPUBLIC OF ANGOLA

AREA	1,246,700 sq km
	(481,351 sq mi)
POPULATION	18,056,000
CAPITAL	Luanda 4,772,000
RELIGION	Indigenous beliefs, Roman
	Catholic, Protestant
LANGUAGE	Portuguese, Bantu
LITERACY	67%
LIFE EXPECTANCY	55 years
GDP PER CAPITA	$5,900

ECONOMY **IND:** petroleum, diamonds, iron ore, phosphates, feldspar, bauxite, uranium, gold, cement, basic metal products, fish processing, food processing, brewing, tobacco products, sugar, textiles, ship repair **AGR:** bananas, sugarcane, coffee, sisal, corn, cotton, manioc (tapioca), tobacco, vegetables, plantains, livestock, forest products, fish **EXP:** crude oil, diamonds, refined petroleum products, coffee, sisal, fish and fish products, timber, cotton

Benin
REPUBLIC OF BENIN

AREA	112,622 sq km
	(43,483 sq mi)
POPULATION	9,599,000
CAPITAL	Porto-Novo (official)
	267,000, Cotonou (seat of
	government) 844,000
RELIGION	Catholic, Muslim, Vodoun,
	Protestant
LANGUAGE	French, Fon, Yoruba
LITERACY	35%
LIFE EXPECTANCY	60 years
GDP PER CAPITA	$1,500

ECONOMY **IND:** textiles, food processing, construction materials, cement **AGR:** cotton, corn, cassava (tapioca), yams, beans, palm oil, peanuts, cashews, livestock **EXP:** cotton, cashews, shea butter, textiles, palm products, seafood

Botswana
REPUBLIC OF BOTSWANA

AREA	581,730 sq km
	(224,606 sq mi)
POPULATION	2,098,000
CAPITAL	Gaborone 232,000
RELIGION	Christian
LANGUAGE	Setswana, Kalanga
LITERACY	81%
LIFE EXPECTANCY	56 years
GDP PER CAPITA	$16,300

ECONOMY **IND:** diamonds, copper, nickel, salt, soda ash, potash, coal, iron ore, silver, livestock processing, textiles **AGR:** livestock, sorghum, maize, millet, beans, sunflowers, groundnuts **EXP:** diamonds, copper, nickel, soda ash, meat, textiles

Burkina Faso
BURKINA FASO

AREA	274,200 sq km
	(105,869 sq mi)
POPULATION	17,275,000
CAPITAL	Ouagadougou 1,908,000
RELIGION	Muslim, Catholic, animist
LANGUAGE	French, native African
	languages
LITERACY	22%
LIFE EXPECTANCY	54 years
GDP PER CAPITA	$1,500

ECONOMY **IND:** cotton lint, beverages, agricultural processing, soap, cigarettes, textiles, gold **AGR:** cotton, peanuts, shea nuts, sesame, sorghum, millet, corn, rice, livestock **EXP:** cotton, livestock, gold

Burundi
REPUBLIC OF BURUNDI

AREA	27,830 sq km
	(10,745 sq mi)
POPULATION	10,557,000
CAPITAL	Bujumbura 393,000
RELIGION	Christian, indigenous
	beliefs, Muslim
LANGUAGE	Kirundi, French, Swahili
LITERACY	59%
LIFE EXPECTANCY	59 years
GDP PER CAPITA	$400

ECONOMY **IND:** blankets, shoes, soap, assembly of imported components, public works construction, food processing **AGR:** coffee, cotton, tea, corn, sorghum, sweet potatoes, bananas, manioc (tapioca), beef, milk, hides **EXP:** coffee, tea, sugar, cotton, hides

Cameroon
REPUBLIC OF CAMEROON

AREA	475,440 sq km
	(183,567 sq mi)
POPULATION	20,130,000
CAPITAL	Yaoundé 1,801,000
RELIGION	Indigenous beliefs,
	Christian, Muslim
LANGUAGE	24 major African language
	groups, English, French
LITERACY	68%
LIFE EXPECTANCY	55 years
GDP PER CAPITA	$2,300

ECONOMY **IND:** petroleum production and refining, aluminum production, food processing, light consumer goods, textiles, lumber, ship repair **AGR:** coffee, cocoa, cotton, rubber, bananas, oilseed, grains, root starches, livestock, timber **EXP:** crude oil and petroleum products, lumber, cocoa beans, aluminum, coffee, cotton

Cape Verde
REPUBLIC OF CAPE VERDE

AREA	4,033 sq km (1,557 sq mi)
POPULATION	524,000
CAPITAL	Praia 135,000
RELIGION	Roman Catholic, Protestant
LANGUAGE	Portuguese, Crioulo
LITERACY	77%
LIFE EXPECTANCY	71 years
GDP PER CAPITA	$4,000

ECONOMY **IND:** food and beverages, fish processing, shoes and garments, salt mining, ship repair **AGR:** bananas, corn, beans, sweet potatoes, sugarcane, coffee, peanuts, fish **EXP:** fuel, shoes, garments, fish, hides

Central African Republic
CENTRAL AFRICAN REPUBLIC

AREA	622,984 sq km
	(240,534 sq mi)
POPULATION	5,057,000
CAPITAL	Bangui 734,000
RELIGION	Indigenous beliefs,
	Protestant, Roman Catholic,
	Muslim
LANGUAGE	French, Sangho
LITERACY	49%
LIFE EXPECTANCY	50 years
GDP PER CAPITA	$800

ECONOMY **IND:** gold and diamond mining, logging, brewing, textiles, footwear, bicycle and motorcycle assembly **AGR:** timber, cotton, coffee, tobacco, manioc (tapioca), yams, millet, corn, bananas, timber **EXP:** diamonds, timber, cotton, coffee, tobacco

Chad
REPUBLIC OF CHAD

AREA	1,284,000 sq km
	(495,752 sq mi)
POPULATION	10,976,000
CAPITAL	N'Djamena 829,000
RELIGION	Muslim, Catholic, Protestant
LANGUAGE	French, Arabic, Sara
LITERACY	26%
LIFE EXPECTANCY	49 years
GDP PER CAPITA	$1,900

ECONOMY **IND:** oil, cotton textiles, meatpacking, brewing, natron (sodium carbonate), soap, cigarettes, construction materials **AGR:** cotton, sorghum, millet, peanuts, rice, potatoes, manioc (tapioca), cattle, sheep, goats, camels **EXP:** oil, cattle, cotton, gum arabic

Comoros
UNION OF THE COMOROS

AREA	2,235 sq km (863 sq mi)
POPULATION	737,000
CAPITAL	Moroni 40,000
RELIGION	Sunni Muslim
LANGUAGE	Arabic, French, Shikomoro
LITERACY	57%
LIFE EXPECTANCY	63 years
GDP PER CAPITA	$1,200

ECONOMY **IND:** fishing, tourism, perfume distillation **AGR:** vanilla, cloves, ylang-ylang (perfume essence), copra, coconuts, bananas, cassava (tapioca) **EXP:** vanilla, ylang-ylang (perfume essence), cloves, copra

Congo
REPUBLIC OF THE CONGO

AREA	342,000 sq km
	(132,046 sq mi)
POPULATION	4,366,000
CAPITAL	Brazzaville 1,323,000
RELIGION	Christian, animist
LANGUAGE	French, Lingala,
	Monokutuba, Kikongo
LITERACY	84%
LIFE EXPECTANCY	55 years
GDP PER CAPITA	$4,600

ECONOMY **IND:** petroleum extraction, cement, lumber, brewing, sugar, palm oil, soap, flour, cigarettes **AGR:** cassava (tapioca), sugar, rice, corn, peanuts, vegetables, coffee, cocoa, forest products **EXP:** petroleum, lumber, plywood, sugar, cocoa, coffee, diamonds

Côte d'Ivoire (Ivory Coast)
REPUBLIC OF
CÔTE D'IVOIRE

AREA	322,463 sq km
	(124,503 sq mi)
POPULATION	21,952,000
CAPITAL	Yamoussoukro (official)
	885,000, Abidjan (adminis-
	trative) 4,125,000
RELIGION	Muslim, Christian, none
LANGUAGE	French, Dioula
LITERACY	49%
LIFE EXPECTANCY	57 years
GDP PER CAPITA	$1,600

ECONOMY **IND:** foodstuffs, beverages, wood products, oil refining, gold mining, truck and bus assembly, textiles, fertilizer, building materials, electricity **AGR:** coffee, cocoa beans, bananas, palm kernels, corn, rice, manioc (tapioca), sweet potatoes, sugar, cotton, rubber, timber **EXP:** cocoa, coffee, timber, petroleum, cotton, bananas, pineapples, palm oil, fish

Democratic Republic of the Congo
DEMOCRATIC REPUBLIC OF THE CONGO

AREA	2,344,858 sq km
	(905,350 sq mi)
POPULATION	73,599,000
CAPITAL	Kinshasa 8,754,000
RELIGION	Roman Catholic, Protestant,
	Kimbanguist, Muslim
LANGUAGE	French, Lingala, Kingwana,
	Kikongo, Tshiluba
LITERACY	67%
LIFE EXPECTANCY	56 years
GDP PER CAPITA	$300

ECONOMY **IND:** mining (diamonds, gold, copper, cobalt, coltan, zinc, tin, diamonds), mineral processing, consumer products (including textiles, plastics, footwear, cigarettes, metal products, processed foods and beverages), timber, cement, commercial ship repair **AGR:** coffee, sugar, palm oil, rubber, tea, cotton, cocoa, quinine, cassava (tapioca), manioc, bananas, plantains, peanuts, root crops, corn, fruits, wood products **EXP:** diamonds, gold, copper, cobalt, wood products, crude oil, coffee

Djibouti
REPUBLIC OF DJIBOUTI

AREA	23,200 sq km
	(8,953 sq mi)
POPULATION	774,000
CAPITAL	Djibouti 514,000
RELIGION	Muslim
LANGUAGE	French, Arabic, Somali,
	Afar
LITERACY	68%
LIFE EXPECTANCY	62 years
GDP PER CAPITA	$2,600

ECONOMY **IND:** construction, agricultural processing **AGR:** fruits, vegetables, goats, sheep, camels, animal hides **EXP:** reexports, hides and skins, coffee (in transit)

Egypt
ARAB REPUBLIC OF EGYPT

AREA	1,001,450 sq km
	(386,560 sq mi)
POPULATION	83,688,000
CAPITAL	Cairo 11,001,000
RELIGION	Muslim
LANGUAGE	Arabic, English, French
LITERACY	71%
LIFE EXPECTANCY	73 years
GDP PER CAPITA	$6,500

ECONOMY **IND:** textiles, food processing, tourism, chemicals, pharmaceuticals, hydrocarbons, construction, cement, metals, light manufactures **AGR:** cotton, rice, corn, wheat, beans, fruits, vegetables, cattle, water buffalo, sheep, goats **EXP:** crude oil and petroleum products, cotton, textiles, metal products, chemicals, processed food

Equatorial Guinea
REPUBLIC OF
EQUATORIAL GUINEA

AREA	28,051 sq km (10,830 sq mi)
POPULATION	686,000
CAPITAL	Malabo 187,000
RELIGION	Roman Catholic, Protestant
LANGUAGE	Spanish, French, Fang, Bubi
LITERACY	87%
LIFE EXPECTANCY	63 years
GDP PER CAPITA	$19,300

ECONOMY **IND:** petroleum, natural gas, sawmilling **AGR:** coffee, cocoa, rice, yams, cassava (tapioca), bananas, palm oil nuts, livestock, timber **EXP:** petroleum products, timber

Eritrea
STATE OF ERITREA

AREA	117,600 sq km (45,405 sq mi)
POPULATION	6,086,000
CAPITAL	Asmara 697,000
RELIGION	Muslim, Coptic Christian, Roman Catholic, Protestant
LANGUAGE	Tigrinya, Arabic, English, Tigre, Kunama, Afar
LITERACY	59%
LIFE EXPECTANCY	63 years
GDP PER CAPITA	$700

ECONOMY **IND:** food processing, beverages, clothing and textiles, light manufacturing, salt, cement **AGR:** sorghum, lentils, vegetables, corn, cotton, tobacco, sisal, livestock, goats, fish **EXP:** livestock, sorghum, textiles, food, small manufactures

Ethiopia
FEDERAL DEMOCRATIC
REPUBLIC OF ETHIOPIA

AREA	1,104,300 sq km (426,370 sq mi)
POPULATION	93,816,000
CAPITAL	Addis Ababa 2,930,000
RELIGION	Orthodox, Muslim, Protestant
LANGUAGE	Amarigna, Orominga, Tigrigna
LITERACY	43%
LIFE EXPECTANCY	57 years
GDP PER CAPITA	$1,100

ECONOMY **IND:** food processing, beverages, textiles, leather, chemicals, metals processing, cement **AGR:** cereals, pulses, coffee, oilseed, cotton, sugarcane, potatoes, khat, cut flowers, hides, cattle, sheep, goats, fish **EXP:** coffee, khat, gold, leather products, live animals, oilseeds

Gabon
GABONESE REPUBLIC

AREA	267,667 sq km (103,346 sq mi)
POPULATION	1,608,000
CAPITAL	Libreville 797,000
RELIGION	Christian, animist
LANGUAGE	French, Fang, Myene, Nzebi, Bapounou/Eschira, Bandjabi
LITERACY	63%
LIFE EXPECTANCY	52 years
GDP PER CAPITA	$16,000

ECONOMY **IND:** petroleum extraction and refining, manganese, gold, chemicals, ship repair, food and beverages, textiles, lumber and plywood, cement **AGR:** cocoa, coffee, sugar, palm oil, rubber, cattle, okoume (a tropical softwood), fish **EXP:** crude oil, timber, manganese, uranium

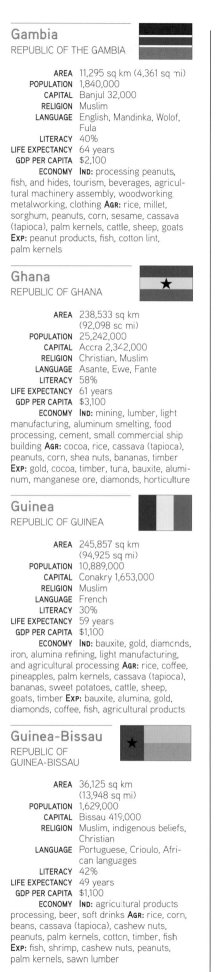

Gambia
REPUBLIC OF THE GAMBIA

AREA	11,295 sq km (4,361 sq mi)
POPULATION	1,840,000
CAPITAL	Banjul 32,000
RELIGION	Muslim
LANGUAGE	English, Mandinka, Wolof, Fula
LITERACY	40%
LIFE EXPECTANCY	64 years
GDP PER CAPITA	$2,100

ECONOMY **IND:** processing peanuts, fish, and hides, tourism, beverages, agricultural machinery assembly, woodworking metalworking, clothing **AGR:** rice, millet, sorghum, peanuts, corn, sesame, cassava (tapioca), palm kernels, cattle, sheep, goats **EXP:** peanut products, fish, cotton lint, palm kernels

Ghana
REPUBLIC OF GHANA

AREA	238,533 sq km (92,098 sq mi)
POPULATION	25,242,000
CAPITAL	Accra 2,342,000
RELIGION	Christian, Muslim
LANGUAGE	Asante, Ewe, Fante
LITERACY	58%
LIFE EXPECTANCY	61 years
GDP PER CAPITA	$3,100

ECONOMY **IND:** mining, lumber, light manufacturing, aluminum smelting, food processing, cement, small commercial ship building **AGR:** cocoa, rice, cassava (tapioca), peanuts, corn, shea nuts, bananas, timber **EXP:** gold, cocoa, timber, tuna, bauxite, aluminum, manganese ore, diamonds, horticulture

Guinea
REPUBLIC OF GUINEA

AREA	245,857 sq km (94,925 sq mi)
POPULATION	10,889,000
CAPITAL	Conakry 1,653,000
RELIGION	Muslim
LANGUAGE	French
LITERACY	30%
LIFE EXPECTANCY	59 years
GDP PER CAPITA	$1,100

ECONOMY **IND:** bauxite, gold, diamonds, iron, alumina refining, light manufacturing, and agricultural processing **AGR:** rice, coffee, pineapples, palm kernels, cassava (tapioca), bananas, sweet potatoes, cattle, sheep, goats, timber **EXP:** bauxite, alumina, gold, diamonds, coffee, fish, agricultural products

Guinea-Bissau
REPUBLIC OF
GUINEA-BISSAU

AREA	36,125 sq km (13,948 sq mi)
POPULATION	1,629,000
CAPITAL	Bissau 419,000
RELIGION	Muslim, indigenous beliefs, Christian
LANGUAGE	Portuguese, Crioulo, African languages
LITERACY	42%
LIFE EXPECTANCY	49 years
GDP PER CAPITA	$1,100

ECONOMY **IND:** agricultural products processing, beer, soft drinks **AGR:** rice, corn, beans, cassava (tapioca), cashew nuts, peanuts, palm kernels, cotton, timber, fish **EXP:** fish, shrimp, cashew nuts, peanuts, palm kernels, sawn lumber

Kenya
REPUBLIC OF KENYA

AREA	580,367 sq km (224,080 sq mi)
POPULATION	43,013,000
CAPITAL	Nairobi 3,523,000
RELIGION	Protestant, Roman Catholic, Muslim, indigenous beliefs
LANGUAGE	English, Kiswahili, indigenous languages
LITERACY	85%
LIFE EXPECTANCY	63 years
GDP PER CAPITA	$1,700

ECONOMY **IND:** small-scale consumer goods, agricultural products, horticulture, oil refining, aluminum, steel, lead, cement, commercial ship repair, tourism **AGR:** tea, coffee, corn, wheat, sugarcane, fruit, vegetables, dairy products, beef, pork, poultry, eggs **EXP:** tea, horticultural products, coffee, petroleum products, fish, cement

Lesotho
KINGDOM OF LESOTHO

AREA	30,355 sq km (11,720 sq mi)
POPULATION	1,930,000
CAPITAL	Maseru 268,000
RELIGION	Christian, indigenous beliefs
LANGUAGE	Sesotho, English, Zulu, Xhosa
LITERACY	85%
LIFE EXPECTANCY	52 years
GDP PER CAPITA	$1,400

ECONOMY **IND:** food, beverages, textiles, apparel assembly, construction, tourism **AGR:** corn, wheat, pulses, sorghum, barley, livestock **EXP:** manufactures (clothing, footwear, vehicles), wool and mohair, food and live animals

Liberia
REPUBLIC OF LIBERIA

AREA	111,369 sq km (43,000 sq mi)
POPULATION	3,888,000
CAPITAL	Monrovia 827,000
RELIGION	Christian, Muslim
LANGUAGE	English, some 20 ethnic group languages
LITERACY	58%
LIFE EXPECTANCY	57 years
GDP PER CAPITA	$400

ECONOMY **IND:** rubber processing, palm oil processing, timber, diamonds **AGR:** rubber, coffee, cocoa, rice, cassava (tapioca), palm oil, sugarcane, bananas, sheep, goats, timber **EXP:** rubber, timber, iron, diamonds, cocoa, coffee

Libya
LIBYA

AREA	1,759,540 sq km (679,358 sq mi)
POPULATION	6,734,000
CAPITAL	Tripoli 1,108,000
RELIGION	Sunni Muslim
LANGUAGE	Arabic, Italian, English
LITERACY	83%
LIFE EXPECTANCY	78 years
GDP PER CAPITA	$14,100

ECONOMY **IND:** petroleum, petrochemicals, aluminum, iron and steel, food processing, textiles, handicrafts, cement **AGR:** wheat, barley, olives, dates, citrus, vegetables, peanuts, soybeans, cattle **EXP:** crude oil, refined petroleum products, natural gas, chemicals

Madagascar
REPUBLIC OF MADAGASCAR

AREA	587,041 sq km (226,657 sq mi)
POPULATION	22,586,000
CAPITAL	Antananarivo 1,879,000
RELIGION	Indigenous beliefs, Christian
LANGUAGE	French, Malagasy, English
LITERACY	69%
LIFE EXPECTANCY	64 years
GDP PER CAPITA	$900

ECONOMY **IND:** meat processing, seafood, soap, breweries, tanneries, sugar, textiles, glassware, cement, automobile assembly plant, paper, petroleum, tourism **AGR:** coffee, vanilla, sugarcane, cloves, Christian rice, cassava (tapioca), beans, bananas, peanuts, livestock products **EXP:** coffee, vanilla, shellfish, sugar, cotton cloth, chromite, petroleum products

Malawi
REPUBLIC OF MALAWI

AREA	118,484 sq km (45,747 sq mi)
POPULATION	16,323,000
CAPITAL	Lilongwe 865,000
RELIGION	Christian, Muslim
LANGUAGE	Chichewa, Chinyanja, Chiyao, Chitumbuka
LITERACY	63%
LIFE EXPECTANCY	52 years
GDP PER CAPITA	$900

ECONOMY **IND:** tobacco, tea, sugar, sawmill products, cement, consumer goods **AGR:** tobacco, sugarcane, cotton, tea, corn, potatoes, cassava (tapioca), sorghum, pulses, groundnuts, Macadamia nuts, cattle, goats **EXP:** tobacco, tea, sugar, cotton, coffee, peanuts, wood products, apparel

Mali
REPUBLIC OF MALI

AREA	1,240,192 sq km (478,838 sq mi)
POPULATION	14,534,000
CAPITAL	Bamako 1,699,000
RELIGION	Muslim
LANGUAGE	French, Bambara
LITERACY	46%
LIFE EXPECTANCY	53 years
GDP PER CAPITA	$1,300

ECONOMY **IND:** food processing, construction, phosphate and gold mining **AGR:** cotton, millet, rice, corn, vegetables, peanuts, cattle, sheep, goats **EXP:** cotton, gold, livestock

Mauritania
ISLAMIC REPUBLIC OF
MAURITANIA

AREA	1,030,700 sq km (397,953 sq mi)
POPULATION	3,359,000
CAPITAL	Nouakchott 870,000
RELIGION	Muslim
LANGUAGE	Arabic, Pulaar, Soninke, Wolof, French, Hassaniya
LITERACY	51%
LIFE EXPECTANCY	62 years
GDP PER CAPITA	$2,200

ECONOMY **IND:** fish processing, oil production, iron ore, gold, copper **AGR:** dates, millet, sorghum, rice, corn, cattle, sheep **EXP:** iron ore, fish and fish products, gold, copper, petroleum

Mauritius
REPUBLIC OF MAURITIUS

AREA 2,040 sq km (788 sq mi)
POPULATION 1,313,000
CAPITAL Port Louis 159,000
RELIGION Hindu, Roman Catholic, Muslim
LANGUAGE Creole, Bhojpuri, French, English
LITERACY 84%
LIFE EXPECTANCY 75 years
GDP PER CAPITA $15,000
ECONOMY IND: food processing (largely sugar milling), textiles, clothing, mining, chemicals, metal products, transport equipment, nonelectrical machinery, tourism AGR: sugarcane, tea, corn, potatoes, bananas, pulses, cattle, goats, fish EXP: clothing and textiles, sugar, cut flowers, molasses, fish

Morocco
KINGDOM OF MOROCCO

AREA 446,550 sq km (172,413 sq mi)
POPULATION 32,309,000
CAPITAL Rabat 1,802,000
RELIGION Muslim
LANGUAGE Arabic, Berber dialects, French
LITERACY 52%
LIFE EXPECTANCY 76 years
GDP PER CAPITA $5,100
ECONOMY IND: phosphate rock mining and processing, food processing, leather goods, textiles, construction, energy, tourism AGR: barley, wheat, citrus fruits, grapes, vegetables, olives, livestock, wine EXP: clothing and textiles, electric components, inorganic chemicals, transistors, crude minerals, fertilizers (including phosphates), petroleum products, citrus fruits, vegetables, fish

Mozambique
REPUBLIC OF MOZAMBIQUE

AREA 799,380 sq km (308,641 sq mi)
POPULATION 23,516,000
CAPITAL Maputo 1,655,000
RELIGION Catholic, Protestant, Muslim
LANGUAGE Emakhuwa, Portuguese, Xichangana
LITERACY 48%
LIFE EXPECTANCY 52 years
GDP PER CAPITA $1,100
ECONOMY IND: food, beverages, chemicals (fertilizer, soap, paints), aluminum, petroleum products, textiles, cement, glass, asbestos, tobacco AGR: cotton, cashew nuts, sugarcane, tea, cassava (tapioca), corn, coconuts, sisal, citrus and tropical fruits, potatoes, sunflowers, beef, poultry EXP: aluminum, prawns, cashews, cotton, sugar, citrus, timber, bulk electricity

Namibia
REPUBLIC OF NAMIBIA

AREA 824,292 sq km (318,259 sq mi)
POPULATION 2,166,000
CAPITAL Windhoek 335,000
RELIGION Christian, indigenous beliefs
LANGUAGE English, Afrikaans, German
LITERACY 85%
LIFE EXPECTANCY 52 years
GDP PER CAPITA $7,300
ECONOMY IND: meatpacking, fish processing, dairy products, mining (diamonds, lead, zinc, tin, silver, tungsten, uranium, copper) AGR: millet, sorghum, peanuts, grapes, livestock, fish EXP: diamonds, copper, gold, zinc, lead, uranium, cattle, processed fish, karakul skins

Niger
REPUBLIC OF NIGER

AREA 1,267,000 sq km (489,189 sq mi)
POPULATION 17,079,000
CAPITAL Niamey 1,048,000
RELIGION Muslim
LANGUAGE French, Hausa, Djerma
LITERACY 29%
LIFE EXPECTANCY 54 years
GDP PER CAPITA $800
ECONOMY IND: uranium mining, cement, brick, soap, textiles, food processing, chemicals, slaughterhouses AGR: cowpeas, cotton, peanuts, millet, sorghum, cassava (tapioca), rice, cattle, sheep, goats, camels, donkeys, horses, poultry EXP: uranium ore, livestock, cowpeas, onions

Nigeria
FEDERAL REPUBLIC OF NIGERIA

AREA 923,768 sq km (356,667 sq mi)
POPULATION 170,124,000
CAPITAL Abuja 1,995,000
RELIGION Muslim, Christian, indigenous beliefs
LANGUAGE English, Hausa, Yoruba, Igbo, Fulani
LITERACY 68%
LIFE EXPECTANCY 52 years
GDP PER CAPITA $2,600
ECONOMY IND: crude oil, coal, tin, columbite, rubber products, wood, hides and skins, textiles, cement and other construction materials, food products, footwear, chemicals, fertilizer, printing, ceramics, steel AGR: cocoa, peanuts, cotton, palm oil, corn, rice, sorghum, millet, cassava (tapioca), yams, rubber, cattle, sheep, goats, pigs, timber, fish EXP: petroleum and petroleum products, cocoa, rubber

Rwanda
REPUBLIC OF RWANDA

AREA 26,338 sq km (10,169 sq mi)
POPULATION 11,690,000
CAPITAL Kigali 939,000
RELIGION Roman Catholic, Protestant, Adventist
LANGUAGE Kinyarwanda, French, English, Kiswahili
LITERACY 70%
LIFE EXPECTANCY 58 years
GDP PER CAPITA $1,300
ECONOMY IND: cement, agricultural products, small-scale beverages, soap, furniture, shoes, plastic goods, textiles, cigarettes AGR: coffee, tea, pyrethrum (insecticide made from chrysanthemums), bananas, beans, sorghum, potatoes, livestock EXP: coffee, tea, hides, tin ore

Sao Tome and Principe
DEMOCRATIC REPUBLIC OF SAO TOME AND PRINCIPE

AREA 964 sq km (372 sq mi)
POPULATION 183,000
CAPITAL São Tomé 68,000
RELIGION Catholic, none
LANGUAGE Portuguese
LITERACY 85%
LIFE EXPECTANCY 63 years
GDP PER CAPITA $2,000
ECONOMY IND: light construction, textiles, soap, beer, fish processing, timber AGR: cocoa, coconuts, palm kernels, copra, cinnamon, pepper, coffee, bananas, papayas, beans, poultry, fish EXP: cocoa, copra, coffee, palm oil

Senegal
REPUBLIC OF SENEGAL

AREA 196,722 sq km (75,954 sq mi)
POPULATION 12,970,000
CAPITAL Dakar 2,863,000
RELIGION Muslim
LANGUAGE French, Wolof, Pulaar, Jola, Mandinka
LITERACY 39%
LIFE EXPECTANCY 60 years
GDP PER CAPITA $1,900
ECONOMY IND: agricultural and fish processing, phosphate mining, fertilizer production, petroleum refining, iron ore, zircon, gold, construction materials, ship construction and repair AGR: peanuts, millet, corn, sorghum, rice, cotton, tomatoes, green vegetables, cattle, poultry, pigs, fish EXP: fish, groundnuts (peanuts), petroleum products, phosphates, cotton

Seychelles
REPUBLIC OF SEYCHELLES

AREA 455 sq km (176 sq mi)
POPULATION 90,000
CAPITAL Victoria 21,000
RELIGION Roman Catholic
LANGUAGE Creole, English
LITERACY 92%
LIFE EXPECTANCY 74 years
GDP PER CAPITA $24,700
ECONOMY IND: fishing, tourism, processing of coconuts and vanilla, coir (coconut fiber) rope, boat building, printing, furniture, beverages AGR: coconuts, cinnamon, vanilla, sweet potatoes, cassava (tapioca), copra, bananas, poultry, tuna EXP: canned tuna, frozen fish, cinnamon bark, copra, petroleum products (reexports)

Sierra Leone
REPUBLIC OF SIERRA LEONE

AREA 71,740 sq km (27,699 sq mi)
POPULATION 5,486,000
CAPITAL Freetown 901,000
RELIGION Muslim, indigenous beliefs, Christian
LANGUAGE English, Mende, Temne, Krio
LITERACY 35%
LIFE EXPECTANCY 57 years
GDP PER CAPITA $800
ECONOMY IND: diamond mining, small-scale manufacturing (beverages, textiles, cigarettes, footwear), petroleum refining, small commercial ship repair AGR: rice, coffee, cocoa, palm kernels, palm oil, peanuts, poultry, cattle, sheep, pigs, fish EXP: diamonds, rutile, cocoa, coffee, fish

Somalia
SOMALIA

AREA 637,657 sq km (246,199 sq mi)
POPULATION 10,086,000
CAPITAL Modagishu 1,500,000
RELIGION Sunni Muslim
LANGUAGE Somali, Arabic, Italian, English
LITERACY 38%
LIFE EXPECTANCY 51 years
GDP PER CAPITA $600
ECONOMY IND: sugar refining, textiles, wireless communication AGR: bananas, sorghum, corn, coconuts, rice, sugarcane, mangoes, sesame seeds, beans, cattle, sheep, goats, fish EXP: livestock, bananas, hides, fish, charcoal, scrap metal

South Africa
REPUBLIC OF SOUTH AFRICA

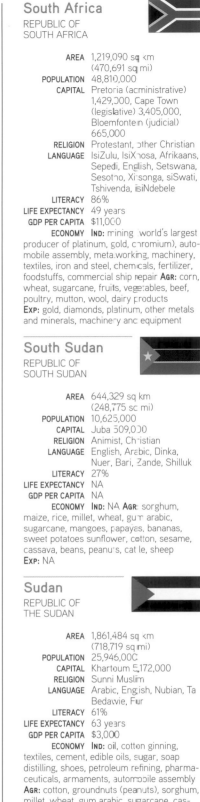

AREA 1,219,090 sq km (470,691 sq mi)
POPULATION 48,810,000
CAPITAL Pretoria (administrative) 1,429,000, Cape Town (legislative) 3,405,000, Bloemfontein (judicial) 665,000
RELIGION Protestant, other Christian
LANGUAGE IsiZulu, IsiXhosa, Afrikaans, Sepedi, English, Setswana, Sesotho, Xitsonga, siSwati, Tshivenda, isiNdebele
LITERACY 86%
LIFE EXPECTANCY 49 years
GDP PER CAPITA $11,000
ECONOMY IND: mining world's largest producer of platinum, gold, chromium), automobile assembly, metalworking, machinery, textiles, iron and steel, chemicals, fertilizer, foodstuffs, commercial ship repair AGR: corn, wheat, sugarcane, fruits, vegetables, beef, poultry, mutton, wool, dairy products EXP: gold, diamonds, platinum, other metals and minerals, machinery and equipment

South Sudan
REPUBLIC OF SOUTH SUDAN

AREA 644,329 sq km (248,775 sq mi)
POPULATION 10,625,000
CAPITAL Juba 509,000
RELIGION Animist, Christian
LANGUAGE English, Arabic, Dinka, Nuer, Bari, Zande, Shilluk
LITERACY 27%
LIFE EXPECTANCY NA
GDP PER CAPITA NA
ECONOMY IND: NA AGR: sorghum, maize, rice, millet, wheat, gum arabic, sugarcane, mangoes, papayas, bananas, sweet potatoes sunflower, cotton, sesame, cassava, beans, peanuts, cattle, sheep EXP: NA

Sudan
REPUBLIC OF THE SUDAN

AREA 1,861,484 sq km (718,719 sq mi)
POPULATION 25,946,000
CAPITAL Khartoum 5,172,000
RELIGION Sunni Muslim
LANGUAGE Arabic, English, Nubian, Ta Bedawie, Fur
LITERACY 61%
LIFE EXPECTANCY 63 years
GDP PER CAPITA $3,000
ECONOMY IND: oil, cotton ginning, textiles, cement, edible oils, sugar, soap distilling, shoes, petroleum refining, pharmaceuticals, armaments, automobile assembly AGR: cotton, groundnuts (peanuts), sorghum, millet, wheat, gum arabic, sugarcane, cassava (tapioca), mangos, papaya, bananas, sweet potatoes, sesame, sheep and other livestock EXP: oil and petroleum products, cotton, sesame, livestock, groundnuts, gum arabic, sugar

Swaziland
KINGDOM OF SWAZILAND

AREA 17,364 sq km (6,704 sq mi)
POPULATION 1,387,000
CAPITAL Mbabane (administrative) 63,000, Lobamba (royal and legislative) 4,000
RELIGION Zionist, Roman Catholic, Muslim
LANGUAGE English, siSwati
LITERACY 82%
LIFE EXPECTANCY 49 years
GDP PER CAPITA $5,200
ECONOMY IND: coal, wood pulp, sugar, soft drink concentrates, textiles and apparel AGR: sugarcane, cotton, corn, tobacco, rice, citrus, pineapples, sorghum, peanuts, cattle, goats, sheep EXP: soft drink concentrates, sugar, wood pulp, cotton yarn, refrigerators, citrus and canned fruit

Tanzania
UNITED REPUBLIC OF TANZANIA

AREA	947,300 sq km (365,753 sq mi)
POPULATION	43,602,000
CAPITAL	Dar es Salaam (administrative) 3,349,000; Dodoma (legislative) 191,000
RELIGION	Muslim, indigenous beliefs, Christian
LANGUAGE	Kiswahili, Swahili, English, Arabic
LITERACY	69%
LIFE EXPECTANCY	53 years
GDP PER CAPITA	$1,500

ECONOMY IND: agricultural processing (sugar, beer, cigarettes, sisal twine); diamond, gold, and iron mining, salt, soda ash; cement, o l refining, shoes, apparel, wood products, fertilizer **AGR:** coffee, sisal, tea, cotton, pyrethrum (insecticide made from chrysanthemums), cashew nuts, tobacco, cloves, corn, wheat, cassava (tapioca), bananas, fruits, vegetables; cattle, sheep, goats **EXP:** gold, coffee, cashew nuts, manufactures, cotton

Togo
TOGOLESE REPUBLIC

AREA	56,785 sq km (21,925 sq mi)
POPULATION	6,961,000
CAPITAL	Lomé 1,667,000
RELIGION	indigenous beliefs, Christian, Muslim
LANGUAGE	French, Ewe, Mina, Kabye, Dagomba
LITERACY	61%
LIFE EXPECTANCY	63 years
GDP PER CAPITA	$900

ECONOMY IND: phosphate mining, agricultural processing, cement, handicrafts, textiles, beverages **AGR:** coffee, cocoa, cotton, yams, cassava (tapioca), corn, beans, rice, millet, sorghum; livestock; fish **EXP:** reexports cotton, phosphates, coffee, cocoa

Tunisia
TUNISIAN REPUBLIC

AREA	163,610 sq km (63,170 sq mi)
POPULATION	10,733,000
CAPITAL	Tunis 767,000
RELIGION	Muslim
LANGUAGE	Arabic, French
LITERACY	74%
LIFE EXPECTANCY	75 years
GDP PER CAPITA	$9,500

ECONOMY IND: petroleum, mining (particularly phosphate and iron ore), tourism, textiles, footwear, agribusiness, beverages **AGR:** olives, olive oil, grain, tomatoes, citrus fruit, sugar beets, dates, almonds; beef, dairy products **EXP:** clothing, semi-finished goods and textiles, agricultural products, mechanical goods, phosphates and chemicals, hydrocarbons, electrical equipment

Uganda
REPUBLIC OF UGANDA

AREA	241,038 sq km (93,065 sq mi)
POPULATION	35,873,000
CAPITAL	Kampala 1,598,000
RELIGION	Roman Catholic, Protestant, Muslim
LANGUAGE	English, Ganda, Luganda, Swahili, Arabic
LITERACY	67%
LIFE EXPECTANCY	53 years
GDP PER CAPITA	$1,300

ECONOMY IND: sugar, brewing, tobacco, cotton textiles; cement, steel production **AGR:** coffee, tea, cotton, tobacco, cassava (tapioca), potatoes, corn, millet, pulses, cut flowers; beef, goat meat, milk, poultry **EXP:** coffee, fish and fish products, tea, cotton, flowers, horticultural products; gold

Zambia
REPUBLIC OF ZAMBIA

AREA	752,618 sq km (290,586 sq mi)
POPULATION	14,309,000
CAPITAL	Lusaka 1,451,000
RELIGION	Christian, Muslim, Hindu
LANGUAGE	Bemba, Nyanja, Tonga, Lozi, Lunda, Kaonde, Luvale, English
LITERACY	81%
LIFE EXPECTANCY	53 years
GDP PER CAPITA	$1,600

ECONOMY IND: copper mining and processing, construction, foodstuffs, beverages, chemicals, textiles, fertilizer, horticulture **AGR:** corn, sorghum, rice, peanuts, sunflower seed, vegetables, flowers, tobacco, cotton, sugarcane, cassava (tapioca), coffee; cattle, goats, pigs, poultry, milk, eggs, hides **EXP:** copper, cobalt, electricity; tobacco, flowers, cotton

Zimbabwe
REPUBLIC OF ZIMBABWE

AREA	390,757 sq km (150,871 sq mi)
POPULATION	12,620,000
CAPITAL	Harare 1,632,000
RELIGION	Syncretic, Christian, indigenous beliefs
LANGUAGE	English, Shona, Sindebele
LITERACY	91%
LIFE EXPECTANCY	52 years
GDP PER CAPITA	$500

ECONOMY IND: mining (coal, gold, platinum, copper, nickel, tin, diamonds, clay, numerous metallic and nonmetallic ores), steel; wood products, cement, chemicals, fertilizer, clothing and footwear, foodstuffs, beverages **AGR:** corn, cotton, tobacco, wheat, coffee, sugarcane, peanuts; sheep, goats, pigs **EXP:** platinum, cotton, tobacco, gold, ferroalloys, textiles/clothing

DEPENDENCIES

Mayotte, Réunion
(FRANCE)

Mayotte and Réunion are now recognized as French regions, having equal status to the 22 metropolitan regions that make up European France. Please see "France" for facts about Mayotte and Réunion.

St. Helena
(U.K.)
SAINT HELENA, ASCENSION, AND TRISTAN DA CUNHA

AREA	308 sq km (119 sq mi)
POPULATION	7,700
CAPITAL	Jamestown 400
RELIGION	Protestant, Roman Catholic
LANGUAGE	English
LITERACY	97%
LIFE EXPECTANCY	79 years
GDP PER CAPITA	$2,500

ECONOMY IND: construction, crafts (furniture, lacework, fancy woodwork), fishing, philatelic sales **AGR:** coffee, corn, potatoes, vegetables; timber; fish, lobster; livestock **EXP:** fish (frozen, canned, and salt-dried skipjack, tuna), coffee, handicrafts

Western Sahara
(MOROCCO)
WESTERN SAHARA

AREA	266,000 sq km (102,703 sq mi)
POPULATION	523,000
CAPITAL	Laayoune 200,000
RELIGION	Muslim
LANGUAGE	Arabic
LITERACY	NA
LIFE EXPECTANCY	62 years
GDP PER CAPITA	$2,500

ECONOMY IND: phosphate mining, handicrafts **AGR:** fruits and vegetables, camels, sheep, goats, fish **EXP:** phosphates

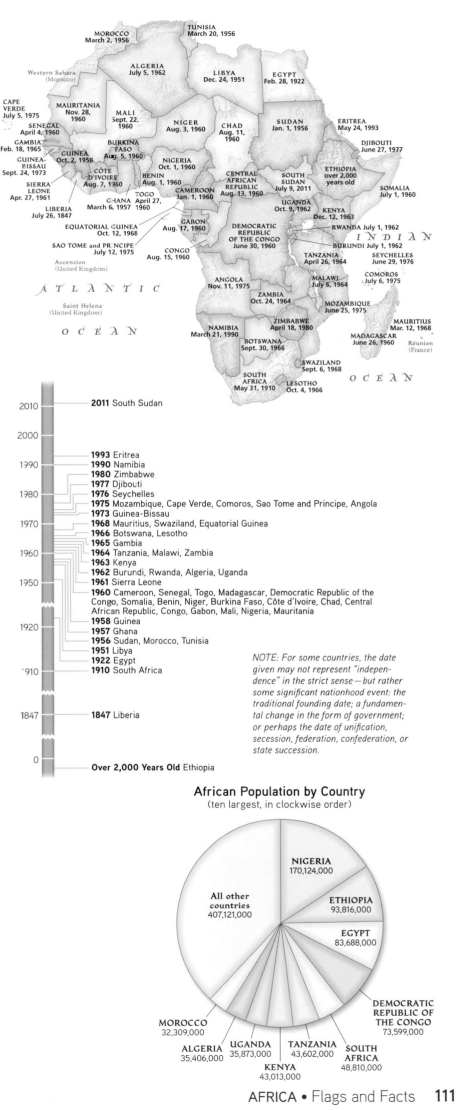

2010	
	2011 South Sudan
2000	
1990	**1993** Eritrea
	1990 Namibia
	1980 Zimbabwe
1980	**1977** Djibouti
	1976 Seychelles
	1975 Mozambique, Cape Verde, Comoros, Sao Tome and Principe, Angola
	1973 Guinea-Bissau
1970	**1968** Mauritius, Swaziland, Equatorial Guinea
	1966 Botswana, Lesotho
	1965 Gambia
1960	**1964** Tanzania, Malawi, Zambia
	1963 Kenya
	1962 Burundi, Rwanda, Algeria, Uganda
1950	**1961** Sierra Leone
	1960 Cameroon, Senegal, Togo, Madagascar, Democratic Republic of the Congo, Somalia, Benin, Niger, Burkina Faso, Côte d'Ivoire, Chad, Central African Republic, Congo, Gabon, Mali, Nigeria, Mauritania
1920	**1958** Guinea
	1957 Ghana
	1956 Sudan, Morocco, Tunisia
	1951 Libya
	1922 Egypt
1910	**1910** South Africa
1847	**1847** Liberia
0	**Over 2,000 Years Old** Ethiopia

NOTE: For some countries, the date given may not represent "independence" in the strict sense—but rather some significant nationhood event: the traditional founding date; a fundamental change in the form of government; or perhaps the date of unification, secession, federation, confederation, or state succession.

African Population by Country
(ten largest, in clockwise order)

NIGERIA 170,124,000
ETHIOPIA 93,816,000
EGYPT 83,688,000
DEMOCRATIC REPUBLIC OF THE CONGO 73,599,000
SOUTH AFRICA 48,810,000
TANZANIA 43,602,000
KENYA 43,013,000
UGANDA 35,873,000
ALGERIA 35,406,000
MOROCCO 32,309,000
All other countries 407,121,000

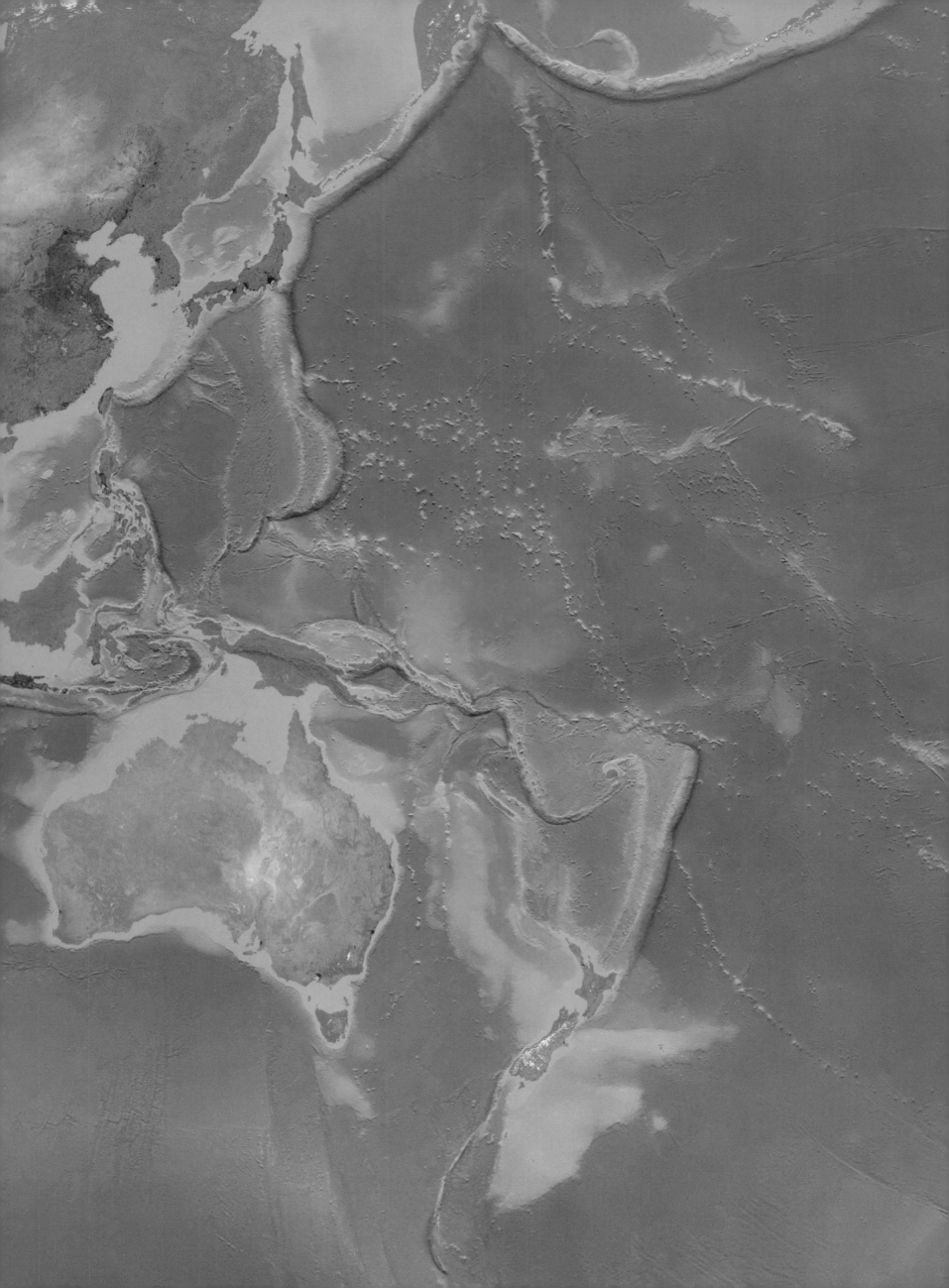

Australia and Oceania

AUSTRALIA IS A CONTINENT OF EXTREMES—smallest and flattest, it's also the only continent-nation, with a landmass equal to that of the lower 48 states of the U.S. Yet it is less populous than any other continent except Antarctica. And more than 80 percent of its people inhabit only the 1 percent of the continent that stretches along the southeast and south coasts. The sun-scorched outback that swells across the Australian interior has daunted virtually all comers, except the Aborigines. Traditionally hunter-gatherers, the Aborigines for eons—long before the arrival of Europeans—considered it home, both spiritually and physically.

The continent itself has been on a kind of planetary walkabout since it broke away from the supercontinent of Gondwana about 65 million years ago. Isolated, dry, and scorched by erosion, Australia developed its own unique species. Kangaroos, koalas, and duck-billed platypuses are well-known examples, but it also boasts rare plants, including 600 species of eucalyptus. The land surface has been stable enough to preserve some of the world's oldest rocks and mineral deposits, while the two islands of its neighboring nation New Zealand are younger and tell of a more violent geology that raised high volcanic mountains above deep fjords. Both nations share a past as British colonies, but each has in recent decades transformed itself from a ranching-based society into a fully industrialized and service-oriented economy.

Sitting at the southwestern edge of Oceania, Australia, with its growing ties to Asia and the Pacific Rim, is the economic powerhouse in this region. By contrast the islands of Oceania—more than 10,000 of them sprawling across the vast stretches of the central and South Pacific—are in various states of nationhood or dependency, prosperity or poverty, and often ignored, if not outright exploited. Their diverse populations and cultures are testament to the seafaring peoples who began settling these islands several thousand years ago, again long before the explorations and exploitations of Europeans in the 16th through the 19th century.

Geographers today divide Oceania into three major ethnographic regions. The largest, Polynesia, or "many islands," composes an immense oceanic triangle, with apexes at Hawai'i in the north, Easter Island in the east, and New Zealand in the southwest. The second Oceanic region, Melanesia, derives its name from the Greek words for "black islands"—either a reference to its dark, lush landscapes or what European explorers described as the dark skin of most of its inhabitants. North and east of Australia, Melanesia encompasses such groups as the Bismarck Archipelago, the Solomon Islands, the Santa Cruz Islands, Vanuatu, the Fiji Islands, and New Caledonia. North of Melanesia, Micronesia contains a widely scattered group of small islands and coral atolls, as well as the world's deepest ocean point—the 35,827-foot-deep (10,920-meter-deep) Challenger Deep—located in the southern Mariana Trench off the southwest coast of Guam. Micronesia stretches across more than 3,000 miles (4,830 kilometers) of the western Pacific, with volcanic peaks that reach 2,500 feet (760 meters). Palau; Nauru; and the Caroline, Mariana, Marshall, and Gilbert Islands all form this third subdivision of Oceania.

CONTINENTAL DATA

TOTAL NUMBER OF COUNTRIES: 1

DATE OF INDEPENDENCE:
January 1, 1901

AREA OF AUSTRALIA:
7,741,220 sq km (2,988,885 sq mi)

PERCENT URBAN POPULATION: 73%

POPULATION OF AUSTRALIA:
22,016,000

POPULATION DENSITY:
2.8 per sq km (7.4 per sq mi)

LARGEST CITY BY POPULATION:
Sydney, Australia 4,429,000

GDP PER CAPITA:
Australia $32,900

AVERAGE LIFE EXPECTANCY: 81 years

AVERAGE LITERACY RATE: 93%

CONTINENTAL DATA

AREA: 7,687,000 sq km (2,968,000 sq mi)

GREATEST NORTH-SOUTH EXTENT:
3,138 km (1,950 mi)

GREATEST EAST-WEST EXTENT:
3,983 km (2,475 mi)

HIGHEST POINT:
Mount Kosciuszko, New South Wales
2,228 m (7,310 ft)

LOWEST POINT:
Lake Eyre -16 m (-52 ft)

LOWEST RECORDED TEMPERATURE:
Charlotte Pass, New South Wales
-23°C (-9.4°F), June 29, 1994

HIGHEST RECORDED TEMPERATURE:
Cloncurry, Queensland 53.3°C
(128°F), January 16, 1889

LONGEST RIVERS:
• Murray 2,375 km (1,476 mi)
• Murrumbidgee 1,485 km (923 mi)
• Darling 1,472 km (915 mi)

LARGEST NATURAL LAKES (AUS.):
• Lake Eyre 0-9,690 sq km
  (0-3,741 sq mi)
• Lake Torrens 0-5,745 sq km
  (0-2,218 sq mi)
• Lake Gairdner 0-4,351 sq km
  (0-1,680 sq mi)

EARTH'S EXTREMES

LOCATED IN AUSTRALIA:
• Longest Reef:
  Great Barrier Reef 2,300 km (1,429 mi)

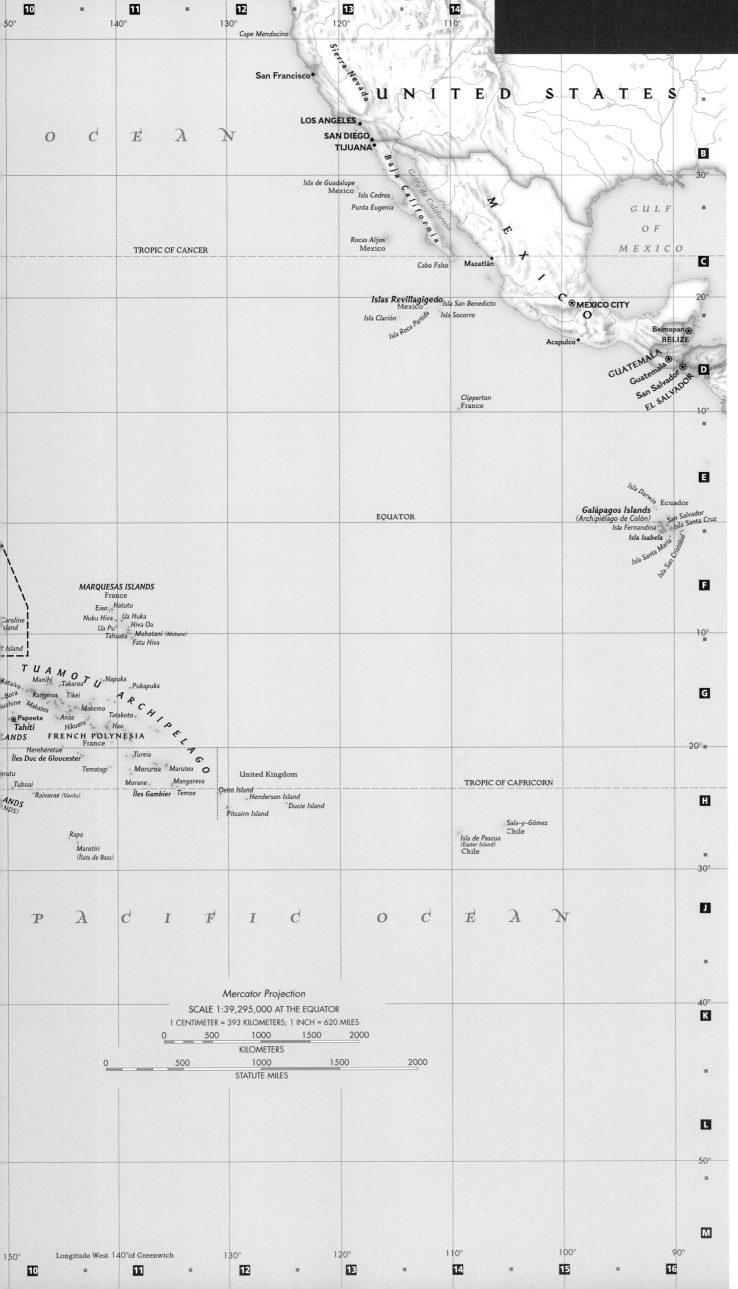

10   11   12   13   14
150°   140°   130°   120°   110°

Cape Mendocino

Sierra Nevada

San Francisco •

U N I T E D   S T A T E S

LOS ANGELES •
SAN DIEGO •
TIJUANA •

O C E A N

Baja California

Golfo de California

Isla de Guadalupe
Mexico
Isla Cedros
Punta Eugenia

M E X I C O

GULF
OF
MEXICO

B
30°

Rocas Alijos
Mexico

TROPIC OF CANCER

Cabo Falso   • Mazatlán

C

Islas Revillagigedo
Mexico
Isla San Benedicto

Isla Clarión
Isla Socorro

⊛ MEXICO CITY

20°

O

Belmopan •
BELIZE

Isla Roca Partida

Acapulco •

D

GUATEMALA ⊛

Guatemala
San Salvador •
EL SALVADOR

Clipperton
France

10°

Galápagos Islands
(Archipiélago de Colón)

Isla Darwin   Ecuador

Isla Fernandina
Isla Isabela

San Salvador
Isla Santa Cruz

E

EQUATOR

Isla Santa María

Isla San Cristóbal

F

MARQUESAS ISLANDS
France

Eiao   Hatutu
Nuku Hiva   Ua Huka
Ua Pu   Hiva Oa
Tahuata   Mohotani (Motane)
Fatu Hiva

10°

Caroline
Island

Island

G

Mataiva   Manihi   Napuka
Bora   Takaroa   Pukapuka
Rangiroa   Tikei
uahine   Makatea   Makemo
Papeete   Anaa   Tatakoto
Tahiti   Hikueru   Hao
FRENCH POLYNESIA
France

T U A M O T U   A R C H I P E L A G O

ANDS

20°

Hereheretue
Îles Duc de Gloucester

Tureia

arutu   Tematagi   Moruroa   Marutea
Tubuai   Morane   Mangareva
Raivavae (Vavitu)   Îles Gambier   Temoe

United Kingdom

TROPIC OF CAPRICORN

ANDS
NDS)

Oeno Island
Henderson Island
Pitcairn Island   Ducie Island

H

Rapa
Marotiri
(Îlots de Bass)

Sala-y-Gómez
Chile

Isla de Pascua
(Easter Island)
Chile

30°

P A C I F I C   O C E A N

J

Mercator Projection

SCALE 1:39,295,000 AT THE EQUATOR

1 CENTIMETER = 393 KILOMETERS; 1 INCH = 620 MILES

0   500   1000   1500   2000
KILOMETERS

0   500   1000   1500   2000
STATUTE MILES

40°
K

50°
L

M

150°   Longitude West 140° of Greenwich   130°   120°   110°   100°   90°

10   11   12   13   14   15   16

REGIONAL DATA

Total number of countries: 13

First independent country:
Samoa, January 1, 1962

"Youngest" country:
Palau, October 1, 1994

Largest country by area:
Solomon Islands 28,370 sq km
(10,954 sq mi)

Smallest country by area:
Nauru 21 sq km (8 sq mi)

Percent urban population: 39%

Most populous country:
Fiji 842,000

Least populous country:
Tuvalu 10,000

**Most densely populated
country:**
Nauru 619 per sq km
(1,625 per sq mi)

**Least densely populated
country:**
Solomon Islands 17 per sq km
(43 per sq mi)

Largest city by population:
Suva, Fiji 210,000

Highest GDP per capita:
Palau $6,717

Lowest GDP per capita:
Solomon Islands $600

**Average life expectancy
in Oceania:** 67 years

**Average literacy rate
in Oceania:** 89%

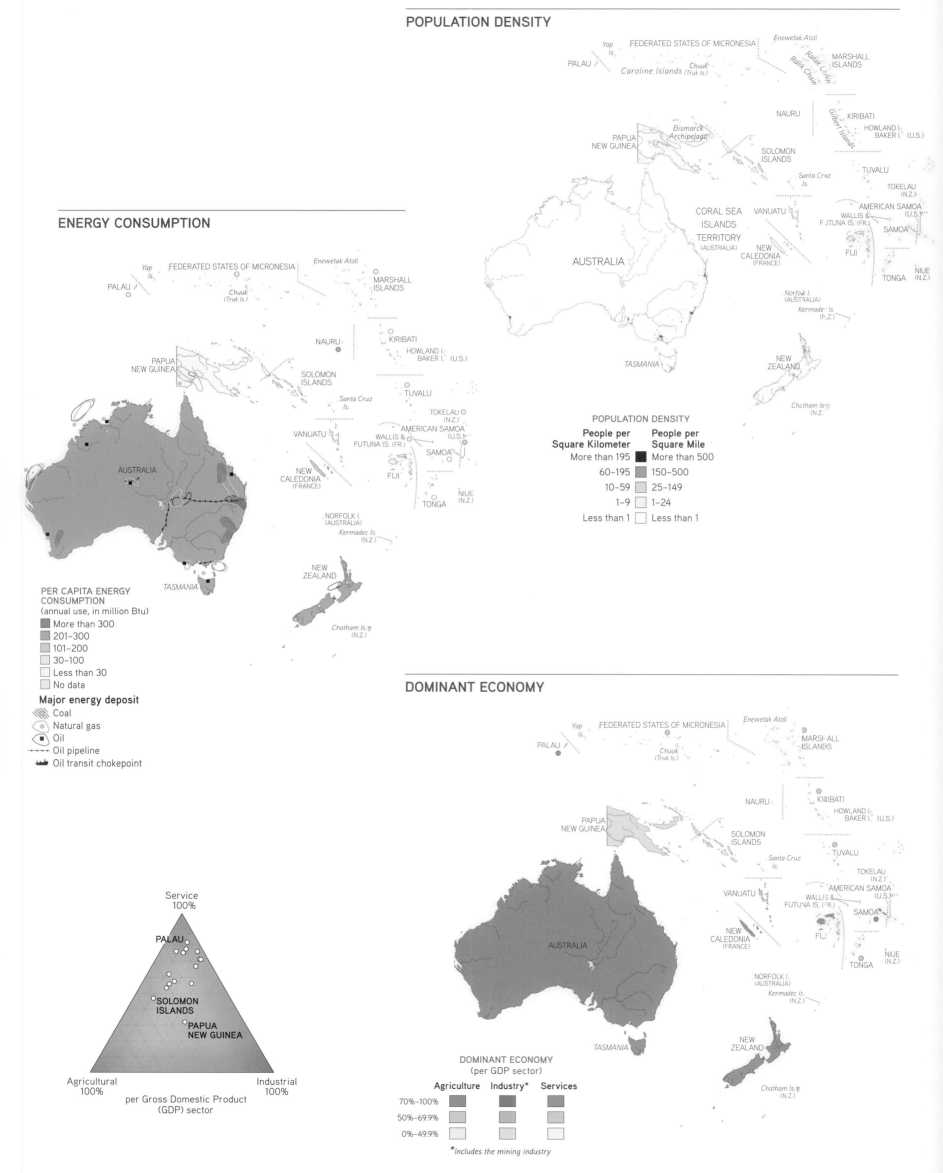

POPULATION DENSITY

POPULATION DENSITY

People per Square Kilometer		People per Square Mile
More than 195	■	More than 500
60–195	■	150–500
10–59	■	25–149
1–9	□	1–24
Less than 1	□	Less than 1

ENERGY CONSUMPTION

PER CAPITA ENERGY CONSUMPTION
(annual use, in million Btu)

- ■ More than 300
- ■ 201–300
- ■ 101–200
- □ 30–100
- □ Less than 30
- □ No data

Major energy deposit

- Coal
- Natural gas
- Oil
- Oil pipeline
- Oil transit chokepoint

DOMINANT ECONOMY

Service 100%

PALAU

SOLOMON ISLANDS

PAPUA NEW GUINEA

Agricultural 100%

Industrial 100%

per Gross Domestic Product (GDP) sector

DOMINANT ECONOMY
(per GDP sector)

	Agriculture	Industry*	Services
70%–100%	■	■	■
50%–69.9%	■	■	■
0%–49.9%	□	□	□

*Includes the mining industry

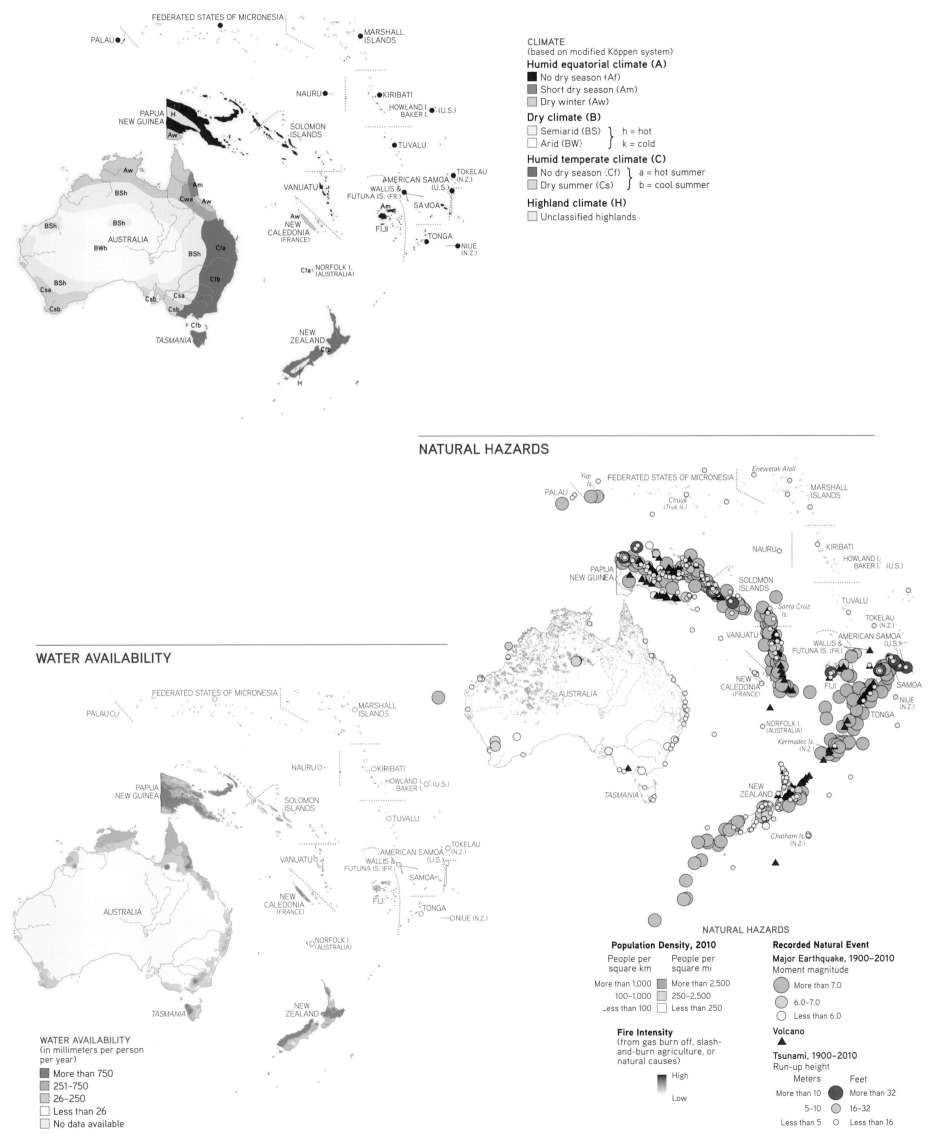

CLIMATE ZONES

FEDERATED STATES OF MICRONESIA

PALAU

MARSHALL ISLANDS

NAURU

KIRIBATI

HOWLAND I.
BAKER I. (U.S.)

PAPUA NEW GUINEA

H

Aw

SOLOMON ISLANDS

TUVALU

TOKELAU (N.Z.)

AMERICAN SAMOA (U.S.)

VANUATU

WALLIS & FUTUNA IS. (FR.)

SAMOA

Aw

Am

NEW CALEDONIA (FRANCE)

Am

FIJI

TONGA

NIUE (N.Z.)

Aw

Am

Cwa

Aw

BSh

BSh

AUSTRALIA

BSh

BWh

BSh

BSh

Csa

Csb

Csa

Csb

Csb

Cfa

Cfb

Cfa

NORFOLK I. (AUSTRALIA)

Cfb

TASMANIA

NEW ZEALAND

Cfb

H

CLIMATE
(based on modified Köppen system)

Humid equatorial climate (A)
- No dry season (Af)
- Short dry season (Am)
- Dry winter (Aw)

Dry climate (B)
- Semiarid (BS) } h = hot
- Arid (BW)   } k = cold

Humid temperate climate (C)
- No dry season (Cf) } a = hot summer
- Dry summer (Cs)   } b = cool summer

Highland climate (H)
- Unclassified highlands

NATURAL HAZARDS

Yap Is.

Enewetak Atoll

FEDERATED STATES OF MICRONESIA

PALAU

Chuuk (Truk Is.)

MARSHALL ISLANDS

NAURU

KIRIBATI

HOWLAND I.
BAKER I. (U.S.)

PAPUA NEW GUINEA

SOLOMON ISLANDS

Santa Cruz Is.

TUVALU

TOKELAU (N.Z.)

VANUATU

AMERICAN SAMOA (U.S.)

WALLIS & FUTUNA IS. (FR.)

AUSTRALIA

NEW CALEDONIA (FRANCE)

FIJI

SAMOA

NIUE (N.Z.)

NORFOLK I. (AUSTRALIA)

TONGA

Kermadec Is. (N.Z.)

TASMANIA

NEW ZEALAND

Chatham Is. (N.Z.)

WATER AVAILABILITY

FEDERATED STATES OF MICRONESIA

PALAU

MARSHALL ISLANDS

NAURU

KIRIBATI

HOWLAND I.
BAKER I. (U.S.)

PAPUA NEW GUINEA

SOLOMON ISLANDS

TUVALU

TOKELAU (N.Z.)

VANUATU

AMERICAN SAMOA (U.S.)

WALLIS & FUTUNA IS. (FR.)

SAMOA

AUSTRALIA

NEW CALEDONIA (FRANCE)

FIJI

TONGA

NIUE (N.Z.)

NORFOLK I. (AUSTRALIA)

TASMANIA

NEW ZEALAND

WATER AVAILABILITY
(in millimeters per person
per year)
- More than 750
- 251–750
- 26–250
- Less than 26
- No data available

NATURAL HAZARDS

Population Density, 2010

People per square km	People per square mi
More than 1,000	More than 2,500
100–1,000	250–2,500
Less than 100	Less than 250

Fire Intensity
(from gas burn off, slash-
and-burn agriculture, or
natural causes)

High

Low

Recorded Natural Event

Major Earthquake, 1900–2010
Moment magnitude
- More than 7.0
- 6.0–7.0
- Less than 6.0

Volcano
▲

Tsunami, 1900–2010
Run-up height

Meters	Feet
More than 10	More than 32
5–10	16–32
Less than 5	Less than 16

COUNTRIES

Australia
COMMONWEALTH OF AUSTRALIA

AREA	7,741,220 sq km (2,988,885 sq mi)
POPULATION	22,016,000
CAPITAL	Canberra 384,000
RELIGION	Protestant, Catholic, none
LANGUAGE	English
LITERACY	99%
LIFE EXPECTANCY	82 years
GDP PER CAPITA	$40,800

ECONOMY **IND:** mining, industrial and transportation equipment, food processing, chemicals, steel **AGR:** wheat, barley, sugarcane, fruits, cattle, sheep, poultry **EXP:** coal, iron ore, gold, meat, wool, alumina, wheat, machinery and transport equipment

Fiji
REPUBLIC OF FIJI

AREA	18,274 sq km (7,056 sq mi)
POPULATION	890,000
CAPITAL	Suva 174,000
RELIGION	Protestant, Hindu
LANGUAGE	English, Fijian, Hindustani
LITERACY	94%
LIFE EXPECTANCY	72 years
GDP PER CAPITA	$4,600

ECONOMY **IND:** tourism, sugar, clothing, copra, gold, silver, lumber, small cottage industries **AGR:** sugarcane, coconuts, cassava (tapioca), rice, sweet potatoes, bananas, cattle, pigs, horses, goats, fish **EXP:** sugar, garments, gold, timber, fish, molasses, coconut oil

Kiribati
REPUBLIC OF KIRIBATI

AREA	811 sq km (313 sq mi)
POPULATION	102,000
CAPITAL	Tarawa 43,000
RELIGION	Roman Catholic, Protestant
LANGUAGE	I-Kiribati, English
LITERACY	NA
LIFE EXPECTANCY	65 years
GDP PER CAPITA	$6,200

ECONOMY **IND:** fishing, handicrafts **AGR:** copra, taro, breadfruit, sweet potatoes, vegetables, fish **EXP:** copra, coconuts, seaweed, fish

Marshall Islands
REPUBLIC OF THE MARSHALL ISLANDS

AREA	181 sq km (70 sq mi)
POPULATION	68,500
CAPITAL	Majuro 30,000
RELIGION	Protestant, Assembly of God
LANGUAGE	Marshallese, English
LITERACY	94%
LIFE EXPECTANCY	72 years
GDP PER CAPITA	$2,500

ECONOMY **IND:** copra, tuna processing, tourism, craft items (from seashells, wood, and pearls) **AGR:** coconuts, tomatoes, melons, taro, breadfruit, fruits, pigs, chickens **EXP:** copra cake, coconut oil, handicrafts, fish

Micronesia
FEDERATED STATES OF MICRONESIA

AREA	702 sq km (271 sq mi)
POPULATION	106,000
CAPITAL	Palikir 7,000
RELIGION	Roman Catholic, Protestant
LANGUAGE	English, Chuukese, Kosrean, Pohnpeian, Yapese, Ulithian, Woleaian, Nukuoro, Kapingamarangi
LITERACY	89%
LIFE EXPECTANCY	72 years
GDP PER CAPITA	$2,200

ECONOMY **IND:** tourism, construction, fish processing, specialized aquaculture, craft items (from shell, wood, and pearls) **AGR:** black pepper, tropical fruits and vegetables, coconuts, bananas, cassava (tapioca), sakau (kava), Kosraen citrus, betel nuts, sweet potatoes, pigs, chickens, fish **EXP:** fish, garments, bananas, black pepper, sakau (kava), betel nut

Nauru
REPUBLIC OF NAURU

AREA	21 sq km (8 sq mi)
POPULATION	9,400
CAPITAL	Yaren 5,000
RELIGION	Protestant, Roman Catholic
LANGUAGE	Nauruan, English
LITERACY	NA
LIFE EXPECTANCY	66 years
GDP PER CAPITA	$5,000

ECONOMY **IND:** phosphate mining, offshore banking, coconut products **AGR:** coconuts **EXP:** phosphates

New Zealand
NEW ZEALAND

AREA	267,710 sq km (103,363 sq mi)
POPULATION	4,328,000
CAPITAL	Wellington 391,000
RELIGION	Protestant, none, Roman Catholic
LANGUAGE	English, Maori
LITERACY	99%
LIFE EXPECTANCY	81 years
GDP PER CAPITA	$27,900

ECONOMY **IND:** food processing, wood and paper products, textiles, machinery, transportation equipment, banking and insurance, tourism, mining **AGR:** dairy products, lamb and mutton, wheat, barley, potatoes, pulses, fruits, vegetables, wool, beef, fish **EXP:** dairy products, meat, wood and wood products, fish, machinery

Palau
REPUBLIC OF PALAU

AREA	459 sq km (177 sq mi)
POPULATION	21,000
CAPITAL	Melekeok 1,000
RELIGION	Roman Catholic, Protestant, none
LANGUAGE	Palauan, Filipino, English
LITERACY	92%
LIFE EXPECTANCY	72 years
GDP PER CAPITA	$8,100

ECONOMY **IND:** tourism, craft items (from shell, wood, pearls), construction, garment making **AGR:** coconuts, copra, cassava (tapioca), sweet potatoes, fish **EXP:** shellfish, tuna, copra, garments

Papua New Guinea
INDEPENDENT STATE OF PAPUA NEW GUINEA

AREA	462,840 sq km (178,703 sq mi)
POPULATION	6,310,000
CAPITAL	Port Moresby 314,000
RELIGION	Protestant, Roman Catholic
LANGUAGE	Tok Pisin, English, Hiri Motu, 860 indigenous languages
LITERACY	57%
LIFE EXPECTANCY	66 years
GDP PER CAPITA	$2,500

ECONOMY **IND:** copra crushing, palm oil processing, plywood production, wood chip production, gold, silver, copper, crude oil production, petroleum refining, construction, tourism **AGR:** coffee, cocoa, copra, palm kernels, tea, sugar, rubber, sweet potatoes, fruit, vegetables, vanilla, shell fish, poultry, pork **EXP:** oil, gold, copper ore, logs, palm oil, coffee, cocoa, crayfish, prawns

Samoa
INDEPENDENT STATE OF SAMOA

AREA	2,831 sq km (1,093 sq mi)
POPULATION	194,000
CAPITAL	Apia 36,000
RELIGION	Protestant, Roman Catholic, Mormon
LANGUAGE	Samoan, English
LITERACY	100%
LIFE EXPECTANCY	73 years
GDP PER CAPITA	$6,000

ECONOMY **IND:** food processing, building materials, auto parts **AGR:** coconuts, bananas, taro, yams, coffee, cocoa **EXP:** fish, coconut oil and cream, copra, taro, automotive parts, garments, beer

Solomon Islands
SOLOMON ISLANDS

AREA	28,896 sq km (11,157 sq mi)
POPULATION	585,000
CAPITAL	Honiara 72,000
RELIGION	Protestant, Roman Catholic
LANGUAGE	Melanesian pidgin, English
LITERACY	75%
LIFE EXPECTANCY	74 years
GDP PER CAPITA	$3,300

ECONOMY **IND:** fish (tuna), mining, timber **AGR:** cocoa beans, coconuts, palm kernels, rice, potatoes, vegetables, fruit, timber, cattle, pigs, fish **EXP:** timber, fish, copra, palm oil, cocoa

Tonga
KINGDOM OF TONGA

AREA	747 sq km (288 sq mi)
POPULATION	106,000
CAPITAL	Nuku'alofa 24,000
RELIGION	Christian
LANGUAGE	Tongan, English
LITERACY	99%
LIFE EXPECTANCY	75 years
GDP PER CAPITA	$7,500

ECONOMY **IND:** tourism, construction, fishing **AGR:** squash, coconuts, copra, bananas, vanilla beans, cocoa, coffee, ginger, black pepper, fish **EXP:** squash, fish, vanilla beans, root crops

Tuvalu
TUVALU

AREA	26 sq km (10 sq mi)
POPULATION	10,600
CAPITAL	Funafuti 5,000
RELIGION	Protestant
LANGUAGE	Tuvaluan, English, Samoan, Kiribati
LITERACY	NA
LIFE EXPECTANCY	65 years
GDP PER CAPITA	$3,400

ECONOMY **IND:** fishing, tourism, copra **AGR:** coconuts, fish **EXP:** copra, fish

Vanuatu
REPUBLIC OF VANUATU

AREA	12,189 sq km (4,706 sq mi)
POPULATION	226,000
CAPITAL	Port-Vila 44,000
RELIGION	Protestant, Roman Catholic
LANGUAGE	local languages (more than 100), Bislama, English, French
LITERACY	74%
LIFE EXPECTANCY	65 years
GDP PER CAPITA	$4,900

ECONOMY **IND:** food and fish freezing, wood processing, meat canning **AGR:** copra, coconuts, cocoa, coffee, taro, yams, fruits, vegetables, beef, fish **EXP:** copra, beef, cocoa, timber, kava, coffee

DEPENDENCIES

American Samoa
(U.S.)

TERRITORY OF AMERICAN SAMOA

AREA	199 sq km (77 sq mi)
POPULATION	68,100
CAPITAL	Pago Pago 60,000
RELIGION	Christian Congregationalist, Protestant, Roman Catholic
LANGUAGE	Samoan, English
LITERACY	97%
LIFE EXPECTANCY	74 years
GDP PER CAPITA	$8,000

ECONOMY **IND:** tuna canneries (largely supplied by foreign fishing vessels), handicrafts **AGR:** bananas, coconuts, vegetables, taro, breadfruit, yams, copra, pineapples, papayas, dairy products, livestock **EXP:** canned tuna

Cook Islands
(NEW ZEALAND)

COOK ISLANDS

AREA	236 sq km (91 sq mi)
POPULATION	10,800
CAPITAL	Avarua 10,300
RELIGION	Protestant, Roman Catholic
LANGUAGE	English, Maori
LITERACY	95%
LIFE EXPECTANCY	75 years
GDP PER CAPITA	$9,100

ECONOMY **IND:** fruit processing, tourism, fishing, clothing, handicrafts **AGR:** copra, citrus, pineapples, tomatoes, beans, pawpaws, bananas, yams, taro, coffee, pigs, poultry **EXP:** copra, papayas, fresh and canned citrus fruit, coffee, fish, pearls and pearl shells, clothing

French Polynesia
(FRANCE)

OVERSEAS LANDS OF FRENCH POLYNESIA

AREA	4,167 sq km (1,609 sq mi)
POPULATION	275,000
CAPITAL	Papeete 133,000
RELIGION	Protestant, Roman Catholic
LANGUAGE	French, Polynesian
LITERACY	98%
LIFE EXPECTANCY	76 years
GDP PER CAPITA	$18,000

ECONOMY **IND:** tourism, pearls, agricultural processing, handicrafts, phosphates **AGR:** fish, coconuts, vanilla, vegetables, fruits, coffee, poultry, beef, dairy products **EXP:** cultured pearls, coconut products, mother-of-pearl, vanilla, shark meat

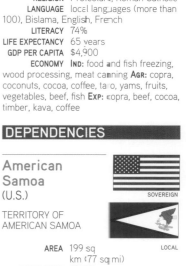

Guam
(U.S.)

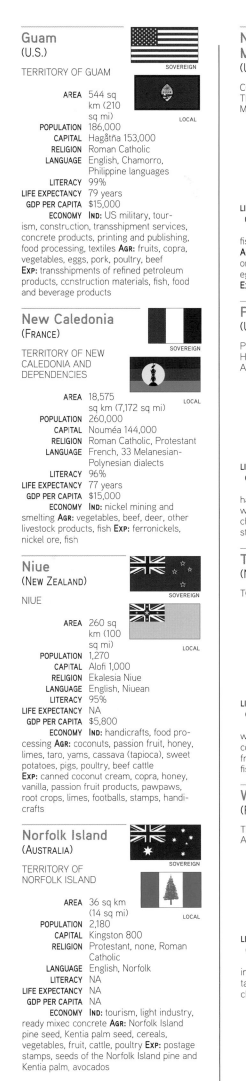

TERRITORY OF GUAM

SOVEREIGN

LOCAL

AREA	544 sq km (210 sq mi)
POPULATION	186,000
CAPITAL	Hagåtña 153,000
RELIGION	Roman Catholic
LANGUAGE	English, Chamorro, Philippine languages
LITERACY	99%
LIFE EXPECTANCY	79 years
GDP PER CAPITA	$15,000

ECONOMY **IND:** US military, tourism, construction, transshipment services, concrete products, printing and publishing, food processing, textiles **AGR:** fruits, copra, vegetables, eggs, pork, poultry, beef **EXP:** transshipments of refined petroleum products, construction materials, fish, food and beverage products

New Caledonia
(FRANCE)

TERRITORY OF NEW CALEDONIA AND DEPENDENCIES

SOVEREIGN

LOCAL

AREA	18,575 sq km (7,172 sq mi)
POPULATION	260,000
CAPITAL	Nouméa 144,000
RELIGION	Roman Catholic, Protestant
LANGUAGE	French, 33 Melanesian-Polynesian dialects
LITERACY	96%
LIFE EXPECTANCY	77 years
GDP PER CAPITA	$15,000

ECONOMY **IND:** nickel mining and smelting **AGR:** vegetables, beef, deer, other livestock products, fish **EXP:** ferronickels, nickel ore, fish

Niue
(NEW ZEALAND)

NIUE

SOVEREIGN

LOCAL

AREA	260 sq km (100 sq mi)
POPULATION	1,270
CAPITAL	Alofi 1,000
RELIGION	Ekalesia Niue
LANGUAGE	English, Niuean
LITERACY	95%
LIFE EXPECTANCY	NA
GDP PER CAPITA	$5,800

ECONOMY **IND:** handicrafts, food processing **AGR:** coconuts, passion fruit, honey, limes, taro, yams, cassava (tapioca), sweet potatoes, pigs, poultry, beef cattle **EXP:** canned coconut cream, copra, honey, vanilla, passion fruit products, pawpaws, root crops, limes, footballs, stamps, handicrafts

Norfolk Island
(AUSTRALIA)

TERRITORY OF NORFOLK ISLAND

SOVEREIGN

LOCAL

AREA	36 sq km (14 sq mi)
POPULATION	2,180
CAPITAL	Kingston 800
RELIGION	Protestant, none, Roman Catholic
LANGUAGE	English, Norfolk
LITERACY	NA
LIFE EXPECTANCY	NA
GDP PER CAPITA	NA

ECONOMY **IND:** tourism, light industry, ready mixed concrete **AGR:** Norfolk Island pine seed, Kentia palm seed, cereals, vegetables, fruit, cattle, poultry **EXP:** postage stamps, seeds of the Norfolk Island pine and Kentia palm, avocados

Northern Mariana Islands
(U.S.)

COMMONWEALTH OF THE NORTHERN MARIANA ISLANDS

SOVEREIGN

LOCAL

AREA	464 sq km (179 sq mi)
POPULATION	53,900
CAPITAL	Saipan 48,000
RELIGION	Christian
LANGUAGE	Philippine languages, Chinese, Chamorro, English
LITERACY	97%
LIFE EXPECTANCY	77 years
GDP PER CAPITA	$12,500

ECONOMY **IND:** banking, construction, fishing, garment, tourism, handicrafts **AGR:** vegetables and melons, fruits and nuts, ornamental plants, livestock, poultry and eggs, fish and aquaculture products **EXP:** garments

Pitcairn Islands
(U.K.)

PITCAIRN, HENDERSON, DUCIE, AND OENO ISLANDS

SOVEREIGN

LOCAL

AREA	47 sq km (18 sq mi)
POPULATION	48
CAPITAL	Adamstown 48
RELIGION	Seventh-Day Adventist
LANGUAGE	English, Pitkern
LITERACY	NA
LIFE EXPECTANCY	NA
GDP PER CAPITA	NA

ECONOMY **IND:** postage stamps, handicrafts, beekeeping, honey **AGR:** honey, wide variety of fruits and vegetables, goats, chickens, fish **EXP:** fruits, vegetables, curios, stamps

Tokelau
(NEW ZEALAND)

TOKELAU

SOVEREIGN

LOCAL

AREA	12 sq km (5 sq mi)
POPULATION	1,370
CAPITAL	none
RELIGION	Congregational Christian Church, Roman Catholic
LANGUAGE	Tokelauan, English
LITERACY	NA
LIFE EXPECTANCY	NA
GDP PER CAPITA	$1,000

ECONOMY **IND:** copra production, woodworking, plaited craft goods, stamps, coins, fishing **AGR:** coconuts, copra, breadfruit, papayas, bananas, pigs, poultry, goats, fish **EXP:** stamps, copra, handicrafts

Wallis and Futuna
(FRANCE)

TERRITORY OF THE WALLIS AND FUTUNA ISLANDS

SOVEREIGN

LOCAL

AREA	142 sq km (55 sq mi)
POPULATION	15,500
CAPITAL	Matā'utu 1,000
RELIGION	Roman Catholic
LANGUAGE	Wallisian, Futunian, French
LITERACY	50%
LIFE EXPECTANCY	79 years
GDP PER CAPITA	$3,800

ECONOMY **IND:** copra, handicrafts, fishing, lumber **AGR:** coconuts, breadfruit, yams, taro, bananas, pigs, goats, fish **EXP:** copra, chemicals, construction materials

UNINHABITED DEPENDENCIES

Baker Island
(U.S.)

BAKER ISLAND

AREA	1.4 sq km (0.5 sq mi)
POPULATION	none

Howland Island
(U.S.)

HOWLAND ISLAND

AREA	1.6 sq km (0.6 sq mi)
POPULATION	none

Jarvis Island
(U.S.)

JARVIS ISLAND

AREA	4.5 sq km (1.7 sq mi)
POPULATION	none

Johnston Atoll
(U.S.)

JOHNSTON ATOLL

AREA	2.6 sq km (1.0 sq mi)
POPULATION	none

Kingman Reef
(U.S.)

KINGMAN REEF

AREA	1.0 sq km (0.4 sq mi)
POPULATION	none

Midway Islands
(U.S.)

MIDWAY ISLANDS

AREA	6.2 sq km (2.4 sq mi)
POPULATION	none

Palmyra Atoll
(U.S.)

PALMYRA ATOLL

AREA	11.9 sq km (4.6 sq mi)
POPULATION	none

Wake Island
(U.S.)

WAKE ISLAND

AREA	6.5 sq km (2.5 sq mi)
POPULATION	none

DATES OF NATIONAL INDEPENDENCE AND POPULATION

Midway Islands
(U.S.)

TROPIC OF CANCER

Wake Island
• (U.S.)

PHILIPPINE

Northern
Mariana
Islands
(U.S.)

Johnston Atoll •
(U.S.)

S E A

Guam
(U.S.)

MARSHALL ISLANDS
Oct. 21, 1986

PALAU
Oct. 1, 1994

FEDERATED STATES
OF MICRONESIA
Nov. 3, 1986

Howland
Island (U.S.)
• Baker Island (U.S.)

EQUATOR

NAURU
Jan. 31, 1968

K   I   R   I   B   A
July 12, 1979

New Guinea

PAPUA NEW GUINEA
Sept. 16, 1975

**SOLOMON
ISLANDS**
July 7, 1978

TUVALU
Oct. 1, 1978

Tokelau
(New Zealand)

Wallis &
Futuna
Is.(Fr.)

SAMOA
Jan. 1,
1962

American
Samoa
(U.S.)

VANUATU
July 30, 1980

TONGA
June 4, 1970

Niue
(N.Z.)

FIJI
Oct. 10, 1970

C O R A L   S E A

New Caledonia
(France)

TROPIC OF CAPRICORN

A U S T R A L I A
Jan. 1, 1901

Norfolk Island
(Australia)

I N D I A N   O C E A N

*T A S M A N
S E A*

NEW ZEALAND
Sept. 26, 1907

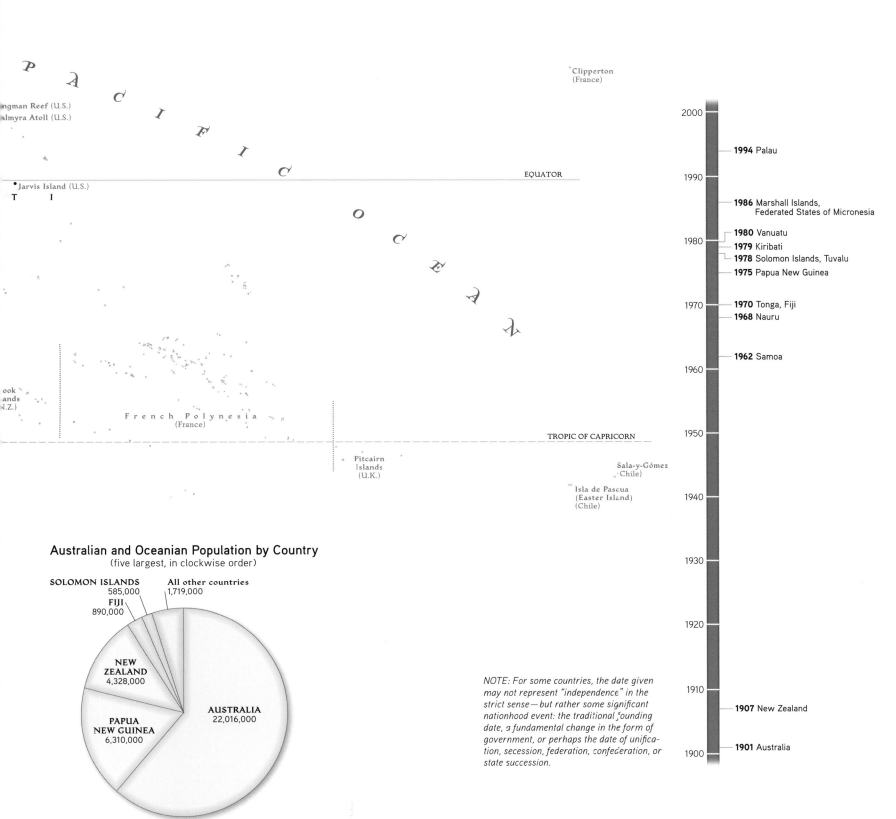

TROPIC OF CANCER

Hawai'i (U.S.)

OCEANIA:
Oceania is not a continent, but rather a vast island realm between Asia and the Americas. Definitions vary as to what island groups make up Oceania, however, it usually consists of islands in the central and southern Pacific Ocean. Australia, a continent, is often included as a part of Oceania. Although, the island nations of Japan, the Philippines, and Indonesia are not considered part of Oceania because of their cultural links to Asia. The island of New Guinea, the world's second largest island, is split between Asia and Oceania, with Indonesia administering the western side of the island and the independent country of Papua New Guinea occupying the eastern side. Papua New Guinea is the largest and most populous island country in Oceania, with six million inhabitants speaking some 800 different languages.

Both physical and cultural geography play a role in dividing Oceania into three regions: Melanesia ("black islands"), Micronesia ("small islands"), and Polynesia ("many islands").

European explorers used the term "Melanesia" to describe the dark-skinned inhabitants of the southwestern Pacific islands, south of the Equator, extending from Papua New Guinea to Fiji. In contrast to Melanesia's large islands, Micronesia consists of small coral and volcanic islands located north of the Equator, starting with Palau and reaching north to the Northern Mariana Islands and east to the Marshall Islands. Polynesia, east of Melanesia and Micronesia, is at the heart of the Pacific, with thousands of islands stretching from New Zealand in the south to the Hawaiian Islands in the north and to Chile's Easter Island in the east.

P A C I F I C

Clipperton (France)

ngman Reef (U.S.)
almyra Atoll (U.S.)

2000

— **1994** Palau

1990

— **1986** Marshall Islands, Federated States of Micronesia

Jarvis Island (U.S.)
T   I

EQUATOR

O C E A N

— **1980** Vanuatu
1980
— **1979** Kiribati
— **1978** Solomon Islands, Tuvalu
— **1975** Papua New Guinea

1970
— **1970** Tonga, Fiji
— **1968** Nauru

— **1962** Samoa

1960

ook
ands
N.Z.)

French Polynesia
(France)

TROPIC OF CAPRICORN
1950

Pitcairn
Islands
(U.K.)

Sala-y-Gómez
Chile

1940

Isla de Pascua
(Easter Island)
(Chile)

1930

Australian and Oceanian Population by Country
(five largest, in clockwise order)

SOLOMON ISLANDS
585,000

All other countries
1,719,000

FIJI
890,000

1920

NEW
ZEALAND
4,328,000

AUSTRALIA
22,016,000

NOTE: For some countries, the date given may not represent "independence" in the strict sense—but rather some significant nationhood event: the traditional founding date, a fundamental change in the form of government, or perhaps the date of unification, secession, federation, confederation, or state succession.

1910

— **1907** New Zealand

PAPUA
NEW GUINEA
6,310,000

— **1901** Australia
1900

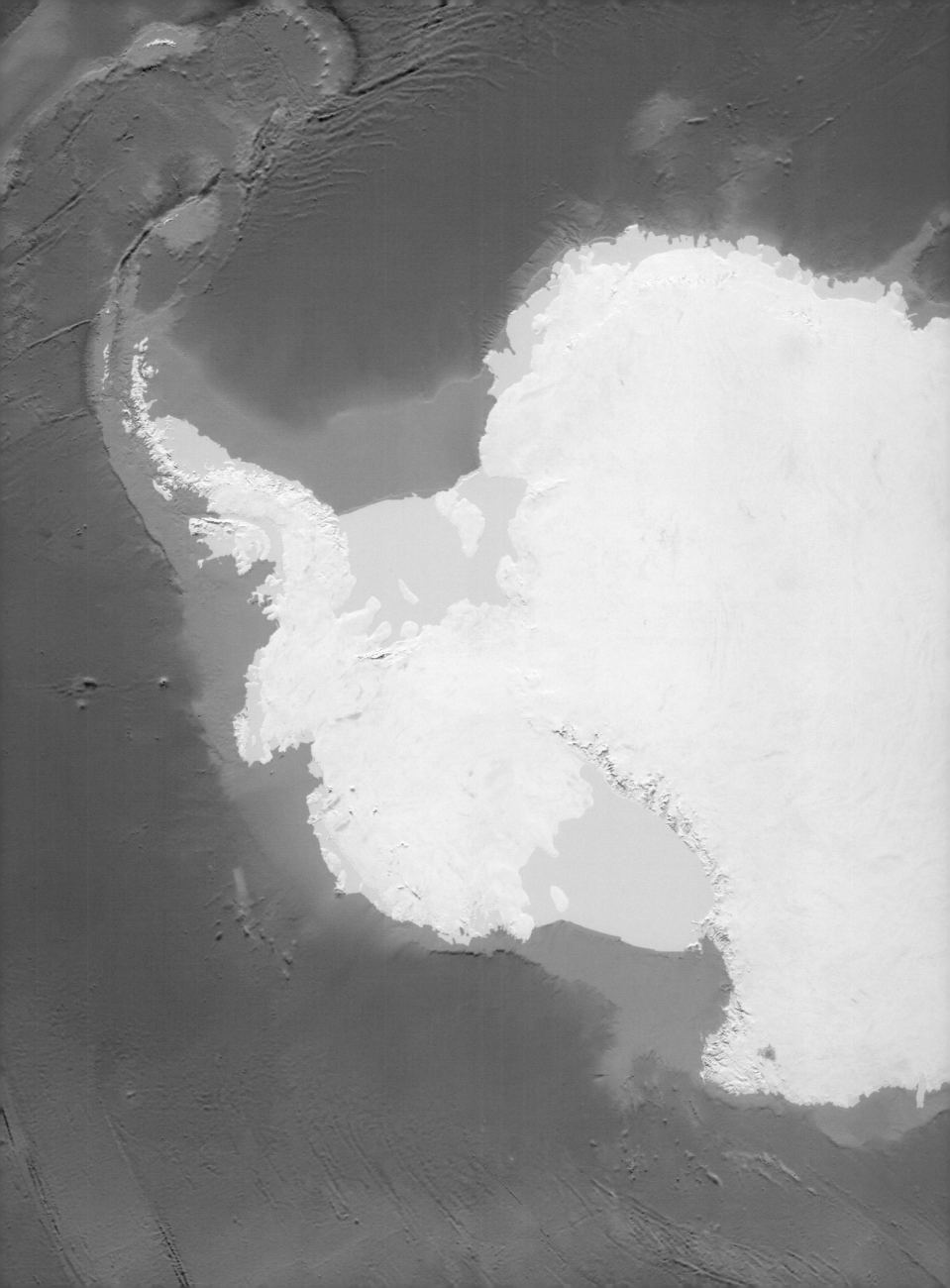

Antarctica

ANTARCTICA, AT THE SOUTHERN extreme of the world, ranks as the coldest, highest, driest, and windiest of Earth's continents. At the South Pole the continent experiences the extremes of day and night, banished from sunlight half the year, bathed in continuous light the other half. As best we know, no indigenous peoples ever lived on this continent. Unlike the Arctic, an ocean surrounded by continents, Antarctica is a continent surrounded by ocean. The only people who live there today, mostly scientists and support staff at research stations, ruefully call Antarctica "the Ice," and with good reason. All but 2 percent of the continent is covered year-round in ice up to 15,000 feet (4,570 meters) thick.

Not until the early 20th century did men explore the heart of the Antarctic to find an austere beauty and an unmatched hardship. "The crystal showers carpeted the pack ice and the ship," wrote Frank Hurley, "until she looked like a tinseled beauty on a field of diamonds." Wrote Apsley Cherry-Garrard in his book, *The Worst Journey in the World*, "Polar exploration is . . . the cleanest and most isolated way of having a bad time . . . [ever] devised." Despite its remoteness, Antarctica has been called the frontier of today's ecological crisis. Temperatures are rising, and a hole in the ozone (caused by atmospheric pollutants) allows harmful ultraviolet radiation to bombard land and sea.

The long tendril of the Antarctic Peninsula reaches to within 700 miles (1,130 kilometers) of South America, separated by the tempestuous Drake Passage, where furious winds build mountainous waves. This "banana belt" of the Antarctic is not nearly so cold as the polar interior, where a great plateau of ice reaches 10,000 feet (3,050 meters) above sea level and winter temperatures can drop lower than -112°F (-80°C). In the Antarctic summer (December to March), light fills the region, yet heat is absent. Glaciers flow from the icy plateau, coalescing into massive ice shelves; the largest of these, the Ross Ice Shelf, is the size of France.

Antarctica's ice cap holds some 70 percent of the Earth's fresh water. Yet despite all this ice and water, the Antarctic interior averages only two inches (five centimeters) of precipitation a year, making it the largest desert in the world. The little snow that does fall, however, almost never melts. The immensely heavy ice sheet, averaging over 1 mile (1.6 kilometers) thick, compresses the land surface over most of the continent to below sea level. The weight actually deforms the South Pole, creating a slightly pear-shaped Earth.

Beneath the ice exists a continent of valleys, lakes, islands, and mountains, little dreamed of until the compilation of more than 2.5 million ice-thickness measurements revealed startling topography below. Ice and sediment cores provide insight into the world's ancient climate and allow for comparison with conditions today. Studies of the Antarctic ice sheet help predict future sea levels, important news for the three billion people who live in coastal areas. If the ice sheet were to melt, global seas would rise by an estimated 200 feet (61 meters), inundating many oceanic islands and gravely altering the world's coastlines.

Antarctica's animal life has adapted extremely well to the harsh climate. Seasonal feeding and energy storage in fat exemplify this specialization. Well-known animals of the far south include seals, whales, and distinctive birds such as flightless penguins, albatrosses, terns, and petrels.

127

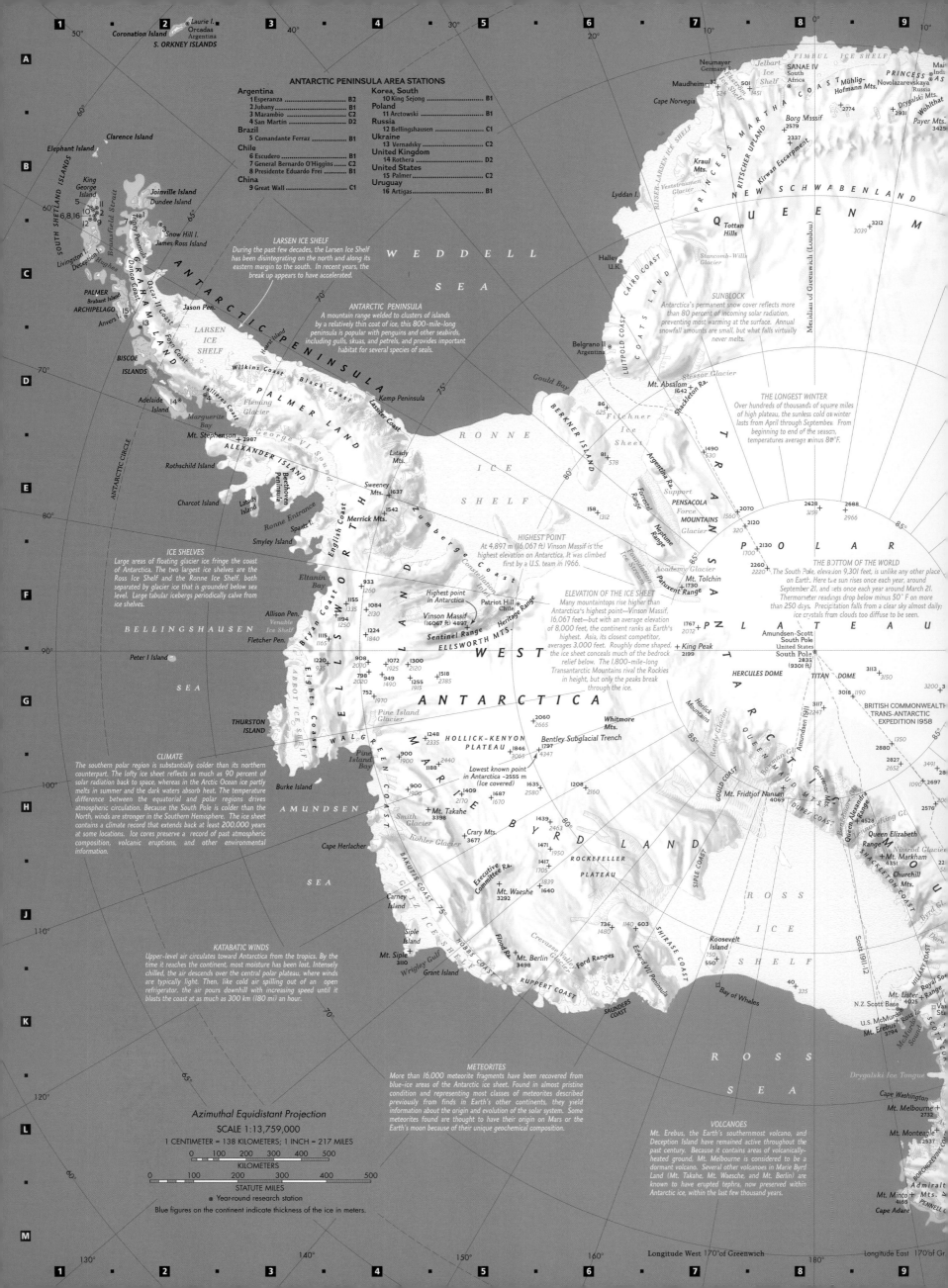

ANTARCTIC PENINSULA AREA STATIONS

Argentina
1 Esperanza B2
2 Jubany B1
3 Marambio C2
4 San Martín D2
Brazil
5 Comandante Ferraz B1
Chile
6 Escudero B1
7 General Bernardo O'Higgins C2
8 Presidente Eduardo Frei B1
China
9 Great Wall C1

Korea, South
10 King Sejong B1
Poland
11 Arctowski B1
Russia
12 Bellingshausen C1
Ukraine
13 Vernadsky C2
United Kingdom
14 Rothera D2
United States
15 Palmer C2
Uruguay
16 Artigas B1

LARSEN ICE SHELF
During the past few decades, the Larsen Ice Shelf has been disintegrating on the north and along its eastern margin to the south. In recent years, the break up appears to have accelerated.

ANTARCTIC PENINSULA
A mountain range welded to clusters of islands by a relatively thin coat of ice, this 800-mile-long peninsula is popular with penguins and other seabirds, including gulls, skuas, and petrels, and provides important habitat for several species of seals.

SUNBLOCK
Antarctica's permanent snow cover reflects more than 80 percent of incoming solar radiation, preventing most warming at the surface. Annual snowfall amounts are small, but what falls virtually never melts.

THE LONGEST WINTER
Over hundreds of thousands of square miles of high plateau, the sunless cold of winter lasts from April through September. From beginning to end of the season, temperatures average minus 80°F.

ICE SHELVES
Large areas of floating glacier ice fringe the coast of Antarctica. The two largest ice shelves are the Ross Ice Shelf and the Ronne Ice Shelf, both separated by glacier ice that is grounded below sea level. Large tabular icebergs periodically calve from ice shelves.

HIGHEST POINT
At 4,897 m (16,067 ft) Vinson Massif is the highest elevation on Antarctica. It was climbed first by a U.S. team in 1966.

ELEVATION OF THE ICE SHEET
Many mountaintops rise higher than Antarctica's highest point—Vinson Massif, 16,067 feet—but with an average elevation of 8,000 feet, the continent ranks as Earth's highest. Asia, its closest competitor, averages 3,000 feet. Roughly dome shaped, the ice sheet conceals much of the bedrock relief below. The 1,800-mile-long Transantarctic Mountains rival the Rockies in height, but only the peaks break through the ice.

THE BOTTOM OF THE WORLD
The South Pole, elevation 9,301 feet, is unlike any other place on Earth. Here the sun rises once each year, around September 21, and sets once each year around March 21. Thermometer readings drop below minus 50°F on more than 250 days. Precipitation falls from a clear sky almost daily; ice crystals from clouds too diffuse to be seen.

CLIMATE
The southern polar region is substantially colder than its northern counterpart. The lofty ice sheet reflects as much as 90 percent of solar radiation back to space, whereas in the Arctic Ocean ice partly melts in summer and the dark waters absorb heat. The temperature difference between the equatorial and polar regions drives atmospheric circulation. Because the South Pole is colder than the North, winds are stronger in the Southern Hemisphere. The ice sheet contains a climate record that extends back at least 200,000 years at some locations. Ice cores preserve a record of past atmospheric composition, volcanic eruptions, and other environmental information.

BRITISH COMMONWEALTH TRANS-ANTARCTIC EXPEDITION 1958

KATABATIC WINDS
Upper-level air circulates toward Antarctica from the tropics. By the time it reaches the continent, most moisture has been lost. Intensely chilled, the air descends over the central polar plateau, where winds are typically light. Then, like cold air spilling out of an open refrigerator, the air pours downhill with increasing speed until it blasts the coast at as much as 300 km (180 mi) an hour.

METEORITES
More than 16,000 meteorite fragments have been recovered from blue-ice areas of the Antarctic ice sheet. Found in almost pristine condition and representing most classes of meteorites described previously from finds in Earth's other continents, they yield information about the origin and evolution of the solar system. Some meteorites found are thought to have their origin on Mars or the Earth's moon because of their unique geochemical composition.

VOLCANOES
Mt. Erebus, the Earth's southernmost volcano, and Deception Island have remained active throughout the past century. Because it contains areas of volcanically-heated ground, Mt. Melbourne is considered to be a dormant volcano. Several other volcanoes in Marie Byrd Land (Mt. Takahe, Mt. Waesche, and Mt. Berlin) are known to have erupted tephra, now preserved within Antarctic ice, within the last few thousand years.

Azimuthal Equidistant Projection
SCALE 1:13,759,000
1 CENTIMETER = 138 KILOMETERS; 1 INCH = 217 MILES

0 100 200 300 400 500
KILOMETERS

0 100 200 300 400 500
STATUTE MILES

⊛ Year-round research station
Blue figures on the continent indicate thickness of the ice in meters.

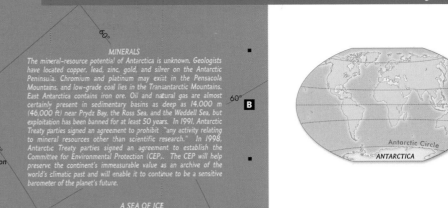

MINERALS

The mineral-resource potential of Antarctica is unknown. Geologists have located copper, lead, zinc, gold, and silver on the Antarctic Peninsula. Chromium and platinum may exist in the Pensacola Mountains, and low-grade coal lies in the Transantarctic Mountains. East Antarctica contains iron ore. Oil and natural gas are almost certainly present in sedimentary basins as deep as 14,000 m (46,000 ft) near Prydz Bay, the Ross Sea, and the Weddell Sea, but exploitation has been banned for at least 50 years. In 1991, Antarctic Treaty parties signed an agreement to prohibit "any activity relating to mineral resources other than scientific research." In 1998, Antarctic Treaty parties signed an agreement to establish the Committee for Environmental Protection (CEP). The CEP will help preserve the continent's immeasurable value as an archive of the world's climatic past and will enable it to continue to be a sensitive barometer of the planet's future.

A SEA OF ICE

When winter comes, the ocean surface around Antarctica begins to freeze. Spreading over an average of 77,700 square kilometers (30,000 sq mi) a day, the ring of sea ice eventually covers more than 18 million square kilometers (7 million sq mi), an area larger than the continent itself. Reducing the ocean's absorption of atmospheric carbon dioxide and blocking ocean-atmosphere heat exchange, sea ice plays a role in shaping regional climate which in turn has impacts over much of the globe.

AMERY ICE SHELF

While ice shelves on the Antarctic Peninsula have retreated dramatically in recent decades, others—including Amery Ice Shelf, fed by the massive Lambert Glacier—have grown larger.

MILDER SHORES
At Australia's Mawson Station the average temperature approaches a toasty 12°F. Year-round, typical highs and lows are separated by only about 10°F.

ICE CORING
In 2003 Russian and American scientists drilled to 3650 m (11,975 ft), and European scientists obtained ice samples estimated to be 1 million years old. Other recently recovered cores record changes in temperature and atmospheric gases dating back 160,000 years. French scientists who analyzed the cores found a correlation between rising temperatures and carbon dioxide (CO_2) levels in ancient times. Because the atmospheric CO_2 level has risen from 280 parts per million (ppm) at the start of the industrial revolution to more than 365 ppm today, the onset of a global warming cycle is thought to be caused in part by increased burning of fossil fuels, which releases CO_2. Along with methane and other gases, CO_2 helps trap solar heat that would otherwise radiate back to space. There is disagreement about whether the rise in global temperatures during the past century confirms this predicted greenhouse effect.

World's coldest place:
annual average temperature -74°C (-94°F)

ICE DESERT
Although Antarctica stores some 72 percent of the world's fresh water as ice, precipitation on six million sq km (2.3 million sq mi) of the continent's interior averages less than five cm a year, similar to the amount of rainfall in the driest part of the Sahara.

The north and south geomagnetic poles, distinct from the more familiar geographic and magnetic poles, mark the axis of the Earth's magnetic field.

A record low temperature of minus 89.2°C (-128.6°F) was recorded here on July 21, 1983.

OUTLET GLACIERS
Numerous named and unnamed outlet glaciers flow from the Antarctic ice sheet into ice shelves or directly into the ocean. Byrd Glacier and Lambert Glacier are considered to be the two largest.

MARS METEORITE
The two areas that have yielded the most meteorites from blue-ice areas are the Allan Hills and the Queen Fabiola Mountains. The ALH 84-001 meteorite, found in Allan Hills, came from Mars and may harbor fossilized bacteria-like organisms.

THICKEST ICE
Echo-sounding from aircraft has identified an ice thickness of 4,776 m (15,670 ft). Bedrock was found at 2,341 m below sea level.

SHIFTING SHORELINES
Antarctica is a mapmaker's nightmare: By the time its outline is drawn, it is likely to have changed significantly. Less than half the shoreline is rock or ice firmly grounded on rock. Floating ice shelves and advancing and retreating glaciers make up nearly 60 percent of the coast. Massive icebergs regularly calve from the ice shelves, knocking divots the size of small U.S. states from the outline of the continent.

MAGNETIC POLE
Compasses in the Southern Hemisphere point to this spot. The magnetic pole moves a few kilometers a year as the Earth's magnetic field changes.

A gale of cold air from the ice plateau, sometimes blowing at 300 km (180 mi) an hour, makes this one of the windiest places on Earth.

CONTINENTAL DATA

AREA: 13,209,000 sq km (5,100,000 sq mi)

GREATEST EXTENT: 5,500 km (3,400 mi), from Trinity Peninsula to Cape Poinsett

HIGHEST POINT: Vinson Massif 4,897 m (16,066 ft)

LOWEST POINT: Bentley Subglacial Trench -2,555 m (-8,383 ft), ice covered

LOWEST RECORDED TEMPERATURE: Vostok -89.2°C (-128.6°F), July 21, 1983

HIGHEST RECORDED TEMPERATURE: Vanda Station, N.Z. (closed), Scott Coast 15°C (59°F), January 5, 1974

EARTH'S EXTREMES LOCATED IN ANTARCTICA:
- Coldest Place on Earth: Ridge A, annual average temperature -74°C (-94°F)
- Coldest Recorded Temperature on Earth: Vostok -89.2°C (-128.6°F), July 21, 1983

ANTARCTIC TREATY

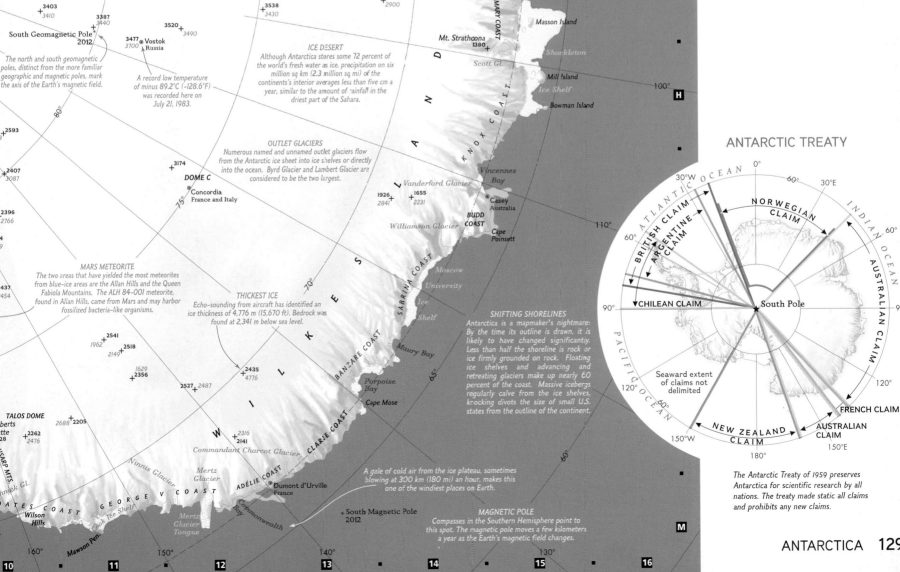

The Antarctic Treaty of 1959 preserves Antarctica for scientific research by all nations. The treaty made static all claims and prohibits any new claims.

Appendix

Airline Distances in Kilometers

	BEIJING	CAIRO	CAPE TOWN	CARACAS	HONG KONG	HONOLULU	LONDON	MELBOURNE	MEXICO CITY	MONTRÉAL	MOSCOW	NEW DELHI	NEW YORK	PARIS	RIO DE JANEIRO	ROME	SAN FRANCISCO	SINGAPORE	STOCKHOLM	TOKYO
BEIJING		7557	12947	14411	1972	8171	8160	9093	12478	10490	5809	3788	11012	8236	17325	8144	9524	4465	6725	2104
CAIRO	7557		7208	10209	8158	14239	3513	13966	12392	8733	2899	4436	9042	3215	9882	2135	12015	8270	3404	9587
CAPE TOWN	12947	7208		10232	11867	18562	9635	10338	13703	12744	10101	9284	12551	9307	6075	8417	16487	9671	10334	14737
CARACAS	14411	10209	10232		16380	9694	7500	15624	3598	3932	9940	14221	3419	7621	4508	8363	6286	18361	8724	14179
HONG KONG	1972	8158	11867	16380		8945	9646	7392	14155	12462	7158	3770	12984	9650	17710	9300	11121	2575	8243	2893
HONOLULU	8171	14239	18562	9694	8945		11653	8862	6098	7915	11342	11930	7996	11988	13343	12936	3857	10824	11059	6208
LONDON	8160	3513	9635	7500	9646	11653		16902	8947	5240	2506	6724	5586	341	9254	1434	8640	10860	1436	9585
MELBOURNE	9093	13966	10338	15624	7392	8862	16902		13557	16730	14418	10192	16671	16793	13227	15987	12644	6050	15593	8159
MEXICO CITY	12478	12392	13703	3598	14155	6098	8947	13557		3728	10740	14679	3362	9213	7669	10260	3038	16623	9603	11319
MONTRÉAL	10490	8733	12744	3932	12462	7915	5240	16730	3728		7077	11286	533	5522	8175	6601	4092	14816	5900	10409
MOSCOW	5809	2899	10101	9940	7158	11342	2506	14418	10740	7077		4349	7530	2492	11529	2378	9469	8426	1231	7502
NEW DELHI	3788	4436	9284	14221	3770	11930	6724	10192	14679	11286	4349		11779	6601	14080	5929	12380	4142	5579	5857
NEW YORK	11012	9042	12551	3419	12984	7996	5586	16671	3362	533	7530	11779		5851	7729	6907	4140	15349	6336	10870
PARIS	8236	3215	9307	7621	9650	11988	341	16793	9213	5522	2492	6601	5851		9146	1108	8975	10743	1546	9738
RIO DE JANEIRO	17325	9882	6075	4508	17710	13343	9254	13227	7669	8175	11529	14080	7729	9146		9181	10647	15740	10682	18557
ROME	8144	2135	8417	8363	9300	12936	1434	15987	10260	6601	2378	5929	6907	1108	9181		10071	10030	1977	9881
SAN FRANCISCO	9524	12015	16487	6286	11121	3857	8640	12644	3038	4092	9469	12380	4140	8975	10647	10071		13598	8644	8284
SINGAPORE	4465	8270	9671	18361	2575	10824	10860	6050	16623	14816	8426	4142	15349	10743	15740	10030	13598		9646	5317
STOCKHOLM	6725	3404	10334	8724	8243	11059	1436	15593	9603	5900	1231	5579	6336	1546	10682	1977	8644	9646		8193
TOKYO	2104	9587	14737	14179	2893	6208	9585	8159	11319	10409	7502	5857	10870	9738	18557	9881	8284	5317	8193	

Abbreviations

Adm.	Administrative
Af.	Africa
Afghan.	Afghanistan
Agr.	Agriculture
Ala.	Alabama
Alas.	Alaska
Alban.	Albania
Alg.	Algeria
Alta.	Alberta
Arch.	Archipelago, Archipiélago
Arg.	Argentina
Ariz.	Arizona
Ark.	Arkansas
Arm.	Armenia
Atl. Oc.	Atlantic Ocean
Aust.	Austria
Austral.	Australia
Azerb.	Azerbaijan
B.	Baai, Baía, Baie, Bahía, Bay, Bu'ayrat
B.C.	British Columbia
Belg.	Belgium
Bol.	Bolivia
Bosn. & Herzg.	Bosnia and Herzegovina
Braz.	Brazil
Bulg.	Bulgaria
C.	Cabo, Cap, Cape, Capo
Calif.	California
Can.	Canada
Cen. Af. Rep.	Central African Republic
C.H.	Court House
Chan.	Channel
Chap.	Chapada
CIS	Commonwealth of Independent States
Cmte.	Comandante
Cnel.	Coronel
Co.-s.	Cerro-s
Col.	Colombia
Colo.	Colorado
Conn.	Connecticut
Cord.	Cordillera
C.R.	Costa Rica
Cr.	Creek, Crique
C.S.I. Terr.	Coral Sea Islands Territory
D.C.	District of Columbia
Del.	Delaware
Den.	Denmark
Dom. Rep.	Dominican Republic
D.R.C.	Democratic Republic of the Congo
E.	East-ern
Ecua.	Ecuador
El Salv.	El Salvador
Eng.	England
Ens.	Ensenada
Eq.	Equatorial
Est.	Estonia
Eth.	Ethiopia
Exp.	Exports
Falk. Is.	Falkland Islands
Fd.	Fiord, Fiordo, Fjord
Fin.	Finland
Fk.	Fork
Fla.	Florida
Fn.	Fortín
Fr.	France, French
F.S.M.	Federated States of Micronesia
ft	feet
Ft.	Fort
G.	Golfe, Golfo, Gulf
Ga.	Georgia
Ger.	Germany
Gl.	Glacier
Gr.	Greece
Gral.	General
Hbr.	Harbor, Harbour
Hist.	Historic, -al
Hond.	Honduras
Hts.	Heights
Hung.	Hungary
Hwy.	Highway
I.-s.	Île-s, Ilha-s, Isla-s, Island-s, Isle, Isol-a, -e
Ice.	Iceland
I.H.S.	International Historic Site
Ill.	Illinois
Ind.	Indiana
Ind.	Industry
Ind. Oc.	Indian Ocean
Intl.	International
Ire.	Ireland
It.	Italy
Jap.	Japan
Jct.	Jonction, Junction
Kans.	Kansas
Kaz.	Kazakhstan
Kep.	Kepulauan
Ky.	Kentucky
Kyrg.	Kyrgyzstan
L.	Lac, Lago, Lake, Límni, Loch, Lough
La.	Louisiana
Lab.	Labrador
Lag.	Laguna
Latv.	Latvia
Leb.	Lebanon
Lib.	Libya
Liech.	Liechtenstein
Lith.	Lithuania
Lux.	Luxembourg
m	meters
Maced.	Macedonia
Madag.	Madagascar
Maurit.	Mauritius
Mass.	Massachusetts
Md.	Maryland
Me.	Maine
Medit. Sea	Mediterranean Sea
Mex.	Mexico
Mgne.	Montagne
Mich.	Michigan
Minn.	Minnesota
Miss.	Mississippi
Mo.	Missouri
Mon.	Monument
Mont.	Montana
Mor.	Morocco
Mt.-s.	Mont-s, Mount-ain-s
N.	North-ern
NA	Not Available
Nat.	National
Nat. Mem.	National Memorial
Nat. Mon.	National Monument
N.B.	National Battlefield
N.B.	New Brunswick
N.C.	North Carolina
N. Dak.	North Dakota
N.E.	Northeast
Nebr.	Nebraska
Neth.	Netherlands
Nev.	Nevada
Nfld.	Newfoundland
N.H.	New Hampshire
Nicar.	Nicaragua
Nig.	Nigeria
N. Ire.	Northern Ireland
N.J.	New Jersey
N. Mex.	New Mexico
N.M.P.	National Military Park
N.M.S.	National Marine Sanctuary
Nor.	Norway
N.P.	National Park
N.S.	Nova Scotia
N.S.W.	New South Wales
N.V.M.	National Volcanic Monument
N.W.T.	Northwest Territories
N.Y.	New York
N.Z.	New Zealand
O.	Ostrov, Oued
Oc.	Ocean
Okla.	Oklahoma
Ont.	Ontario
Oreg.	Oregon
Oz.	Ozero
Pa.	Pennsylvania
Pac. Oc.	Pacific Ocean
Pak.	Pakistan
Pan.	Panama
Para.	Paraguay
Pass.	Passage
Peg.	Pegunungan
P.E.I.	Prince Edward Island
Pen.	Peninsula, Péninsule
Pk.	Peak
P.N.G.	Papua New Guinea
Pol.	Poland
Pol.	Poluostrov
Port.	Portugal, Portuguese
P.R.	Puerto Rico
Prov.	Province, Provincial
Pt.-e.	Point-e
Pta.	Ponta, Punta
Qnsld.	Queensland
Que.	Quebec
R.	Río, River, Rivière
Ra.-s.	Range-s
Rec.	Recreation
Rep.	Republic
Res.	Reservoir, Reserve, Reservatório
R.I.	Rhode Island
Rom.	Romania
Russ.	Russia
S.	South-ern
Sa.-s.	Serra, Sierra-s
S. Af.	South Africa
Sask.	Saskatchewan
S.C.	South Carolina
Scot.	Scotland
Sd.	Sound
S. Dak.	South Dakota
Sev.	Severn-yy, -aya, -oye
Sk.	Shankou
Slov.	Slovenia
Sp.	Spain, Spanish
Spr.-s.	Spring-s
Sta.	Santa
St.-e.	Saint-e, Sankt, Sint
Str.-s.	Straat, Strait-s
Switz.	Switzerland
Syr.	Syria
Taj.	Tajikistan
Tas.	Tasmania
Tenn.	Tennessee
Terr.	Territory
Tex.	Texas
Tg.	Tanjung
Thai.	Thailand
Trin.	Trinidad
Tun.	Tunisia
Turk.	Turkey
Turkm.	Turkmenistan
U.A.E.	United Arab Emirates
U.K.	United Kingdom
Ukr.	Ukraine
U.N.	United Nations
Uru.	Uruguay
U.S.	United States
Uzb.	Uzbekistan
Va.	Virginia
Vdkhr.	Vodokhranilishche
Vdskh.	Vodoskhowshche
Venez.	Venezuela
V.I.	Virgin Islands
Vic.	Victoria
Viet.	Vietnam
Vol.	Volcán, Volcano
Vt.	Vermont
W.	Wadi, Wâd, Webi
W.	West-ern
Wash.	Washington
Wis.	Wisconsin
W. Va.	West Virginia
Wyo.	Wyoming
Yug.	Yugoslavia
Zakh.	Zakhod-ni, -nyaya, -nye
Zimb.	Zimbabwe

QUICK REFERENCE CHART FOR METRIC TO ENGLISH CONVERSION

| 1 METER | 1 METER = 100 CENTIMETERS |
| 1 FOOT | 1 FOOT = 12 INCHES |

| 1 KILOMETER | 1 KILOMETER = 1,000 METERS |
| 1 MILE | 1 MILE = 5,280 FEET |

METERS	1	10	20	50	100	200	500	1,000	2,000	5,000	10,000
FEET	3.28	32.8	65.6	164	328	656	1,640	3,280	6,560	16,400	32,800
KILOMETERS	1	10	20	50	100	200	500	1,000	2,000	5,000	10,000
MILES	0.62	6.2	12.4	31	62	124	310	620	1,240	3,100	6,200

CONVERSION FROM METRIC MEASURES

SYMBOL	WHEN YOU KNOW	MULTIPLY BY	TO FIND	SYMBOL
LENGTH				
cm	centimeters	0.39	inches	in
m	meters	3.28	feet	ft
m	meters	1.09	yards	yd
km	kilometers	0.62	miles	mi
AREA				
cm^2	square centimeters	0.16	square inches	in^2
m^2	square meters	10.76	square feet	ft^2
m^2	square meters	1.20	square yards	yd^2
km^2	square kilometers	0.39	square miles	mi^2
ha	hectares	2.47	acres	—
MASS				
g	grams	0.04	ounces	oz
kg	kilograms	2.20	pounds	lb
t	metric tons	1.10	short tons	—
VOLUME				
mL	milliliters	0.06	cubic inches	in^3
mL	milliliters	0.03	liquid ounces	liq oz
L	liters	2.11	pints	pt
L	liters	1.06	quarts	qt
L	liters	0.26	gallons	gal
m^3	cubic meters	35.31	cubic feet	ft^3
m^3	cubic meters	1.31	cubic yards	yd^3
TEMPERATURE				
°C	degrees Celsius (centigrade)	9/5 then add 32	degrees Fahrenheit	°F

CONVERSION TO METRIC MEASURES

SYMBOL	WHEN YOU KNOW	MULTIPLY BY	TO FIND	SYMBOL
LENGTH				
in	inches	2.54	centimeters	cm
ft	feet	0.30	meters	m
yd	yards	0.91	meters	m
mi	miles	1.61	kilometers	km
AREA				
in^2	square inches	6.45	square centimeters	cm^2
ft^2	square feet	0.09	square meters	m^2
yd^2	square yards	0.84	square meters	m^2
mi^2	square miles	2.59	square kilometers	km^2
—	acres	0.40	hectares	ha
MASS				
oz	ounces	28.35	grams	g
lb	pounds	0.45	kilograms	kg
—	short tons	0.91	metric tons	t
VOLUME				
in^3	cubic inches	16.39	milliliters	mL
liq oz	liquid ounces	29.57	milliliters	mL
pt	pints	0.47	liters	L
qt	quarts	0.95	liters	L
gal	gallons	3.79	liters	L
ft^3	cubic feet	0.03	cubic meters	m^3
yd^3	cubic yards	0.76	cubic meters	m^3
TEMPERATURE				
°F	degrees Fahrenheit	5/9 after subtracting 32	degrees Celsius (centigrade)	°C

World Temperature and Rainfall

Average daily high and low temperatures and monthly rainfall for selected world locations:

CANADA

Location	Jan H	Jan L	Jan R	Feb H	Feb L	Feb R	Mar H	Mar L	Mar R	Apr H	Apr L	Apr R	May H	May L	May R	Jun H	Jun L	Jun R	Jul H	Jul L	Jul R	Aug H	Aug L	Aug R	Sep H	Sep L	Sep R	Oct H	Oct L	Oct R	Nov H	Nov L	Nov R	Dec H	Dec L	Dec R
CALGARY, Alberta	-4	-16	14	-2	-14	15	3	-9	20	11	-3	27	17	3	54	20	7	82	24	9	65	23	8	57	18	3	40	12	-1	18	3	-9	16	-2	-13	14
CHARLOTTETOWN, P.E.I.	-3	-11	100	-3	-12	83	1	-7	83	7	-1	77	14	4	79	20	10	75	24	14	78	23	14	86	18	10	91	13	5	106	6	0	06	0	-7	111
CHURCHILL, Manitoba	-23	-31	15	-22	-30	12	-15	-25	18	-6	-15	23	2	-5	27	11	1	43	17	7	55	16	7	62	9	2	53	2	-4	44	-9	-16	31	-18	-26	18
EDMONTON, Alberta	-9	-18	23	-5	-15	18	0	-9	19	10	-1	24	17	5	45	21	9	79	23	12	87	22	10	64	17	5	36	11	0	20	0	-8	18	-6	-15	22
FORT NELSON, B.C.	-18	-27	23	-11	-23	21	-2	-15	21	8	-4	20	16	3	44	21	8	65	23	10	76	21	8	58	15	3	39	6	-4	28	-9	-17	26	-16	-24	23
GOOSE BAY, Nfld.	-12	-22	1	-10	-21	4	-4	-15	4	3	-7	15	10	0	46	17	5	97	21	10	119	19	9	98	14	4	87	6	-2	58	0	-8	21	-9	-18	7
HALIFAX, Nova Scotia	0	-8	139	0	-9	121	3	-5	123	8	0	109	14	5	110	19	10	96	22	13	93	22	14	103	19	10	93	13	5	127	8	1	42	2	-5	141
MONTRÉAL, Quebec	-6	-15	71	-4	-13	66	2	-7	71	11	1	74	18	8	69	24	13	84	26	16	87	25	14	91	20	10	84	13	4	76	5	-2	90	-3	-11	85
MOOSONEE, Ontario	-14	-27	39	-12	-25	32	-5	-19	37	3	-8	36	11	0	55	18	5	72	22	9	79	20	8	78	15	5	77	6	0	66	-1	-9	53	-11	-21	41
OTTAWA, Ontario	-6	-16	67	-5	-15	59	1	-8	67	11	0	60	19	7	72	24	12	82	27	15	86	25	13	80	20	9	77	13	3	69	4	-3	70	-4	-12	74
PRINCE RUPERT, B.C.	4	-3	237	6	-1	198	7	0	202	9	2	179	12	5	133	14	8	110	16	10	115	16	10	149	15	8	218	11	5	345	7	1	297	5	-1	275
QUÉBEC, Quebec	-7	-17	85	-6	-16	75	0	-9	79	8	-1	76	17	5	93	22	10	108	25	13	112	23	12	109	18	7	113	11	2	89	3	-4	100	-5	-13	104
REGINA, Saskatchewan	-12	-23	17	-9	-21	13	-2	-13	18	10	-3	20	18	3	45	23	9	77	26	11	59	25	10	44	19	4	35	11	-2	20	0	-11	16	-8	-19	14
SAINT JOHN, N.B.	-3	-14	141	-2	-14	115	3	-7	111	10	-1	111	17	4	116	22	9	103	25	12	100	24	11	100	19	7	108	14	2	118	6	-3	149	-1	-10	157
ST. JOHN'S, Nfld.	-1	-8	69	-1	-9	69	1	-6	74	5	-2	80	10	1	91	16	6	95	20	11	78	20	11	122	16	8	125	11	3	147	6	0	122	2	-5	91
TORONTO, Ontario	-1	-8	68	-1	-9	60	3	-4	66	11	2	65	17	7	71	23	13	68	26	16	77	25	15	70	21	11	73	14	5	62	7	0	70	1	-6	67
VANCOUVER, B.C.	5	0	146	8	1	121	10	2	102	13	5	69	17	8	56	19	11	47	22	13	31	22	13	37	19	10	60	14	6	116	9	3	155	6	1	172
WHITEHORSE, Yukon	-14	-23	17	-9	-18	13	-2	-13	13	5	-5	9	13	1	30	18	5	30	20	8	37	18	6	39	12	3	31	4	-3	21	-6	-13	20	-12	-20	19
WINNIPEG, Manitoba	-13	-23	21	-10	-21	19	-2	-13	26	9	-2	34	18	5	55	23	10	81	26	14	74	25	12	66	19	6	55	12	1	35	-1	-9	26	-9	-18	22
YELLOWKNIFE, N.W.T.	-24	-32	14	-20	-30	12	-12	-24	11	-1	-13	10	10	0	16	18	8	20	21	12	35	18	10	39	10	4	29	1	-4	32	-10	-18	23	-20	-28	17

UNITED STATES

Location	Jan H	Jan L	Jan R	Feb H	Feb L	Feb R	Mar H	Mar L	Mar R	Apr H	Apr L	Apr R	May H	May L	May R	Jun H	Jun L	Jun R	Jul H	Jul L	Jul R	Aug H	Aug L	Aug R	Sep H	Sep L	Sep R	Oct H	Oct L	Oct R	Nov H	Nov L	Nov R	Dec H	Dec L	Dec R
ALBANY, New York	-1	-12	61	1	-10	59	7	-4	76	14	2	77	21	7	86	26	13	83	29	15	80	27	14	87	23	10	78	17	4	77	9	-1	30	2	-8	74
AMARILLO, Texas	9	-6	13	12	-4	14	16	0	23	22	6	28	26	11	71	31	16	88	33	19	70	32	18	74	28	14	50	23	7	35	15	0	15	10	-5	15
ANCHORAGE, Alaska	-6	-13	20	-3	-11	21	1	-8	17	6	-2	15	12	4	17	16	8	26	18	11	47	17	10	62	13	5	66	5	-2	47	-3	-9	29	-5	-12	28
ASPEN, Colorado	0	-18	32	2	-16	26	5	-11	35	10	-6	28	16	-2	39	22	1	34	25	5	44	25	4	45	21	0	34	15	-5	36	6	-10	31	1	-15	32
ATLANTA, Georgia	10	0	117	13	1	117	18	6	139	23	10	103	26	15	100	30	19	92	31	21	134	31	21	93	28	18	91	23	11	77	17	6	95	12	2	105
ATLANTIC CITY, N.J.	5	-6	83	6	-5	78	11	0	98	16	4	86	22	10	82	27	15	63	29	18	103	29	18	103	25	13	78	19	7	72	13	2	84	7	-3	81
AUGUSTA, Maine	-2	-11	76	0	-10	71	4	-5	84	11	1	92	19	7	95	23	12	85	26	16	85	25	15	84	20	10	80	14	4	92	7	-1	114	0	-8	93
BIRMINGHAM, Alabama	11	0	128	14	1	114	19	6	150	24	10	114	27	14	112	31	18	97	32	21	132	32	20	95	29	17	105	24	10	75	18	5	103	13	2	120
BISMARCK, N. Dak.	-7	-19	12	-3	-15	11	4	-8	20	13	-1	37	20	6	56	25	11	74	29	14	59	28	12	44	22	6	38	15	0	21	4	-8	4	-4	-16	12
BOISE, Idaho	2	-6	38	9	-3	28	12	0	32	16	3	31	22	7	31	27	11	22	32	14	8	31	14	9	25	9	16	18	4	18	9	-1	35	3	-5	35
BOSTON, Massachusetts	2	-6	95	3	-5	91	8	0	100	13	5	93	19	10	84	25	15	79	28	18	73	27	18	92	23	14	82	17	8	87	11	4	110	5	-3	105
BROWNSVILLE, Texas	21	10	37	22	11	36	26	15	16	29	19	41	31	22	64	33	24	74	34	24	69	34	24	69	32	23	134	30	19	89	26	15	41	22	11	30
BURLINGTON, Vermont	-4	-14	46	-3	-13	44	4	-6	55	12	1	71	20	7	78	24	13	85	27	15	90	26	14	101	21	9	85	14	4	77	7	-1	76	-1	-9	59
CHARLESTON, S.C.	14	3	88	16	4	80	20	9	114	24	12	71	28	17	97	31	21	155	32	23	180	32	22	176	29	20	135	25	14	77	21	8	63	16	5	82
CHARLESTON, W. Va.	5	-5	87	7	-4	82	14	2	100	19	6	85	24	11	99	28	15	92	30	18	126	29	17	102	26	14	81	20	7	67	14	2	85	8	-2	85
CHEYENNE, Wyoming	3	-9	10	5	-8	11	7	-6	26	13	-1	35	18	4	64	24	9	56	28	13	51	27	12	42	22	7	31	16	1	19	8	-5	5	4	-9	10
CHICAGO, Illinois	-1	-10	48	1	-7	42	8	-1	72	15	5	97	22	10	83	27	16	103	29	19	103	28	18	89	24	14	79	18	7	70	9	1	73	2	-6	65
CINCINNATI, Ohio	3	-6	89	5	-4	67	12	1	97	18	7	94	24	12	101	28	17	99	30	19	102	30	18	86	26	14	75	19	8	62	12	3	81	5	-3	75
CLEVELAND, Ohio	1	-7	62	2	-6	58	8	-2	78	15	4	85	21	9	90	26	14	89	28	17	88	27	16	86	23	12	80	17	7	65	10	2	80	3	-4	70
DALLAS, Texas	13	1	47	15	4	58	20	8	74	25	13	105	29	18	125	33	22	86	35	24	56	35	24	60	31	20	82	26	14	100	19	8	64	14	3	60
DENVER, Colorado	6	-9	14	8	-7	16	11	-3	34	17	1	45	22	6	63	27	11	43	31	15	47	30	14	38	25	9	28	19	2	26	11	-4	23	7	-8	15
DES MOINES, Iowa	-2	-12	26	1	-9	30	8	-2	57	17	4	85	23	11	103	28	16	108	30	19	97	29	18	105	24	13	80	18	6	58	9	-1	46	0	-9	31
DETROIT, Michigan	-1	-7	42	1	-7	43	7	-2	62	14	4	75	21	10	69	26	15	85	29	18	86	27	18	87	23	14	78	17	7	55	9	2	67	2	-4	67
DULUTH, Minnesota	-9	-19	31	-6	-16	21	1	-9	44	9	-2	59	17	4	84	22	9	105	25	13	102	23	12	101	18	7	95	11	2	62	2	-6	48	-6	-15	32
EL PASO, Texas	13	1	11	17	1	11	21	5	8	26	9	7	31	14	9	36	18	17	36	20	38	34	19	39	31	16	34	26	10	20	19	4	11	14	1	14
FAIRBANKS, Alaska	-19	-28	14	-14	-26	11	-5	-19	9	5	-6	7	15	3	15	21	10	35	22	11	45	19	8	46	13	2	28	0	-8	21	-12	-21	18	-17	-26	19
HARTFORD, Connecticut	1	-9	83	2	-7	79	8	-2	97	16	3	97	22	9	95	27	14	85	29	17	86	28	16	104	24	11	101	18	5	96	11	0	105	3	-6	93
HELENA, Montana	-1	-12	15	3	-9	12	7	-5	18	13	-1	24	19	4	45	24	9	53	29	12	28	28	11	27	21	5	28	15	0	19	6	-6	14	0	-12	16
HONOLULU, Hawai'i	27	19	80	27	19	68	28	20	72	28	20	32	29	21	25	30	22	10	31	23	15	32	23	14	31	23	18	31	22	53	29	21	67	27	19	89
HOUSTON, Texas	16	4	98	19	6	75	22	10	88	26	15	91	29	18	142	32	21	133	34	22	85	34	22	95	31	20	106	28	14	120	22	10	97	18	6	91
INDIANAPOLIS, Indiana	1	-8	69	4	-6	61	11	0	92	17	5	94	23	11	98	28	16	98	30	19	111	29	17	88	25	13	74	19	6	69	11	1	89	4	-5	77
JACKSONVILLE, Florida	18	5	83	19	6	89	23	10	100	26	13	77	29	17	92	32	21	140	33	22	164	33	22	186	31	21	199	27	15	99	23	10	52	19	6	65
JUNEAU, Alaska	-1	-7	139	1	-5	116	4	-3	113	9	0	105	13	4	109	16	7	88	18	9	120	17	8	160	13	6	217	8	3	255	3	-2	186	0	-5	153
KANSAS CITY, Missouri	2	-9	30	5	-6	32	12	0	67	18	7	88	24	12	138	29	17	102	32	20	115	30	19	99	26	14	120	20	8	83	11	1	56	4	-6	43
LAS VEGAS, Nevada	14	0	14	17	4	12	20	7	13	25	10	5	31	16	5	38	21	3	41	25	9	40	23	13	35	19	7	28	12	6	20	6	7	14	1	10
LITTLE ROCK, Arkansas	9	-1	85	12	1	88	17	6	120	23	11	134	26	15	141	31	20	84	33	22	83	32	21	80	28	18	85	23	11	102	16	6	153	10	1	123
LOS ANGELES, California	19	9	70	19	10	61	19	10	51	20	12	20	21	14	3	22	15	1	24	17	1	25	18	2	25	17	5	24	15	7	21	12	38	19	9	43
LOUISVILLE, Kentucky	5	-5	85	7	-3	88	14	2	113	20	7	101	24	13	114	29	17	90	31	20	106	30	19	84	27	15	76	21	8	68	14	3	92	7	-2	89
MEMPHIS, Tennessee	9	-1	118	12	2	114	17	6	136	23	11	142	27	16	126	32	21	98	34	23	101	33	22	87	29	18	83	24	11	74	17	6	124	11	2	135
MIAMI, Florida	24	15	52	25	16	53	26	18	63	28	20	82	30	22	150	31	24	227	32	25	152	32	25	198	31	24	215	29	22	178	27	19	80	25	16	47
MILWAUKEE, Wisconsin	-3	-11	32	-1	-8	31	5	-3	54	12	2	87	18	7	73	24	13	87	27	17	85	26	16	94	22	12	95	15	6	66	7	-1	65	0	-7	53
MINNEAPOLIS, Minnesota	-6	-16	21	-3	-13	22	4	-5	45	14	2	58	21	9	80	26	14	103	29	17	97	27	16	95	21	10	70	15	4	49	5	-4	37	-4	-12	24
NASHVILLE, Tennessee	8	-3	108	10	-1	100	16	4	127	22	9	104	26	14	118	30	18	99	32	21	99	31	20	85	28	16	89	23	9	67	16	4	101	10	-1	112
NEW ORLEANS, Louisiana	16	5	136	18	7	147	22	11	124	26	15	119	29	18	135	32	22	147	33	23	167	32	23	157	30	21	138	26	15	76	22	11	101	18	7	132
NEW YORK, New York	3	-4	80	4	-3	76	9	1	99	15	7	94	21	12	93	26	17	80	29	21	101	28	20	107	24	16	85	18	10	81	12	5	95	6	-1	90
OKLAHOMA CITY, Okla.	8	-4	28	11	-1	36	17	4	61	22	9	76	26	14	145	31	19	107	34	21	74	34	21	65	29	17	97	23	10	83	16	4	43	10	-2	37
OMAHA, Nebraska	-1	-12	18	2	-9	21	9	-2	61	17	5	73	23	11	118	28	16	105	30	19	96	29	18	95	24	13	90	18	6	60	9	-1	35	1	-9	23
PENSACOLA, Florida	15	5	109	17	7	126	21	11	150	25	15	112	29	19	105	32	22	168	32	23	187	32	23	176	30	21	166	26	15	102	21	11	91	17	7	105
PHILADELPHIA, Pa.	3	-5	82	5	-4	70	11	1	95	17	6	88	23	12	94	28	17	87	30	20	108	29	19	97	25	15	86	19	8	67	13	3	85	6	-2	86
PHOENIX, Arizona	19	3	21	22	5	21	25	7	30	29	9	7	33	13	5	38	18	3	39	23	21	38	22	30	36	18	23	30	12	14	23	7	13	19	3	28
PITTSBURGH, Pa.	1	-7	66	3	-7	60	9	-1	85	16	4	80	21	9	92	26	14	91	28	16	98	27	16	83	24	12	74	17	6	61	10	1	63	4	-4	71
PORTLAND, Oregon	7	1	133	11	2	105	13	4	92	16	5	61	20	8	53	23	12	38	27	14	15	27	14	25	24	11	41	18	7	76	11	4	157	8	2	149
PROVIDENCE, R.I.	3	-7	101	4	-6	91	8	-2	111	14	3	102	20	9	89	25	14	90	28	17	77	27	17	102	23	12	88	16	6	93	12	2	117	5	-4	110
RALEIGH, N.C.	9	-2	89	11	0	88	17	4	94	22	8	70	26	13	96	29	18	91	31	20	111	30	20	110	27	16	79	22	9	73	17	4	75	12	0	79
RAPID CITY, S. Dak.	2	-12	10	4	-10	12	8	-6	26	14	0	52	20	6	84	25	12	89	30	15	63	29	13	43	23	7	32	16	1	26	8	-5	12	3	-11	10
RENO, Nevada	7	-6	28	11	-4	24	14	-2	20	18	1	11	23	5	17	28	8	11	33	11	7	32	10	6	26	5	9	20	1	10	12	-3	19	8	-7	27
ST. LOUIS, Missouri	3	-6	50	6	-4	54	13	2	84	19	8	97	25	13	100	30	19	103	32	21	92	31	20	76	27	16	73	20	9	70	13	3	73	5	-3	64
SALT LAKE CITY, Utah	2	-7	32	6	-4	30	11	0	45	16	3	52	23	8	46	29	13	23	35	18	18	32	17	21	26	11	27	19	5	34	10	-1	34	3	-6	34
SAN DIEGO, California	19	9	56	19	10	41	19	12	50	20	13	20	21	15	5	22	17	2	25	19	1	25	20	2	25	19	5	24	16	9	21	12	30	19	9	50
SAN FRANCISCO, Calif.	14	8	112	16	9	77	16	9	78	17	10	34	17	10	10	18	11	4	18	12	1	19	12	2	20	13	7	20	13	28	17	11	73	14	8	91

RED FIGURES: Average daily high temperature (°C) **BLUE FIGURES:** Average daily low temperature (°C) **BLACK FIGURES:** Average monthly rainfall (mm)
1 millimeter = 0.039 inches

	JAN.			FEB.			MARCH			APRIL			MAY			JUNE			JULY			AUG.			SEPT.			OCT.			NOV.			DEC.		
UNITED STATES																																				
SANTA FE, *New Mexico*	6	-10	11	9	-7	9	13	-5	12	18	-1	13	24	4	23	29	9	31	31	12	52	29	11	64	25	7	38	20	1	32	13	-5	14	7	-9	12
SEATTLE, *Washington*	7	2	141	10	3	107	12	4	94	14	5	64	18	8	42	21	11	38	24	13	20	24	13	27	21	11	47	15	8	89	10	5	149	7	2	149
SPOKANE, *Washington*	1	-6	52	5	-3	39	9	-1	37	14	2	28	19	6	35	24	10	33	28	12	15	28	12	16	22	8	20	15	2	31	5	-2	51	1	-6	57
TAMPA, *Florida*	21	10	54	22	11	73	25	14	90	28	16	44	31	20	76	32	23	143	32	24	189	32	24	196	32	23	160	29	18	60	25	14	46	22	11	54
VICKSBURG, *Mississippi*	14	2	155	16	3	131	21	8	160	25	12	147	29	16	130	32	20	88	33	22	106	33	21	80	30	18	85	26	12	106	20	8	126	16	4	168
WASHINGTON, *D.C.*	6	-3	71	8	-2	66	14	3	90	19	8	72	25	14	94	29	19	80	31	22	97	31	21	104	27	17	84	21	10	78	15	5	76	8	0	79
WICHITA, *Kansas*	4	-7	19	8	-5	23	14	1	57	20	7	57	25	12	99	30	18	105	34	21	82	33	20	78	27	15	85	21	8	62	13	1	37	6	-5	29
MIDDLE AMERICA																																				
ACAPULCO, *Mexico*	29	21	8	31	21	1	31	21	0	31	22	1	32	23	36	32	24	325	32	24	231	32	24	236	31	24	353	31	23	170	31	22	30	31	21	10
BALBOA, *Panama*	31	22	34	32	22	16	32	22	14	32	23	73	31	23	198	30	23	203	31	23	176	31	23	200	30	23	197	29	23	271	29	23	260	31	23	133
CHARLOTTE AMALIE, *V.I.*	28	23	50	27	22	41	28	23	49	28	23	53	29	24	105	30	25	67	31	26	71	31	26	112	31	26	132	31	25	139	29	24	131	28	23	69
GUATEMALA CITY, *Guatemala*	23	12	4	25	12	5	27	14	10	28	14	32	29	16	110	27	16	257	26	16	197	26	16	193	26	16	235	24	16	98	23	14	33	22	13	13
GUAYMAS, *Mexico*	23	13	17	24	14	6	26	16	5	29	18	1	31	21	2	34	24	1	34	27	46	35	27	71	35	26	28	32	22	17	28	18	8	23	13	18
HAVANA, *Cuba*	26	18	71	26	18	46	27	19	46	29	21	58	30	22	119	31	23	165	32	24	124	32	24	135	31	24	150	29	23	173	27	21	79	26	19	58
KINGSTON, *Jamaica*	30	19	29	30	19	24	30	20	23	31	21	39	31	22	104	32	23	96	32	23	46	32	23	107	32	23	127	31	23	181	31	22	95	31	21	41
MANAGUA, *Nicaragua*	33	21	2	33	21	3	35	22	4	36	23	3	35	24	136	32	23	237	32	23	132	32	23	121	33	23	213	32	23	315	32	22	42	32	22	10
MÉRIDA, *Mexico*	28	17	30	29	17	23	32	19	18	33	21	20	34	22	81	33	23	142	33	23	132	33	23	142	32	23	173	31	22	97	29	19	33	28	18	33
MEXICO CITY, *Mexico*	19	6	8	21	6	5	24	8	11	25	11	19	26	12	49	24	13	106	23	12	129	23	12	121	23	12	110	21	10	44	20	8	15	19	6	7
MONTERREY, *Mexico*	20	9	18	22	11	23	24	14	16	29	17	29	31	20	40	33	22	68	32	22	62	33	22	76	30	21	151	27	18	78	22	13	26	18	10	20
NASSAU, *Bahamas*	25	18	48	25	18	43	26	19	41	27	21	65	29	22	132	31	23	178	31	24	153	32	24	170	31	24	180	29	23	171	27	21	71	26	19	43
PORT-AU-PRINCE, *Haiti*	31	20	32	31	20	50	32	21	79	32	22	156	32	22	218	33	23	96	34	23	73	34	23	139	33	23	166	32	22	164	31	22	84	31	21	35
PORT OF SPAIN, *Trinidad*	29	19	69	30	19	41	31	19	46	31	21	53	32	21	94	31	22	193	31	21	218	31	22	246	31	22	193	31	22	170	31	21	183	30	21	124
SAN JOSÉ, *Costa Rica*	24	14	11	24	14	5	26	15	14	26	17	46	27	17	224	26	17	276	25	17	215	26	16	243	26	16	326	25	16	323	25	16	148	24	14	42
SAN JUAN, *Puerto Rico*	27	21	75	27	21	56	27	21	59	28	22	95	29	23	156	29	24	112	29	24	115	29	24	133	30	24	136	29	24	140	29	23	148	27	22	118
SAN SALVADOR, *El Salv.*	32	16	7	33	16	7	34	17	13	34	18	53	33	19	179	31	19	315	32	18	312	32	19	307	31	19	317	31	18	230	31	17	40	32	16	12
SANTO DOMINGO, *Dom. Rep.*	29	19	57	29	19	43	29	19	49	29	21	77	30	22	179	31	22	154	31	22	155	31	23	162	31	22	173	31	22	164	30	21	111	29	19	63
TEGUCIGALPA, *Honduras*	25	13	9	27	14	4	29	14	8	30	17	32	29	18	151	28	18	159	28	17	82	28	17	87	28	17	185	27	17	135	26	16	38	25	15	12
SOUTH AMERICA																																				
ANTOFAGASTA, *Chile*	24	17	0	24	17	0	23	16	0	21	14	0	19	13	0	18	11	1	17	11	1	17	11	1	18	12	0	19	13	0	21	14	0	22	16	0
ASUNCIÓN, *Paraguay*	35	22	150	34	22	133	33	21	142	29	18	145	25	14	120	22	12	73	23	12	51	26	14	48	28	16	83	30	17	136	32	18	144	34	21	142
BELÉM, *Brazil*	31	22	351	30	22	412	31	23	441	31	23	370	31	23	282	31	22	164	31	22	154	31	22	122	32	22	129	32	22	105	32	22	101	32	22	202
BOGOTÁ, *Colombia*	19	9	48	20	9	52	19	10	81	19	11	119	19	11	103	18	11	61	18	10	47	18	10	48	19	9	58	19	10	142	19	10	115	19	9	67
BRASÍLIA, *Brazil*	27	18	262	27	18	213	28	18	202	28	17	103	26	13	20	25	11	4	26	11	4	28	13	6	31	16	35	28	18	140	28	19	238	26	18	329
BUENOS AIRES, *Arg.*	29	17	93	28	17	81	26	16	117	22	12	90	18	8	77	14	5	64	14	6	59	16	6	65	18	8	78	21	10	97	24	13	89	28	16	96
CARACAS, *Venezuela*	24	13	41	25	13	27	26	14	22	27	16	20	27	17	36	26	17	52	26	16	53	26	16	53	27	16	48	26	16	47	25	16	50	26	14	58
COM. RIVADAVIA, *Arg.*	26	13	16	25	13	11	22	11	21	18	8	21	13	6	34	11	3	21	11	3	25	12	3	22	14	5	13	19	9	13	22	10	13	24	12	15
CÓRDOBA, *Argentina*	31	16	110	30	16	102	28	14	96	24	11	45	21	7	25	18	3	10	18	3	10	21	4	13	23	7	27	25	11	69	28	13	97	30	16	118
GUAYAQUIL, *Ecuador*	31	21	224	31	22	278	31	22	287	32	22	180	31	20	53	31	20	17	29	19	2	30	18	0	31	19	2	30	20	3	31	20	3	31	21	30
LA PAZ, *Bolivia*	17	6	130	17	6	105	18	6	72	18	4	47	18	3	13	17	1	6	17	1	9	17	2	14	18	3	29	19	4	40	19	6	50	18	6	93
LIMA, *Peru*	28	19	1	28	19	1	28	19	1	27	17	0	23	16	1	20	14	2	19	14	4	19	13	3	20	14	3	22	14	2	23	16	1	26	17	1
MANAUS, *Brazil*	31	24	264	31	24	262	31	24	298	31	24	283	31	24	204	31	24	103	32	24	67	33	24	46	33	24	63	33	24	111	33	24	161	32	24	220
MARACAIBO, *Venezuela*	32	23	5	32	23	5	33	23	6	33	24	39	33	25	65	34	25	55	34	24	25	34	25	53	34	25	76	33	24	119	33	24	55	33	24	22
MONTEVIDEO, *Uruguay*	28	17	95	28	16	100	26	15	111	22	12	83	18	9	76	15	6	74	14	6	86	15	6	84	17	8	90	20	9	98	23	12	78	26	15	84
PARAMARIBO, *Suriname*	29	22	209	29	22	149	29	22	168	30	23	219	30	23	307	30	23	302	31	23	227	32	23	163	33	23	80	33	23	82	32	23	117	30	22	204
PUNTA ARENAS, *Chile*	14	7	35	14	7	28	12	5	39	10	4	41	7	2	42	5	1	32	4	-1	34	6	1	33	8	2	28	11	3	24	12	4	29	14	6	32
QUITO, *Ecuador*	22	8	113	22	8	128	22	8	154	21	8	176	21	8	124	22	7	48	22	7	20	23	7	24	23	7	78	22	8	127	22	7	109	22	8	103
RECIFE, *Brazil*	30	25	62	30	25	102	30	24	197	29	24	252	28	23	301	28	23	302	27	22	254	27	22	156	28	23	78	29	24	36	29	24	29	29	25	40
RIO DE JANEIRO, *Brazil*	29	23	135	29	23	124	28	22	134	27	21	109	25	19	78	24	18	52	24	17	45	24	18	46	24	18	62	25	19	82	26	20	100	28	22	137
SANTIAGO, *Chile*	29	12	3	29	11	3	27	9	5	23	7	13	18	5	64	14	3	84	15	3	76	17	4	56	19	6	30	22	7	15	26	9	8	28	11	5
SÃO PAULO, *Brazil*	27	17	225	28	18	208	27	17	160	26	14	71	23	12	67	22	11	54	22	9	35	23	11	48	23	12	77	24	14	117	26	15	139	27	16	185
VALPARAÍSO, *Chile*	22	13	0	22	13	0	21	12	0	19	11	22	17	10	38	16	9	100	16	8	111	16	8	42	17	9	27	18	10	15	21	11	15	22	12	1
EUROPE																																				
AJACCIO, *Corsica*	13	3	76	14	4	58	16	5	66	18	7	56	21	10	41	25	14	23	27	16	71	28	16	18	26	15	43	22	11	97	18	7	112	15	4	79
AMSTERDAM, *Neth.*	4	1	79	5	1	44	8	3	89	11	6	39	16	10	50	18	13	60	21	15	73	20	15	60	18	13	80	13	9	104	8	5	76	5	2	72
ATHENS, *Greece*	13	6	48	14	7	41	16	8	41	20	11	23	25	16	18	30	20	7	33	23	5	33	23	8	29	19	10	24	15	53	19	12	55	15	8	62
BARCELONA, *Spain*	13	6	38	14	7	38	16	9	47	18	11	47	21	14	44	25	18	38	28	21	28	28	21	44	25	19	76	21	15	96	16	11	51	13	8	44
BELFAST, *N. Ireland*	6	2	83	7	2	55	9	3	59	12	4	51	15	6	56	18	9	65	18	11	79	18	11	78	16	9	82	13	7	85	9	4	75	7	3	84
BELGRADE, *Serbia*	3	-3	42	5	-2	39	11	2	43	18	7	57	23	12	73	26	15	84	28	17	63	28	17	53	24	13	47	18	8	50	11	4	55	5	0	52
BERLIN, *Germany*	2	-3	43	3	-3	38	8	0	38	13	4	41	19	8	49	22	12	64	24	14	71	23	13	62	20	10	44	13	6	44	7	2	46	3	-1	48
BIARRITZ, *France*	11	4	106	12	4	93	15	6	92	16	8	95	18	11	97	22	14	93	23	16	64	24	16	74	22	15	102	19	11	129	15	7	135	12	5	134
BORDEAUX, *France*	9	2	76	11	2	65	15	4	66	17	6	65	20	9	71	24	12	65	25	14	52	26	14	59	23	12	70	18	8	87	13	5	88	9	3	86
BRINDISI, *Italy*	12	6	57	13	7	61	15	8	67	18	11	35	22	14	26	26	18	20	29	21	9	29	21	25	26	18	47	22	15	71	18	11	72	14	8	65
BRUSSELS, *Belgium*	4	-1	82	7	0	51	10	2	81	14	5	53	18	8	74	22	11	74	23	12	58	22	12	42	21	11	69	15	7	85	9	3	61	6	0	68
BUCHAREST, *Romania*	1	-7	44	4	-5	37	10	-1	35	18	5	46	23	10	65	27	14	86	30	16	56	30	15	56	25	11	35	18	6	28	10	2	45	4	-3	42
BUDAPEST, *Hungary*	1	-4	41	4	-2	36	10	2	41	17	7	49	22	11	69	26	15	71	28	16	53	27	16	53	23	12	45	16	7	52	8	3	58	4	-1	49
CAGLIARI, *Sardinia*	14	7	53	15	7	52	17	9	45	19	11	35	23	14	27	27	18	10	30	21	3	30	21	10	27	19	29	23	15	57	19	11	56	16	9	55
CANDIA, *Crete*	16	9	94	16	9	76	17	10	41	20	12	23	23	15	18	27	19	3	29	21	1	29	22	3	27	19	18	24	17	43	21	14	69	18	11	102
COPENHAGEN, *Denmark*	2	-2	42	2	-3	25	5	-1	35	10	3	40	16	8	42	19	11	52	22	14	67	21	14	75	18	11	51	12	7	53	7	3	52	4	1	51
DUBLIN, *Ireland*	7	2	64	8	2	51	10	3	52	12	5	49	14	7	56	18	9	55	19	11	65	19	11	77	17	10	62	14	7	73	10	4	69	8	3	69
DURAZZO, *Albania*	11	6	76	12	6	84	13	8	99	17	13	56	22	17	41	25	21	48	28	23	13	28	22	48	24	18	43	20	14	180	14	11	216	12	8	185
EDINBURGH, *Scotland*	6	1	55	6	1	41	8	2	47	11	4	39	14	6	50	17	9	50	18	11	64	18	11	69	16	9	63	12	7	62	9	4	63	7	2	61
FLORENCE, *Italy*	9	2	64	11	3	62	14	5	69	19	8	71	23	12	73	27	15	56	30	18	34	30	17	47	26	15	83	20	11	99	14	7	103	11	4	79
GENEVA, *Switzerland*	4	-2	55	6	-1	53	10	2	60	15	5	63	19	9	76	23	13	81	25	15	72	24	14	90	21	12	90	14	7	91	8	3	81	4	0	66
HAMBURG, *Germany*	2	-2	61	3	-2	40	7	-1	52	13	3	47	18	7	55	21	11	74	22	13	81	22	12	79	19	10	68	13	6	62	7	3	65	4	0	71
HELSINKI, *Finland*	-3	-9	46	-4	-9	37	0	-7	35	6	-1	37	14	4	42	19	9	46	22	13	62	20	12	75	15	8	67	8	3	69	3	-1	66	-1	-5	55
LISBON, *Portugal*	14	8	95	15	8	87	17	10	85	20	12	60	21	13	44	25	15	18	27	17	4	28	17	5	26	17	33	22	14	75	17	11	100	15	9	97
LIVERPOOL, *England*	7	2	69	7	2	48	9	3	38	11	5	41	14	8	56	17	11	51	19	13	71	18	13	79	16	11	66	13	8	76	9	5	76	7	3	64
LONDON, *England*	7	2	62	7	2	36	11	8	50	13	4	43	17	7	45	21	11	46	23	13	46	22	12	44	19	11	43	14	7	73	9	4	45	7	2	59
LUXEMBOURG, *Lux.*	3	-1	66	4	-1	54	10	1	55	14	4	53	18	8	66	21	11	65	23	13	70	22	12	69	19	10	62	13	6	70	7	3	71	4	0	74
MADRID, *Spain*	9	2	45	11	2	43	15	5	37	18	7	45	21	10	40	27	15	25	31	17	9	30	17	10	25	14	29	19	10	46	13	5	64	9	2	47
MARSEILLE, *France*	10	2	49	12	2	40	15	5	45	18	8	46	22	11	46	26	15	26	29	17	15	28	17	24	25	15	63	20	10	94	15	6	76	11	3	59

World Temperature and Rainfall

Average daily high and low temperatures and monthly rainfall for selected world locations:

EUROPE

Location	JAN.			FEB.			MARCH			APRIL			MAY			JUNE			JULY			AUG.			SEPT.			OCT.			NOV.			DEC.		
MILAN, *Italy*	5	0	61	8	2	58	13	6	72	18	10	85	23	14	98	27	17	81	29	20	68	28	19	81	24	16	82	17	11	116	10	6	106	6	2	75
MUNICH, *Germany*	1	-5	49	3	-5	43	9	-1	52	14	3	70	18	7	101	21	11	123	23	13	127	23	12	112	20	9	83	13	4	62	7	0	54	2	-4	51
NANTES, *France*	8	2	79	9	2	62	13	4	62	15	6	54	19	9	61	22	12	55	24	14	50	24	13	54	21	12	70	16	8	89	11	5	91	8	3	86
NAPLES, *Italy*	12	4	94	13	5	81	15	6	76	18	9	66	22	12	46	26	16	46	29	18	15	29	18	18	26	16	71	22	12	130	17	9	114	14	6	137
NICE, *France*	13	4	77	13	5	73	15	7	73	17	9	64	20	13	49	24	16	37	27	18	19	27	18	32	25	16	65	21	12	111	17	8	117	13	5	88
OSLO, *Norway*	-2	-7	41	-1	-7	31	4	-4	34	10	1	36	16	6	45	20	10	59	22	13	75	21	12	86	16	8	72	9	3	71	3	-1	57	0	-4	49
PALERMO, *Italy*	16	8	44	16	8	35	17	9	30	20	11	29	24	14	14	27	18	9	30	21	2	30	21	8	28	19	28	25	16	59	21	12	66	18	10	68
PALMA DE MALLORCA, *Spain*	14	6	39	15	6	35	17	8	37	19	10	35	22	13	34	26	17	20	29	20	8	29	20	18	27	18	52	23	14	77	18	10	54	15	8	54
PARIS, *France*	6	1	46	7	1	39	12	4	41	16	6	44	20	10	56	23	13	57	25	15	57	24	14	55	21	12	53	16	8	57	10	5	54	7	2	49
PRAGUE, *Czech. Rep.*	1	-4	21	3	-2	19	7	1	26	13	4	36	18	9	59	22	11	68	23	14	67	23	14	62	18	11	41	12	7	30	5	2	27	1	-2	23
RIGA, *Latvia*	-4	-10	32	-3	-10	24	2	-7	26	10	1	35	16	6	42	21	9	58	22	11	72	21	11	68	17	8	66	11	4	54	4	-1	52	-2	-7	39
ROME, *Italy*	11	5	80	13	5	71	15	7	69	19	10	67	23	13	52	28	17	34	30	20	16	30	19	24	26	17	69	22	13	113	16	9	111	13	6	97
SEVILLE, *Spain*	15	6	56	17	7	74	20	9	84	24	11	58	27	13	33	32	17	23	36	20	3	36	20	3	32	18	28	26	14	66	20	10	94	16	7	71
SOFIA, *Bulgaria*	2	-4	34	4	-3	34	10	1	38	16	5	54	21	10	69	24	14	78	27	16	56	26	15	43	22	11	40	17	8	35	9	3	52	4	-2	44
SPLIT, *Croatia*	10	5	80	11	5	65	14	7	65	18	11	62	23	16	62	27	19	48	30	22	28	30	22	43	26	19	66	21	14	87	15	10	111	12	7	113
STOCKHOLM, *Sweden*	-1	-5	31	-1	-5	25	3	-4	26	8	1	29	14	6	34	19	11	44	22	14	64	20	13	66	15	9	49	9	5	51	5	1	44	2	-2	39
VALENCIA, *Spain*	15	6	23	16	6	38	18	8	23	20	10	30	23	13	28	26	17	33	29	20	10	29	20	13	27	18	56	23	13	41	19	10	64	16	7	33
VALETTA, *Malta*	14	10	84	15	10	58	16	11	38	18	13	20	22	16	10	26	19	3	29	22	1	29	23	5	27	22	33	24	19	69	20	16	91	16	12	99
VENICE, *Italy*	6	1	51	8	2	53	12	5	61	17	10	71	21	14	81	25	17	84	27	19	66	27	18	66	24	16	66	19	11	94	12	7	89	8	3	66
VIENNA, *Austria*	1	-4	38	3	-3	36	8	1	46	15	6	51	19	10	71	23	14	69	25	15	76	24	15	69	20	11	51	14	7	25	7	3	48	3	-1	46
WARSAW, *Poland*	0	-6	28	0	-6	26	6	-2	31	12	3	37	20	9	50	23	12	66	24	15	77	23	14	72	19	10	47	13	5	41	6	1	38	2	-3	35
ZÜRICH, *Switzerland*	2	-3	61	5	-2	61	10	1	68	15	4	85	19	8	101	23	12	127	25	14	128	24	13	124	20	11	98	14	6	83	7	2	71	3	-2	72

ASIA

Location	JAN.			FEB.			MARCH			APRIL			MAY			JUNE			JULY			AUG.			SEPT.			OCT.			NOV.			DEC.		
ADEN, *Yemen*	27	23	8	27	23	7	29	24	8	31	26	4	34	28	3	35	29	1	34	28	2	33	27	3	34	28	4	32	26	2	29	24	2	27	23	4
ALMATY, *Kazakhstan*	-5	-14	33	-3	-12	23	4	-6	56	13	3	102	20	10	94	24	14	66	27	16	36	27	14	30	22	8	25	13	2	51	4	-5	48	-2	-9	33
ANKARA, *Turkey*	4	-4	49	6	-3	52	11	-1	45	17	4	44	23	9	56	26	12	37	30	15	13	31	15	8	26	11	28	21	7	21	14	3	28	6	-2	63
ARKHANGEL'SK, *Russia*	-12	-20	30	-10	-18	28	-4	-13	28	5	-4	18	12	2	33	17	6	48	20	10	66	19	10	69	12	5	56	4	-1	48	-2	-7	41	-8	-15	33
BAGHDAD, *Iraq*	16	4	27	18	6	28	22	9	27	29	14	19	36	19	7	41	23	0	43	24	0	43	24	0	40	21	0	33	16	3	25	11	20	18	6	26
BALIKPAPAN, *Indonesia*	29	23	243	30	23	221	30	23	249	29	23	226	29	23	258	29	23	252	28	23	259	29	23	257	29	23	201	29	23	186	29	23	176	29	23	245
BANGKOK, *Thailand*	32	20	11	33	22	28	34	24	31	35	25	72	34	25	189	33	24	152	32	24	158	32	24	187	32	24	320	31	24	231	31	22	57	31	20	9
BEIJING, *China*	2	-9	4	5	-7	5	12	-1	8	20	7	18	27	13	33	31	18	78	32	22	224	31	21	170	27	14	58	21	7	18	10	-1	9	3	-7	3
BEIRUT, *Lebanon*	17	11	187	17	11	151	19	12	96	22	14	51	26	18	19	28	21	2	31	23	0	32	23	0	30	23	6	27	21	48	23	16	119	18	13	176
BRUNEI	30	24	371	30	24	193	31	24	198	32	24	249	32	24	277	31	24	241	31	25	229	31	24	185	31	24	300	31	24	368	31	24	386	30	24	330
CHENNAI (MADRAS), *India*	29	19	29	31	20	9	33	22	9	35	26	17	38	28	44	38	27	52	36	26	99	35	26	124	34	25	125	32	24	285	29	22	345	29	21	138
CHONGQING, *China*	9	5	18	13	7	21	18	11	38	23	16	94	27	19	148	29	22	174	34	24	151	35	25	128	28	22	144	22	16	103	16	12	49	13	8	23
COLOMBO, *Sri Lanka*	30	22	84	31	22	64	31	23	114	31	24	255	31	26	335	29	25	190	29	25	129	29	25	96	29	25	158	29	24	353	29	23	308	29	22	152
DAMASCUS, *Syria*	12	2	39	14	4	32	18	6	23	24	9	13	29	13	5	33	16	1	36	18	0	37	18	0	33	16	0	27	12	9	19	8	26	13	4	42
DAVAO, *Philippines*	31	22	117	32	22	110	32	22	109	33	22	149	32	23	223	31	23	205	31	22	171	31	22	161	32	22	177	32	22	184	32	22	39	31	22	139
DHAKA, *Bangladesh*	26	13	8	28	15	21	32	20	58	33	23	116	33	24	267	32	26	358	31	26	399	31	26	317	32	26	256	31	24	164	29	19	30	26	14	6
HANOI, *Vietnam*	20	13	20	21	14	30	23	17	64	28	21	91	32	24	104	33	26	284	33	26	302	32	26	386	31	24	254	29	22	89	26	18	56	22	15	71
HO CHI MINH CITY, *Viet.*	32	21	14	33	22	4	34	23	9	35	24	51	33	24	213	32	24	309	31	24	295	31	24	271	31	23	342	31	23	261	31	23	19	31	22	47
HONG KONG, *China*	18	13	27	17	13	44	19	16	75	24	19	140	28	23	298	29	26	399	31	26	371	31	26	377	29	25	297	27	23	119	23	18	38	20	15	25
IRKUTSK, *Russia*	-16	-26	13	-12	-25	10	-4	-17	8	6	-7	15	13	1	33	20	7	56	21	10	79	20	9	71	14	2	43	5	-6	18	-7	-17	15	-16	-24	15
ISTANBUL, *Turkey*	8	3	91	9	3	69	11	3	62	16	7	42	21	12	30	25	16	28	28	18	24	28	19	31	24	16	48	20	13	66	15	9	92	11	5	114
JAKARTA, *Indonesia*	29	23	342	29	23	302	30	23	210	31	24	135	31	24	108	31	23	90	31	23	59	31	23	48	31	23	69	31	23	106	30	23	139	29	23	208
JEDDAH, *Saudi Arabia*	29	19	5	29	18	1	29	19	1	33	21	1	35	23	1	36	24	0	37	27	1	36	25	1	35	24	1	33	22	25	30	19	30	30	19	30
JERUSALEM, *Israel*	13	5	140	13	6	111	18	8	116	23	10	17	27	14	6	29	16	0	31	18	0	31	18	0	29	17	0	27	15	11	21	11	58	15	7	129
KABUL, *Afghanistan*	2	-8	33	4	-6	54	12	1	70	19	6	66	26	11	21	31	13	1	33	16	5	33	15	1	29	11	2	22	6	4	17	1	11	8	-3	21
KARACHI, *Pakistan*	25	13	7	26	14	10	29	19	10	32	23	3	34	26	0	34	28	10	33	27	90	31	26	58	31	25	27	33	23	3	31	18	3	27	14	5
KATHMANDU, *Nepal*	18	2	17	19	4	15	25	7	30	28	12	37	30	16	102	29	19	201	29	20	375	28	20	325	28	19	189	27	13	56	23	7	2	19	3	10
KOLKATA (CALCUTTA), *India*	27	13	12	29	15	25	34	21	32	36	24	53	36	25	129	33	26	291	32	26	329	32	26	338	32	26	266	32	23	131	29	18	21	26	13	7
KUNMING, *China*	16	3	11	18	4	14	21	7	17	24	11	20	26	14	90	25	17	175	25	17	205	25	17	203	24	15	126	21	12	78	18	7	40	17	3	13
LAHORE, *Pakistan*	21	4	25	22	7	24	28	12	27	35	17	15	40	22	17	41	26	39	38	27	155	36	26	135	36	23	63	35	15	10	28	8	3	23	4	14
LHASA, *China*	7	-10	0	9	-7	4	12	-2	4	16	1	6	19	5	24	24	9	72	23	9	132	22	9	128	21	7	58	17	1	9	13	-5	1	9	-9	1
MANAMA, *Bahrain*	20	14	14	21	15	16	24	17	11	29	21	8	33	26	1	36	28	0	37	29	0	38	29	0	36	27	0	32	24	0	28	21	7	22	16	10
MANDALAY, *Myanmar*	28	13	2	31	15	13	36	19	7	38	25	35	37	26	142	34	26	124	34	26	83	33	25	113	33	24	155	32	23	125	29	19	45	27	14	10
MANILA, *Philippines*	30	21	21	31	21	10	33	22	15	34	23	30	34	24	123	33	24	262	31	24	423	31	24	421	31	24	353	31	23	197	31	22	135	30	21	65
MOSCOW, *Russia*	-9	-16	38	-6	-14	36	0	-8	28	10	1	40	19	8	56	21	11	74	23	13	76	22	12	74	16	7	48	9	3	69	2	-3	43	-5	-10	41
MUMBAI (BOMBAY), *India*	28	19	3	28	19	1	30	22	1	32	24	2	33	27	14	32	26	518	29	25	647	29	24	384	29	24	276	32	24	55	32	23	15	31	21	2
MUSCAT, *Oman*	25	19	28	25	19	18	28	22	10	32	26	10	37	30	1	38	31	3	36	31	1	33	29	1	34	28	0	34	27	3	30	23	0	26	20	18
NAGASAKI, *Japan*	9	2	75	10	2	87	14	5	124	19	10	190	23	14	191	26	18	326	29	23	284	31	23	187	27	20	236	22	14	108	17	9	89	12	4	80
NEW DELHI, *India*	21	7	23	24	9	20	31	14	15	36	20	10	41	26	15	39	28	68	36	27	200	34	26	200	34	24	123	34	18	19	29	11	3	23	8	10
NICOSIA, *Cyprus*	15	5	70	16	5	50	19	7	35	24	10	24	29	14	26	34	18	9	37	21	1	37	21	2	33	18	6	28	14	23	22	10	31	17	7	74
ODESA, *Ukraine*	0	-6	25	2	-4	18	5	-1	18	12	6	28	19	12	28	23	16	48	26	18	41	26	18	36	21	14	28	16	9	36	10	4	28	4	-2	28
PHNOM PENH, *Cambodia*	31	21	7	32	22	9	34	23	32	34	24	73	33	24	149	33	24	149	32	24	151	32	24	157	31	24	231	31	24	259	30	23	129	30	22	38
PONTIANAK, *Indonesia*	31	23	275	32	23	213	32	23	242	33	24	280	32	23	279	32	23	228	32	23	178	32	23	206	32	23	245	32	23	356	31	23	385	31	23	321
RIYADH, *Saudi Arabia*	21	8	14	23	9	10	28	13	30	32	18	30	38	22	13	42	25	0	42	26	0	42	24	0	39	22	0	34	16	1	29	13	5	21	9	11
ST. PETERSBURG, *Russia*	-7	-13	25	-5	-12	23	0	-8	23	8	1	25	15	6	41	20	11	51	21	13	64	20	13	71	15	9	53	9	4	46	2	-2	36	-3	-8	30
SANDAKAN, *Malaysia*	29	23	454	29	23	271	30	23	200	31	23	118	32	23	153	32	23	196	32	23	185	32	23	240	32	23	263	31	23	356				30	23	470
SAPPORO, *Japan*	-2	-12	100	-1	-11	79	3	-6	70	11	0	61	16	4	59	21	10	65	24	14	86	26	16	117	22	11	136	16	4	114	8	-2	106	1	-7	102
SEOUL, *South Korea*	0	-9	21	3	-7	28	8	-2	49	17	5	105	22	11	88	27	16	151	29	21	384	31	22	263	26	15	160	19	7	49	11	0	46	3	-7	24
SHANGHAI, *China*	8	1	47	8	1	61	13	4	85	19	10	95	25	15	104	28	19	174	32	23	145	32	23	137	28	19	138	23	14	69	17	7	52	12	2	37
SINGAPORE, *Singapore*	30	23	239	31	23	165	31	24	174	31	24	166	31	24	171	31	24	163	31	24	150	31	24	171	31	24	164	31	23	191	31	23	250	31	23	269
TAIPEI, *China*	19	12	95	18	12	141	21	14	162	25	17	162	28	21	209	32	23	280	33	24	248	33	24	277	31	23	201	27	19	112	24	16	76	21	14	76
T'BILISI, *Georgia*	6	-2	16	7	-1	21	12	2	30	18	7	52	23	12	83	27	15	73	31	19	49	31	19	40	26	15	44	20	9	39	13	4	32	8	0	21
TEHRAN, *Iran*	7	-3	42	10	0	37	15	4	39	22	9	33	28	14	19	34	19	3	37	22	2	36	22	2	32	18	2	24	12	9	17	6	24	11	1	32
TEL AVIV-YAFO, *Israel*	17	9	165	18	9	64	19	10	58	23	12	13	27	16	3	29	18	0	31	21	0	31	21	0	30	20	1	29	18	14	25	15	85	19	11	144
TOKYO, *Japan*	8	-2	50	9	-1	72	12	2	106	17	8	129	22	12	144	24	17	176	28	21	136	30	22	149	26	19	216	21	13	194	16	6	96	11	1	54
ULAANBAATAR, *Mongolia*	-19	-32	1	-13	-29	1	-4	-22	3	7	-8	5	13	-2	8	21	7	25	22	11	74	21	8	48	14	2	20	6	-8	5	-6	-20	3	-16	-28	3
VIENTIANE, *Laos*	28	14	7	30	17	18	33	19	41	34	23	88	32	23	212	32	24	216	31	24	254	31	24	244				31	23	81	29	18	15	28	16	5
VLADIVOSTOK, *Russia*	-11	-18	8	-6	-14	10	1	-7	18	8	1	30	13	6	53	17	11	74	22	16	84	24	18	119	20	13	109	13	5	48	2	-4	30	-7	-13	15

CELSIUS scale: 50° 40° 30° 20° 10° 0° -10° -20° -30° -40° -50°

RED FIGURES: Average daily high temperature (°C) **BLUE FIGURES:** Average daily low temperature (°C) **BLACK FIGURES:** Average monthly rainfall (mm)
1 millimeter = 0.039 inches

	JAN.			FEB.			MARCH			APRIL			MAY			JUNE			JULY			AUG.			SEPT.			OCT.			NOV.			DEC.		
ASIA																																				
WUHAN, *China*	8	1	41	9	2	57	14	6	92	21	13	136	26	18	165	31	23	212	34	26	165	34	25	114	29	21	73	23	16	74	17	9	49	11	3	30
YAKUTSK, *Russia*	-43	-47	8	-33	-40	5	-18	-29	3	-3	-14	8	9	-1	10	19	9	28	23	12	41	19	9	33	10	1	28	-5	-12	13	-26	-31	10	-39	-43	8
YANGON (RANGOON), *Myanmar*	32	18	4	33	19	4	36	22	17	36	24	47	33	25	307	30	24	478	29	24	535	29	24	511	30	24	368	31	24	183	31	23	62	31	19	11
YEKATERINBURG, *Russia*	-14	-21	8	-10	-17	10	-4	-12	5	6	-3	8	14	4	15	18	9	48	21	12	38	18	10	53	12	5	46	3	-2	23	-7	-12	10	-12	-18	8
AFRICA																																				
ABIDJAN, *Côte D'Ivoire*	31	23	22	32	24	47	32	24	110	32	24	142	31	24	309	29	23	543	28	23	238	28	22	36	28	23	74	29	23	172	31	23	168	31	23	85
ACCRA, *Ghana*	31	23	15	31	24	29	31	24	57	31	24	90	31	24	136	29	23	199	27	23	50	27	22	19	27	23	43	29	23	64	31	24	34	31	24	20
ADDIS ABABA, *Ethiopia*	24	6	17	24	8	38	25	9	68	25	10	86	25	10	86	23	9	132	21	10	268	21	10	281	22	9	186	24	7	28	23	6	11	23	5	10
ALEXANDRIA, *Egypt*	18	11	52	19	11	28	21	13	13	23	15	4	26	18	1	28	21	0	29	23	0	31	23	0	30	23	1	28	20	8	25	17	35	21	13	55
ALGIERS, *Algeria*	15	9	93	16	9	73	17	11	67	20	13	52	23	15	34	26	18	14	28	21	2	29	22	5	27	21	33	23	17	77	19	13	96	16	11	114
ANTANANARIVO, *Madagascar*	26	16	287	26	16	262	26	16	194	24	14	57	23	12	18	21	10	9	20	9	8	21	9	10	23	11	16	27	12	61	27	14	153	27	16	290
ASMARA, *Eritrea*	23	7	0	24	8	0	25	9	1	26	11	7	26	12	23	26	12	48	22	12	114	22	12	123	23	13	49	22	12	4	22	10	3	22	9	0
BAMAKO, *Mali*	33	16	0	36	19	0	39	22	3	39	24	19	39	24	59	34	23	131	32	22	229	31	22	307	32	22	198	34	22	63	34	18	7	33	17	0
BANGUI, *Cen. Af. Rep.*	32	20	20	34	21	39	33	22	107	33	22	133	32	21	163	31	21	143	29	21	181	29	21	225	31	21	190	31	21	202	31	20	93	32	19	29
BEIRA, *Mozambique*	32	24	267	32	24	259	31	23	263	30	22	117	28	18	67	26	16	40	25	16	34	26	17	33	28	18	25	31	22	34	31	22	121	31	23	243
BENGHAZI, *Libya*	17	10	66	18	11	41	21	12	20	23	14	5	26	17	3	28	20	1	29	22	1	29	22	1	28	21	3	27	19	18	23	16	46	19	12	66
BUJUMBURA, *Burundi*	29	20	97	29	20	97	29	20	126	29	20	129	29	20	64	29	19	11	30	19	3	30	19	17	31	20	43	31	20	62	29	20	98	29	20	100
CAIRO, *Egypt*	18	8	5	21	9	4	24	11	4	28	14	2	33	17	1	35	20	0	36	21	0	35	22	0	32	20	0	30	18	1	26	14	3	20	10	6
CAPE TOWN, *South Africa*	26	16	16	26	16	15	25	14	22	22	12	50	19	9	92	18	8	105	17	7	91	18	8	83	18	9	54	21	11	40	23	13	24	24	14	19
CASABLANCA, *Morocco*	17	7	57	18	8	53	19	9	51	21	11	38	22	13	21	24	16	6	26	18	0	27	19	1	26	17	6	24	14	34	21	11	65	18	8	73
CONAKRY, *Guinea*	31	22	1	31	23	1	32	23	6	32	23	21	32	24	141	30	23	503	28	22	1210	28	22	1016	29	23	664	31	23	318	31	24	106	31	23	14
DAKAR, *Senegal*	26	18	1	27	17	1	27	18	0	27	18	0	29	20	1	31	23	15	31	24	75	31	24	215	32	24	146	32	24	42	30	23	3	27	19	4
DAR ES SALAAM, *Tanzania*	31	25	66	31	25	66	31	24	130	30	23	290	29	22	188	29	20	33	28	19	31	28	19	30	28	19	30	29	21	41	30	22	74	31	24	91
DURBAN, *South Africa*	27	21	119	27	21	126	27	20	132	26	18	84	24	14	56	23	12	34	22	11	35	22	13	49	23	15	73	24	17	110	25	18	118	26	19	120
HARARE, *Zimbabwe*	26	16	190	26	16	177	26	14	107	26	13	33	23	9	10	21	7	3	21	7	1	23	8	2	26	12	7	28	14	32	27	16	93	26	16	173
JOHANNESBURG, *South Africa*	26	14	150	25	14	129	24	13	110	22	10	48	19	6	24	17	4	6	17	4	10	20	5	10	23	9	25	25	12	65	25	13	126	26	14	141
KAMPALA, *Uganda*	28	18	58	28	18	68	27	18	128	26	18	185	26	17	134	25	17	71	25	17	55	26	16	87	27	17	100	27	17	119	27	17	142	27	17	95
KHARTOUM, *Sudan*	32	15	0	34	16	0	38	19	0	41	22	0	42	25	4	41	26	7	38	25	49	37	24	69	39	25	21	40	24	5	36	20	0	33	17	0
KINSHASA, *D.R.C.*	31	21	138	31	22	148	32	22	184	32	22	220	31	22	145	29	19	5	27	18	3	29	18	4	31	20	40	31	21	133	31	22	235	30	21	156
KISANGANI, *D.R.C.*	31	21	97	31	21	107	31	21	172	31	21	190	31	21	162	30	21	128	29	19	114	28	20	178	29	20	164	30	20	233	29	20	207	30	20	105
LAGOS, *Nigeria*	31	23	27	32	25	44	32	26	98	32	25	146	31	24	252	29	23	414	28	23	253	28	23	69	28	23	153	29	23	197	31	24	66	31	24	25
LIBREVILLE, *Gabon*	31	23	164	31	22	137	32	23	248	32	23	232	31	22	181	29	21	24	28	20	3	29	21	6	29	22	69	30	22	332	30	22	378	31	22	197
LIVINGSTONE, *Zambia*	29	19	175	29	19	160	29	18	95	30	15	25	28	11	5	25	7	1	25	7	0	28	10	0	32	15	2	34	19	26	33	19	78	31	19	176
LUANDA, *Angola*	28	23	34	29	24	35	30	24	90	29	24	127	28	23	18	25	20	0	23	18	0	23	18	1	24	19	2	26	22	6	28	23	32	28	23	23
LUBUMBASHI, *D.R.C.*	28	16	253	28	17	256	28	16	210	28	14	51	27	10	4	26	7	1	26	6	0	28	8	0	32	11	6	33	14	31	31	16	150	28	17	272
LUSAKA, *Zambia*	26	17	213	26	17	172	26	17	104	26	15	22	25	12	3	23	10	0	23	9	0	25	12	0	29	15	1	31	18	14	29	18	86	27	17	200
LUXOR, *Egypt*	23	6	0	26	7	0	30	10	0	35	15	0	40	21	0	41	21	0	42	23	0	41	23	0	39	22	0	37	18	1	31	12	0	26	7	0
MAPUTO, *Mozambique*	30	22	153	31	22	134	29	21	99	28	19	52	27	16	29	25	13	18	24	13	15	26	14	13	27	16	32	28	18	51	28	19	78	29	21	94
MARRAKECH, *Morocco*	18	4	27	20	6	31	23	9	36	26	11	32	29	14	17	33	17	7	38	19	2	38	20	3	33	17	7	28	14	20	23	9	37	19	6	28
MOGADISHU, *Somalia*	30	23	0	30	23	0	31	24	8	32	26	58	32	25	59	29	23	78	28	23	67	28	23	42	29	23	21	30	24	30	31	24	40	30	24	9
MONROVIA, *Liberia*	30	23	5	29	23	3	31	23	112	31	23	297	30	22	340	27	23	917	27	22	615	27	23	472	27	22	759	28	22	640	29	23	208	30	23	74
NAIROBI, *Kenya*	25	12	45	26	13	43	25	14	73	24	14	160	22	13	119	21	12	30	21	11	13	21	11	13	24	11	26	24	13	42	23	13	121	23	13	77
N'DJAMENA, *Chad*	34	14	0	37	16	0	40	21	0	42	23	8	40	25	31	38	24	62	33	22	150	31	22	215	33	22	91	36	21	22	36	17	0	33	14	0
NIAMEY, *Niger*	34	14	0	37	18	0	41	22	3	42	25	6	41	27	35	38	25	75	34	23	143	32	23	187	34	23	90	38	23	16	38	18	1	34	15	0
NOUAKCHOTT, *Mauritania*	29	14	1	31	15	3	32	17	1	32	18	1	34	21	1	33	23	3	32	23	13	32	24	104	34	24	23	33	22	10	32	18	3	28	13	1
TIMBUKTU, *Mali*	31	13	0	34	14	0	38	19	0	42	22	1	43	26	4	43	27	19	39	25	62	36	24	79	39	24	33	40	23	3	37	18	0	32	13	0
TRIPOLI, *Libya*	16	8	69	17	9	40	19	11	27	22	14	13	24	16	5	27	19	1	29	22	0	30	22	1	29	22	11	27	18	38	23	14	60	18	9	81
TUNIS, *Tunisia*	14	6	62	16	7	52	18	8	46	21	11	38	24	13	22	29	17	10	32	20	3	33	21	7	31	19	32	25	15	55	20	11	54	16	7	63
WADI HALFA, *Sudan*	24	9	0	27	10	0	31	14	0	36	18	0	40	22	1	41	24	0	41	25	1	41	25	0	40	24	0	37	21	0	30	15	0	25	11	0
YAOUNDÉ, *Cameroon*	29	19	26	29	19	55	29	19	140	29	19	193	28	19	216	27	19	163	27	19	62	27	18	80	27	19	216	27	18	292	28	19	120	28	19	28
ZANZIBAR, *Tanzania*	32	24	75	33	24	61	33	25	150	30	25	350	29	24	251	28	23	54	28	22	44	28	22	39	29	22	48	30	23	86	32	24	201	32	24	145
ZOMBA, *Malawi*	27	18	299	27	18	269	26	18	230	26	17	85	24	14	23	22	12	13	22	12	8	24	13	8	27	15	8	29	18	29	29	19	124	27	18	281
ATLANTIC ISLANDS																																				
ASCENSION ISLAND	29	23	4	31	23	8	31	24	23	31	24	27	31	23	10	29	23	14	29	22	12	28	22	10	28	22	8	28	22	7	28	22	4	29	22	3
FALKLAND ISLANDS	13	6	71	13	5	58	12	4	64	9	3	66	7	1	66	5	-1	53	4	-1	51	5	-1	51	7	1	38	9	2	41	11	3	51	12	4	71
FUNCHAL, *Madeira Is.*	19	13	87	18	13	88	19	13	79	19	14	43	21	16	22	22	17	9	24	19	2	24	19	3	24	19	27	23	18	85	22	16	106	19	14	87
HAMILTON, *Bermuda Is.*	20	14	112	20	14	119	20	14	122	22	15	104	24	18	117	27	21	112	29	23	114	30	23	137	29	22	132	26	21	147	23	17	127	21	16	119
LAS PALMAS, *Canary Is.*	21	14	28	22	14	21	22	15	15	22	16	10	23	17	3	24	18	1	25	19	1	26	21	0	26	21	6	26	19	18	24	18	37	22	16	32
NUUK, *Greenland*	-7	-12	36	-7	-13	43	-4	-11	41	-1	-7	30	4	-2	43	8	1	36	11	3	56	11	3	79	6	1	84	2	-3	64	-2	-7	48	-5	-10	38
PONTA DELGADA, *Azores*	17	12	105	17	11	91	17	12	87	18	12	62	20	13	57	22	15	36	25	17	25	26	18	34	25	17	75	22	16	97	20	14	108	18	12	98
PRAIA, *Cape Verde*	25	20	1	25	19	2	26	20	0	26	21	0	27	21	0	28	22	0	28	24	7	29	24	63	29	25	88	29	24	44	28	23	15	26	22	5
REYKJAVÍK, *Iceland*	2	-2	86	3	-2	75	4	-1	76	6	1	56	10	4	42	12	7	45	14	9	51	14	8	62	11	6	71	7	3	88	4	0	83	2	-2	84
THULE, *Greenland*	-17	-27	7	-20	-29	8	-19	-28	4	-13	-23	4	-2	-9	5	5	-1	6	8	2	14	6	1	17	1	-6	13	-5	-13	11	-11	-19	11	-18	-27	5
TRISTAN DA CUNHA	19	15	103	20	16	110	19	14	133	18	14	137	16	12	153	14	11	153	14	10	54	13	9	162	13	9	157	15	11	148	16	12	124	18	14	131
PACIFIC ISLANDS																																				
APIA, *Samoa*	30	24	437	29	24	360	30	23	356	30	24	236	29	23	174	29	23	135	29	23	100	29	24	111	29	23	144	29	24	206	30	23	259	29	23	374
AUCKLAND, *New Zealand*	23	16	70	23	16	86	22	15	77	19	13	96	17	11	115	14	9	126	13	8	131	14	8	112	16	9	94	17	11	93	19	12	82	21	14	78
DARWIN, *Australia*	32	25	396	32	25	331	33	25	282	33	24	97	33	23	18	31	21	3	31	19	1	32	21	4	33	23	15	34	25	60	34	26	130	33	26	239
DUNEDIN, *New Zealand*	19	10	81	19	10	70	17	9	78	15	7	75	12	5	78	9	4	78	9	3	70	11	3	61	13	5	61	15	6	70	17	7	79	18	9	81
GALÁPAGOS IS., *Ecuador*	30	22	20	30	24	36	31	24	28	31	24	18	30	23	1	28	22	1	27	21	1	27	19	1	27	19	1	27	19	1	27	20	1	28	21	1
GUAM, *Mariana Is.*	29	24	138	29	23	116	29	24	121	31	24	108	31	25	164	31	25	150	30	24	274	30	24	368	30	24	374	30	24	334	30	25	231	29	24	160
HOBART, *Australia*	22	12	51	22	12	38	20	11	46	17	9	51	14	7	46	12	5	51	11	4	51	13	5	49	15	6	47	17	8	60	19	9	52	21	11	57
MELBOURNE, *Australia*	26	14	48	26	14	47	24	13	52	20	11	57	17	8	58	14	7	49	13	6	49	15	6	50	17	8	59	19	9	67	22	11	60	24	12	59
NAHA, *Okinawa*	19	13	125	19	13	126	21	15	159	24	18	165	27	20	252	29	24	280	32	25	178	31	25	270	31	24	175	27	21	165	24	18	133	21	14	111
NOUMÉA, *New Caledonia*	30	22	111	29	23	130	29	22	155	28	21	121	26	19	106	25	18	107	24	17	91	24	16	73	26	17	56	27	18	53	28	20	55	30	21	77
PAPEETE, *Tahiti*	32	22	335	32	22	292	32	22	165	32	22	173	31	21	124	30	21	81	30	20	66	30	20	48	30	21	58	31	21	86	31	22	165	31	22	302
PERTH, *Australia*	29	17	9	29	17	13	27	16	19	24	14	45	21	12	122	18	10	182	17	9	174	18	9	136	19	10	80	21	12	53	24	14	21	27	16	13
PORT MORESBY, *P.N.G.*	32	24	179	31	24	196	31	24	190	31	24	120	30	24	65	29	23	39	28	23	27	28	23	26	29	23	33	30	24	35	31	24	56	32	24	121
SUVA, *Fiji*	30	23	305	30	23	293	30	23	367	29	23	342	28	22	261	27	21	166	26	20	142	26	20	184	27	21	200	27	21	217	28	22	266	29	23	296
SYDNEY, *Australia*	26	18	103	26	18	111	24	17	131	22	14	130	19	11	123	16	9	129	16	8	103	17	9	80	19	11	69	22	13	83	23	16	81	25	17	78
WELLINGTON, *New Zealand*	21	13	79	21	13	80	19	12	85	17	11	98	14	8	121	13	7	124	12	6	139	12	6	121	14	8	99	16	9	105	17	10	88	19	12	90

Aaglet	well
Aain	spring
Aauinat	spring
Āb	river, water
Ache	stream
Açude	reservoir
Ada,-si	island
Adrar	mountain-s, plateau
Aguada	dry lake bed
Aguelt	water hole, well
'Ain, Aïn	spring, well
Aïoun-et	spring-s, well
Aivi	mountain
Ákra, Akrotírion	cape, promontory
Alb	mountain, ridge
Alföld	plain
Alin'	mountain range
Alpe-n	mountain-s
Altiplanicie	high-plain, plateau
Alto	hill-s, mountain-s, ridge
Älv-en	river
Āmba	hill, mountain
Anou	well
Anse	bay, inlet
Ao	bay, cove, estuary
Ap	cape, point
Archipel, Archipiélago	archipelago
Arcipelago, Arkhipelag	archipelago
Arquipélago	archipelago
Arrecife-s	reef-s
Arroio, Arroyo	brook, gully, rivulet, stream
Ås	ridge
Ava	channel
Aylagy	gulf
'Ayn	spring, well

Ba	intermittent stream, river
Baai	bay, cove, lagoon
Bāb	gate, strait
Badia	bay
Bælt	strait
Bagh	bay
Bahar	drainage basin
Bahía	bay
Bahr, Baḥr	bay, lake, river, sea, wadi
Baía, Baie	bay
Bajo-s	shoal-s
Ban	village
Bañado-s	flooded area, swamp-s
Banc, Banco-s	bank-s, sandbank-s, shoal-s
Band	lake
Bandao	peninsula
Baño-s	hot spring-s, spa
Baraj-ı	dam, reservoir
Barra	bar, sandbank
Barrage, Barragem	dam, lake, reservoir
Barranca	gorge, ravine
Bazar	marketplace
Ben, Benin	mountain
Belt	strait
Bereg	bank, coast, shore
Berg-e	mountain-s
Bil	lake
Biq'at	plain, valley
Bir, Bîr, Bi'r	spring, well
Birket	lake, pool, swamp
Bjerg-e	mountain-s, range
Boca, Bocca	channel, river, mouth
Bocht	bay
Bodden	bay
Boğaz, -i	strait
Bögeni	reservoir
Boka	gulf, mouth
Bol'sh-oy, -aya, -oye	big
Bolsón	inland basin
Boubairet	lagoon, lake
Bras	arm, branch of a stream

Braț, -ul	arm, branch of a stream
Bre, -en	glacier, ice cap
Bredning	bay, broad water
Bruch	marsh
Bucht	bay
Bugt-en	bay
Buḥayrat, Buheirat	lagoon, lake, marsh
Bukhta, Bukta, Bukt-en	bay
Bulak, Bulaq	spring
Bum	hill, mountain
Burnu, Burun	cape, point
Busen	gulf
Buuraha	hill-s, mountain-s
Buyuk	big, large

Cabeza-s	head-s, summit-s
Cabo	cape
Cachoeira	rapids, waterfall
Cal	hill, peak
Caleta	cove, inlet
Campo-s	field-s, flat country
Canal	canal, channel, strait
Caño	channel, stream
Cao Nguyen	mountain, plateau
Cap, Capo	cape
Capitán	captain
Càrn	mountain
Castillo	castle, fort
Catarata-s	cataract-s, waterfall-s
Causse	upland
Çay	brook, stream
Cay-s, Cayo-s	island-s, key-s, shoal-s
Cerro-s	hill-s, peak-s
Chaîne, Chaînons	mountain chain, range
Chapada-s	plateau, upland-s
Chedo	archipelago
Chenal	river channel
Chersónisos	peninsula
Chhung	bay
Chi	lake
Chiang	bay
Chiao	cape, point, rock
Ch'ih	lake
Chink	escarpment
Chott	intermittent salt lake, salt marsh
Chou	island
Ch'ü	canal
Ch'üntao	archipelago, islands
Chute-s	cataract-s, waterfall-s
Chyrvony	red
Cima	mountain, peak, summit
Ciudad	city
Co	lake
Col	pass
Collina, Colline	hill, mountains
Con	island
Cordillera	mountain chain
Corno	mountain, peak
Coronel	colonel
Corredeira	cascade, rapids
Costa	coast
Côte	coast, slope
Coxilha, Cuchilla	range of low hills
Crique	creek, stream
Csatorna	canal, channel
Cul de Sac	bay, inlet

Da	great, greater
Daban	pass
Dağ, -ı, Dagh	mountain
Dağlar, -ı	mountains
Dahr	cliff, mesa
Dake	mountain, peak
Dal-en	valley
Dala	steppe
Dan	cape, point
Danau	lake
Dao	island
Dar'ya	lake, river
Daryācheh	lake, marshy lake

Dasht	desert, plain
Dawan	pass
Dawḥat	bay, cove, inlet
Deniz, -i	sea
Dent-s	peak-s
Deo	pass
Desēt	hummock, island, land-tied island
Desierto	desert
Détroit	channel, strait
Dhar	hills, ridge, tableland
Ding	mountain
Distrito	district
Djebel	mountain, range
Do	island-s, rock-s
Doi	hill, mountain
Dome	ice dome
Dong	village
Dooxo	floodplain
Dzong	castle, fortress

Eiland-en	island-s
Eilean	island
Ejland	island
Elv	river
Embalse	lake, reservoir
Emi	mountain, rock
Enseada, Ensenada	bay, cove
Ér	rivulet, stream
Erg	sand dune region
Est	east
Estación	railroad station
Estany	lagoon, lake
Estero	estuary, inlet, lagoon, marsh
Estrecho	strait
Étang	lake, pond
Eylandt	island
Ežeras	lake
Ezers	lake

Falaise	cliff, escarpment
Farvand-et	channel, sound
Fell	mountain
Feng	mount, peak
Fiord-o	inlet, sound
Fiume	river
Fjäll-et	mountain
Fjällen	mountains
Fjärd-en	fjord
Fjardar, Fjörður	fjord
Fjeld	mountain
Fjell-ene	mountain-s
Fjöll	mountain-s
Fjord-en	inlet, fjord
Fleuve	river
Fljót	large river
Flói	bay, marshland
Foci	river mouths
Főcsatorna	principal canal
Förde	fjord, gulf, inlet
Forsen	rapids, waterfall
Fortaleza	fort, fortress
Fortín	fortified post
Foss-en	waterfall
Foum	pass, passage
Foz	mouth of a river
Fuerte	fort, fortress
Fwafwate	waterfalls

Gacan-ka	hill, peak
Gal	pond, spring, waterhole, well
Gang	harbor
Gangri	peak, range
Gaoyuan	plateau
Garaet, Gara'et	lake, lake bed, salt lake
Gardaneh	pass
Garet	hill, mountain
Gat	channel
Gata	bay, inlet, lake
Gattet	channel, strait
Gaud	depression, saline tract

Gave	mountain stream
Gebel	mountain-s, range
Gebergte	mountain range
Gebirge	mountains, range
Geçidi	mountain pass, passage
Geçit	mountain pass, passage
Gezâir	islands
Gezîra-t, Gezîret	island, peninsula
Ghats	mountain range
Ghubb-at, -et	bay, gulf
Giri	mountain
Gletscher	glacier
Gobernador	governor
Gobi	desert
Gol	river, stream
Göl, -ü	lake
Golets	mountain, peak
Golf, -e, -o	gulf
Gor-a, -y, Gór-a, -y	mountain,-s
Got	point
Gowd	depression
Goz	sand ridge
Gran, -de	great, large
Gryada	mountains, ridge
Guan	pass
Guba	bay, gulf
Guelta	well
Gum	desert
Guntō	archipelago
Gunung	mountain
Gura	mouth, passage
Guyot	table mount

Haḍabat	plateau
Haehyŏp	strait
Haff	lagoon
Hai	lake, sea
Haihsia	strait
Haixia	channel, strait
Hakau	reef, rock
Hakuchi	anchorage
Halvø, Halvøy-a	peninsula
Hama	beach
Hamada, Ḥammādah	rocky desert
Hamn	harbor, port
Hāmūn, Hamun	depression, lake
Hana	cape, point
Hantō	peninsula
Har	hill, mound, mountain
Ḥarrat	lava field
Hasi, Hassi	spring, well
Hauteur	elevation, height
Hav-et	sea
Havn, Havre	harbor, port
Hawr	lake, marsh
Hāyk'	lake, reservoir
Hegy, -ség	mountain, -s, range
Heiau	temple
Ho	canal, lake, river
Hoek	hook, point
Hög-en	high, hill
Höhe, -n	height, high
Høj	height, hill
Holm, -e, Holmene	island-s, islet -s
Holot	dunes
Hon	island-s
Hor-a, -y	mountain, -s
Horn	horn, peak
Houma	point
Hoved	headland, peninsula, point
Hraun	lava field
Hsü	island
Hu	lake, reservoir
Huk	cape, point
Hüyük	hill, mound

Idehan	sand dunes
Île-s, Ilha-s, Illa-s, Îot-s	island-s, islet-s
Îet, Ilhéu-s	islet, -s
Irhil	mountain-s
'Irq	sand dune-s
Isblink	glacier, ice field

Is-en	glacier
Isla-s, Islote	island-s, islet
Isol-a, -e	island, -s
Istmo	isthmus
Iwa	island, islet, rock

Jabal, Jebel	mountain-s, range
Järv, -i, Jaure, Javrre	lake
Jazā'ir, Jazīrat, Jazīreh	island-s
Jehīl	lake
Jezero, Jezioro	lake
Jiang	river, stream
Jiao	cape
Jibāl	hill, mountain, ridge
Jima	island-s, rock-s
Jøkel, Jökull	glacier, ice cap
Joki, Jokka	river
Jökulsá	river from a glacier
Jūn	bay

Kaap	cape
Kafr	village
Kaikyō	channel, strait
Kaise	mountain
Kaiwan	bay, gulf, sea
Kanal	canal channel
Kangri	mountain, peak
Kap, Kapp	cape
Kavīr	salt desert
Kefar	village
Kênet'	lagoon, lake
Kep	cape, point
Kepulauan	archipelago, islands
Khalīg, Khalīj	bay, gulf
Khirb-at, -et	ancient site, ruins
Khrebet	mountain range
Kinh	canal
Klint	bluff, cliff
Kō	bay, cove, harbor
Ko	island, lake
Koh	island, mountain, range
Köl-i	lake
Kólpos	gulf
Kong	mountain
Körfez, -i	bay, gulf
Kosa	spit of land
Kou	estuary, river mouth
Kowtal-e	pass
Krasn-yy, -aya, -oye	red
Kryazh	mountain range, ridge
Kuala	estuary, river mouth
Kuan	mountain pass
Kūh, Kūhhā	mountain-s, range
Kul', Kuli	lake
Kum	sandy desert
Kundo	archipelago
Kuppe	hill-s, mountain-s
Kust	coast, shore
Kyst	coast
Kyun	island

La	pass
Lac, Lac-ul, -us	lake
Lae	cape, point
Lago, -a	lagoon, lake
Lagoen, Laguna	lagoon
Laguna-s	lagoon-s, lake-s
Laht	bay, gulf, harbor
Laje	reef, rock ledge
Laut	sea
Lednik	glacier
Leida	channel
Lhari	mountain
Li	village
Liedao	archipelago, islands
Liehtao	archipelago, islands
Liman-ı	bay, estuary
Límni	lake
Ling	mountain-s, range
Linn	pool, waterfall
Lintasan	passage
Liqen	lake
Llano-s	plain-s
Loch, Lough	lake, arm of the sea

Loma-s — hill-s, knoll-s

Mal — mountain, range
Mal-yy, -aya, -oye — little, small
Mamarr — pass, path
Man — bay
Mar, Mare — large lake, sea
Marsa, Marsá — bay, inlet
Masabb — mouth of river
Massif — massif, mountain-s
Mauna — mountain
Mēda — plain
Meer — lake, sea
Melkosopochnik — undulating plain
Mesa, Meseta — plateau, tableland
Mierzeja — sandspit
Minami — south
Mios — island
Misaki — cape, peninsula, point
Mochun — passage
Mong — town, village
Mont-e, -i, -s — mount, -ain, -s
Montagne, -s — mount, -ain, -s
Montaña, -s — mountain, -s
More — sea
Morne — hill, peak
Morro — bluff, headland, hill
Motu, -s — islands
Mouïet — well
Mouillage — anchorage
Muang — town, village
Mui — cape, point
Mull — headland, promontory

Munkhafad — depression
Munte — mountain
Munţi-i — mountains
Muong — town, village
Mynydd — mountain
Mys — cape

Nacional — national
Nada — gulf, sea
Næs, Näs — cape, point
Nafūd — area of dunes, desert
Nagor'ye — mountain range, plateau
Nahar, Nahr — river, stream
Nakhon — town
Namakzār — salt waste
Ne — island, reef, rock-s
Neem — cape, point, promontory
Nes, Ness — peninsula, point
Nevado-s — snow-capped mountain-s
Nez — cape, promontory
Ni — village
Nísi, Nísia, Nisís, Nísoi — island-s, islet-s
Nisídhes — islets
Nizhn-iy, -yaya, -eye — lower
Nizmennost' — low country
Noord — north
Nord-re — north-ern
Nørre — north-ern
Nos — cape, nose, point
Nosy — island, reef, rock
Nov-yy, -aya, -oye — new
Nudo — mountain
Numa — lake
Nunatak, -s, -ker — peak-s surrounded by ice cap
Nur — lake, salt lake
Nuruu — mountain range, ridge
Nut-en — peak
Nuur — lake

Ö-n, Ø-er — island-s
Oblast' — administrative division, province, region
Oceanus — ocean
Odde-n — cape, point
Øer-ne — islands
Oglat — group of wells

Oguilet — well
Ór-os, -i — mountain, -s
Órmos — bay, port
Ort — place, point
Øst-er — east
Ostrov, -a, Ostrv-o, -a — island, -s
Otoci, Otok — islands, island
Ouadi, Oued — river, watercourse
Øy-a — island
Øyane — islands
Ozer-o, -a — lake, -s

Pää — mountain, point
Palus — marsh
Pampa-s — grassy plain-s
Pantà — lake, reservoir
Pantanal — marsh, swamp
Pao, P'ao — lake
Parbat — mountain
Parque — park
Pas, -ul — pass
Paso, Passo — pass
Passe — channel, pass
Pasul — pass
Pedra — rock
Pegunungan — mountain range
Pellg — bay, bight
Peña — cliff, rock
Pendi — basin
Penedo-s — rock-s
Péninsule — peninsula
Peñón — point, rock
Pereval — mountain pass
Pertuis — strait
Peski — sands, sandy region
Phnom — hill, mountain, range
Phou — mountain range
Phu — mountain
Piana-o — plain
Pic, Pik, Piz — peak
Picacho — mountain, peak
Pico-s — peak-s
Pistyll — waterfall
Piton-s — peak-s
Pivdennyy — southern
Plaja, Playa — beach, inlet, shore
Planalto, Plato — plateau
Planina — mountain, plateau
Plassen — lake
Ploskogor'ye — plateau, upland
Pointe — point
Polder — reclaimed land
Poluostrov — peninsula
Pongo — water gap
Ponta, -l — cape, point
Ponte — bridge
Poolsaar — peninsula
Portezuelo — pass
Porto — port
Poulo — island
Praia — beach, seashore
Presa — reservoir
Presidente — president
Presqu'île — peninsula
Prokhod — pass
Proliv — strait
Promontorio — promontory
Průsmyk — mountain pass
Przylądek — cape
Puerto — bay, pass, port
Pulao — island-s
Pulau, Pulo — island
Pun — peak
Puncak — peak, summit, top
Punt, Punta, -n — point, -s
Puu — hill, mountain
Puy — peak

Qā' — depression, marsh, mud flat
Qal'at — fort
Qal'eh — castle, fort
Qanâ — canal
Qārat — hill-s, mountain-s

Qaşr — castle, fort, hill
Qila — fort
Qiryat — settlement, suburb
Qolleh — peak
Qooriga — anchorage, bay
Qoz — dunes, sand ridge
Qu — canal
Quebrada — ravine, stream
Qullai — peak, summit
Qum — desert, sand
Qundao — archipelago, islands
Qurayyāt — hills

Raas — cape, point
Rabt — hill
Rada — roadstead
Rade — anchorage, roadstead
Rags — point
Ramat — hill, mountain
Rand — ridge of hills
Rann — swamp
Raqaba — wadi, watercourse
Ras, Râs, Ra's — cape
Ravnina — plain
Récif-s — reef-s
Regreg — marsh
Represa — reservoir
Reservatório — reservoir
Restinga — barrier, sand area
Rettō — chain of islands
Ri — mountain range, village
Ría — estuary
Ribeirão — stream
Río, Rio — river
Rivière — river
Roca-s — cliff, rock-s
Roche-r, -s — rock-s
Rosh — mountain, point
Rt — cape, point
Rubha — headland
Rupes — scarp

Saar — island
Saari, Sar — island
Sabkha-t, Sabkhet — lagoon. marsh, salt lake
Sagar — lake, sea
Sahara, Şaḥrā' — desert
Sahl — plain
Saki — cape, point
Salar — salt flat
Salina — salt pan
Salin-as, -es — salt flat-s, salt marsh-es
Salto — waterfall
Sammyaku — mountain range
San — hill, mountain
San, -ta, -to — saint
Sandur — sandy area
Sankt — saint
Sanmaek — mountain range
São — saint
Sarīr — gravel desert
Sasso — mountain, stone
Savane — savanna
Scoglio — reef, rock
Se — reef, rock-s, shoal-s
Sebjet — salt lake, salt marsh
Sebkha — salt lake, salt marsh
Sebkhet — lagoon, salt lake
See — lake, sea
Selat — strait
Selkä — lake, ridge
Semenanjung — peninsula
Sen — mountain
Seno — bay, gulf
Serra, Serranía — range of hills or mountains
Severn-yy, -aya, -oye — northern
Sgurr — peak
Sha — island, shoal
Sha'ib — ravine, watercourse
Shamo — desert

Shan — island-s, mountain-s, range
Shankou — mountain pass
Shanmo — mountain range
Sharm — cove, creek, harbor
Shaṭṭ — large river
Shi — administrative division, municipality
Shima — island-s, rock-s
Shō — island, reef, rock
Shotō — archipelago
Shott — intermittent salt lake
Shuiku — reservoir
Shuitao — channel
Shyghanaghy — bay, gulf
Sierra — mountain range
Silsilesi — mountain chain, ridge
Sint — saint
Sinus — bay, sea
Sjö-n — lake
Skarv-et — barren mountain
Skerry — rock
Slieve — mountain
Sø — lake
Sønder, Søndre — south-ern
Sopka — conical mountain, volcano
Sor — lake, salt lake
Sør, Sör — south-ern
Sory — salt lake, salt marsh
Spitz-e — peak, point, top
Sredn-iy, -yaya, -eye — central, middle
Stagno — lake, pond
Stantsiya — station
Stausee — reservoir
Stenón — channel, strait
Step'-i — steppe-s
Štít — summit, top
Stor-e — big, great
Straat — strait
Straum-en — current-s
Strelka — spit of land
Stretet, Stretto — strait
Su — reef, river, rock, stream
Sud — south
Sudo — channel, strait
Suidō — channel, strait
Şummān — rocky desert
Sund — sound, strait
Sunden — channel, inlet, sound
Svyat-oy, -aya, -oye — holy, saint
Sziget — island

Tagh — mountain-s
Tall — hill, mound
T'an — lake
Tanezrouft — desert
Tang — plain, steppe
Tangi — peninsula, point
Tanjong, Tanjung — cape, point
Tao — island-s
Tarso — hill-s, mountain-s
Tassili — plateau, upland
Tau — mountain-s, range
Taūy — hills, mountains
Tchabal — mountain-s
Te Ava — tidal flat
Tel-l — hill, mound
Telok, Teluk — bay
Tepe, -si — hill, peak
Tepuí — mesa, mountain
Terara — hill, mountain, peak
Testa — bluff, head
Thale — lake
Thang — plain, steppe
Tien — lake
Tierra — land, region
Ting — hill, mountain
Tir'at — canal
Tó, Tō — lake, pool
To, Tō — island-s, rock-s
Tonle — lake
Tope — hill, mountain, peak

Top-pen — peak-s
Träsk — bog, lake
Tso — lake
Tsui — cape, point
Tübegi — peninsula
Tulu — hill, mountain
Tunturi-t — hill-s, mountain-s

Uad — wadi, watercourse
Udde-m — point
Ujong, Ujung — cape, point
Umi — bay, lagoon, lake
Ura — bay, inlet, lake
'Urūq — dune area
Uul, Uula — mountain, range
'Uyûn — springs

Vaara — mountain
Vaart — canal
Vær — fishing station
Vaïn — channel, strait
Valle, Vallée — valley, wadi
Vallen — waterfall
Valli — lagoon, lake
Vallis — valley
Vanua — land
Varre — mountain
Vatn, Vatten, Vatnet — lake, water
Veld — grassland, plain
Verkhn-iy, -yaya, -eye — higher, upper
Vesi — lake, water
Vest-er — west
Via — road
Vidda — plateau
Vig, Vík, Vik, -en — bay, cove
Vinh — bay, gulf
Vodokhranilishche — reservoir
Vodoskhovyshche — reservoir
Volcan, Volcán — volcano
Vostochn-yy, -aya, -oye — eastern
Vötn — stream
Vozvyshennost' — plateau, upland
Vozyera — lake-s
Vrchovina — mountains
Vrch-y — mountain-s
Vrh — hill, mountain
Vrŭkh — mountain
Vyaliki — big, large
Vysočina — highland

Wabē — stream
Wadi, Wâdi, Wādī — valley, watercourse
Wâhât, Wāḥat — oasis
Wald — forest, wood
Wan — bay, gulf
Water — harbor
Webi — stream
Wiek — cove, inlet

Xia — gorge, strait
Xiao — lesser, little

Yanchi — salt lake
Yang — ocean
Yarymadasy — peninsula
Yazovir — reservoir
Yŏlto — island group
Yoma — mountain range
Yü — island
Yumco — lake
Yunhe — canal
Yuzhn-yy, -aya, -oye — southern

Zaki — cape, point
Zaliv — bay, gulf
Zan — mountain, ridge
Zangbo — river, stream
Zapadn-yy, -aya, -oye — western
Zatoka — bay, gulf
Zee — bay, sea
Zemlya — land

The following system is used to locate a place on a map in the *National Geographic Concise Atlas of the World*. The boldface type after an entry refers to the page on which the map is found. The letter-number combination refers to the grid on which the particular place-name is located. The edge of each map is marked horizontally with numbers and vertically with letters. In between, at equally spaced intervals, are index squares (■). If these squares were connected with lines, each page would be divided into a grid. Take Cartagena, Colombia, for example. The index entry reads "**Cartagena**, *Col.* **68** A2." On page 68, Cartagena is located within the grid square where row A and column 2 intersect (see below).

Carson City, *Nev., U.S.* **56** E3
Carson Sink, *Nev., U.S.* **58** E3
Cartagena, *Col.* **68** A2
Cartagena, *Sp.* **78** K3
Cartier Island, *W. Austral., Austral.* **116** B5
Cartwright, *Nfld. and Lab., Can.*

A place-name may appear on several maps, but the index lists only the best presentation. Usually, this means that a feature is indexed to the largest-scale map on which it appears in its entirety. (Note: Rivers are often labeled multiple times even on a single map. In such cases, the rivers are indexed to labels that are closest to their mouths.) The name of the country or continent in which a feature lies is shown in italic type and is usually abbreviated. (A full list of abbreviations appears on page 130.)

The index lists more than proper names. Some entries include a description, as in "**Elba**, *island, It.* **78** J6" and "**Amazon**, *river, Braz.-Peru* **70** D8." In languages other than English, the description of a physical feature may be part of the name; e.g., the "'Erg" in "**Chech, 'Erg**, *Alg.-Mali* **104** E4," means "sand dune region." The glossary of Foreign Terms on pages 136–137 translates such terms into English.

When a feature or place can be referred to by more than one name, both may appear in the index with cross-references. For example, the entry for Cairo, Egypt reads "**Cairo** *see* **El Qâhira**, *Egypt* **102** D9." That entry is "**El Qâhira (Cairo)**, *Egypt* **102** D9."

A Ridge *Antarctica* **129** F10
Aansluit, *S. Af.* **103** P8
Aba, *D.R.C.* **102** J9
Aba, *Nig.* **102** J5
Ābādān, *Iran* **90** G4
Abaetetuba, *Braz.* **68** D9
Abaiang, *island, Kiribati* **118** E6
Abakan, *Russ.* **90** E9
Abancay, *Peru* **68** G3
Ābaya, Lake, *Eth.* **104** H10
Abbot Ice Shelf, *Antarctica* **128** G3
Abéché, *Chad* **102** G7
Abemama, *island, Kiribati* **118** E6
Abeokuta, *Nig.* **102** H4
Aberdeen, *S. Dak., U.S.* **56** C9
Aberdeen, *U.K.* **78** D4
Aberdeen, *Wash., U.S.* **56** B3
Abidjan, *Càote d'Ivoire* **102** J3
Abilene, *Tex., U.S.* **56** H8
Abingden Downs, *homestead, Qnsld., Austral.* **115** D12
Abitibi, *river, Can.* **52** H8
Abitibi, Lake, *Can.* **52** H8
Abkhazia, *region, Ga.* **79** H12
Abomey, *Benin* **102** H4
Abou Deïa, *Chad* **102** H7
Absalom, Mount, *Antarctica* **128** D7
Absaroka Range, *Mont.-Wyo., U.S.* **58** D6
Absheron Peninsula, *Azerb.* **81** H14
Abu Ballâș, *peak, Egypt* **104** E8
Abu Dhabi *see* Abū Ẓaby, *U.A.E.* **90** H4
Abuja, *Nig.* **102** H5
Abunã, *Braz.* **68** F5
Abū Ẓaby (Abu Dhabi), *U.A.E.* **90** H4
Academy Glacier, *Antarctica* **128** F7
Acapulco, *Mex.* **51** P5
Acarigua, *Venez.* **68** A4
Accra, *Ghana* **102** J4
Achacachi, *Bol.* **68** G4
Achinsk, *Russ.* **90** E9
Aconcagua, Cerro, *Arg.-Chile* **71** L4
A Coruña, *Sp.* **78** H2
Acraman, Lake, *S. Austral., Austral.* **116** J9
Açu, *Braz.* **68** E11
Ada, *Okla., U.S.* **56** G9
Adams, Mount, *Wash., U.S.* **58** B3
'Adan, *Yemen* **90** J3
Adana, *Turk.* **79** K11
Adare, Cape, *Antarctica* **128** M9
Adavale, *Qnsld., Austral.* **115** G12
Ad Dahnā', *region, Saudi Arabia* **92** G4
Ad Dakhla, *W. Sahara* **102** E1
Ad Dammām, *Saudi Arabia* **90** H4
Ad Dawḥah (Doha), *Qatar* **90** H4
Addis Ababa *see* Ādīs Ābeba, *Eth.* **102** H10
Adelaide, *S. Austral., Austral.* **115** K10
Adelaide Island, *Antarctica* **128** D2
Adelaide River, *N. Terr., Austral.* **114** B7
Adélie Coast, *Antarctica* **129** M12
Aden, Gulf of, *Af.-Asia* **92** J3
Adieu, Cape, *S. Austral., Austral.* **116** J8
Ādīgrat, *Eth.* **102** G10
Adirondack Mountains, *N.Y., U.S.* **59** C15
Ādīs Ābeba (Addis Ababa), *Eth.* **102** H10
Adıyaman, *Turk.* **79** K12
Admiralty Island, *Alas., U.S.* **58** L5
Admiralty Islands, *P.N.G.* **118** F3
Admiralty Mountains, *Antarctica* **128** M9
Adrar, *Alg.* **102** E4
Adrar des Iforas, *mountains, Alg.-Mali* **104** F4
Adriatic Sea, *Europe* **80** J7
Ādwa, *Eth.* **102** G10
Aegean Sea, *Gr.-Turk.* **80** K9
Afghanistan, *Asia* **90** G6
Afognak Island, *Alas., U.S.* **58** M3
Afyon, *Turk.* **79** K10
Agadez, *Niger* **102** G5
Agadir, *Mor.* **102** D3
Agattu, *island, U.S.* **53** R2
Agen, *Fr.* **78** H4
Agnes Creek, *homestead, S. Austral., Austral.* **114** G8
Agnew, *W. Austral., Austral.* **114** H4
Agra, *India* **90** H7
Agrihan, *island, N. Mariana Is.* **118** C3
Aguán, *river, Hond.* **53** P8
Aguas Blancas, *Chile* **68** J4
Aguascalientes, *Mex.* **51** N5
Aguelhok, *Mali* **102** F4
Aguja Point, *Peru* **70** E1
Agulhas, Cape, *S. Af.* **105** R7
Ahaggar Mountains, *Alg.* **104** F5
Ahmadabad, *India* **90** J7
Ahvāz, *Iran* **90** G4
Aiken, *S.C., U.S.* **57** G14
Aileron, *N. Terr., Austral.* **114** F8
Ailinglapalap Atoll, *Marshall Is.* **118** E5
Ailuk Atoll, *Marshall Is.* **118** D6
Ainsworth, *Nebr., U.S.* **56** E8
Aiquile, *Bol.* **68** H5
Aïr Massif, *mountains, Niger* **104** F5
Aitutaki Atoll, *Cook Is.* **118** G9
Aix-en-Provence, *Fr.* **78** H5
Ajaccio, *Fr.* **78** J5
Ajajú, *river, Braz.-Col.* **70** C3
Ajdābiyā, *Lib.* **102** D7
Ajo, *Ariz., U.S.* **56** H4
Akbulak, *Russ.* **79** E14
Akchâr, *region, Maurit.* **104** F1
Akhḑar, Jabal al, *Lib.* **104** D7
Akhtuba, *river, Russ.* **81** G13
Akhtubinsk, *Russ.* **79** F13
Akimiski Island, *Can.* **52** G8
Akita, *Jap.* **91** E13
Akjoujt, *Maurit.* **102** F2
Akobo, *S. Sudan* **102** H9
Akron, *Ohio, U.S.* **57** E13
Aksu, *China* **90** G8
Akureyri, *Ice.* **78** A3
Alabama, *river, Ala., U.S.* **59** H12
Alabama, *U.S.* **57** H12
Alagoinhas, *Braz.* **68** F11
Alajuela, *C.R.* **51** Q8
Alakanuk, *Alas., U.S.* **56** K1
Alamagan, *island, N. Mariana Is.* **118** D3
Alamogordo, *N. Mex., U.S.* **56** H7
Alamosa, *Colo., U.S.* **56** F7
Åland Islands, *Fin.* **80** D8
Alaska, *U.S.* **56** K3
Alaska, Gulf of, *Alas., U.S.* **58** M4
Alaska Peninsula, *Alas., U.S.* **58** M2
Alaska Range, *Alas., U.S.* **58** L3
Alatyr', *Russ.* **79** E12
Albacete, *Sp.* **78** J3
Albania, *Europe* **78** J8
Albany, *Ga., U.S.* **57** H13
Albany, *N.Y., U.S.* **57** D15
Albany, *Oreg., U.S.* **56** C3
Albany, *W. Austral., Austral.* **114** L3
Al Başrah, *Iraq* **90** G4
Albatross Bay, *Qnsld., Austral.* **117** B11
Al Bayḑā' (Beida), *Lib.* **102** D7
Albemarle Sound, *N.C., U.S.* **59** F15
Albert, Lake, *D.R.C.-Uganda* **104** J9
Albert, Lake, *S. Austral., Austral.* **117** L10
Alberta, *Can.* **50** F4
Albert Lea, *Minn., U.S.* **57** D10
Albert Nile, *river, Uganda* **104** J9
Albina Point, *Angola* **105** M6
Alborán, *island, Sp.* **78** K2
Alboran Sea, *Mor.-Sp.* **80** K2
Ålborg, *Den.* **78** E6
Albuquerque, *N. Mex., U.S.* **56** G6
Albury, *N.S.W., Austral.* **115** L13
Alcoota, *homestead, N. Terr., Austral.* **114** F9
Aldabra Islands, *Seychelles* **105** L12
Aldan, *river, Russ.* **93** D11
Aldan, *Russ.* **91** D11
Aleg, *Maurit.* **102** F2
Alegrete, *Braz.* **69** K7
Aleksandrovsk Sakhalinskiy, *Russ.* **91** D13
Alençon, *Fr.* **78** G4
Alenquer, *Braz.* **68** D7
'Alenuihāhā Channel, *Hawaii, U.S.* **59** L12
Aleppo *see* Ḩalab, *Syr.* **90** F3
Alert, *Nunavut, Can.* **50** B7
Ålesund, *Nor.* **78** C6
Aleutian Islands, *U.S.* **53** R3
Aleutian Range, *Alas., U.S.* **58** M2
Alexander Archipelago, *Alas., U.S.* **58** M5
Alexander Bay, *S. Af.* **103** Q7
Alexander Island, *Antarctica* **128** E3
Alexandria *see* El Iskandarîya, *Egypt* **102** D9
Alexandria, *La., U.S.* **57** J11
Alexandria, *Va., U.S.* **57** E15
Alexandrina, Lake, *S. Austral., Austral.* **117** L10
Al Farciya, *W. Sahara* **102** E2
Algeciras, *Sp.* **78** K2
Algena, *Eritrea* **102** F10
Alger (Algiers), *Alg.* **102** C5
Algeria, *Af.* **102** E4
Algha, *Kaz.* **79** E14
Algiers *see* Alger, *Alg.* **102** C5
Algoa Bay, *S. Af.* **105** Q8
Al Harūj al Aswad, *region, Lib.* **104** E7
Al Ḩijāz, *region, Saudi Arabia* **90** G3
Al Ḩudaydah, *Yemen* **90** H3
Al Hufūf, *Saudi Arabia* **90** H4
Äli Bayramlı, *Azerb.* **79** H14
Alicante, *Sp.* **78** K3
Alice, *Qnsld., Austral.* **115** F13
Alice, *Tex., U.S.* **56** K9
Alice Downs, *homestead, W. Austral., Austral.* **114** D6
Alice Springs, *N. Terr., Austral.* **114** F8
Alijos Rocks, *Mex.* **53** M3
Al Jaghbūb, *Lib.* **102** D8
Al Jawf, *Lib.* **102** E8
Al Khums, *Lib.* **102** D6
Al Kuwayt, *Kuwait* **90** G4
Allahabad, *India* **90** J8
Allakaket, *Alas., U.S.* **56** K3
Allan Hills, *Antarctica* **128** K10
Allegheny, *river, N.Y.-Penn., U.S.* **59** D14
Allegheny Mountains, *U.S.* **59** F14
Alliance, *Nebr., U.S.* **56** E8
Allison Peninsula, *Antarctica* **128** F3
Almaden, *Qnsld., Austral.* **115** D13
Al Madīnah (Medina), *Saudi Arabia* **90** G3
Al Manāmah (Manama), *Bahrain* **90** H4
Al Marj, *Lib.* **102** D7
Almaty, *Kaz.* **90** F7
Al Mawşil, *Iraq* **90** F4
Almenara, *Braz.* **68** G10
Almería, *Sp.* **78** K3
Al'met'yevsk, *Russ.* **79** D13
Al Mukallā, *Yemen* **90** J3
Alor, *island, Indonesia* **118** F1
Alor Setar, *Malaysia* **91** L10
Aloysius, Mount, *W. Austral., Austral.* **116** G7
Alpena, *Mich., U.S.* **57** C13
Alpine, *Tex., U.S.* **56** J7
Alps, *mountains, Europe* **80** H6
Alroy Downs, *homestead, N. Terr., Austral.* **114** D9
Alta, *Nor.* **78** A8
Alta Floresta, *Braz.* **68** F7
Altamaha, *river, Ga., U.S.* **59** H14
Altamira, *Braz.* **68** D8
Altar Desert, *Mex.-U.S.* **53** L3
Altay, *China* **90** F9
Altay, *Mongolia* **90** F9
Altay Mountains, *Asia* **92** F9
Altiplano, *plateau, Bol.-Peru* **70** G4
Alto Araguaia, *Braz.* **68** G7
Alto Garças, *Braz.* **68** G7
Alto Molócuè, *Mozambique* **103** M10
Alton, *Ill., U.S.* **57** F11
Altoona, *Penn., U.S.* **57** E14
Alto Parnaíba, *Braz.* **68** F9
Altun Shan, *China* **92** G9
Al Ubayyiḑ *see* El Obeid, *Sudan* **102** G9
Al Uwaynāt, *Lib.* **102** E6
Alvorada, *Braz.* **68** F8
Amadeus, Lake, *N. Terr., Austral.* **116** F7
Amadeus Depression, *N. Terr., Austral.* **116** G7
Amadi, *S. Sudan* **102** J9
Amami Ō Shima, *Jap.* **118** B1
Amapá, *Braz.* **68** C8
Amarillo, *Tex., U.S.* **56** G8
Amata, *S. Austral., Austral.* **114** G8
Amazon, *river, Braz.-Peru* **70** D8
Amazon, Mouths of the, *Braz.* **70** C8
Amazon, Source of the, *Peru* **70** G3
Amazonas (Amazon), *river, Braz.-Peru* **68** D8
Amazon Basin, *S. America* **70** D3
Ambanja, *Madag.* **103** M12
Ambarchik, *Russ.* **91** B11
Ambargasta, Salinas de, *Arg.* **71** K5
Ambon, *Indonesia* **91** L14
Ambovombe, *Madag.* **103** P11
Ambre, Cap d', *Madag.* **105** M12
Ambriz, *Angola* **103** L6
American Falls Reservoir, *Idaho, U.S.* **58** D5
American Highland, *Antarctica* **129** E13
American Samoa, *Pac. Oc.* **118** G8
Americus, *Ga., U.S.* **57** H13
Amery Ice Shelf, *Antarctica* **129** E13
Ames, *Iowa, U.S.* **57** E10
Amguid, *Alg.* **102** E5
Amiens, *Fr.* **78** F5
Aminuis, *Namibia* **103** P7
Amistad Reservoir, *Mex.-U.S.* **58** J8
'Ammān, *Jordan* **90** F3
Ammaroo, *homestead, N. Terr., Austral.* **114** E9
Amolar, *Braz.* **68** H7
Amos, *Que., Can.* **50** H8
Amravati, *India* **90** J7
Amritsar, *India* **90** H7
Amsterdam, *Neth.* **78** F5
Am Timan, *Chad* **102** H7
Amu Darya, *river, Turkm.-Uzb.* **92** F6
Amundsen Bay, *Antarctica* **129** B13
Amundsen Gulf, *Can.* **52** D4
Amundsen-Scott South Pole, *station, Antarctica* **128** F8
Amundsen Sea, *Antarctica* **128** H3
Amur, *river, China-Russ.* **93** D12
Amur-Onon, Source of the, *Mongolia* **93** F10
Anaa, *island, Fr. Polynesia* **119** G10
Anadyr', *river, Russ.* **93** B12
Anadyr', *Russ.* **91** A12
Anadyr, Gulf of, *Russ.* **93** A12
Anadyrskiy Zaliv (Gulf of Anadyr), *Russ.* **91** A12
Analalava, *Madag.* **103** M12
Anápolis, *Braz.* **68** G8
Anatahan, *island, N. Mariana Is.* **118** D3
Anatolia (Asia Minor), *region, Turk.* **92** E3
Anatom, *island, Vanuatu* **118** H6
Anchorage, *Alas., U.S.* **56** L3
Ancona, *It.* **78** J6
Ancud, *Chile* **69** N4
Andaman Islands, *India* **92** K9
Andaman Sea, *Asia* **92** K10
Andamooka, *S. Austral., Austral.* **114** J10
Anderson, *S.C., U.S.* **57** G13
Andes, *mountains, S. America* **70** G3
Andoany (Hell-Ville), *Madag.* **103** M12
Andoas, *Peru* **68** D2
Andorra, *Andorra* **78** J4
Andorra, *Europe* **78** J4
Andradina, *Braz.* **68** H8
Andreanof Islands, *U.S.* **53** R3
Androka, *Madag.* **103** P11
Andros Island, *Bahamas* **53** M9
Anefis I-n-Darane, *Mali* **102** F4
Aneto, Pico de, *Sp.* **80** H4
Aney, *Niger* **102** F5
Angamos Point, *Chile* **70** J4
Angara, *river, Russ.* **92** E9
Angarsk, *Russ.* **90** E10
Angel Falls, *Venez.* **70** B5
Angermanälven, *river, Sweden* **80** C7
Angers, *Fr.* **78** G4
Ango, *D.R.C.* **102** J8
Angoche, *Mozambique* **103** M11
Angola, *Af.* **103** M7
Angora *see* Ankara, *Turk.* **79** J11
Aniak, *Alas., U.S.* **56** L2
Anil, *Braz.* **68** D10
Anixab, *Namibia* **103** N6
Ankara (Angora), *Turk.* **79** J11
Ann, Cape, *Antarctica* **129** B14
Ann, Cape, *Mass., U.S.* **59** D16
Annaba, *Alg.* **102** C5
An Nafūd, *region, Saudi Arabia* **92** G3
An Najaf, *Iraq* **90** G4
Annam Cordillera, *Laos-Viet.* **93** J11
Anna Plains, *homestead, W. Austral., Austral.* **114** E4
Annapolis, *Md., U.S.* **57** E15
Ann Arbor, *Mich., U.S.* **57** D13
An Nāşirīyah, *Iraq* **90** G4
Annean, Lake, *W. Austral., Austral.* **116** H3
Anningie, *homestead, N. Terr., Austral.* **114** E8
Annitowa, *homestead, N. Terr., Austral.* **114** E9
Annobón, *island, Eq. Guinea* **105** K5
Anqing, *China* **91** G12
Anshan, *China* **91** F12
Anshun, *China* **91** H11
Anson Bay, *N. Terr., Austral.* **116** B7
Antalya, *Turk.* **79** K10
Antananarivo, *Madag.* **103** N12
Antarctic Peninsula, *Antarctica* **128** C2
Anthony Lagoon, *homestead, N. Terr., Austral.* **114** D9
Anticosti Island, *Can.* **52** G10
Antigua and Barbuda, *N. America* **51** N12
Antipodes Islands, *N.Z.* **118** L6
Antofagasta, *Chile* **68** J4
Antsirabe, *Madag.* **103** N12
Antsirañana, *Madag.* **103** M12
Antwerpen, *Belg.* **78** F5
Anuta (Cherry Island), *Solomon Is.* **118** G6
Anvers Island, *Antarctica* **128** C2
Anvik, *Alas., U.S.* **56** K2
Anxi, *China* **90** G9
Aomori, *Jap.* **91** E13
Aoulef, *Alg.* **102** E4
Aozou, *Chad* **102** F7
Aozou Strip, *Chad* **102** F7
Apalachee Bay, *Fla., U.S.* **59** J13
Apalachicola, *Fla., U.S.* **57** J13
Apatity, *Russ.* **78** B9
Apatzingán, *Mex.* **51** N5
Apennines, *mountains, It.* **80** H6
Appennini *see* Apennines, *mountains, It.* **78** H6
Apia, *Samoa* **118** G7
Apollo Bay, *Vic., Austral.* **115** M12
Appalachian Mountains, *U.S.* **59** G13
Appalachian Plateau, *U.S.* **59** F13
Appleton, *Wis., U.S.* **57** D11
Apucarana, *Braz.* **68** J8
Apure, *river, Venez.* **70** B4

Acknowledgments

WORLD THEMATIC SECTION

Structure of the Earth
pp. 22–23

CONSULTANTS
Laurel M. Bybell
U.S. Geological Survey (USGS)

Robert I. Tilling
U.S. Geological Survey (USGS)

GRAPHICS
CONTINENTS ADRIFT IN TIME: Christopher R. Scotese/PALEOMAP Project

CUTAWAY OF THE EARTH: Tibor G. Tóth

TECTONIC BLOCK DIAGRAMS: Susan Sanford

PLATE TECTONICS AND GEOLOGIC TIME: *National Geographic Atlas of the World*, 9th ed. Washington, D.C.: The National Geographic Society, 2011.

Climate
pp. 24–27

CONSULTANTS
William Burroughs

H. Michael Mogil
Certified Consulting Meteorologist (CCM)

Vladimir Ryabinin
World Climate Research Programme

GRAPHICS
TOPOGRAPHY: Chapel Design & Marketing and XNR Productions

GLOBAL AIR TEMPERATURE CHANGES, 1850–2010: Reproduced by kind permission of the Climatic Research Unit.

SATELLITE IMAGES
Images originally created for the GLOBE program by NOAA's National Geophysical Data Center, Boulder, Colorado, U.S.A.

CLOUD COVER: International Satellite Cloud Climatology Project (ISCCP); National Aeronautics and Space Administration (NASA); Goddard Institute for Space Studies (GISS). PRECIPITATION: Global Precipitation Climatology Project (GPCP); International Satellite Land Surface Climatology Project (ISLSCP). SOLAR ENERGY: Earth Radiation Budget Experiment (ERBE); Greenhouse Effect Detection Experiment (GEDEX). TEMPERATURE: National Center for Environmental Prediction (NCEP); National Center for Atmospheric Research (NCAR); National Weather Service (NWS).

PHOTOGRAPHS
PAGE 25, Sharon G. Johnson

Population
pp. 28–31

CONSULTANTS
Carl Haub
Population Reference Bureau

Gregory Yetman
Center for International Earth Science Information Network (CIESIN), Columbia University

GENERAL REFERENCES
Center for International Earth Science Information Network (CIESIN), Columbia University: www.ciesin.org

International Migrant Stock: The 2008 Revision. Population Division of the Department of Economic and Social Affairs of the United Nations Secretariat. New York: United Nations, 2009.

Population Reference Bureau: www.prb.org

United Nations World Population Prospects: The 2010 Revision Population Database: esa.un.org/unpd/wpp

World Urbanization Prospects: The 2009 Revision. Population Division of the Department of Economic and Social Affairs of the United Nations Secretariat. New York: United Nations, 2010.

GRAPHICS
POPULATION DENSITY: Center for International Earth Science Information Network (CIESIN), Columbia University, and Centro Internacional de Agricultura Tropical (CIAT), 2010. Gridded Population of the World Version 3 (GPWv3): Population Density Grids—World Population Density, 2010 [map]. Palisades, New York: Socioeconomic Data and Applications Center (SEDAC), Columbia University. Available at http://sedac.ciesin.columbia.edu/gpw. Accessed November 2011.

SATELLITE IMAGES
LIGHTS OF THE WORLD: Composite image: MODIS imagery; ETOPO-2 relief; NOAA/NGDC and DMSP lights at night data.

Religions
pp. 32–33

CONSULTANTS
William M. Bodiford
University of California—Los Angeles

Todd Johnson
Center for the Study of Global Christianity, Gordon-Conwell Theological Seminary

GENERAL REFERENCES
World Christian Database: Center for the Study of Global Christianity, Gordon-Conwell Theological Seminary (www.worldchristiandatabase.org)

GRAPHICS
MAJOR RELIGIONS: *National Geographic Collegiate Atlas of the World*, 2nd ed. Washington, D.C.: The National Geographic Society, 2011.

PHOTOGRAPHS
PAGE 32, (LE), Jodi Cobb, National Geographic Photographer (RT), James L. Stanfield
PAGES 32–33, Tony Heiderer
PAGE 33, (LE), Thomas J. Abercrombie; (RT), Annie Griffiths Belt

Economy
pp. 34–35

CONSULTANTS
William Beyers
University of Washington

Michael Finger
World Trade Organization (WTO)

Richard R. Fix
World Bank

Susan Martin
Institute for the Study of International Migration

GENERAL REFERENCES
CIA *World Factbook:* www.cia.gov/library/publications

International Monetary Fund: www.imf.org

International Telecommunication Union: www.itu.int

International Trade Statistics, 2011. Geneva, Switzerland: World Trade Organization.

UNESCO Institute for Statistics: www.uis.unesco.org

World Development Indicators, 2011. Washington, D.C.: World Bank.

Note: GDP and GDP (PPP) data on this spread are from the IMF.

GRAPHICS
LABOR MIGRATION: *National Geographic Collegiate Atlas of the World*, 2nd ed. Washington, D.C.: The National Geographic Society, 2011.

Trade
pp. 36–37

CONSULTANTS
Michael Finger and Peter Werner
World Trade Organization (WTO)

United Nations Conference on Trade and Development (UNCTAD)

GENERAL REFERENCES
International Trade Statistics, 2011. Geneva, Switzerland: World Trade Organization.

United Nations Conference on Trade and Development: www.unctad.org

World Trade Organization: www.wto.org

GRAPHICS
GROWTH OF WORLD TRADE: World Trade Organization

Health and Education
pp. 38–39

CONSULTANTS
Carlos Castillo-Salgado
Pan American Health Organization (PAHO)/
World Health Organization (WHO)

George Ingram and Annababette Wils
Education Policy and Data Center

Margaret Kruk
United Nations Millennium Project and University of Michigan School of Public Health

Ruth Levine
Center for Global Development

GENERAL REFERENCES
2010 World Population Data Sheet, Population Reference Bureau.

Education Policy and Data Center: www.epdc.org

Human Development Report, 2011. New York: United Nations Development Programme (UNDP), 2011.

UN Millennium Development Goals: www.un.org/millenniumgoals

The State of the World's Children 2011. New York: UNICEF, 2011.

The World Health Report 2010. Annex table 5. Selected national health accounts indicators. Geneva: World Health Organization, 2010.

World Bank list of economies, 2011. Washington, D.C.: World Bank.

World Health Organization: www.who.int

Youth (15–24) and Adult (15+) Literacy Rates by Country and by Gender. New York: UNESCO Institute for Statistics, 2011.

GRAPHICS
ACCESS TO IMPROVED SANITATION: *The State of the World's Children, 2011.* New York: UNICEF, 2011.

DEVELOPING HUMAN CAPITAL: Adapted from Human Capital Projections developed by Education Policy and Data Center.

Conflict and Terror
pp. 40–41

CONSULTANTS
Barbara Harff
U.S. Naval Academy

Monty G. Marshall
Center for Systemic Peace; Societal-Systems Research Inc.

Christian Oxenboll
United Nations High Commissioner for Refugees (UNHCR)

GENERAL REFERENCES
Marshall, Monty G. and Benjamin R. Cole. *Global Report 2011: Conflict, Governance, and State Fragility.* Vienna, VA: Center for Systemic Peace, 2011.

Carnegie Endowment for International Peace: www.carnegieendowment.org/npp

James Martin Center for Nonproliferation Studies: cns.miis.edu

United Nations High Commissioner for Refugees (UNHCR): www.unhcr.org

United Nations Peacekeeping: www.un.org/Depts/dpko

Environmental Stresses
pp. 42–43

CONSULTANT
Christian Lambrechts
Division of Early Warning and Assessmen (DEWA), United Nations Environmental Program (UNEP)

GENERAL REFERENCES
Acidification and eutrophication of developing country ecosystems. Swedish University of Agricultural Sciences (SLU), 2002.

EM-DAT: The OFDA/CRED International Disaster Database. Université Catholique de Louvain, Brussels, Belgium: www.emdat.be

Energy Information Administration. U.S. Department of Energy: www.eia.doe.gov

Global Forest Resources Assessment. Forestry Department of the Food and Agriculture Organization of the United Nations, 2010.

Halpern, et al, *A Global Map of Human Impact on Marine Ecosystems* Science (15 Feb. 2008): Vol. 319, no. 5865, pp. 948–952.

State of the World's Forests. World Resources Institute: www.wri.org

United Nations Environment Programme-World Conservation and Monitoring Program (UNEP-WCMC): www.unep-wcmc.org

GRAPHICS
HUMAN FOOTPRINT: Wildlife Conservation Society. www.wcs.org/humanfootprint

SATELLITE IMAGES
DEPLETION OF THE OZONE LAYER: NASA Ozone Watch, Goddard Space Flight Center.

CONTINENTAL AND U.S. THEMATIC MAPS

North America, pages 54–55; South America, pages 72–73; Europe, pages 82–83; Asia, pages 94–95; Africa, pages 106–107; Australia and Oceania, pages 120–121;

POPULATION DENSITY: Landscan 2009™ Population Dataset created by UT-Battelle, LLC, the management and operating contractor of the Oak Ridge National Laboratory acting on behalf of the U.S. Department of Energy under Contract No. DE-AC05-00OR22725.

DOMINANT ECONOMY: CIA, *The World Factbook*

ENERGY CONSUMPTION: EIA (U.S. Energy Administration)

CLIMATE ZONES: H. J. de Blij, P. O. Muller, and John Wiley & Sons, Inc.

NATURAL HAZARDS: USGS Earthquake Hazard Program; Global Volcanism Program, Smithsonian Institution; National Geophysical Data Center/World Data Center (NGDC/WDC) Historical Tsunami Database; DMSP Lights at Night data.

WATER AVAILABILITY: Aaron Wolf, Oregon State University

United States, pages 60–61:

POPULATION DENSITY: U.S. Census Bureau

POPULATION CHANGE: U.S. Census Bureau

WATERSHEDS: *HydroSHEDS,* United States Geological Survey: hydrosheds.cr.usgs.gov

FEDERAL LANDS: National Park Service; Bureau of Land Management; USDA Forest Service; U.S. Fish and Wildlife Service; Bureau of Indian Affairs; Department of Defense; Department of Energy; NOAA.

FLAGS AND FACTS

Carl Haub
Population Reference Bureau

Whitney Smith
Flag Research Center

DATES OF NATIONAL INDEPENDENCE

Leo Dillon
Department of State, Office of the Geographer

Carl Haub
Population Reference Bureau

ART AND ILLUSTRATIONS

COVER AND PAGES 2–3: Bathymetric Relief: ETOPO1, 1 Arc-Minute Global Relief Model, March 2009. National Oceanic and Atmospheric Administration (NOAA), National Geophysical Data Center (NGDC). Topographic Relief: GTOPO30, United States Geological Survey (USGS).

PAGES 7 AND 160: Globes, Tibor G. Tóth (data from The Living Earth, Inc.).

SATELLITE IMAGES

PAGES 10–11, 48–49, 66–67, 76–77, 88–89, 100–101, 122–113, AND 126–127: Globes and Continental Satellite Images: Blue Marble Next Generation, NASA's Earth Observatory; Population density data from Landscan 2009™ Population Dataset created by UT-Battelle, LLC, the management and operating contractor of the Oak Ridge National Laboratory acting on behalf of the U.S. Department of Energy under Contract No. DE-AC05-00OR22725.

PAGES 20–21: ETOPO-2 relief; Digital Chart of the World.

PAGE 24: *Images originally created for the GLOBE program by NOAA's National Geophysical Data Center, Boulder, Colorado, U.S.A. For more detail, see listings under Climate acknowledgments on page 158.*

PAGE 28: Lights of the World: Composite image: MODIS imagery; ETOPO-2 relief; NOAA/NGDC and DMSP lights at night data.

PAGE 42: Depletion of the Ozone Layer: NASA Ozone Watch, Goddard Space Flight Center.

PHOTOGRAPHS

PAGE 25, Sharon G. Johnson
PAGE 32, (LE), Jodi Cobb/National Geographic Photographer
PAGE 32, (RT), James L. Stanfield
PAGES 32–33, Tony Heiderer
PAGE 33, (LE), Thomas J. Abercrombie
PAGE 33, (RT), Annie Griffiths Belt

PHYSICAL AND POLITICAL MAPS

Bureau of the Census, U.S. Department of Commerce

Bureau of Land Management, U.S. Department of the Interior

Central Intelligence Agency (CIA)

National Geographic Maps

National Geospatial-Intelligence Agency (NGA)

National Park Service, U.S. Department of the Interior

Office of the Geographer, U.S. Department of State

U.S. Board on Geographic Names (BGN)

U.S. Geological Survey, U.S. Department of the Interior

PRINCIPAL REFERENCE SOURCES

Columbia Gazetteer of the World. Cohen, Saul B., ed. New York: Columbia University Press, 1998.

Encarta World English Dictionary. New York: St. Martin's Press and Microsoft Encarta, 1999.

Human Development Report, 2011. New York: United Nations Development Programme (UNDP), 2011.

International Trade Statistics, 2011. Geneva, Switzerland: World Trade Organization.

McKnight, Tom L. *Physical Geography: A Landscape Appreciation.* 5th ed. Upper Saddle River, New Jersey: Prentice Hall, 1996.

National Geographic Atlas of the World, 9th ed. Washington, D.C.: The National Geographic Society, 2011.

Strahler, Alan and Arthur Strahler. *Physical Geography: Science and Systems of the Human Environment.* 2nd ed. John Wiley & Sons, Inc, 2002.

Tarbuck, Edward J. and Frederick K. Lutgens. *Earth: An Introduction to Physical Geology.* 7th ed. Upper Saddle River, New Jersey: Prentice Hall, 2002.

World Development Indicators, 2011. Washington, D.C.: World Bank.

The World Factbook 2012. Washington, D.C.: Central Intelligence Agency, 2012.

The World Health Report 2010. Geneva: World Health Organization, 2010.

World Investment Report, 2011. New York and Geneva: United Nations Conference on Trade and Development, 2011.

PRINCIPAL ONLINE SOURCES

Cambridge Dictionaries Online
dictionary.cambridge.org

Central Intelligence Agency
www.cia.gov

CIESIN
www.ciesin.org

Conservation International
www.conservation.org

International Monetary Fund
www.imf.org

Merriam-Webster OnLine
www.m-w.com

National Aeronautics and Space Administration
www.nasa.gov

National Atmospheric and Oceanic Administration
www.noaa.gov

National Climatic Data Center
www.ncdc.noaa.gov

National Geophysical Data Center
www.ngdc.noaa.gov

National Park Service
www.nps.gov

National Renewable Energy Laboratory
www.nrel.gov

Population Reference Bureau
www.prb.org

United Nations
www.un.org

UN Conference on Trade and Development
www.unctad.org

UN Development Programme
www.undp.org

UN Educational, Cultural, and Scientific Organization
www.unesco.org

UNEP-WCMC
www.unep-wcmc.org

UN Millennium Development Goals
www.un.org/millenniumgoals

UN Population Division
www.un.org/esa/population

UN Refugee Agency
www.unhcr.org

UN Statistics Division
unstats.un.org

U.S. Board on Geographic Names
geonames.usgs.gov

U.S. Geological Survey
www.usgs.gov

World Bank
www.worldbank.org

World Health Organization
www.who.int

World Trade Organization
www.wto.org

KEY TO FLAGS AND FACTS

The National Geographic Society, whose cartographic policy is to recognize de facto countries, counted 195 independent nations at the end of 2011. At the end of each chapter of the *Concise Atlas of the World* there is a fact box for every independent nation and for most dependencies located on the continent or region covered in that chapter. Each box includes the flag of a political entity, as well as important statistical data. Boxes for some dependencies show two flags—a local one and the sovereign flag of the administering country. Dependencies are non-independent political entities associated in some way with a particular independent nation.

The statistical data provide highlights of geography, demography, and economy. These details offer a brief overview of each political entity; they present general characteristics and are not intended to be comprehensive studies. The structured nature of the text results in some generic collective or umbrella terms. The industry category, for instance, includes services in addition to traditional manufacturing sectors. Space limitations dictate the amount of information included. For example, the only languages listed for the U.S. are English and Spanish, although many others are spoken. The North America chapter also includes concise fact boxes for U.S. states, showing the state flag, population, and capital.

Fact boxes are arranged alphabetically by the conventional short forms of the country or dependency names. Country and dependency boxes are grouped separately. The conventional long forms of names appear below the conventional short form; if there are no long forms, the short forms are repeated. Except where otherwise noted below, all demographic data are derived from the CIA *World Factbook.*

AREA accounts for the total area of a country or dependency, including all land and inland water delimited by international boundaries, intranational boundaries, or coastlines. Figures in square kilometers are from the CIA *World Factbook.* Square miles were calculated by using the conversion factor of 0.3861 square miles to 1 square kilometer.

POPULATION figures for independent nations and dependencies are July 2012 estimates from the CIA *World Factbook.* Next to CAPITAL is the name of the seat of government, followed by the city's population. Capital city populations for both independent nations and dependencies are from *World Urbanization Prospects: The 2009 Revision,* and represent the populations of metropolitan areas. In the POPULATION category, the figures for U.S. state populations are 2011 U.S. Census estimates. POPULATION figures for countries, dependencies, and U.S. states are rounded to the nearest thousand.

Under RELIGION, the most widely practiced faith appears first. "Traditional" or "indigenous" connotes beliefs of important local sects, such as the Maya in Middle America. Under LANGUAGE, if a country has an official language, it is listed first. Often, a country may list more than one official language. Otherwise both RELIGION and LANGUAGE are in rank ordering.

LITERACY generally indicates the percentage of the population above the age of 15 who can read and write. There are no universal standards of literacy, so these estimates are based on the most common definition available for a nation.

LIFE EXPECTANCY represents the average number of years a group of infants born in the same year can be expected to live if the mortality rate at each age remains constant in the future. (Data from the CIA *World Factbook.*)

GDP PER CAPITA is Gross Domestic Product divided by midyear population estimates. GDP estimates for independent nations and dependencies use the purchasing power parity (PPP) conversion factor designed to equalize the purchasing powers of different currencies.

Individual income estimates such as GDP PER CAPITA are among the many indicators used to assess a nation's well-being. As statistical averages, they hide extremes of poverty and wealth. Furthermore, they take no account of factors that affect quality of life, such as environmental degradation, educational opportunities, and health care.

ECONOMY information for the independent nations and dependencies is divided into three general categories: Industry, Agriculture, and Exports. Because of structural limitations, only the primary industries (Ind), agricultural commodities (Agr), and exports (Exp) are reported. Agriculture serves as an umbrella term for not only crops but also livestock, products, and fish. In the interest of conciseness, agriculture for the independent nations presents, when applicable, four major crops, followed respectively by leading entries for livestock, products, and fish.

NA indicates that data are not available.

NATIONAL GEOGRAPHIC

Concise
Atlas of the World

THIRD EDITION

Published by the National Geographic Society

John M. Fahey, Jr
Chairman of the Board and Chief Executive Officer

Timothy T. Kelly
President

Declan Moore
Executive Vice President; President, Publishing and Digital Media

Melina Gerosa Bellows
Executive Vice President; Chief Creative Officer, Books, Kids, and Family

National Geographic Maps

Charles D. Regan, Jr.
Senior Vice President, General Manager

Daniel J. Ortiz
Vice President, Publisher

Kevin P. Allen
Vice President, Production Services

Books Division

Hector Sierra
Senior Vice President and General Manager

Anne Alexander
Senior Vice President and Editorial Director

Jonathan Halling
Design Director, Books and Children's Publishing

Marianne R. Koszorus
Design Director, Books

R. Gary Colbert
Production Director

Jennifer A. Thornton
Director of Managing Editorial

Staff for This Atlas

Carl Mehler
Project Editor and Director of Maps

Laura Exner, Thomas L. Gray, Joseph F. Ochlak, Nicholas P. Rosenbach
Map Editors

Nathan Eidem, Steven D. Gardner, and XNR Productions
Map Research and Compilation

Matt Chwastyk
Map Production Manager

Steven D. Gardner, James Huckenpahler, Michael McNey, Gregory Ugiansky, and XNR Productions
Map Production

Marty Ittner
Book Design

Judith Klein, Rebecca Lescaze, Victoria Garrett Jones
Text Editors

Elisabeth B. Booz, Patrick Booz, William Burroughs, Carlos Castillo-Salgado, Michael Finger, Noel Grove, K.M. Kostyal, Monty G. Marshall, Antony Shugaar, Robert I. Tilling
Contributing Writers

Elisabeth B. Booz, Nathan Eidem, Steven D. Gardner, Joseph F. Ochlak, Nicholas P. Rosenbach
Text Researchers

Tibor G. Tóth
Contributing Relief Artist

Manufacturing and Quality Management

Christopher A. Liedel
Chief Financial Officer

Phillip L. Schlosser
Senior Vice President

Chris Brown
Vice President

Robert L. Barr
Manager

Printed and Bound by Elcograf, Verona, Italy